Venus and Serena weren't always superstars.

The tennis courts were damaged, dirty, and sometimes dangerous. Soda cans, beer bottles, and fast-food wrappers had to be swept away before play could begin. Broken glass was everywhere, weeds poked out of the ground, and cracks covered the cement.

Sometimes, gunshots rang out.

Richard Williams told his daughters, Venus and Serena, to ignore the distractions. *Just enjoy yourselves and work on improving your game.*

"Never mind the noise, Meeka," he told Serena, using her nickname, trying to reassure her. "Just play."

His strategy worked. Most days, Venus and Serena had so much fun volleying with each other that they barely noticed their challenging surroundings. Playing tennis somehow transported Venus and Serena to a calm, happy place.

From these humble beginnings began a lifelong love affair between the Williams sisters and a sport they would dominate like no other two players in history. They would need to overcome a series of unexpected obstacles to achieve greatness, however.

OTHER BOOKS YOU MAY ENJOY

RISING ABOVE

Inspiring Women in Sports

GREGORY ZUCKERMAN

with Gabriel and Elijah Zuckerman

PUFFIN BOOKS

PUFFIN BOOKS
An imprint of Penguin Random House LLC, New York

First published in the United States of America by Philomel Books,
an imprint of Penguin Random House LLC, 2018
Published by Puffin Books, an imprint of Penguin Random House LLC, 2019

Visit us online at penguinrandomhouse.com

THE LIBRARY OF CONGRESS HAS CATALOGED THE PHILOMEL BOOKS EDITION AS
FOLLOWS:
Names: Zuckerman, Gregory, author. | Zuckerman, Elijah, author.
| Zuckerman, Gabriel, author.
Title: Rising above. Inspiring women in sports / Gregory Zuckerman ;
with Elijah and Gabriel Zuckerman.
Other titles: Inspiring women in sports
Description: New York, NY : Philomel Books, 2018. | Audience: Age 8–12.
| Audience: Grade 3 to 7.
Identifiers: LCCN 2017037902 | ISBN 9780399547478 (hardback)
| ISBN 9780399547492 (ebook)
Subjects: LCSH: Women athletes—United States—Biography—Juvenile literature.
| African American women athletes—Biography—Juvenile literature. | BISAC:
JUVENILE NONFICTION / Biography & Autobiography / Sports & Recreation. |
JUVENILE NONFICTION / Girls & Women. | JUVENILE NONFICTION / Social
Issues / Physical & Emotional Abuse
(see also Social Issues / Sexual Abuse).
Classification: LCC GV697.A1 Z83 2018 | DDC 796.0922 [B]—dc23
LC record available at https://lccn.loc.gov/2017037902

Puffin Books ISBN 9780399547485

Printed in the United States of America

3 5 7 9 10 8 6 4

Edited by Brian Geffen.
Text set in 12.5-point Apollo MT Std.

To the superstars in our lives—
Savtah Ricki, Savtah Tova,
Aunt Aviva, Aunt Shoshana,
and, of course,
Mom

CONTENTS

SIMONE BILES

At the age of two, Simone Biles was taken from her mother.

Shanon Biles, who suffered from drug and alcohol addictions, never properly cared for Simone and her three other kids. Simone's father had abandoned the family and wasn't around. With Shanon absent much of the time, too often there was no one looking after the children.

Shanon was arrested multiple times during Simone's childhood. Twice, Shanon was caught stealing cases of baby formula at a local Target store; another time she was arrested for shoplifting children's clothing. Since her four children were left alone so often, regularly playing in the streets in their Columbus, Ohio, neighborhood with no supervision, neighbors began calling social services, urging the city to step in to help Simone and her siblings.

Some of Simone's earliest memories were of hunger pangs. Even when she visited relatives, Simone had a hard time finding enough to eat. Once, she visited her uncle and poured tap water into a bowl of cereal because there was no milk in the home.

Even at a young age, Simone became frustrated by her living conditions.

For most girls, a visit from a neighborhood cat brings joy. But when a local cat sauntered by Simone's yard, she felt resentment—the cat seemed content and well fed even as Simone and her siblings struggled for food. Years later, Simone would still feel antipathy toward cats, though she knew her feelings weren't justified.

"This cat was always being fed—and at the time, we were hungry a lot, so I was always kind of mad at this cat," Simone recalls in her book, *Courage to Soar*.

One day, a social worker came and sat with the four kids on the front steps of their house.

"We're placing you kids in foster care so Shanon can try to get better," the social worker said.

As they sat in the back of the car, driving away from their home, Simone and her siblings were too scared to speak, a searing memory that remained with Simone the rest of her life.

Little Simone was frightened as she prepared for the unknown, moving in with a group of strangers. Simone soon realized she had nothing to worry about. Living with her foster family, Simone and her siblings enjoyed three full meals a day for the first time and got to play with a backyard swing. Simone remembers soaring high and doing backflips after jumping off the swing midair, amazing onlookers who couldn't believe someone so young was attempting such daring tricks. Her foster parents, whom Simone called Miss Doris and Mr. Leo, wouldn't let little Simone jump on their trampoline, however, because they were worried she might get injured. Simone watched with envy as the family's older, biological children somersaulted with glee off the trampoline.

Simone's foster parents "were doing their best to

keep us safe but I just knew I could do the moves the older kids did," Simone recalls. "I was always running and jumping, cartwheeling, and somersaulting."

On Christmas Eve 2002, when Simone was five, she got a real surprise. Her grandfather Ron Biles brought her and her siblings to live with him and his second wife, Nellie, in Spring, Texas, about thirty miles from Houston.

It wasn't supposed to be a permanent thing. The family hoped Simone's mother could kick her addictions and learn to care for her kids. But an attempted reunion ended after Shanon failed new drug tests. The following year, Simone's grandparents legally adopted her, along with her younger sister, Adria, while their two siblings moved in with Ron's sister.

At first, Nellie had been reluctant to adopt the girls, unsure how they'd integrate with her existing family. She also worried she wouldn't be a good mother. Nellie prayed that she could love Simone and her sister as much as she loved her own sons.

It turned out there was no need for concern. "I don't know the exact date [it happened]," Nellie says, "but my heart just made room" for Simone and her siblings.

Simone felt loved. She began calling her grandparents Mom and Dad. Finally, she was well fed and cared for.

"I was happy," she says. "I knew because the knots I usually felt in my tummy were gone."

There even was a trampoline in the backyard of her new home. Simone bounced, twirled, flipped, and somersaulted for hours, her beaded braids flying. She tried different moves, some quite daring, to see if she could land on her feet. She usually succeeded.

Simone's situation was unusual, but she embraced it. "I thought every kid was adopted . . . to me it's just normal," she says. "I want to know why my mother did what she did. But those aren't questions for me because that was her lifestyle [before I was] even born."

One day, when Simone was five, her day care center decided to take the kids on a field trip to a farm. It rained that day, however, so they changed their plans and headed for a gym called Bannon's Gymnastix in nearby Houston.

From the moment she entered the gym, Simone was enthralled. She was tiny for her age but the equipment seemed perfect for her size—there were low beams and a low bar along with floor vaults and mats. Simone saw someone jump backward, use her hands, and then land while standing upright—something gymnasts called a back handspring—so she tried her own back-flip. Simone pulled it off, over and over again, landing on her feet each time and even adding a little twist at the end.

A woman who worked at the gym raced over, amazed at what she was seeing from such a young girl. She gave Simone a few simple instructions, telling her to point her toes and keep her knees together, and in-vited Simone to come back to the gym for some formal classes. Before long, gymnastics consumed Simone's life. Practice, gymnastics classes, more practice, and even more classes. She couldn't get enough.

Fearless, surprisingly strong, and full of energy, Simone had discovered the perfect sport for her per-sonality and body type. Even at such a young age, a local coach, Aimee Boorman, believed that with hard work Simone had a chance to develop into a special talent.

"Her physical stature and her energy are what caught my eye," Coach Boorman says. "The biggest obstacle with coaching her was her desire, or lack of desire, for repetition. Most high-level gymnasts are comfortable with doing very high numbers of repetition, but not so much in Simone's case. Luckily, she didn't require them."

As Simone worked to perfect her routines, she noticed her body changing and her muscles expanding. Some kids teased Simone about her bulky, well-built physique. Even in the world of gymnastics, small and powerful wasn't seen as an ideal body type at the time.

As she got bigger and stronger, Simone turned self-conscious. "I definitely wasn't one of the cool kids," she writes in *Courage to Soar*. Sometimes when she was around young people her age, Simone wore baggy clothing, such as an athletic jacket on top of her outfit, to mask her muscular physique. "I always hid it," Simone later told *New York* magazine.

Spending more time in the gym with others focused

on the sport helped Simone build confidence. It took a while but the more she practiced and succeeded at gymnastics, the more she learned to ignore how others viewed her.

"Once I started going to the gym more, I realized that . . . it wasn't weird. I have these muscles because I do the sport that I do," she says.

The critiquing of her body and her abilities never quite stopped, though.

In 2013, Simone turned sixteen and began competing in the senior elite category of amateur gymnastics. She dealt with early challenges, including difficulties with the horizontal bars. Legendary coach Martha Karolyi once watched Simone practice and told Coach Aimee Boorman that "this kid has no bars . . . She can tumble great, but that's it."

Coach Boorman encouraged Simone to ignore the criticism and keep working to improve her technique. "Her family and I always told her that she could stop doing gymnastics whenever she wanted," Coach Boorman says, "but if she was going to put her energy in it, she should try to be the best that she could be."

Simone took the lessons to heart. Soon, she began dominating competitions and gaining broad acclaim, especially after winning gold at meets in Italy and Germany. Sometimes, she didn't even need to be at her best during practice to win subsequent competitions.

In July 2013, Simone traveled to Hoffman Estates, Illinois, to compete in the Secret US Classic, a meet that's a tune-up for the USA Gymnastics National Championships. At the Secret competition Simone would face real pressure for the first time. Nearly eleven thousand fans packed into the Sears Centre Arena to watch Simone compete against 2012 Olympic gold medalists Kyla Ross and McKayla Maroney as well as other top gymnasts.

Early on, Simone fell on the uneven bars and then bobbled and almost tumbled off the balance beam, shocking fans in the stands. Simone still had the floor exercise ahead, usually her strength, so she tried to shake off the early, embarrassing mistakes.

Wearing a multicolored outfit, Simone flashed a

confident smile as she began the floor exercise. She nailed her first few jumps—she was precise in her movements and seemed in control and in sync with the music. Fans and judges could see her upbeat personality, the goal of every competitor in the exercise, and Simone seemed on her way to an impressive performance.

"You got it, Simone!" a fan yelled to encourage her.

Ninety seconds into the routine, however, something startling happened. Simone lost her balance after a jump, landing clumsily. Just twenty seconds later, after attempting a full-twisting double-back somersault, Simone landed so awkwardly that she almost fell on her face. Simone had to put both hands out to protect her face from smashing into the mat.

It was *that* bad.

"Oooh," the crowd shouted, feeling bad for her.

Simone couldn't hide the crushed, despondent look on her face as she left the floor. Unable to stop thinking about her mistakes, Simone felt uncomfortable and awkward as she prepared for her next event, the vault, which would conclude the competition. Simone was so clearly off her game that Coach Boorman pulled her from the competition before she even could attempt a single vault.

"She just about tried to kill herself on her vault warm-up," Coach Boorman told a reporter. "She could have done something that could've ended her career right then and there if I let her compete . . . her mind wasn't where it needed to be."

Simone finished in thirteenth place out of fifteen competitors, the worst meet of Simone's senior career.

"I think I was just trying to live up to everyone's expectations that I kind of got lost in competing," Simone later explained. "I was just so stressed. I didn't know how to deal with a lot of it."

On her way out, Simone overheard another coach critiquing her performance.

"She's too fat," the male coach said. "How does she expect to compete like that? Maybe if she didn't look like she'd swallowed a deer, she wouldn't have fallen."

Humiliated, Simone rushed behind the curtains and cried.

"It was really hard, because growing up, I never

felt overweight or fat," Simone later told *People* magazine. "It shocked me."

Once again, Coach Boorman told Simone to ignore the criticisms. Her weight was the same as when she won earlier competitions. A lack of preparation and conditioning had led to her poor performance, Coach Boorman insisted, not her size.

"You can't train like this and expect the results to show," national team coordinator Karolyi added, shaking her head with disapproval. "I believe in you . . . Turn the page."

Later, when Simone met other gymnasts like gold medalists Aly Raisman and Gabby Douglas she learned she wasn't the only athlete dealing with body shaming.

"You name it and she got trampled," says Gabby Douglas's mother, Natalie Hawkins, in reference to stinging critiques her daughter faced on social media about her hair, her skin, her body shape, and more. "Gabrielle's had her heart broken."

Because female gymnasts usually are young women competing in formfitting outfits, even as their bodies are still developing, they often feel insecure and super-conscious of the opinions of coaches, parents, fans, and others.

"It's hard growing up in a sport where you compete with very little clothing on your body and everyone is staring at [your body] no matter how good you are," Simone says. "People will always say you don't look good *enough*."

Yet over time, Simone learned to ignore the criticisms and snide remarks.

"In a way it actually shaped me for the better," she says, referring to the comments about her weight. "It just taught me to rise above and to love my body no matter what."

Later, when she was an established gymnast, Simone tweeted: "You all can judge my body all you want, but at the end of the day it's MY body. I love it & I'm comfortable in my skin."

To Simone, her poor showing at the Secret was a crushing blow. So many people had predicted she'd have a star performance, and she'd expected so much of herself, but she'd failed. Simone's adoptive mother—by then Simone just saw her as her mother—noticed that Simone started doubting herself and found excuses for her performance. Gymnastics is a tough sport—judges nitpick and search for the tiniest mistakes, Simone's mother knew.

Sensing that she was bottling up her worries, Simone's parents suggested that she meet with a sports psychologist to discuss her worries and frustrations.

"You just turned sixteen and you have the whole world looking at you and they expect a certain level of performance," Coach Boorman said of Simone in an interview with writer Dvora Meyers. "You're not a normal kid, and you don't have normal problems."

At first, Simone resisted seeing the psychologist. "You all think I'm crazy," Simone said, according to her mother.

Eventually, she agreed to go. The psychologist taught Simone various strategies to handle her stress, such as breathing techniques. They were invaluable tools for an athlete because in sports, mental toughness is just as important as, if not more important than, physical toughness.

Her coaches gave her sharp criticisms after the Secret event. Instead of reacting with anger or hurt, however, Simone viewed the coaches' comments as pep talks and helpful critiques. The coaches still believed in her and Simone knew they were right about how she needed to improve her practice habits.

"Simone made up her mind that she was going to be great," Coach Boorman says. "She didn't want to have another performance like that."

With the national and world championships ahead, Karolyi invited Simone and Coach Boorman to the Karolyi Ranch in Texas for one-on-one training sessions. Karolyi told Simone that the difference between being a great gymnast and a world-class competitor was the practice necessary to get to the next level. But Karolyi also told Simone that it's okay to fail. Take a chance, try to win the upcoming competitions, but if it doesn't happen it's not the end of the world, Karolyi said.

Individual attention from Karolyi helped improve

Simone's mental outlook, as did continuing work with the sports psychologist. The pressure building on Simone seemed to lift. She decided to get back to enjoying herself.

"You kind of just knew that if you went out there and made a mistake, that it's okay," Simone says.

Just three months after her embarrassing performance at the Secret Classic, Simone traveled to the Sports Palace in Antwerp, Belgium, the world's second-most visited event hall after New York's Madison Square Garden, to compete in the World Championships against stars around the world, including Kyla Ross, who had won the Secret.

Simone and Ross went back and forth, vying for the gold medal, Simone's strength and athleticism matched by Ross's polish and elegance. Both had scores of about 60 points and Ross led by just 0.016 points ahead of the final floor exercise. It would come down to this one, last event.

Wearing a bright pink outfit, Simone launched into a powerful routine. Her landings weren't perfect. Her toe-point needed work—gymnasts receive a 0.10-point deduction just for failing to point their toes. But fans were wowed by Simone's powerful effort; thousands in the crowd rhythmically clapped along to the music as Simone leaped, twisted, and strutted. Simone left the floor with a huge smile. Ross was smooth and graceful, making hardly any mistakes, but her routine couldn't match Simone's physicality and degree of difficulty.

The results flashed on the stadium's board as the competitors embraced—Simone finished with a score of 60.216 points, edging out Ross at 59.332 points. Simone had won the all-around gold medal, the first African American woman to become all-around champion. And it all took place during her rookie year, no less. Simone had just hoped to make the national team that year, but now she was an international champion.

It was the first of three world all-around titles Simone would win, a turning point in her career. It had been a challenging road from failure to success, but along the way, she learned that trusting her talent, ignoring the critics, enjoying herself, and sharing her concerns with others brought out her very best.

Simone developed a growing and avid fan base, yet

critics searched for a reason to explain away her talent, focusing on her strength and ignoring her obvious grace. Following the world championship victory, Italian gymnast Carlotta Ferlito even suggested that the color of Simone's skin had helped her achieve success and fame.

Ferlito said she and teammate Vanessa Ferrari should "also paint our skin black so that we could win, too." David Ciaralli, spokesman for the Italian Gymnastics Federation, added that black gymnasts are "known to be more powerful," giving them an unfair advantage.

The comments were quickly condemned by fans and others, and Ferlito apologized. But the criticisms pointed to underlying racism in parts of the gymnastics world that Simone still had to deal with, some said.

By 2016, Simone had dominated the world of gymnastics in a way no one ever had. Simone even had perfected a move that no male or female gymnast had ever completed, a double flip in a layout position with a half twist and a blind landing, a move that makes it look as though she's flying. Because only she could pull it off, the move became known as "the Biles."

As the Summer Olympics in Rio de Janeiro, Brazil, approached, Simone, just nineteen years old and four feet, eight inches tall, was the clear favorite. A key reason she was so good: Simone attempted more-difficult routines than almost all of her competitors. In 2006, the sport's governing body rewrote its point system to increase the awards for attempting difficult routines, something Simone specialized in. That change helped Simone.

Simone "attempts trickier elements than anyone, and she pulls them off cleaner than anyone almost every time," the *Wall Street Journal* said. "It's an unbeatable combination."

Early on at the Olympics, Simone anchored a dominant US team victory and destroyed the rest of the field in the individual all-around competition. Simone knew she would have a greater challenge if she was going to win a third gold in the vault. She had won multiple world championships in the balance beam and floor exercise, but never in the vault. In fact, no American had ever won a gold in the event.

Months earlier, Simone was struggling so much with

her intricate and extremely difficult Cheng vault that she resorted to scrapping the move and trying an entirely new vault. In the end, she decided to try to fix the Cheng.

But as Simone walked with Coach Boorman onto the Rio Olympic Arena's floor, the coach sensed Simone was ready for something special.

"She got a little more giggly," the coach told a reporter, "and that's usually her thing."

Simone, the last to perform, aced her Cheng after landing her Amanar vault, both high in difficulty and executed so well that she racked up enough points to blow away her competition. Simone beat silver medalist Maria Paseka of Russia by 0.703 points and bronze medalist Giulia Steingruber by 0.75 points, an enormous difference.

How dominant was the victory? In the two previous Summer Games, the gaps between the gold and silver medalists were 0.108 points and 0.075 points.

Simone came as close to perfection as anyone in the history of women's gymnastics.

"She's definitely the best that I have ever seen,"

said Mary Lou Retton, the legendary gold medalist.

With three gold medals earned, Simone headed into her second-to-last event, the balance beam. Fans started to wonder: Could she do the unthinkable and win gold in all five of her events?

It was not to meant to be. Simone performed well, but she was not the victor this time around. She won bronze, her fourth medal of the competition, but wasn't crushed missing out on gold in the event.

"I'm not disappointed in the medal that I received because anyone would love to have a bronze at an Olympics Games," Simone said.

Simone bounced back to dominate on the beam, unleashing her signature Biles move, finishing the Olympics with four gold medals and a bronze, becoming the fourth American female gymnast to win five medals in a single Olympics.

Simone was selected to carry the US flag during the closing ceremony. So many fellow athletes stopped her along the way to congratulate her or take a photo with her that the closing ceremony was delayed for her arrival.

• • •

Simone's Olympic Games domination amazed the world and resulted in new acclaim. Some called Simone the greatest gymnast ever. Others called her the Michael Jordan of gymnastics.

Even as Simone was cheered around the world, a new challenge emerged. Just after the Olympics, hackers released the medical files of various Olympians, a leak that showed Simone was taking a drug that was on the prohibited list of the World Anti-Doping Agency. The hack was aimed at embarrassing Simone and causing a scandal, but instead of ignoring the issue or denying she had taken the drug, Simone acknowledged taking medication since childhood for ADHD. She had permission for the drug and wasn't ashamed, she added.

"Having ADHD, and taking medicine for it is nothing to be ashamed of nothing that I'm afraid to let people know," Simone tweeted.

Simone wasn't embarrassed about her difference.

"I was born with my body for a reason," she says.

In fact, the same body type that some rival coaches had mocked earlier in her career now was praised.

"Her body is nearly ideal for the sport," the *Wall Street Journal* wrote in 2016.

The compliment underscores an important lesson—ignore critics and doubters and be comfortable in your own skin.

It's no longer "weird" for girls to have muscles, Simone says. "Now people are like, 'Do you lift? Are you a gymnast? You have a good body.' People just appreciate it more, and we're just a little bit more confident as we get older."

Other top gymnasts emphasize a similar message about the importance of embracing one's unique body type.

"Shout-out to all the boys from 5th–9th grade who made fun of me for being 'too strong,'" Raisman posted on Instagram in 2016, after winning a silver medal. "My muscular arms that were considered weird and gross when I was young have made me one of the best gymnasts on the planet. Thanks for forcing me to learn to love myself and my body. Don't ever let anyone tell you how you should or shouldn't look."

Simone hopes young women who feel a lack of

confidence about how they look or are subject to body shaming by peers or others can learn to ignore the negative comments and doubters.

"Don't even listen, love your body!" she says. "You were born with it, God has blessed it. Don't pay attention to negativity."

Today, Simone is taking things day by day and planning the rest of her life. Her biological mother is drug free, and Simone speaks with her from time to time.

"She is a fun, lighthearted young woman who happens to be incredibly talented," says Coach Boorman, adding that Simone hasn't changed very much. "We talk a few times a week and she is still 'just Simone.'"

Simone emphasizes the importance of finding a passion in life, something you can dedicate yourself to.

"I know it sounds clichéd but don't give up on your goals," Simone says.

She shared a tip for how to keep life's goals in focus.

"Write them down, the small ones as well as the big ones. And don't give up on them!"

But it's not only about dedication for Simone—most

important of all is enjoying what you're doing. After a meet once, Karolyi told Simone she was getting distracted and seemed to be enjoying herself too much. "Tone it down," the star coach said. Simone had to explain that when she's happy and smiling, she's in her zone and at her best.

Simone's ability to enjoy the moment doesn't get in her way—it's a key reason she will go down as perhaps the greatest gymnast in history. It's a way of approaching life that can lead to other kinds of success, as well.

"No matter how old you are, it's never too late to start something you love," Simone says. "Do something good with it! Pursue your dreams and passions!"

And most important of all? "Always have fun," Simone says.

ELENA DELLE DONNE

Elena Delle Donne seemed to have hit the jackpot.

Growing up outside Wilmington, Delaware, Elena had remarkable basketball skills even at a young age. At seven years old, Elena played on a team of eleven-year-old boys. She became so good that colleges sent scouts to watch her games while Elena was still in grade school. In the summer after seventh grade, Elena even received a future college scholarship from the University of North Carolina, though she didn't accept the offer.

A star high school basketball player, Elena set a

national record with eighty consecutive free throws and led her team to three straight Delaware State Championships. Elena, who was born to a family of athletes, was so focused on becoming the nation's best female basketball player that she got up at six in the morning to run; later in the day, she'd lift weights and practice shooting. By senior year, Elena had emerged as the top female high school basketball recruit in the country, a six-foot-five force who had the unique offensive ability to excel inside the paint as well as beyond the three-point line.

Geno Auriemma, the legendary University of Connecticut coach, was so impressed that he offered Elena a scholarship as a guard/forward, making Elena the envy of thousands of young female players around the world. Elena was expected to be a key player as the Huskies tried to capture a sixth national title during the 2008–2009 season before crowds in Connecticut that sometimes swelled to ten thousand. It was clear Elena was the next great female basketball star, a life of wealth and fame surely ahead.

But soon after Elena arrived on Connecticut's campus

in the city of Storrs, she was absolutely miserable. She couldn't stop thinking about her family. Yet it wasn't the typical homesickness that many college students experience being away from home for the first time. Elena was unusually close with her family, partly because they had gone through so much together.

Her older sister, Elizabeth, twenty-four years old at the time, had cerebral palsy and autism. Elena had seen Elizabeth endure more than thirty surgeries to try to help her condition. When she was younger, Elena often would go with her sister—whom they called Lizzie— to physical therapy appointments, sitting quietly and playing while Lizzie worked with specialists.

It was clear to anyone who knew them that Elena and Lizzie had a unique bond that only grew over the years. Because Lizzie also was blind and deaf, it was harder for her to communicate. She relied on touch and smell rather than texts and phone calls. As a result, Elena and Lizzie developed their own hand-over-hand sign language. Elena knew exactly when Lizzie was asking for food or drink.

"Feel and smells . . . it's just more of those types of

senses," Elena told a reporter for ESPN. "It is kind of hard to explain it in words, but it's just everything, like our love, our relationship is completely touch and feel. That's how we communicate with each other."

That unique form of communication just wasn't possible long-distance, though. Indeed, Elena said leaving her sister behind to go to college in Connecticut made her so sad it was like "a big piece of my life missing."

"I look up to Lizzie more than anyone else," Elena told the *Hartford Courant*. "She's an inspiration to me."

After just two days of classes, Elena decided she couldn't take the pain of being away from her family.

"I can't do this," she told her parents.

Adding to her misery, Elena began to feel that in devoting so much of her life to basketball, she had missed the opportunity to try other pursuits. She realized she was becoming tired of basketball being the center of her world. All of a sudden, she felt the need to walk away from the sport.

"I was overdriving myself because I was so into becoming the best," Elena said. "It wasn't fun. It was like a job."

Despite all the hard work she had put into her game and her bright future as a member of the Huskies basketball team, Elena made an abrupt decision to leave Connecticut. She was so unhappy that she bolted in the middle of the night, getting a ride home from an old friend, a decision the *New York Times* called "stunning."

According to Elena, "It was tough and I was scared, but I had to do it." She was crying when she got home early the next morning.

Some criticized Elena for squandering her God-given talent and leaving her school and teammates so hastily. There even were rumors that she was on drugs or pregnant and needed to leave campus. Others wondered if Elena would regret her decision to quit the storied basketball program.

Once she was back home, Elena transferred to the University of Delaware but decided to play volleyball. Elena was burned out on basketball and wanted to try a new sport that appeared to be more fun and less stressful. At her new school, Elena sometimes played volleyball matches in front of fewer than two hundred fans, well short of the massive crowds that attended basketball games at the University of Connecticut, but more important to her, she was near Lizzie and her family once again.

Elena wasn't a great volleyball player, but friends said she finally looked happy. Still, her parents had mixed feelings about her new life. They were thrilled to see her smiling once again, of course. But even they weren't sure Elena had made the right the decision to leave Connecticut and the sport she had dominated, jeopardizing her future in the process.

"If Tom Brady was your son, you would really enjoy that he was a darn good Ping-Pong player, but you'd feel like, 'Why's he playing Ping-Pong?'" Elena's father, Ernie Delle Donne, said at the time, referring to the legendary New England quarterback.

In some ways, such second-guessing wasn't new for Elena. She had dealt with criticism from others in the past. For many years, her height bred insecurity. One of Elena's first memories is a trip to the market as a three-year-old. She was so tall that strangers stopped her mother to criticize her for letting an eight-year-old rely on a pacifier.

Later, a doctor said Elena was getting too tall and recommended injections to stunt her growth. Her mother declined the suggestion, but Elena left the office feeling like something was wrong with her. A few years later, Elena was humiliated when she and classmates measured themselves in science class for a project and Elena dwarfed everyone else. Elena looked so different from her classmates that she became uncomfortable.

These moments were embarrassing for Elena, but it was even more devastating when people made insensitive comments or jokes.

How's the weather up there?

You know, you're really tall.

Sometimes she felt "like a monster," she later told ESPN.

Because she stood out in such an obvious way, Elena decided she couldn't act out, convinced teachers and others would notice any misbehavior, even if the mischief of smaller classmates escaped notice.

Adding to her angst: At times, Elena felt guilty that she'd been born with so much strength and physical blessings while her sister wasn't able-bodied.

Thanks to encouragement from her parents, Elena eventually became less self-conscious of her height and even proud of her body, but it was a process that took some time.

Rather than dwell on the criticisms of her decision to focus on volleyball, Elena focused on her family and on establishing a new life that worked for her. Delaware's campus was a short ride from Wilmington, so Elena was able to return home during the week and remain part of Lizzie's life. Elena drove Lizzie around the family's property on a golf cart and reestablished their unspoken form of communication. More than ever, Lizzie's strength was an inspiration for Elena.

"She's completely put perspective into my life," Elena told ESPN. "When I see her struggling to get up in the morning, struggling to walk on her own—she can't see, she can't speak. What she's able to overcome throughout a day is incredible. Any challenge I ever face, Lizzie has done way more than that. She's my role model; she's my inspiration; and, when things are tough, I think of Lizzie and realize nothing in my life will ever be that tough."

Other people Elena met also encouraged her. One time, while she visited Lizzie at her school, a woman named Dawn, a basketball fan who had cerebral palsy and used a wheelchair, approached her to say hello.

"Elena, do everything you can with your abilities, just like we do."

The words inspired Elena. Rather than feel guilty about her physical gifts, Elena realized she needed to do the most she could with her abilities, just like her sister and others with physical challenges and differences managed to do.

One evening during the winter of 2009, Elena picked up a basketball, walked into an empty gym with a friend, and began taking shots from all over the court. It felt good to just play without worrying about her future.

I miss that feeling, Elena thought.

With her newfound motivation and a renewed love of the sport, Elena began considering the idea of playing basketball once again. Delaware's women's team had never achieved any kind of prominence, but in some ways that may have been an added attraction for

Elena. She'd be free of the expectations she would have faced in Connecticut, where any season that doesn't end in a championship is seen as a disappointment.

It was time to return to the basketball court—and time to rediscover her love of the game.

Elena picked up where she had left off, dominating opponents almost from the start of the 2009 season, quickly emerging as one of the nation's best players. She averaged 26.7 points per game, third highest in all of Division I women's basketball, including a 54-point performance in a loss against James Madison.

It seemed as though Elena had it all. She was back home with her family, in close touch with Lizzie, and having fun playing basketball again. But before long, Elena would have to deal with another, shocking setback.

The next year, during Elena's sophomore year in college, she suddenly began feeling extremely tired. Often, she slept as many as eighteen hours in a single day. Elena lost thirty pounds and was weaker than ever. It seemed like she had an awful flu that just wouldn't go away. In a game against Penn State, Elena asked her coach for permission to leave the game, the first time she'd ever made such a request.

She couldn't even hold her arms up. Elena began to panic.

"I think I'm dying," she told her parents one day.

For a while, doctors couldn't figure out what was wrong. Eventually, it was determined that Elena had contracted Lyme disease, an infectious disease transmitted by a tick bite that can cause fevers, headaches, fatigue, and skin rashes.

Elena began taking about fifty different supplements to keep her disease under control, though it would flare up from time to time for the rest of her life, draining Elena's energy and occasionally causing her to miss games.

"Keeping my body healthy is like a second job," she says.

The disease wouldn't stop her, though. In 2012, Elena led the nation in scoring, with an average of 27.5 points per game and an impressive 53 percent field goal percentage, while also averaging double-digit rebounds and more than two blocks a game. Elena amazed opposing players and coaches with her ability to go hard all game long and do the little things on the court that many top scorers avoided—fighting for offensive rebounds, rotating on defense, guarding an opponent's top scorer, and more.

During her junior year, Elena once again finished as the league's scoring champion with an average of 28.1 points a game. The next year, Elena led the Blue Hens to a perfect 18–0 record in league play, sweeping through the Colonial Athletic Association tournament. Undefeated, Delaware headed into the National Collegiate Athletic Association (NCAA) women's basketball tournament, playing in front of packed houses, mowing down competitors, and advanced to the Final Four, the school's first-ever appearance. In a matchup against the number two seed Kentucky, Elena scored thirty-three points, but it wasn't enough to secure the win and the Blue Hens fell to the Wildcats. Despite the loss, it had been a historic finish for Elena and her teammates. Even President Barack Obama mentioned Elena when he made his tournament predictions, picking Delaware to advance to the regional finals.

After a game that year, Elena headed to the baseline of the court to greet residents of the Wilmington facility for the disabled, where Lizzie spent much of her time. Elena approached each of the residents with a huge smile and friendly hello before embracing Lizzie, who had been helped out of her wheelchair into Elena's arms.

In that moment, it was clear that Elena had made the right decision.

"To see her just smile and to really enjoy life and enjoy herself, there's nothing better," Gene Delle Donne, Elena's brother, said.

Scouts were so confident of Elena's talent that she was drafted as the number two overall pick by the Chicago Sky in 2013. Elena was excited to join the Sky but also torn by how far she would be from home and Lizzie. She decided to split her time between Chicago and Delaware.

Elena dominated the pros, just as she had in college, finishing her rookie season with an average of 18.1 points per game and earning the Women's National

Basketball Association (WNBA) Rookie of the Year Award. It was the first of many accolades to come.

Elena quickly emerged as one of the top players in the league, winning the WNBA's Most Valuable Player award in 2015, the same year she was named an All-Star for the third time in a row. That year, Elena led the league with 23.4 points a game, ranked third in rebounding with 8.4 a game, and shot a career-high 95 percent from the free throw line.

Elena shared with the *Wall Street Journal* one of the secrets to her free throw success, one that young people can apply to other sports and pursuits.

"I actually just tell myself, 'It's going in,'" she said. "Every single time."

Some began comparing Elena to Dallas Mavericks superstar forward Dirk Nowitzki because she had the ball skills, agility, and shooting touch usually associated with shorter players but she also had the post-up skills of taller players, allowing her to score from almost anywhere on the court.

Elena continued to deal with health issues due to her Lyme disease, however. She began an intensive workout regime, including boxing, running up stairs with weights on her shoulders, push-ups, and pull-ups, improving her endurance in the process. Elena also started avoiding foods that caused inflammation to try to keep her disease under control.

"I think it's always surprising to people that I have a chronic illness and I play a professional sport," Elena told the *New York Times*.

In 2016, she averaged 21.5 points a game, along with seven rebounds, helping the Sky reach the play-offs, though Elena missed the postseason after surgery on her right thumb.

In her free time, Elena began running basketball camps for young people. Inspired by Lizzie's strength, Elena opened the camps to every kind of kid—special-needs children as well as able-bodied players.

Despite her success, Elena continued to feel the tug of home. In 2016, Elena indicated it was time to leave Chicago to play closer to Delaware once again. The Sky complied with her request, trading Elena in 2017 to the Washington Mystics—less than two hours from Delaware—for two players and the second-overall pick in that year's draft, a huge package of talent for just one player and a sign of the respect Elena commanded. Analysts said she was the biggest star ever traded in the league's twenty-one-year history.

"Clearly, this is one of the biggest moves in the history of this organization," Mystics coach Mike Thibault said after the trade. "In only four years, Elena has established herself as one of the premier players in the world, as evidenced by her MVP season two years ago. Her impact on and off the court will be invaluable."

Even though the Mystics had been an underperforming team, Elena was thrilled to be closer to home.

"My entire family is super excited, even aunts and uncles," she said. "I've gotten texts, calls, everyone's thrilled. They'll be at a lot of games. Having Lizzie this close by is so great. Now I'm in such close proximity to her. I'm hoping to get her to a game. She hasn't been to one of my professional games."

Elena also was enthused about her next challenge— helping to turn the Mystics into a winning team. "I'm really excited about this next chapter in my career," she said.

It will be yet another test for Elena. But she's no stranger to adversity. If the past is any indication of what's to come, Elena has a bright future ahead of her. After all, she's faced tough, controversial decisions in the past, proving that with strong will and the right mind-set, she can overcome any obstacle thrown her way.

VENUS AND SERENA WILLIAMS

The tennis courts were damaged, dirty, and sometimes dangerous. Soda cans, beer bottles, and fast-food wrappers had to be swept away before play could begin. Broken glass was everywhere, weeds poked out of the ground, and cracks covered the cement.

Sometimes, gunshots rang out.

Richard Williams told his daughters, Venus and Serena, to ignore the distractions. *Just enjoy yourselves and work on improving your game.*

"Never mind the noise, Meeka," he told Serena,

using her nickname, trying to reassure her. "Just play."

His strategy worked. Most days, Venus and Serena had so much fun volleying with each other that they barely noticed their challenging surroundings. Playing tennis somehow transported Venus and Serena to a calm, happy place.

From these humble beginnings began a lifelong love affair between the Williams sisters and a sport they would dominate like no other two players in history. They would need to overcome a series of unexpected obstacles to achieve greatness, however.

Even before the Williams sisters were born, Richard made a decision about how his future children could build better lives for themselves.

Richard was watching the French Open, one of the four major competitions, or Grand Slam tournaments, in professional tennis, on television in 1978 when he heard something startling. The announcer said the tournament's winner, Virginia Ruzici, had won $40,000.

Richard was amazed—that sum of money was more than he made in an entire year.

Two years later, Richard's wife, Oracene, gave birth to a daughter, Venus. Just over a year later, another daughter, Serena, was born. Almost immediately, Richard vowed to do everything he could to help the girls become tennis stars, just like Ruzici.

Living in Compton, a neighborhood in Los Angeles that was becoming known for gangs and random violence, Richard and Oracene had limited ways of helping their daughters learn the game. The couple didn't have enough money to afford proper tennis clothing for Venus and Serena, and tennis lessons were out of the question.

Serena's earliest memory is of holding a racquet while playing on a court in 1984, when she was just three years old and Venus was four. But the only racquets their parents could get their hands on were much too big for the girls. Richard didn't let the challenges stop his daughters, though. While he couldn't afford formal lessons, he had enough money to order instruction books and videos and taught himself the game so he could share lessons with Venus and Serena.

Most days, the girls played on local courts with their father, as did their three half sisters, who also became passionate about tennis. Other times, Richard drove the girls to public courts a little farther away in a neighborhood where it was rare to see African Americans playing. One day, when Serena was seven and Venus was eight, they were practicing on their own on that court when some local boys ran over and began taunting the sisters about their race.

"Blackie One! Blackie Two!" the boys called out.

Venus and Serena didn't know how to react to the hateful words. Before they knew it, however, their older half sister, Tunde, had chased the boys down and confronted them over their slurs. The boys never bothered the girls again.

"People were used to seeing tennis champions who were white," Venus says in the book *Venus & Serena*. "Who was ever going to believe that two black girls from Compton could become the best in the world? But we didn't stop playing, no matter how wacky our dream seemed to other people."

The five Williams girls had to share a single bedroom with four beds, but the cramped living situation helped them forge a lasting bond. It also encouraged them to empathize with their less fortunate neighbors. Something as simple as having new tennis balls was a luxury the girls learned to appreciate.

"Seeing all parts of life makes you well-rounded and gives perspective," Venus says.

Richard owned a security firm and Oracene was a nurse, but over time their primary focus became helping their daughters become tennis greats. Richard pushed the sisters to excel, but Venus says he didn't force them to play the sport. According to Venus, the sisters were told they could quit if they wanted, but they kept coming back for more, practicing harder each time on the court, several hours each day after school. Soon they came to share their father's dream—they hungered to become champions.

"Daddy believed tennis was our ticket up and out of Compton," says Serena. "But he also knew we had to take to it."

As they grew up, the Williams sisters didn't have

many friends or hobbies, but they continued to improve on the court and enjoyed the sport. Before long, all the practice started to pay off and the sisters began gaining notice for their prowess on the court. They were just one year and three months apart in age, but early on it was Venus—taller, quicker, and more athletic at the time than Serena—who seemed on the fast track to stardom. Venus began winning local tournaments and even drawing attention from national media.

"Venus was the phenom, the prodigy, the rising one," Serena writes in her book, *My Life*. "I understood it on some level . . . but on another level it hurt . . . sometimes it felt like nobody believed in me."

Serena wasn't jealous of her sister. Instead, she vowed to work hard on her game to try to join Venus in the spotlight, at least one day.

For her part, Venus says it sometimes was a burden that so many recognized her talent at such a young age. She felt pressure from both her father and tennis commentators who predicted greatness for her and wondered if she could fulfill everyone's hopes for her career.

"There was a lot of hype and it was hard to balance

my expectations, and the expectations of others," Venus says. "For a young person, that's pressure and it can be hard to navigate."

Venus says she found a solution. She decided to ignore what others predicted for her "and focus on what I wanted to accomplish."

Venus dominated her competition, stunning opponents by winning every match she played as a junior player. She turned professional in 1994 at age fourteen and beat a few top players over the next three years, though she didn't advance far in various tournaments she entered.

In 1997, Venus managed to break into the sport's top 100 ranking. By then, she had gained a following for her style of play—a unique blend of power and athleticism—as well as her distinctive look.

Venus was "like nothing ever seen in tennis before: Beads in her hair, incredible wheels and reach, attitude to spare," *Sports Illustrated* wrote.

That year, Venus competed in the US Open for the

first time and made it to the semifinals, where she played Romanian Irina Spirlea, who was ranked seventh in the world. Amid the excitement, Venus was subjected to an uncomfortable moment on the court. During a changeover in that semifinal match, Spirlea intentionally bumped into Venus, an unheard-of insult that stunned fans and television commentators.

Venus managed to overcome the collision and the distraction it had created, beating Spirlea 7–6, 4–6, 7–6 in a dramatic third-set tie break, even after Spirlea held two match points in the tiebreaker. Later, Spirlea told reporters that she had bumped Venus because Venus seemed arrogant. The move likely also was aimed at intimidating Venus. Venus's father accused Spirlea of racism, an obstacle he felt his daughters were dealing with in a sport that had few black stars.

Rather than get into a war of words, Venus took the high road, telling reporters she wouldn't focus on the collision or Spirlea's criticisms.

"I'm sorry she feels that way," Venus said of Spirlea. "It's not a big thing to me."

The Williams sisters' ability to ignore insults and

distractions would serve them well throughout their careers.

Venus lost in the finals of that tournament, but she became the first woman since Pam Shriver to reach a US Open singles final in her very first try, losing to top-ranked Martina Hingis in straight sets. Months later, Venus beat Joannette Kruger to win her first singles tournament. The following year, Venus avenged her loss to Hingis, then the world's top-ranked female, in a dramatic three-set match at the Sydney International, overcoming cramps in the sweltering heat.

Venus's victory sent a clear message to the tennis world that a new superstar had arrived. She finished 1998 as the world's fifth-ranked female tennis player.

Venus's confidence seemed to grow, even as she played more experienced players. On the inside, however, she still battled insecurities. The next year, she was seeded third in the US Open, but she lost to Hingis in the semifinals.

"On the court, I was just so nervous, I let fear take over," Williams later explained. "And the next thing I know, I'm shaking hands [as] the loser."

Venus vowed to never again let fear get in her way.

"Losses are just awful, they're massive," Venus says. "But the only tragedy of losing is not learning from it."

It took Serena slightly longer than her sister to reach tennis's upper echelon. Unlike Venus, Serena lost several matches as a junior. For a while, she was viewed simply as Venus's kid sister. But Serena made up for lost time and joined Venus as a pro in 1995, at age fourteen.

Just three years later, Serena "announced herself to the tennis world," according to *USA Today*, becoming the unexpected US Open champion, beating Hingis in the finals and turning heads for powering the tennis ball in volleys as hard as anyone in the game, even her sister.

Midway through the finals match, Serena belted a forehand winner past Hingis with such force that tennis great John McEnroe, sitting in the commentary booth, could only say: "Excuse me?!"

With the win, Serena became the second African

American woman after Althea Gibson in 1958 to win a Grand Slam singles tournament. Playing together, the Williams sisters also won the US Open doubles title, another sign of their ascendance in the tennis world.

Over the next few years, the sisters would dominate the game, more than fulfilling the expectations of their father. During one stretch, Venus won *thirty-five* consecutive singles matches as well as six tournaments, including Wimbledon and the US Open several times. In 2002, Venus became the world's top-ranked female player. She also won the gold medal in the 2000 Olympic Games in Sydney, Australia. During this period, Venus battled tendinitis in her knee and wrists as well as anemia, a blood condition that often causes weariness. Meanwhile, Serena emerged as a top-10 player and won major tournaments, including the US Open.

In 2001, playing in the Indian Wells Masters in the desert in super-hot Palm Springs, California, Venus came down with heat exhaustion. She was so dehydrated she began to cramp, feeling severe pain. Venus's knee also throbbed with pain. Fans couldn't tell, but she even had trouble breathing when she came off the court after a quarterfinals victory over Elena Dementieva.

In the semifinals, Venus was scheduled to face Serena in a much-anticipated match. But Venus told tournament officials she just couldn't go on, her body was in terrible pain. Aware that the big crowd was eager to see the matchup, the officials didn't take Venus's complaints seriously, however. Some wondered if Venus was trying to get out of a match against her sister. The officials kept stalling, hoping Venus would feel better and the match would go on. Finally, they told the fans the truth—Venus wasn't in the right condition to play and Serena would be awarded the victory.

The crowd was incensed. When Serena arrived at the court to play a strong Belgian player named Kim Clijsters in the finals, boos rained down from the stands, something that almost never happens in tennis. Some fans directed loud, disgusting insults at Serena.

"I heard the word nigger a couple of times," Serena writes in her book. "I couldn't believe it . . . I tried to block it out but it's tough to ignore fourteen thousand screaming people—especially when they're screaming at you!"

Serena wanted to cry but held back tears so the cruel fans wouldn't get satisfaction from knowing they had affected her.

As the match began, fans continued screaming at Serena while cheering for Clijsters. At one point, while resting during a changeover, Serena was so emotionally drained she cried into her towel.

She quickly recovered. Bracing herself, she became determined to persevere. *Okay, Serena, you need to be tough*, she thought to herself.

"If Althea Gibson could fight her way through far worse, I had an obligation to fight through this," Serena says, referring to the trailblazing African American tennis star.

Back in action, Serena double-faulted, a huge miscue that gave the crowd more reason to root against her. Somehow, Serena managed to maintain her composure, though. Then a supportive fan screamed out: "Come on, Serena, you can do it!" A few others also began to cheer for Serena, impressed by her courage in the face of the hostile crowd. They lifted Serena's spirits as she realized that some fans were on her side. Somehow, Serena battled back and scored an improbable victory, winning two of three sets, 4–6, 6–4, 6–2.

In the postmatch press conference, Serena was determined to behave in a more dignified way than the fans had behaved.

"To those of you who didn't cheer," Serena said, "I love you anyway."

"I would not be reduced by these people," Serena writes in her book. "I would rise above them."

After Serena's win, the Williams sisters boycotted the Indian Wells tournament for many years, a sign that they hadn't forgotten how they had been treated.

Starting around 2002, Serena's dominance truly began. At Wimbledon, Serena defeated her sister, who had been the top seed in the tournament, to become the world's number-one-ranked female player. The next year, Serena became only the fifth woman ever to hold all four Grand Slam titles simultaneously. She went on to win multiple tournaments and Grand Slam titles over the next few years, reigning over rivals for most of that period thanks to an unmatched baseline game, powerful serves, and remarkable perseverance.

Soon, though, Venus and Serena would be tested in very troubling ways.

In March 2011, Serena was on her way to a party after the Oscar awards when she began having trouble breathing and was rushed to the hospital.

Serena worried a doctor would walk in and tell her she'd have to stop playing tennis. She was actually in more danger than she realized. Tests revealed she had a pulmonary embolism—a potentially fatal blockage in an artery of her lung. Had she waited a couple of days to go to the hospital, Serena would have been in mortal danger. If left untreated, 30 percent of patients die from pulmonary embolisms, according to the Centers for Disease Control and Prevention.

Doctors performed surgery on Serena and she had to endure a difficult recovery.

"It got to the stage where it felt like I could hardly

breathe. Some days I didn't get out of bed at all," she later told the *Guardian*. "I just laid on a couch thinking why has this happened to me."

Serena says recovering from the embolism was hard, but it gave her useful perspective in life, reminding her to appreciate each day. At the time, doctors said the embolism could affect Serena's ability to breathe and make her more susceptible to bruising and bleeding, but as she slowly recovered she vowed to become a champion once again.

After about a year of healing, Serena returned to the court, wowing those same doctors.

Coincidentally, also around the beginning of 2011, Venus began noticing something worrisome happening to her own body. She woke up bone tired and couldn't seem to shake the fatigue the rest of the day.

Venus was just thirty-three at the time. And she was a world-class athlete. It didn't make sense that she had so little energy. Venus and her family began to worry that she had a serious disease. She had trouble just getting out of bed and began blaming herself for not having more energy and motivation.

Am I just lazy? Venus asked herself.

"[At the time] I could never, ever get in shape and I couldn't understand why," Venus says. "It was very difficult."

After months of tests and doctor visits, Venus was diagnosed with Sjögren's syndrome, a debilitating autoimmune disease more common in women than men that afflicts four million Americans. In some ways, the diagnosis was good news for Venus and her family. They had worried she might have a serious disease, maybe one that was life-threatening. It was a relief to finally know what the problem was.

But Sjögren's syndrome can cause joint pain, fatigue, dry eyes, and dry mouth. Worst of all, it's incurable. Soon, Venus was forced to quit the tennis tour and saw her ranking fall to a lowly 103 in the world.

"Not being able to practice has most definitely affected my game," she told a reporter at the time. "I can't get all those extra little things you need, and it's hard to get motivated if you don't feel well, too."

By 2014, Venus was rebuilding her career, winning

tournaments and climbing the rankings. She was a thirty-four-year-old, seven-time Grand Slam champion who will go down in history as among the greatest tennis players ever, but Venus realized her battle with Sjögren's was the toughest in her life and she needed to dig deep and adopt a new attitude—in terms of both the game she loved and her life.

"My motto now is that it all adds up, so if I can only do a little bit this day, it will add up, and it's better than if I get discouraged and don't do anything," she told CNN. "That's when I really start sliding downhill."

In the summer of 2016, Venus and Serena flew to London to compete at Wimbledon, another of the four Grand Slam tournaments. They each had overcome so much, but skeptics doubted their chances of success in the prestigious competition. Venus was coming off a comeback year highlighted by three titles, finishing 2015 ranked in the top ten for the first time in six years. Still, at age thirty-six, Venus was positively ancient in the world of tennis. Serena, at thirty-five, was coming off a losing streak, and, like her sister, some thought she was also too old to be a champion.

Venus managed to beat her first two opponents. In the third round, her age was put to the test as she went up against nineteen-year-old Daria Kasatkina, a player born just before Venus played her first Wimbledon in 1997. The veteran managed to outlast Kasatkina, winning in a third-set tiebreaker to advance. Venus continued to win and went on a surprising run, reaching the semifinals before losing to the fourth-ranked player in the world, Angelique Kerber.

Venus would not go home empty-handed. The Williams sisters won the doubles title and Venus improved her individual ranking to number six in the world, reestablishing herself as a tennis star.

Meanwhile, Serena was dominant throughout the tournament, advancing easily to the singles championship round. In the Wimbledon finals against Angelique Kerber, at a key moment in the match, the score was 3–3 in the second set, with Serena serving, and Kerber had break point, when Serena sent a 117-mile-per-hour serve past Kerber's backhand side, stunning the crowd. A few moments later, Serena dialed it up further, sending a 124-mile-per-hour serve past Kerber. The explosive serves were turning points in the match, helping Serena capture her seventh Wimbledon championship and her twenty-second victory in a major tennis tournament.

In early 2017, Serena beat Venus 6–4, 6–4 to win the Australian Open. For Venus, it was her first major final since 2009, a sign she was still one of the best players in the world, while Serena set an Open-era record for the most Grand Slam titles won by an individual and was again the world's top-ranked female.

After Serena beat Elena Vesnina in the semifinals of the 2016 Wimbledon tournament, she was asked in a post-match press conference if she now should be considered "one of the greatest female athletes of all time."

The question reflected Serena's historic accomplishments. But something seemed to bother Serena, who used the opportunity to make an important point about the value of female athletes.

"I prefer the words 'one of the greatest athletes of all time,'" Serena responded.

Indeed, Serena already had recorded a remarkable accomplishment—at thirty-four she was the oldest player in the Open era to hold the number one ranking, female *or* male.

Serena's point was clear: Gender shouldn't define how women are valued or appreciated. A woman shouldn't be considered a great athlete *for a woman*. She should be viewed as a great athlete. That can be said of female athletes as well as of female doctors, lawyers, and others who excel in life, even those who never pick up a racquet, ball, or glove.

Yet even today, women are often discriminated against, especially in the workplace, with many women still receiving substantially less money than men for doing the same jobs. Fed up with this inequality, Serena has become an important face in the movement for equal pay for men and women.

Once, when Serena was asked about her frequent calls for equal pay and treatment for male and female athletes, she said she would like to "see people, the public, the press, other athletes in general, just realize and respect women for who they are and what we are and what we do."

All champions enjoy lifting trophies over their heads as crowds cheer. But in some ways, Serena and Venus say they've derived so much pleasure from those moments because of the struggles they've weathered.

"Only I know the challenges I've overcome and the long path I've been on," Venus says, referring to dealing with Sjögren's syndrome and other issues.

Venus, who has won seven Grand Slam singles titles and four Olympic gold medals and held the number one world ranking on three separate occasions, says there's only one way to conquer obstacles, find success in life, and become a leader: Identify a sport, hobby, academic interest, or something else you love and are good at, and then put maximum effort into improving each day.

"Following your dreams and tapping into your passion will always lead you to personal success and ultimately happiness," Venus says.

Just make sure to ignore the inevitable doubters

and skeptics, and listen to parents, coaches, and others who support you and provide guidance on ways you can achieve greatness.

"Don't let outsiders bring negativity into your mind and your life," Venus says.

With that message in mind, Venus is setting her sights on the 2020 Olympics, when she'll be forty. Venus says she wants to represent the US once more, because playing in the Olympics is what has made her happiest in her career.

"Stay true to yourself and do something *you* love," Venus says. "And know you *can* go beyond where you think you can go, and it's worth it. Never give up."

As kids, with the encouragement of their father, the Williams sisters set out on a journey to become tennis stars. They had the passion, the drive to excel, and most important of all—a dream. Today, that dream has become a reality as the Williams sisters will go down in history as two of the greatest athletes—female or male—of all time.

MO'NE DAVIS

For many years, girls were ridiculed for their abilities on the baseball field. They were too small, too weak, and too slow and could never compete with boys, skeptics said.

During the summer of 2014, however, the unlikely exploits of a thirteen-year-old named Mo'ne Davis helped change the perception of fans, baseball experts, and others, likely for good.

Growing up in South Philadelphia, Mo'ne had little interest in dolls, art, or dance classes. She was a born athlete who was happiest playing almost any kind of sport.

Mo'ne wasn't a baseball prodigy, though, and never aimed to be any kind of pioneer for other young women.

Early on, she didn't even like baseball very much, preferring basketball or other sports. In fact, when she played baseball she often struggled.

"I usually swung and missed on a tee," Mo'ne says. "Not a lot of people threw to me because I couldn't catch or throw; it was a little embarrassing."

In 2008, when Mo'ne was seven, she was playing football with her cousins and older brother one day when Steve Bandura, the program director at the Marian Anderson Recreation Center in South Philadelphia, walked by the field.

Watching Mo'ne effortlessly throw a football with a perfect spiral, run hard, and tackle the boys, Coach Bandura was instantly impressed with her athleticism. Coach Bandura asked Mo'ne to join a basketball practice at the center. Mo'ne agreed, and when she showed up at practice, she watched as the boys, including her older cousin, tried to keep up with a complicated "three-man weave" basketball drill. Within minutes, Mo'ne, the only girl on the court, joined in on the action.

"She went through it like she had been doing it a

thousand times," an impressed Bandura later told the *Philadelphia Tribune.*

Mo'ne fit in so well that Coach Bandura invited her to become a member of the team, which also played soccer and baseball in local leagues. But Mo'ne's mother, Lakeisha McLean, vetoed the idea.

"When she found out it was all boys, Mom didn't want me to play," Mo'ne says. "She was afraid I'd get hurt, she kept saying no. She was not happy about it."

Mo'ne was persistent, however, asking her mother for permission on an almost daily basis. She couldn't forget the fun she had playing with the team and wanted more.

"I'll be *fine,*" Mo'ne insisted to her mother.

Eventually, her mother gave in and let Mo'ne join Coach Bandura's team.

"I wore her down," Mo'ne says. "I just really wanted to play, I just wanted to try something new."

Soon, Mo'ne wasn't just the team's only female member, she also was one of its best players. But when she played rival squads in various sports, Mo'ne often heard skepticism or even mockery from opposing players.

"Guys were thinking they were stronger and faster in soccer, so whenever I did something good [on the field] they gave a shocked look. It was the coolest thing ever," Mo'ne says.

Sometimes, even parents of rival teams made negative comments about how the lone girl on the field wouldn't be able to keep up with the boys.

"A lot of parents trash talked on the side," she says. "I heard it but didn't pay any attention or I'd start laughing, to show them I didn't really care . . . whatever they said was just funny [to me]."

Mo'ne played a variety of sports for Coach Bandura, including baseball, but basketball remained Mo'ne's favorite. In fact, she almost quit baseball at age nine.

"I wasn't really into baseball until I was nine or ten," she says. "I wasn't the best on the team, I was just another player."

When playing baseball, Mo'ne usually was an outfielder. One day, though, Coach Bandura, perhaps remembering Mo'ne's impressive football-throwing ability, asked her if she wanted to pitch. From the start, Mo'ne had impressive control and accuracy, but she didn't have much velocity. The coach said he didn't mind.

"Throw strikes," he told her. "Let your teammates field the ball."

The Anderson Monarchs practiced almost daily and Mo'ne kept working on her pitching mechanics. Over time, she began to throw much harder, impressing her coach and teammates.

"Somehow my arm got stronger," Mo'ne says. "Coach Steve said I had a good arm so I kept coming to practice to improve."

Back at school, Mo'ne's friends were supportive of her sports ambitions, saying it was cool she was playing with boys. That bolstered Mo'ne's confidence. But some were worried for her, just like Mo'ne's mother had been.

"Aren't you scared of getting hurt?" a friend asked.

Mo'ne reassured her that she would be fine.

As the Monarchs' starting pitcher, Mo'ne didn't hide the fact that she was the only girl on the team. She even wore a distinctive, hot-pink baseball glove. It was Mo'ne's favorite color at the time and the glove had been a present from her mother, so Mo'ne wasn't going to hide it or choose a different color. She was comfortable being herself, even if she began to draw attention.

"The first time we played [the Monarchs] I remember looking and wondering why this baseman had a pink glove," said Jesse Balcer, coach of the Fox Rox Baseball Club, which played against Mo'ne's team. "Then I looked closer and thought, wait a minute, that's not a boy, it's a girl!"

One time, as Mo'ne walked out to the mound at the Marian Anderson Recreation Center, she heard the opposing team laughing at her and her glove.

"We're gonna kill them!" Mo'ne remembers them saying. "There's a girl pitching!"

Mo'ne just looked at her teammates and smiled. By then, she was consistently throwing a fastball that topped 60 miles per hour. She knew the boys should have been nervous, not cocky, about facing her. The teasing made Mo'ne even more determined to succeed.

"I was ready to go out there and shut them down," she says.

Mo'ne says she pitched a shutout, leading her team to victory.

Other outings were rougher. In one game when she was around eleven years old, Mo'ne pitched against an aptly named team called the Bombers. Facing a lineup stacked with tough hitters, she was pounded, giving up four home runs in a single inning.

"It was the worst day," she says. "I just kept throwing strikes and somehow I got out of the inning."

Afterward, Mo'ne says she tried to keep her confidence up, reminding herself that even major league pitching stars have bad days.

"I was disappointed because I let my team down, but I told myself this was going to happen at some point," she says.

Around 2011, at age ten, Mo'ne says she realized she was emerging as a dominant player. In tournament games against top-seeded teams, Mo'ne usually was given the start, a clear recognition that she was her team's best pitcher.

"I was like, 'Oh my, I didn't know I could pitch like this,'" she says. "I was good, though I knew there was still room for improvement."

Mo'ne's reputation began to spread and opponents

took notice. Before long, no one was laughing at Mo'ne or the color of her glove.

Skill, training, and discipline were the keys to her developing talent. Mo'ne had to sacrifice for her love of the game. She took a bus at 6:15 a.m. each morning to travel to school. After school, she would go to the recreational center for practice or games. Her work ethic was just as impressive as her ability to dominate the boys, who were as big as six foot three, in her Philadelphia league.

In 2014, Mo'ne and a Philadelphia team she had joined, the Taney Dragons, set out to try to make the Little League World Series (LLWS). In a qualifying game in August of that year, Mo'ne, now thirteen years old, was the starting pitcher and she threw a three-hit, complete game shutout to qualify the Dragons for the LLWS in South Williamsport, Pennsylvania, where the world would be watching. By then, Mo'ne had garnered her share of publicity, including articles in local newspapers.

She wasn't prepared for what was ahead, however.

• • •

From the first game in the World Series, all eyes were on Mo'ne. It wasn't just that she was the first African American girl to compete in tournament history or that she was one of just eighteen female players in LLWS history—fans and analysts were simply in awe of her incredible talent.

Throwing with a compact, over-the-top motion, falling slightly to her left with a style that some compared to former Boston Red Sox star closer Jonathan Papelbon, Mo'ne dominated from the opening game's first inning. Though she later acknowledged dealing with nerves, few in the stands could tell. Mo'ne's fastball reached 70 miles per hour and her curveball hit the exact spots where she'd aimed, as she began mowing down opposing hitters from the team from South Nashville, Tennessee.

By the fifth inning, Mo'ne had only thrown forty-four pitches and seemed fresh and in control, while Nashville's starter had already reached the eighty-five-pitch Little League limit. In the sixth and final inning, Mo'ne struck out the first two batters. The third made it to a full count, three balls and two strikes, but

Mo'ne struck him out, too, finishing off the victory.

In all, Mo'ne had struck out eight batters and allowed no walks and only two hits in the complete game 4–0 shutout victory, her second complete game in a row. With the win, Mo'ne etched her name in the record books by becoming the first girl to toss a shutout in LLWS history.

The performance astounded fans in attendance and those watching on TV. Some began to look up to Mo'ne. In the stands, a young girl on her father's shoulders held a handmade sign up high: "I want to throw like a girl!" The photo was featured in newspapers and shared online and on social media, further evidence of the inspiration Mo'ne was giving to so many, even adults.

"The 13-year-old baseball sensation has emerged as one of the best sports stories of the summer," columnist Jason Gay wrote in the *Wall Street Journal*. "It was a calm, dominant performance . . . it's hard to not be moved by the excitement created by the right-handed ace."

Even major leaguers took notice. American League

MVP Mike Trout saluted her on Twitter: "Mo'ne Davis is straight dominating . . . fun to watch!!!"

Boston Red Sox slugger David Ortiz told ESPN that Mo'ne "throws serious cheese," referring to her fastball.

Praise poured in from other celebrities and athletes like TV show host Ellen DeGeneres, basketball star Kevin Durant, legendary tennis player Billie Jean King, First Lady Michelle Obama and many others. Mo'ne's story captivated the nation because it demonstrated that girls can accomplish any goal they set out for themselves, even on a playing field usually dominated by boys.

"It was the coolest thing ever," Mo'ne says. "I don't think many of these people actually had watched the Little League World series before. It was very overwhelming."

Even as the nation cheered her performance, though, Mo'ne appeared calm and composed. In interviews, she usually gave confident answers, often laced with sly humor.

"I throw my curveball like Clayton Kershaw," she said in one interview, referring to the Los Angeles

Dodgers' flamethrower, "and my fastball like Mo'ne Davis."

Asked by ESPN whether she minded all the new-found attention and interview requests pouring in from all over the world, she had a perfect answer.

"I can always say no," Mo'ne said.

In her next start, Mo'ne wasn't quite as dominant, though she struck out six batters in just over two innings of work in her team's 8–1 loss to a Nevada team considered the best hitting squad in the tournament.

"Everyone knew their lineup was stacked with great players," Mo'ne says. "I went in very nervous but somehow the nerves went away."

In their next game, a do-or-die match against a squad from Chicago, Mo'ne and her Philadelphia team were down by four runs early in the game. But they fought back, cutting down their opponent's lead to one run. Unfortunately, that was as close as they would come. They lost the game and Mo'ne and her teammates were knocked out of the tournament, but the sports world was still buzzing about all she had accomplished and the impact she was having.

That week, Mo'ne became the first Little League baseball player to appear on the cover of *Sports Illustrated*. Later, she earned the Associated Press's Female Athlete of the Year award. Mo'ne even helped inspire a 2016 television show called *Pitch*, about a female pitcher with a chance to the play in the major leagues, a sign of her wider impact on society.

Mo'ne's talent and tenacity helped change the perceptions many had of female athletes, and she even became a role model, something Mo'ne says made her proud.

After the tournament, "a lot of girls say they began trying out" for new sports, Mo'ne says. "I like that I had an opportunity to show we girls can hang with the guys."

Mo'ne couldn't return to the LLWS after her 2014 feat because she was past the tournament's age limit. She continued to play summer ball for the Anderson Monarchs, though. And her success forced fans and baseball experts to consider the possibility that a female player could emerge as a star in the major leagues at some point in the years ahead.

In fact, in 2015, Melissa Mayeux, a sixteen-year-old French shortstop, garnered attention when she became the first female player added to Major League Baseball's international registration list, making her eligible to be signed by an MLB club.

"Davis captivated America," the *Washington Post* wrote. "Thanks to the performances of Davis and Mayeux . . . the wait for fiction to turn into reality is dwindling."

In the years since her historic performance at the 2014 LLWS, Mo'ne has continued to play a variety of sports against boys, enjoying each.

"Winning is winning," she says. "I just enjoy the opportunity to get better."

As a tenth grader, she mostly plays baseball, soccer, and basketball today, but she's decided on a new goal: playing college basketball and then advancing to the WNBA.

Despite her amazing accomplishments, from time to time, she still hears trash talk from rivals or parents on the sidelines.

"It's not every game, just whenever we're beating

a team and parents start getting mad," Mo'ne says.

Mo'ne has a piece of advice for other girls in similar situations: Ignore the skeptics and those who share insults, not inspiration.

"There always will be people who will put you down or try to hurt you," she says. "Just know that life won't always be an uphill arrow, there are some bumps and obstacles, just keep pushing and working hard and staying in school and you will see the hard work rewarded."

BETHANY HAMILTON

Sometimes it's easy to predict how a physical difference or other challenge will serve as an imposing obstacle in life. Other times, however, setbacks arrive unexpectedly. These can be the most difficult challenges one could possibly face because they emerge abruptly, providing no time to prepare or adjust.

As a young teenager, Bethany Hamilton suffered a tragedy that was sudden and shocking. She was so devastated even her family and friends expected Bethany to abandon her life's dream.

But Bethany wasn't willing to give up.

. . .

From an early age, Bethany had a single passion: surfing. Bethany had fun playing soccer and other sports, but there was something different about surfing—for her, the sport is "a pleasure rush indescribable to anyone who has not experienced it."

Bethany lived in Hawaii and began hitting the waves at the age of five, guided by her parents, Tom and Cheri. She was a natural in the water, and at age seven, Bethany could surf and catch waves without any help, winning her first competition on the island of Oahu just a year later.

"My passion for surfing ignited and went off," says Bethany.

Bethany's family wasn't wealthy, but her parents managed to pay for contest entrance fees, car rentals, and other transportation costs. Most important, her parents gave Bethany their full support as she chased her dream.

"My parents were able to get me a surfboard and get me to the beach, and that's all I needed," she says. "My mom and dad weren't financially well off but they provided the best they could and always cheered for me."

When Bethany began to participate in more serious amateur surfing competitions, it became clear
she had a great deal of talent. In 2002, she won the
explorer women's division of the National Scholastic
Surfing Association's (NSSA) Open and Explorer event
on Kauai. It was her first win at a major amateur contest. Yet Bethany was no stranger to success. Even before the NSSA competition, she beat out older surfers
to win the women's division at a contest at Ala Moana
on Oahu.

Beyond her obvious talent, discipline and training were key to Bethany's early success. She worked
hard on her physical condition, which in turn helped
her surfing. But after watching competitors carefully,
Bethany came to realize she'd require something else
to reach the ambitious goals she was setting for herself
in surfing. She also needed a strong mental approach
to the sport.

Rivals were often intimidated when they saw a
huge wave rushing toward them, but Bethany would
steady her nerves and try to stay confident. When
she traveled to compete in a spot where she had never

surfed, Bethany worked hard to stay calm and not let local girls more familiar with the area beat her.

"What separates the best from the rest is the ability to overcome hard stuff," Bethany says. "The ocean is always challenging; it's frustrating at times and your ability to adapt and adjust to changing conditions is crucial."

Bethany's ability to stay cool under pressure would serve her well later in life.

By age thirteen, Bethany seemed to have a bright future. She was a top amateur surfer with a loving and supportive family. Some thought she might even be gifted enough to become a professional surfer. Bethany was dedicated to doing everything she could to pursue her dream.

Then came the terrifying morning that would change everything.

Early on October 31, 2003—Halloween morning—Bethany's mother, Cheri, opened Bethany's bedroom door a crack to ask a question: "Wanna go surfing?"

Within minutes, Bethany was out of bed and dressed for the beach. It was still dark when they headed for a spot on the north shore of Kauai. The waves were too calm, though, and Bethany and her mother were about to drive home when Bethany suggested they check out nearby Tunnels Beach. The waves there weren't much more exciting, but Bethany spotted a friend, Alana Blanchard, and asked if she could stay. Bethany waved good-bye to her mother and paddled out with Alana.

Unable to find challenging waves, Bethany relaxed on her surfboard, her left hand dangling in the cool blue ocean. The crystal-clear water was as peaceful and calm as a backyard swimming pool.

"I had no warning at all, not even the slightest hint of danger on the horizon," she says.

Out of nowhere, Bethany saw a flash of gray. A split second later, she felt two lightning-fast tugs and then tremendous pressure on her left side. Bethany saw the jaws of a huge, fourteen-foot tiger shark covering the top of the surfboard and her entire left arm. Almost immediately, the water around her turned bright red.

Bethany realized her left arm was gone, almost to the armpit.

"It was over in a few seconds . . . There was no pain," Bethany writes in her book. "I felt pressure and kind of a jiggle-jiggle tug, which I know now was the teeth."

Somehow calm, perhaps because she was in a daze, Bethany began furiously paddling back to the beach, relying on her right arm and getting help from Alana and others who saw the attack. Onshore, Alana's father, Holt Blanchard, reacted quickly, wrapping a T-shirt and a surfboard leash around the area of the wound to serve as a tourniquet and stop the bleeding.

He likely saved Bethany's life. But she had lost 60 percent of her blood in the attack and kept passing out as paramedics raced her to the hospital. Soon she would be in surgery as doctors struggled to keep her alive.

Surfers sometimes face dangers from sharks. In 2015, a top men's competitive event in South Africa was canceled after a three-time world champion surfer fought off a shark, punching it and swimming to safety. But shark attacks rarely happen, underscoring how shocked Bethany's family was when they heard about the accident.

The surgeries went well and her doctors were thrilled with her progress and confident she'd be released from the hospital within a week or two. Because she kept herself in top condition, Bethany was better able to survive the huge blood loss, doctors said.

She was shaken by the attack, though. As she recovered, Bethany had early doubts about her future.

"I put on a brave face for everyone, but I can't pretend it didn't get to me at times," Bethany says.

The early challenges were imposing. Bethany suffered some lasting pain from the injury. And she knew she would have to deal with the physical challenge of leading a life with only one arm and relearning to do even simple things, such as tie her shoelaces and put on a shirt.

Bethany also experienced mental anguish. Her life was devoted to surfing and, before the accident, she had hoped to become a competitive surfer. Now her dreams seemed dashed and she didn't know how to handle the sudden change.

"There was pain, doubt, and fear," she says. "The mental side of things was the hardest part, though physically difficult, too, it was all intertwined . . . All these feelings flooded into my head, it was incredibly hard, I didn't know what I would be capable of."

Bethany's family and friends shared her concerns. Her father told a local television station that he wasn't sure if she would continue surfing. Bethany started to consider pursuing other activities. She told her parents she'd like to be a surf photographer and mentioned to a friend that she'd get back into soccer.

"For a while I doubted I would ever surf again," she writes in her book.

One day, Bethany met one of her older brother's friends who had lost a leg to a shark five years earlier and eventually resumed surfing. *If he could do it, maybe I could*, Bethany thought.

"He was my first hint of hope," Bethany says. "I began to think that maybe I could surf with one arm. I was willing to try."

In some ways, she says, surfing had prepared her for the challenges she knew were ahead.

"It's a battle and you have to adjust; surfers really have to be resilient . . . now it would be that much more challenging."

Bethany says her religious faith also helped her. She felt God had a plan for her and was guiding her and helping her adjust to living with only one arm. Members of her church came to her hospital room and helped cheer her up.

"I was grounded in faith and that gave me hope," she says.

Before long, Bethany had come to a decision: She would try to resume her surfing career.

"I don't think I could handle not chasing my dream," she says.

It took months for Bethany to adjust to having just one arm. An occupational therapist taught her how to tie her shoelaces with one hand, get dressed, and take care of herself. The last thing Bethany wanted was the pity of others, so she persevered. At home, though, when the bandages came off and she looked at her stump of an arm for the first time, she almost fainted.

I look like a monster, she remembers thinking.

But Bethany appreciated the fact that she had survived the attack and was healthy in every other way. There was an outpouring of support from around the world from people who had heard about the attack and were amazed by her upbeat attitude. Bethany even appeared on various television shows. Support from Bethany's family, friends, and community gave her encouragement.

The question remained, however: Would she be scared to go back into the ocean? And would she be able to surf?

About a month after leaving the hospital, Bethany agreed to watch some friends surf. Once she arrived at the beach, she decided to try to get back on her surfboard. Bethany was nervous but tried to ignore her nagging self-doubt.

She walked into the surf with her friend Alana and didn't even think about being attacked again. Instead,

Bethany focused on the task at hand, attempting to figure out how to paddle with just one arm. On her first couple of tries, she couldn't get up on the board, which was very discouraging.

Bethany refused to give up.

Then it happened. Bethany managed to balance herself on the board, caught a wave, and began surfing. Tears of joy trickled down her face.

"It's hard for me to describe the joy I felt," Bethany says.

Over the next year, Bethany continued to learn to adjust to her new circumstances and became more comfortable on the board. In many ways, she was learning how to surf all over again. But this time she had to deal with certain restrictions. Instead of paddling with two arms, Bethany learned a more effective way to propel herself by kicking hard with her feet. She and her coach placed a hand strap in the top center of her board so she could grab hold with her right hand and push the board underwater. She had a lifelike prosthetic arm custom made for her, but she almost never used it.

Her courage inspired young people and adults alike all over the world.

In July 2004, Bethany entered the national championship of the NSSA in Huntington Beach, California. She didn't win but she earned the respect of fans, including actor Adam Sandler, as well as fellow competitors.

"One arm or not, this girl proved she's back in the saddle and will be a nationals contender for years to come," wrote Janice Aragon, a blogger for the surfing association.

Indeed, over the next few years, Bethany either won or came close to winning various events, capturing her first national amateur title in 2005 before turning professional in 2007. Since then she has participated in numerous Association of Surfing Professionals and World Tour events, taking second place at the 2009 World Junior Championships.

In the spring of 2016, when Bethany was twenty-six, she was given a wild card berth in an event hosted by the elite World Surf League in a competition in Fiji. The contest didn't start well. In the first-round group,

Bethany finished last, which confirmed to skeptics that her invitation had merely been a publicity stunt, not a recognition of her abilities.

Bethany would have to win a second-chance heat to remain in the competition. She was up against Tyler Wright, the world's number one female surfer and a six-time world champion.

Bethany's first ride was scored 7.1 out of 10, a solid but unremarkable result. But her second ride was a thing of beauty. Bethany started with a quick tube ride under the curl of a wave before executing four slashing turns that wowed the crowd, scoring an impressive 9.0 on the run. Her combined 16.1 topped Wright's 14.9, a shocking upset. Bethany went on to win the third round as well as the quarterfinals. She was eliminated in the semifinals, finishing third overall, but it was Bethany's best competitive result in her career.

Experts were amazed. "Few expected Hamilton to reach the top level of the sport while surfing with just one arm," the *New York Times* wrote that day.

"I knew once I beat Tyler I could beat anyone,"

Bethany told an interviewer after reaching the quarterfinals. "At the end of the day, it's just putting it together and catching the right waves and surfing my best."

It was a sign Bethany was continuing to improve, adapt, and persevere. Bethany, who saw her life story hit the silver screen in 2011 in the movie *Soul Surfer*, acknowledges that she's been able to turn tragedy into triumph.

Through promotions, television appearances, competitions, and marketing, she managed to earn a substantial salary. "I was lucky enough to travel around the world several times before I was even an adult," Bethany acknowledges.

But she continues to face difficulties. "Coping with people's stares . . . answering endless questions . . . learning to [deal] with the frustration of knowing that if I had both arms to paddle, I just might have done a little better in a surf contest," she writes.

Bethany continues to overcome the obstacles thrown her way, allowing her to live a rewarding life. In 2015, Bethany and her husband welcomed a healthy baby boy named Tobias. Bethany was thrilled, of course, but also anxious about how she would manage to deal with a squirming baby.

"What I don't want is for people to pity me or think of me as a person who has had her life ruined," she writes. "It's my reality now, I've learned to accept it. I've moved on."

Bethany says everyone will face battles at some point in their lives.

"We all have sudden struggles," Bethany says. "When hard times come our way, how will we react and what will we fight for?"

Just as she wasn't ready to give up on surfing, Bethany's advice is to cling tight to one's passions when faced with an unexpected challenge.

"I look at the loss of my arm and say, 'Wow, so much good has come out of it, it's worth it in a weird way,'" she says. "Life is so much more than your ambition and goals, it's about giving back to the community and the next generation, and cheering them and their talents."

Bethany made progress when she realized that her

fears were holding her back, not her missing limb. It's a lesson she says can be helpful for others. "So often we're held back by fears of the unknown. If something is uncomfortable or challenging we don't want to give it a chance."

It's understandable to have self-doubt and nervousness about life's challenges. Face your fears and don't let them stop you, Bethany says. Things may work out better than one could ever imagine.

CARLI LLOYD

After 120 grueling minutes of play, the score remained tied at 2–2. The final match in the 2011 Women's World Cup would come down to penalty kicks to decide the winner. A palpable tension filled the stadium as the US and Japanese soccer teams retreated to their benches to prepare for the shootout. Carli Lloyd and her American teammates felt the pressure building.

The US team had endured a difficult journey to get to the finals. They were nearly knocked out in a quarterfinals match against Brazil, surviving after tying the match in the 122nd minute and then winning on penalty kicks in one of most riveting games in the history of the Women's World Cup.

It had been twelve years since the US Women's National Team had reached the finals. Carli knew a single goal could make the difference. She had been benched during early matches of the World Cup but she knew this was the perfect opportunity to solidify her spot on the team and become an instant legend.

Carli prepared for her shot, deciding on a strategy.

"All these mixed emotions are going through your head," she says.

Does the goalkeeper know where you're going? Do you hit it harder or softer?

Focused, Carli approached the ball hard and blasted a powerful shot toward the middle of the goal. The goalkeeper dove to her right, leaving an opening close to the top of the goal, exactly where Carli was aiming. For a moment, it looked like her shot would find net and Carli would be a hero.

Glancing up, however, Carli watched in horror as the ball soared high over the crossbar, badly missing its target. Carli stared ahead, almost in disbelief, cupped her mouth with her left hand, and quietly walked back to join her teammates. The US Women's National

Team had lost to Japan, extending their trophy drought.

For days, Carli was dejected and depressed.

"It was a really tough thing to go through," she said. "I felt kind of like a failure, felt like I let the team down . . . I was pretty devastated."

It was the lowest moment of Carli's life, an experience that would have completely demoralized many players and even ended some careers.

Somehow, Carli would have to find a way to turn this major setback into something more positive.

Growing up in Delran Township, a small town in southern New Jersey, Carli began playing soccer at age five, developing an early love of the sport, constantly working on her game at a field near her home. Carli would practice shot after shot, often on her own. Before long, Carli emerged as perhaps the best young player in the state.

A five-foot-eight midfielder, Carli won two New Jersey State Cups playing for the Medford Strikers Soccer Club and scored twenty-six goals during her senior year in high school as captain of her varsity team, distinguishing herself with superb ball control and dribbling skills, essential traits for an attacking midfielder.

In some ways, soccer came *too* easily to Carli. Growing up, she usually was the best player on her teams, relying on raw, natural ability. Carli received a scholarship to attend Rutgers University and excelled from her first game, starting every match her freshman year and leading the team with fifteen goals. Eventually, she broke the Rutgers scoring records and became a first-team All–Big East choice four straight years.

During her college career, Carli had little need to hone various aspects of her game. She relied on the same skill set she had used to great advantage all her life, playing purely as an attacker, sitting behind the two main strikers with few defensive responsibilities. Carli waited for the ball and had little need for technique. Her offensive game was so strong that coaches and others applauded and congratulated her, rarely asking for more.

After her junior year of college, Carli was selected for the Under-21 Women's National Team, a huge break that opened up the possibility of a professional career. But Carli struggled for the first time in her life. Playing with other talented women, Carli saw that her natural ability was no longer sufficient and she quickly lost confidence. Even worse, Carli blamed her coaches and teammates for her lackluster play.

"When you get to the national team, everybody's that type of player," she told the *Houston Chronicle*. "I couldn't crack through. I just couldn't crack through."

Eventually, Coach Chris Petrucelli, the U-21 coach, cut Carli from the team.

"You're really talented, but there are holes in your game that need to be fixed," Coach Petrucelli told her, referring to her defense and ability to work away from the ball. "You're not ready."

Carli left the room crying. She went home and told her parents that she was going to finish her last year at Rutgers and then quit the sport. Her parents were disappointed after investing so much time and money in their daughter's soccer career and were sad to see her turn her back on a sport that she had been so passionate about.

They encouraged Carli not to give up—hold on a little longer and maybe she could make the senior national team.

"If I can't even make Under-21, how am I gonna make the national team?" Carli responded.

Carli mentally checked out. She spent her final year of college focused on socializing, enjoying college life, and other things she couldn't do before because of the work she'd put into her training and games.

One day in 2003, Carli's father, Stephen, was attending a training session with Carli's brother run by James Galanis, a top coach in the region. Coach Galanis had spent three years playing professional soccer in Australia and previously had been coached by Ferenc Puskas, a Hungarian who was considered one of the greatest players of all time.

Coach Galanis was walking to his car when Stephen approached.

"My daughter needs you," he put simply. "She wants to play for the national team."

Carli had just received news that a player on the U-21 team had been injured and the team's coaches wanted to reevaluate Carli to see if there was any way she could help the team, even in a small role.

Coach Galanis recalled Carli's skills from working with one of her teammates years earlier, but he also remembered the huge flaws in her game. He gave Stephen his number and told him to have Carli call to set up an evaluation.

Carli, still in a funk, took weeks to place the call. When they finally got together and began drills, it was obvious they had a lot of work ahead to get Carli to the point where she could compete for a spot on the national team. In fact, it seemed doubtful she'd ever get to that point. After only twenty minutes of work, Carli was gassed.

Carli was "skilled, had spent time playing with freedom, and had a street savviness and was tactically savvy," Coach Galanis says. But Carli lacked physical fitness and only "worked hard when she wanted to work hard, not all the time."

Carli was a bit of a diva. She had been surrounded

by coaches who used her to help their teams win, but they never pushed her very much to improve.

"I don't think she was being treated like everyone else on the team, because [she was] so skilled," Coach Galanis says. "When she didn't work hard [she] didn't have coaches around her to say that wasn't acceptable . . . Coaches would let her cruise . . . they didn't want to piss her off because she was their star player."

Coach Galanis asked Carli some probing questions.

"Why did you get cut from the team?" he asked.

Carli was full of excuses. "The coach didn't like me [and] the girls were egotistical," she responded.

Coach Galanis wasn't happy with what he heard. Eventually, he sat Carli down for a difficult conversation.

"What do you want to do with your career?" he asked.

"I want to play national for the national team."

"I believe there are five major pillars of [soccer]," he told her. "You have the first two—technical skill and tactical awareness. But you're lacking the last three: work ethic, mental toughness, and 'coachability,'" or good habits on and off the pitch.

"If you can improve your weaknesses and turn them into strengths, then you can become one of the best players in the world," Coach Galanis said.

Carli shot him a look of disbelief. The coach must be joking, Carli thought.

"But this has to be your entire life," Coach Galanis continued. "If I call you on a Saturday night when you are with your friends and I tell you that you need to be at the field in thirty minutes, you say, 'Sorry, guys, I have to go.' This has to come before everything . . . boyfriends, friends, family, everything. Unless you have that commitment, I'm not doing this."

She had never gotten this kind of critique or lecture from a coach. She needed to hear it. Inspired by her coach's words, Carli decided to devote herself to the sport. It would be a turning point in her life.

In addition to improving Carli's fitness, Coach Galanis worked on her technique and in-game focus. After noticing she didn't strike the ball properly, he even worked on adjusting her shooting form.

Because Coach Galanis was convinced Carli could

achieve greatness, she became willing to make the dramatic changes to her game that he requested.

"It was the first time in my career that I felt that someone believed in me to the point where they could actually get me there," Carli says.

The coach didn't even charge Carli or her parents for his help.

"I had to spend so much time with her that I knew it would cost them a fortune even if I charged them $20 an hour," instead of his usual $100 fee, he says. "I also knew that she really had the potential if she listened and applied herself."

Many of Coach Galanis's friends and even his family thought he was foolish for devoting so much time to someone so headstrong who seemed a long shot to make the national team.

"I said she could be the best player in the world, but they kind of chuckled," Coach Galanis remembers. "They thought I was nuts, even Carli's family."

In 2004, Carli started every game for the U-21 team at that year's Nordic Cup in Iceland, finally earning Coach Petrucelli's faith and emerging as a true star.

The next year, she made the senior US Women's National Team, emerging as an attacking and intimidating midfielder.

Carli's first moment in the national spotlight came in the 2008 Olympics in Beijing during the final match against Brazil. Six minutes into extra time, Carli took a booming, left-footed shot that found net, leading the US team to a gold medal. That year, Carli was named US Soccer Athlete of the Year, along with the US Men's National Team goalie Tim Howard.

Coach Galanis was most proud that Carli had battled for over 90 minutes in the scoreless game without getting discouraged, as she likely would have become just a few years earlier. But even after Carli's team won the gold, her training only became more grueling. Every day she did as many as one thousand sit-ups and five hundred push-ups. Her confidence wasn't yet at the level where it needed to be. To most fans, Carli already was a superstar. But she and her coach knew she hadn't yet reached her full potential. Coach Galanis had faith in her and believed she was getting there, however.

Now we're on our way, he thought.

Then came a major setback: the 2011 World Cup Finals and Carli's embarrassing penalty-kick miscue. For days after the match, she was despondent. Coach Galanis tried to cheer her up, reminding Carli that she'd worked tirelessly for five years to improve and helped the US win Olympic gold along with a number of important tournaments.

"This penalty kick does not represent who you are," he emphasized, reminding Carli how well she had played throughout the World Cup. "Anyone can miss a penalty kick; this won't drag you down . . . just get back to work."

"It was really hard because that's the last impression that people have of you," Carli said at the time, referring to the missed kick. "It starts to play mind games with you, but I missed. I had to get over it."

Within a few days, Carli was training again, with an eye toward winning the 2012 Olympics. Her mind still wasn't fully focused on soccer, however. Days before the Olympics began, after playing a poor half in a pretournament match in Philadelphia, Carli got some shocking news from the US coach—she was being benched for another midfielder, Shannon Boxx. In two short years, Carli had gone from player of the year and Olympic hero to just another backup.

This time, Carli didn't sulk or blame others. She returned home and trained day and night with Coach Galanis.

"I could tell she was hurt, big-time," he says. "But I wanted her to feel the pain" to spur Carli to train even harder.

On the third day of training, the coach walked her back to her car.

"Are you all right?" he asked.

Carli began to cry.

"It sucks, after one bad half, this happens," she said. "It's unfair."

"That's the coach's decision, but we're gonna prove her wrong," Coach Galanis responded. "You'll get time, maybe ten minutes, maybe more, but you're going to have your chance to shine."

His perspective made sense to Carli. She resolved to be a good teammate and to be ready when called upon. Arriving at the Olympics, Carli didn't feel sharp enough. As a backup, she wasn't playing full games and didn't think she was in ideal shape. Some athletes are naturally fit; Carli was someone who needed to work hard to stay in game shape.

On her own, Carli snuck out of the team's dorm rooms at five a.m. to improve her fitness. All alone, she'd sprint on sidewalks, past the front lawns of sleeping locals. She put water bottles on the ground to serve as cones and dribble around them, working on sharp cuts. Carli even got the keys to the stadium and worked on her shooting. She also sprinted up and down the stairs. She no longer needed her coach to motivate her; Carli pushed herself.

Seventeen minutes into the tournament opener against France, Boxx got injured and Carli was called into the game, giving her an early chance for redemption. At the time, the US was down 2–0. Playing with newfound ferocity and focus, Carli helped her team engineer a remarkable comeback, getting the ball outside the box and firing in the game winner to help the US advance.

All her training began to pay off during the rest of the tournament. Carli was in the best shape of her life, even as opponents slowed by the end of the tournament, and she scored both goals in the finals against Japan in the US's 2–1 victory. Carli became the only player in history—man or woman—to score game winners in two separate Olympic gold medal matches.

Carli had discovered the secret to success—intense training, patience, and resilience. She had managed to turn setbacks into successes. Her game continued to improve. The next year, Carli became the highest-scoring midfielder in the history of the US women's team.

In the 2015 World Cup, Carli was named team captain for a number of matches, including the final against Japan, scoring six goals in the tournament. She wore the number ten jersey, the premier number in soccer, one that's usually given to the most gifted and creative attacker.

Carli even scored a hat trick in that year's finals to bring victory to the US, amazing fans and commentators.

"It was the greatest individual performance in a

World Cup final ever," *USA Today* wrote. "I don't care if you're a man or woman. It doesn't matter. Scoring a hat trick in 16 minutes in a final, with the third goal being a shot from half field, that's it. That's the end of discussion."

The last goal was absolutely stunning—a daring 54-yard shot from *midfield* that somehow eluded Japanese goalie Ayumi Kaihori, who found herself just a bit far outside the goal. Reuters called it "one of the most remarkable goals ever witnessed in a Women's World Cup."

As the ball went in, Carli flashed one of the biggest smiles fans had ever seen. Of all those in attendance, Coach Galanis alone realized that for all her success, Carli had only recently developed the confidence necessary to dominate such an important match.

Carli was quick to share credit for her success.

"To be honest, for a number of years, even up until recently, I didn't really have the self-belief in myself," she said that year. "I credit a lot obviously to my trainer back home who took me under his wing. He was the only person in my life who fully believed that I could make the national team. I've gone out and busted my butt."

Much of the explanation for Carli's turnaround also is attributable to her ability to recover and learn from the lows of her life, such as the missed penalty kick.

Looking back, Carli says, "I think that [kind of setback] builds character."

After three dominant tournaments, Carli and the women's national team's success ran out during the 2016 Olympics. They managed to make it out of the group stages but could not break a stalemate in a game against Sweden.

It went to a penalty shoot-out. Carli converted the penalty this time, but it was not enough to clinch a win. The team lost in the quarterfinals.

"You did everything you possibly [could]," Coach Galanis told Carli, trying to console her.

A week after the big loss, Carli called her coach, eager to get back to training. Coach Galanis had to force *her* to take a couple of weeks off. Carli once had been someone with ample skill but little work ethic. Through years of physical and mental training, she improved her attitude and never stopped working until she became one of the best soccer players in the world.

By 2017, Carli was a global superstar who twice had won the FIFA Player of the Year award. At thirty-four, she said she had two last goals before walking away from the sport—the 2019 World Cup and the 2020 Olympics.

Asked how she'd been able to overcome various obstacles in her life, and what advice she'd give others dealing with their own issues, Carli took a few moments to contemplate the question before sharing a crucial lesson for young people.

"You've got to work hard to turn negatives into positives," Carli said. "That's really the key in life."

Carli's lesson is valuable for those competing on the sports field as well as those eager for success elsewhere in life.

WILMA RUDOLPH

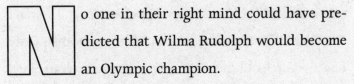o one in their right mind could have predicted that Wilma Rudolph would become an Olympic champion.

For a long time, she could barely walk. Running seemed out of the question.

Wilma was born in 1940 to a poor African American family and grew up in the little town of Clarksville, Tennessee, the twentieth of twenty-two kids. Wilma's father worked as a porter at a railroad station and did odd jobs around town, like painting people's homes, while her mother cleaned the houses of local white families, working six days a week.

Wilma's home lacked electricity and didn't even have indoor plumbing. When the family needed to go to the bathroom they went to an outside shed, called an outhouse.

"We didn't have too much money back then, but we had everything else, especially love," Wilma writes in her autobiography, *Wilma*.

At the time, racism was prevalent in American society. Black people had to drink from separate water fountains and sit in the back on buses. They couldn't eat in the same restaurants as white people, and weren't considered for the same jobs as white applicants. Only one doctor in Clarksville was willing to treat black people.

When Wilma went to a grocery store, white kids sometimes taunted her.

"Hey, nigger, get out of town!"

Wilma's parents taught her and her siblings to "hold their tongue" and not respond. Sometimes, though, she and her friends fought the white bullies.

"The fights were nasty at times, very nasty," she writes.

At age six, Wilma began to notice she was very different from her friends.

"I realized that something was wrong with me," she says.

Wilma had been born prematurely, weighing four and a half pounds. Early on, she always seemed to contract serious illnesses, including scarlet fever, pneumonia, mumps, and whooping cough.

At age four, Wilma was stricken with polio, an infectious disease that today is prevented by vaccination, thanks to the work of Dr. Jonas Salk in the 1950s. At the time, though, there was no cure for polio and it severely weakened thousands of children each year, causing serious developmental problems or even death.

Wilma survived the disease, but her left leg twisted inward and she couldn't straighten it. She also lost strength in her left leg and foot. Wilma did special exercises and her devoted family gave her massages a few times a day, helping her regain strength, though most assumed she would rely on a wheelchair or leg brace her entire life.

"My doctors told me I would never walk again," Wilma later said. "My mother told me I would. I believed my mother."

With the help of her exercises and massages, Wilma did begin walking, astounding her doctors, but she was too weak to go to school. When she played with friends, sometimes they made fun of her for how different she looked.

"Some of them would start teasing me and calling me 'cripple,'" Wilma writes in her book. "But even that didn't bother [me] too often because I always had brothers and sisters around, and they would stick up for me, and the teasing would stop."

Sometimes, though, Wilma was hurt by the cruelty. At first, she cried. Eventually, the mockery gave her a new determination to succeed in life.

Someday I'll do something that will make them all take notice and put them in their places, Wilma recalled thinking.

Unable to walk for long distances, Wilma stayed home most days. Her family didn't have a television and few books were around, so there was little for her to do. Instead, Wilma spent time trying to picture a better life for herself.

"There wasn't really anything to do but dream," she writes.

When Wilma was seven, she was allowed to start second grade, though she still battled health issues. Until she was twelve, Wilma wore a steel brace on her leg, usually from the morning until she went to sleep at night. Wilma also needed to take long bus rides for treatments for her leg.

The goal was to help straighten her leg, and it was certainly working, but the brace made Wilma insecure around other young people. She also couldn't enjoy games on the playground and was forced to watch others run and play sports.

"It always reminded me that something was wrong with me," she later said, referring to the brace.

Finally, at age twelve, Wilma took the brace off for good. Until then, she had little experience with or knowledge of sports. Now Wilma was fully healthy for the first time. She went to a local playground and saw some kids playing basketball and became excited and intrigued.

"I watched them for a while, saw how much fun they were having, studied what they were doing and I said to myself, 'Wilma, tomorrow you're going to see what it feels like to play a little basketball,'" she recalled.

. . .

Wilma had spent years sitting around the house. Now that she was healthy, she threw herself into athletics, first playing on her school's basketball team and then joining the track-and-field team. Running with the team, Wilma noticed she could pass both boys and girls with ease. She even raced past her coach. It was almost like she was a superhero discovering powers she hadn't been aware of.

Wilma was the first at practice and last to leave. Sometimes, she and a boy in her school would climb a fence and sneak into a municipal stadium in the area to do even more running. Wilma was so fast she won every race she entered.

One year in high school, her team entered a meet in Alabama. Wilma was cocky and confident before the race but ended up losing in embarrassing fashion, leaving her despondent for days.

"I can't remember ever being so totally crushed," she writes.

Wilma realized she couldn't rely on natural ability. Lots of girls were fast, it turned out. She would need to outwork them and outsmart them, she decided. Wilma became even more dedicated, sometimes running twenty miles a day over local hills and farmlands. Her coach also taught her proper running techniques. Her stamina and breathing quickly improved.

Once, after winning a big meet in Philadelphia, Wilma had a chance to take a picture with Brooklyn Dodgers star Jackie Robinson, the first black baseball player in the major leagues. Robinson said he had seen Wilma race and couldn't believe she was only in high school.

"You are a fascinating runner and don't let anything or anybody keep you from running," Robinson told an overwhelmed Wilma. "I really think you have a lot of potential."

Just before her junior year in high school in 1956, when Wilma was sixteen, her coach told her something that would have been simply absurd for her to hear a few years back: She had a chance to make the US Olympic team.

Wilma had no idea what the Olympics were, or

even that nations competed against each other in various sports. The next Olympic Games were to be held that very year in Melbourne, Australia, but Wilma had never even heard of the city.

Yet Wilma had faith in her coach. If he believed she had a chance, maybe that meant she really did. The Olympic trials were in two weeks, the coach said, and Wilma agreed to go and do her best, even though he told her the competitors would be young women who were already in college with many more years of experience.

The weather was cold in Washington D.C., the site of the trials. The stadium seemed huge to Wilma, and she was intimidated by the foreign surroundings and sight of her older competitors.

But when the gun went off to signal the start of the race, Wilma ran like lightning, sprinting to a lead in the 200 meters. She did so well she made the team. Wilma was well on her way to proving to the kids in the playground who'd once mocked her that she would do something special in her life.

"From that moment on, it seemed as if I wasn't

afraid to challenge anyone, anywhere," according to Wilma.

Back home, locals were so happy for Wilma that they chipped in to buy her a suitcase, which her family didn't have, as well as some new clothes for her upcoming trip.

The team stopped in Hawaii on their way to Australia, spending a day in Honolulu. As Wilma and two African American teammates walked down the street, window-shopping, a white woman they passed looked horrified.

"What are you natives doing out in the street?" she asked, before picking up her dog and crossing the street, as if to get away from the girls. The experience left her sad the rest of the day, Wilma later said.

It wasn't the first time she had encountered racism. Some of the nicknames she had acquired, such as "The Black Gazelle" and "Mosquito," offended her.

"Racism is part of life, you deal with it," Wilma later told Jackie Joyner-Kersee, another legendary track star.

"She wouldn't let it sap her energy," Jackie says.

Her spirits high, Wilma arrived in Melbourne prepared to compete in the 200-meter race. Unfortunately, her hopes were dashed very quickly. Wilma was eliminated early on in the 200-meter trial heat, shocking and disappointing her. After her loss, she felt as though she'd let down her team, coach, and country. Wilma rooted for her teammates and vowed to come back in four years and win an individual medal.

But Wilma still had a chance to win a medal in the team relay race. When she got the baton in the race, which meant it was her turn to start running, she passed two competitors, helping her team secure a bronze medal and further fueling her determination to return to the Olympics and achieve even greater success.

Over the next few years, Wilma began college at Tennessee State, where she starred on the track team, worked on her running, and became even faster. She wasn't prepared for what would happen at the trials for the 1960 Olympic Games in Rome, Italy, however. She ran the 200 meters, plopped down next to her coach, looked up at the results, and couldn't believe her eyes:

22.9 seconds, a new world record. Wilma ended up making the US team in the 100-meter and 200-meter races, as well as the relay.

On the day before her first race in Rome, disaster struck. While stretching and jogging on a grassy field in the Italian city, Wilma stepped into a hole, turned her ankle, and heard a pop. She began crying, fearing her swollen ankle was broken.

It turned out to be a sprain. Wilma knew she had overcome much more difficult health challenges in her life. Plus, her first race was the shortest of the games, the 100 meters. She was determined to fight through the pain.

"I put it all out of my head," she says.

Tension built in the stadium before the final race. Fans weren't sure how Wilma, who was just twenty years old, would fare against top competitors from the United Kingdom, West Germany, and other nations, or if her ankle would hold up. She got off to a solid start, third in the race, and then turned it on at 50 meters, accelerating past all her rivals. Wilma ended up winning the race in eleven seconds, a world record, as the fans in Rome cheered "Vil-ma, Vil-ma," because they were not used to pronouncing the letter *W*.

Wilma ended up winning gold medals in all three of her Olympic events, becoming the first American woman to win that many gold medals in a single Olympic Games. Suddenly, she was an international star. She and her teammates even met Pope John XXIII in the Vatican after the games, and later she met President John F. Kennedy. Back home, the city of Clarksville hosted a parade in her honor, and over forty thousand people came to cheer on their hometown hero.

It was astounding how much had changed for Wilma in a few short years. Once, some had wondered if she would be able to walk. Now she was renowned as the fastest woman in the world.

Suddenly, Wilma was seen as a role model, especially for black and female athletes. Until Wilma's exploits, track and field was considered a sport for men only. Her remarkable story and unlikely road to success helped build nationwide interest in women's track and field and even gave a boost to the civil rights movement. After the Olympics, for example, Wilma participated in a protest in Clarksville that helped lead to full racial integration of her hometown's restaurants and public facilities. Wilma was a model of dignity and courage who impressed all Americans. Her success proved that it was pure ignorance to believe that minorities were somehow inferior to white people.

Wilma retired in 1962, at the peak of her athletic career, after beating a tough Soviet competitor at a race at Stanford University. She was the world record holder in the 100- and 200-meter events and wanted to "go out in style." A year later, she graduated from college and became an educator and coach.

While she continued to share memories of her exploits, Wilma also emphasized the importance of learning from losses and setbacks.

"Winning is great, sure, but if you are really going to do something in life, the secret is learning how to lose," Wilma once said. "If you can pick up after a crushing defeat, and go on to win again, you are going to be a champion someday."

• • •

Wilma, who passed away in 1994, continues to impact people today, inspiring stars in various sports and others in broader society. Some have read about Wilma, have watched movies featuring her exploits, or were told about her remarkable story.

Others, such as Jackie Joyner-Kersee, were lucky enough to have met Wilma. Jackie is an African American track-and-field star who overcame severe asthma and the loss of her mother as a freshman in college to become one of the US's greatest all-time athletes. Jackie says she first met Wilma during the 1984 Olympic Games when Jackie competed in the heptathlon as well as the long jump and Wilma was a television commentator. Later, Wilma took Jackie under her wing.

Jackie says Wilma paved the way for her own accomplishments, which include three Olympic gold medals, one silver medal, and two bronze medals. Like Wilma, Jackie faced racism during various parts of her career. Some even called her epithets, such as "gorilla," she says.

"I dealt with it all the time and still sometimes do," she says.

Wilma gave Jackie a model of how to deal with bigotry.

"She wasn't bitter, she rose above it. She had that grace and elegance and [was] always smiling," Jackie says. "She said it's important to take the time and breathe and not overreact [to racist comments] because there will be consequences."

Jackie says young people can take inspiration from how Wilma "had polio and still had the will and courage not just to walk, but also to run and then win three gold medals."

"She's a constant reminder that things aren't as bad as you think they are," says Jackie, who today works with inner-city elementary and middle-school kids in East St. Louis.

Wilma taught Jackie that "obstacles can become an excuse." That's true not just in athletics but also in every other aspect of life.

Wilma's lessons are as relevant today as they were back in the 1950s. Almost any kind of obstacle in life can be overcome, no matter how imposing, with persistence, dignity, and a healthy belief in one's own abilities to succeed.

"Never underestimate the power of dreams and the influence of the human spirit," Wilma said. "We are all the same in this notion: The potential for greatness lives within each of us."

RONDA ROUSEY

Ronda Rousey's first battle began with her very first breath.

Ronda was born with her umbilical cord wrapped around her neck. She was blue in the face, her air supply was cut off, and her heart stopped. Doctors rushed to help the baby, concerned she might die, as Ronda's parents watched and cried.

Little Ronda, a born fighter, managed to survive. But the doctor told her parents she suffered potential damage from the lack of oxygen reaching her brain, and Ronda might have to deal with learning disabilities later in life. At the hospital, babies are given a score of 0 to 10 to rate their health on something called an Apgar scale. Ronda's score was zero.

Ronda spent the first few years of her life unable to communicate. Her mother took her to specialists, who said being cut off from oxygen at birth might have created lasting speech difficulties. When Ronda's speech challenges continued at age three, Ronda's parents became very concerned. The sounds and words that came out of her mouth weren't what little Ronda intended.

It took a while, but her brain began to adjust. Eventually, Ronda's brain rewired itself and she began to speak like other kids.

It was the start of a childhood filled with challenges. One day that same year, Ronda's parents took her and her siblings to a hill in their neighborhood in Minot, North Dakota, to go sledding. Her father, Ron, went down first, making sure it was safe for his kids. The ride seemed smooth at first, but then, suddenly, Ron sledded over a tree trunk covered with snow, skidded to a stop at the bottom of the hill and lay flat on his back on the ground, unable to get up or even move. An ambulance came and took him to a local hospital, where doctors determined he had broken his back.

For months, Ron lay in the hospital as doctors tried

to deal with a rare disorder that made it impossible for him to stop bleeding. Even after going home, his condition deteriorated and his back gave him more problems. Ronda watched her father deal with excruciating pain and paralysis.

At age eight, Ronda's mother sat her down on the living room couch to deliver some awful and shocking news.

"Dad went to heaven," she told Ronda.

Unable to deal with the unbearable pain and with no hope in sight, Ronda's father had taken his own life. When Ronda heard the news, her legs collapsed under her and she fell to the ground.

"I cried so hard I felt like I was going to run out of tears," Ronda writes in her book, *My Fight Your Fight*.

Over the next few years, Ronda and her family did their best to recover from the tragedy.

In her period of sadness, Ronda turned to a new hobby—martial arts. Her mother, AnnMaria, had achieved athletic distinction in her youth. In 1984, at age twenty-six, AnnMaria had been the first American to win the world judo championship before giving up the sport. After her husband's death, AnnMaria married a man from California, so the family moved to Santa Monica, near Los Angeles. There, AnnMaria reconnected with old friends from her judo career and Ronda, now eleven years old, decided to follow in her mother's footsteps and try judo. Something about the sport immediately grabbed her.

At the time, Ronda was still dealing with her father's sudden death. She also was adjusting to her new home and school and was getting to know her stepfather. When Ronda played other sports, her mind wandered and she found herself thinking about her difficult life and her father's death. But judo is all about being in the moment. If your mind wanders just a bit, an opponent can pounce, throwing you to the ground in embarrassing fashion. Judo was the perfect sport for a young woman in desperate need of distraction from the upheaval of her life.

Other kids complained about the rigor of the sport, but for Ronda judo seemed almost like a vacation—a chance for her mind to focus on something other than the challenges in her life. After each grueling practice and match, Ronda couldn't wait for more. She also discovered she loved the feeling of victory. Ronda might not have been the best student, but she stood out on the judo mat with her obvious natural talent. Once, she even won a tournament by defeating each of her opponents by *ippon*, a judo term for a quick move that results in instant and dominant victory.

Her mother, AnnMaria, pushed Ronda to excel. Ronda was short and skinny, but her mother told her to ignore coaches and others who doubted her.

"You prove them wrong," AnnMaria told Ronda.

As she practiced and became stronger, kids began to bully Ronda. Some called her "Miss Man," referring to her bulging biceps and shoulders. One day, a boy crept up behind Ronda and grabbed her throat. Ronda reacted with unusual quickness and strength, throwing the boy over her hip onto the cement, stunning him.

Another time, as Ronda lugged her bassoon in the hall, an eighth-grade girl shoved and taunted her, challenging Ronda to a fight. Ronda defended herself and earned respect from her classmates for refusing to accept the abuse. Ronda dropped the eighth grader with a single punch.

Ronda continued to improve her judo skills, and at sixteen she became the youngest competitor on the US national team. She had obvious natural skills, but Ronda also had a sheer will and resilience that few could match. When Ronda broke her right hand she didn't sulk or take time away from the sport. Instead, Ronda developed an unstoppable left hook. After tearing the anterior cruciate ligament (ACL) in her knee, Ronda spent a year practicing her mat work, doing thousands of armbar moves until she had perfected them. This type of dedication would serve her well throughout her athletic career.

"Don't focus on what you can't do," Ronda says. "Focus on what you can do."

Injuries and setbacks, rather than stalling Ronda's progress, turned her into a disciplined, relentless athlete. One of her early coaches, Jimmy Pedro, notes that in judo, competitors often are pinned to the ground and have to fight to get out. Ronda battled harder than almost anyone he had ever seen.

"She had an inability to accept defeat; she hated losing more than she loved winning," he says. "Ronda just refused to accept losing. It bothered her to the point of depression."

In 2003, at age sixteen, Ronda was so focused on making the US Olympic team that she dropped out of school and traveled across the country to live with another top judo coach who resided in New Hampshire. It proved to be a very challenging period for Ronda. Alone at night, she sometimes cried and called her mother, who offered little sympathy. Uncomfortable socializing with the older players, Ronda read science fiction, drew sketches in a notebook, or watched movies on her own.

Ronda was a growing, athletic young woman with a healthy appetite. But she was wary of fighting women in her weight class, who appeared stronger than she was, so Ronda reduced her caloric intake to remain in a lower weight division.

As a result, Ronda was hungry all the time. Her coach stayed on top of her so she wouldn't gain weight. Once, when the coach, who Ronda called "Big Jim," caught Ronda eating graham crackers in the basement, he lashed out.

"You have no discipline!" Ronda recalls the coach telling her.

Racked with guilt after eating full meals, Ronda started trying to make herself vomit up her food in a bathroom toilet. At first it didn't work. But Ronda persisted and the purging became a habit. After a period of constant hunger, Ronda would eat a meal, and then just as she began to feel full, she would force her entire meal out of her stomach, an incredibly dangerous routine that threatened Ronda's long-term health. This very serious eating disorder is known as bulimia.

Ronda's judo skills were improving, despite her developing bulimic condition. By 2004 she had climbed to the top of the national rankings and earned a spot on the US Olympic team, becoming the youngest competitor in the entire Athens Olympic field. Still trying to keep her weight down, Ronda was starving and thirsty as the games began. At one point, she was so dehydrated that her body couldn't even manage to sweat.

Ronda finished ninth in the Olympics, an impressive feat for someone so young, especially considering she was barely eating or drinking at the time. But Ronda, striving for greatness, left Athens dejected. She had expected to win a medal and couldn't shake her disappointment.

"I had lost tournaments before, but I had never felt this level of crushing devastation," Ronda says.

Following the Olympics, Ronda's frustration lingered. She frequently fought with her mother and eventually ran away from home. She stayed with a friend's family but eventually was kicked out, moving from place to place while lugging two duffel bags carrying all her belongings. Lonely and struggling to make her weight level, Ronda turned to a new boyfriend for support. For a while, he gave her comfort. Over time, however, the boyfriend turned emotionally abusive, preying on Ronda's weaknesses, perhaps because he was jealous of her judo success.

"Boy, you're getting fat," he would tease.

In some ways, the turmoil spurred Ronda in her career.

Ronda had a "chip on her shoulder," Jimmy Pedro, her early coach, says. "She was out to prove something. She's good at being the underdog."

Only when Ronda competed did she feel in control and at ease. The fights also gave her an outlet for her mounting frustrations. In April 2006, Ronda won the World Cup tournament in Birmingham, England, her greatest achievement in a year full of triumphs. But as soon as the thrill of a victory faded, Ronda immediately began worrying about how she was going to make her weight level in the next competition. Ronda started wearing plastic sweats and blasting hot water in her bathtub to increase her sweat production. She'd often go two days without food, only drinking black coffee, trying to shed pounds. Other times she would eat and then purge her meal.

All the while, no one in her life warned her to improve her unhealthy lifestyle.

At a tournament in Vienna something surprising happened. Ronda missed the regular weigh-in and was forced to compete at a weight class fifteen pounds above her usual level. Ronda was nervous to go up against bigger fighters, but at least she could eat a full breakfast before fighting. The nourishment seemed to work—Ronda won the entire tournament and turned in one of her best performances ever.

Ronda realized she had unnecessarily weakened herself, potentially causing serious damage to her health, to fight at a lower weight level. It turned out she could handle the larger competitors. Even more important, Ronda was having fun for the first time in a while. Good health translated into good feelings. And the happier she was, the better she performed, a crucial life lesson.

"For the first time in as long as I could remember, I was enjoying myself," Ronda says. "My focus was just on competing and having fun."

Ronda stormed into Beijing for the 2008 Olympics and came away with both a bronze medal and a feeling of accomplishment.

After returning home, Ronda picked up odd jobs and tried to figure out her future. She was working in a bar one night, watching ESPN's *SportsCenter*, when highlights from a mixed martial arts match aired. MMA, a full-contact combat sport that allows punching, kicking, kneeing, and elbowing, borrows from other sports, including judo. At the time, MMA was growing in popularity and Ronda became intrigued.

She asked one of her judo coaches to help her train to compete as an MMA fighter. "You're wasting your talent," he told her. "This plan of yours is never going to work."

Ronda's mother was even less encouraging.

"It's the stupidest . . . idea I've ever heard in my entire life," she said, noting that there were no female fighters in the Ultimate Fighting Championship (UFC), which promoted the most popular MMA events.

Ronda had valuable judo skills but needed to learn many others, including striking, or hitting, opponents. In MMA, fighters use their hands, elbows, legs, and feet to deliver powerful blows. Ronda eventually convinced a coach to work with her, and she focused on her new sport. She had a new goal: to be a star MMA fighter. Juggling three jobs, Ronda pushed herself like never before.

In her first amateur fight in 2010, Ronda approached her opponent in the middle of the ring, or, as they call it in MMA, the cage. Ronda fended off a kick, grabbed her opponent's leg, and threw the woman to the ground. Ronda pounced and her opponent tried to get away. In pain, she tapped on the mat, signaling that she was giving up. Ronda had won in just 23 seconds. She felt overwhelming happiness.

Ronda kept on winning, turning pro five months later. She was quick and talented, but so were many of her competitors. The qualities that separated Ronda from the pack were her drive and willingness to work harder than others. When she was preparing for a match, Ronda endured grueling six-hour training sessions, six days a week. To hone her boxing skills, she hit the heavy bag and did "mitt work," punching a sparring partner's boxing mitts, to hone her reflexes and technique. Ronda also worked on her footwork, sparred with opponents, and worked on various other boxing skills. She stretched, jumped rope, and did two thousand crunches a day to strengthen her abs.

Soon, Ronda was fighting tougher competition

as part of Strikeforce, a top MMA organization. Her first fight, against Sarah D'Alelio, was at the Las Vegas Palms hotel in front of thousands of fans. Ronda quickly locked an armbar—a powerful move in which Ronda placed her legs across D'Alelio's chest, grabbed her arm, and locked it up, pressuring her elbow joint while inflicting intense pain. Ronda was awarded a technical knockout after 25 seconds but it wasn't clear if D'Alelio had "tapped out," or given up.

The decision by the judge caused fans to boo lustily. Ronda resolved to be even more ferocious in future battles, to ensure there were no doubts about who had emerged victorious.

"I was so . . . pissed that I did a cool flying armbar and [the match] was tarnished," Ronda says. "I was like, that's it. I'm not gonna be nice ever."

On March 3, 2012, Ronda took on Miesha Tate, the world champion, in Columbus, Ohio, with 431,000 fans tuned in on Showtime to watch. Tate came out swinging, showing little fear and landing several painful blows. Ronda withstood the barrage and managed to get her arm around Tate's neck, throwing her to the ground and pouncing. Ronda used her powerful thighs to hold Tate down for a while, but Tate recovered, standing over Ronda while landing more blows and weakening Ronda, who was used to quick victories and had never fought so long or endured so much pain in the cage.

But Ronda managed to outlast Tate, winning on another armbar submission to capture the championship. Scanning the crowd, Ronda found her mother, standing and beaming with happiness. Just as fans around the country had embraced Ronda's growing prominence in her new sport, so too had her mother.

"The worst moments of my life brought me to the best times," Ronda says. "Loss. Heartbreak. Injury. I had come to understand every event was necessary to guide me to where I am today."

Ronda was gaining recognition and even appeared on the cover of *ESPN The Magazine*'s annual body issue. But the most popular MMA organization, Ultimate Fighting Championship, still wouldn't consider featuring female fighters. When UFC president Dana White was asked if he ever would allow women to fight, he laughed and said, "Never."

That year, Ronda approached White at an event. Ronda spent 45 minutes trying to convince him to create a women's division. She was passionate, charismatic, and ambitious, describing how she could lead the way and help the women's division gain a following.

Fifteen minutes into the conversation, White says he was convinced. He could tell that twenty-five-year-old Ronda was likable and a potential fan favorite. She had the talent and a determination to be a champion. Put all of that together and she had the makings of a future global star.

"If we're ever going to do it, this is the woman to do so," White later recalled in an interview with ESPN.

Ronda's first UFC fight in February 2013 was a championship bout against Liz Carmouche in UFC's eight-sided enclosure, which it called "the Octagon." Ronda knew it would be difficult. Carmouche was a tough, twenty-eight-year-old US Marine who served three tours of duty in the Middle East, including in war-torn Iraq. Heading into the match, she had an 8–2 career record.

Less than a minute into the fight, Ronda was on the defensive. Carmouche jumped on Ronda's back and she found herself losing balance as Carmouche yanked her neck straight up. Ronda's sinuses popped and her teeth cut into her upper lip. She could feel her jaw dislocating.

"I was literally on the verge of having my neck snapped in half," Ronda recalls.

The screaming crowd waited for Ronda to give up. She refused.

Ronda somehow pushed Carmouche off her back, backflipped to avoid a leg lock, and put Carmouche in a side headlock. Then she delivered a series of painful punches, scoring repeated blows to Carmouche's head, before her opponent tapped out.

In her very first UFC match, Ronda Rousey had shown the world that she was a force to be reckoned with and wouldn't go down easily.

In a highly anticipated 2013 rematch with Tate in Las Vegas's MGM Grand Garden Arena, Ronda landed a flurry of punches, winning the fight in a three-round epic battle that is considered key in cementing the place of women in mixed martial arts.

By 2015 Ronda was 12–0 and was one of the highest-paid athletes in the sports world. One fight lasted 16 seconds, another just 14. Ronda was UFC's top financial draw, headlining matches above top male fighters. The *Wall Street Journal* said she could be considered "one of the most important athletes on the planet" and "a gender pioneer in her sport."

Ronda hosted *Saturday Night Live*, was featured in *Sports Illustrated*'s swimsuit issue, appeared in major motion pictures, and modeled for Buffalo jeans. That year, Ronda was the third-most Googled person.

She had no hint of the dramatic challenges still ahead.

In November 2015, Ronda squared off against Holly Holm in Melbourne, Australia. Ronda was heavily favored going into the match—no one thought Holm had a chance of stealing a win. But in the second round of the highest-attended event in UFC history, Holm, an ex-boxer, stunned Ronda with a devastating high kick to the neck that knocked Ronda out in stunning fashion. She lost the match as well as her undefeated record in a fight the *New York Times* called "an epic shock."

Ronda was 12–1 in her career and remained a world-wide superstar, but inside, she was a mess. It had been a long time since Ronda had suffered a serious setback, and the loss sent her spiraling emotionally. She was so depressed that she went into seclusion, questioned her worth, and even considered suicide, she later told talk show host Ellen DeGeneres.

"What am I anymore?" Ronda asked herself, she tearfully recalled on the show.

Slowly, Ronda set her sights on a comeback. Focused and in the best shape of her life, she took on Amanda Nunes, a Brazilian jiujitsu black belt who had beaten Holm to become the new champion. Four thousand fans came to the prefight weigh-in day, most cheering for Ronda and booing Nunes, who wore a lion's mask while stepping on the scales, an apparent effort to intimidate Ronda.

On a Saturday night at T-Mobile Arena in Las Vegas in late December 2016, thirteen months after Ronda's loss to Holm, Ronda's comeback quest began.

It wasn't meant to be, though. Early on, Nunes pounced on Ronda with a series of jabs to her face that sent her stumbling in the cage. Ronda's reflexes were off. She didn't move her head quickly enough, doing a poor job of defending herself. Nunes pounded Ronda, landing one vicious punch after another with her powerful right hand, an outright pummeling.

Ronda was knocked down and couldn't get up, shocking the crowd. It took 48 seconds for the referee to stop the match and award Nunes the victory. Around the arena, men and women began to cry, sensing the end of an era.

As Ronda leaned on the cage after the fight, bracing herself, Nunes raced over and grabbed her by the shoulders. She was thanking Ronda, not hurting her.

"You did so much for this sport," Nunes said.

White, the UFC chief, also embraced Ronda, despite the blood and sweat that covered much of her body.

"I love you so much and whatever you want to do

next, I got your back," he recalls telling Ronda. "You built this. This doesn't exist without you. You're the best decision I ever made."

After Ronda's loss, fans, commentators, and others discovered a new appreciation for all Ronda had accomplished. At one point, the UFC didn't even want women to battle. But Ronda was a trailblazer, paving the way for others to follow in her footsteps and gain their own fame and fortune from mixed martial arts. She made it acceptable for women to fight in the sport, just like men. She even made it cool, something for a new generation of young girls to aspire to. Strong women now were respected, not harassed. Ronda's legacy was secure.

"Rousey can hold her head high for what she has meant to women's MMA," the *New York Post* wrote the next day. "Nunes, in many ways, is a product of Rousey's impact on MMA . . . Because of Rousey, women have become a top attraction."

Sometimes in life, loss can bring as much respect and appreciation as victory.

• • •

After the brutal loss, Ronda avoided the media and stayed out of the limelight, raising worries among her fans. Her new home in Venice Beach, California, was vandalized with indecipherable black graffiti, adding to her misery. It was clear Ronda was dealing with her most imposing setback yet.

But signs emerged that Ronda was preparing for life's next challenges. She turned thirty and spoke of wanting to get married, have children, and start a new life. Movie roles were waiting for her, along with other projects. Ronda had made tens of millions of dollars from her victories, endorsements, and other projects and was a role model, demonstrating the strength and perseverance of all women. Dana White spoke with her and said she was content and in good spirits.

Ronda released a statement to ESPN indicating she was coming to grips with her shattering loss. She also shared lessons about how to deal with disappointment.

"Returning to not just fighting, but winning, was my entire focus this past year," she wrote. "However, sometimes—even when you prepare and give everything you have and want something so badly—it doesn't work how you planned. I take pride in seeing how far the women's division has come in the UFC and commend all the women who have been part of making this possible, including Amanda. I need to take some time to reflect and think about the future. Thank you for believing in me and understanding."

Around that time, Ronda sent a quote to her fans on Instagram from an address J. K. Rowling, author of the Harry Potter series, gave in 2008 at a Harvard University commencement speech:

"I was set free, because my greatest fear had already been realized, and I was still alive . . . And so rock bottom became the solid foundation on which I rebuilt my life."

Ronda's message: She had suffered a devastating loss and hit rock bottom. But she was alive and kicking and wasn't going to give up. Just as Rowling found that failure in her own pursuits enabled her to focus on her true love, writing, Ronda was suggesting that her life still held opportunity and potential. Giving up wasn't an option. She was going to rebuild and find new success. If it wasn't in the Octagon, it would be somewhere else.

Awards, accolades, and victories are obvious measures of success. But another kind of triumph is the ability to deal with and learn from abject failure. In some ways, Ronda Rousey's greatest strength, even more than her fighting abilities, was her refusal to stay down even after she'd fallen.

SWIN CASH

As she stepped onto the basketball court, Swin Cash could hear the whispers.

She felt out of place. Her sneakers were beaten up and her outfit was a hand-me-down. She could feel other players staring and talking about her.

Swin knew what they were saying.

Born in McKeesport, Pennsylvania, a suburb of Pittsburgh, Swin was raised by her mother, Cynthia, who was just a seventeen-year-old high school student when she gave birth to her first child. She named her Swintayla, or "astounding woman" in Swahili, a language used in parts of the family's native Africa.

At the time, Cynthia was a high school basketball player, a left-handed star dreaming of scoring a scholarship to play ball in college. Determined to keep her life on track, Cynthia returned to the court just two months after giving birth, to the amazement of her coach and teammates. Living at home with her parents, Cynthia placed Swin's crib next to her own bed, leaning on her family for support.

With great focus, Cynthia managed to keep up with her classes, work hard to support her baby, attend to her studies, and play basketball. Even with all of these responsibilities, Cynthia graduated from high school.

Cynthia longed to go to college, but Swin's father wasn't around to help, and as a single mother, she felt pressure to find a job to help support her young daughter. Cynthia reluctantly enrolled in a trade school and took courses at a local community college, hoping to learn about computers. But she had trouble finding a job and her anxiety built.

Eventually, Cynthia found a maintenance job at a senior living center operated by the McKeesport

Housing Authority. She had given up her dream of college and basketball but was thankful to land the job and felt she was teaching Swin a lesson in how to be a responsible parent. Each day, Cynthia pulled on a pair of work pants and an orange Housing Authority T-shirt and left for work. On hot summer days, she pulled a black spandex cap over her head to hold in the sweat.

Cynthia and Swin moved to the Harrison Village projects, a neighborhood that frequently witnessed violence. The region had seen a surge in unemployment after the local steelmaking industry suffered, sparking a flight from the area. Some girls in Swin's school carried knives, while others kept rocks in their socks, to intimidate classmates. Swin's mother encouraged her to focus on building a better life for herself, hoping school, sports, and church would keep Swin out of trouble. "Give your maximum effort and try to avoid the mistakes I made," her mother stressed.

On the basketball court in grade school, Swin modeled her game after her mother's. Swin was a righty but she dribbled with her left hand as much as possible, mimicking her mother. Swin also adopted her mother's fearless style, crashing the boards with abandon and posting up aggressively. After school and on weekends, the mother and daughter went at it in ferocious games of one-on-one, neither giving an inch.

Cynthia almost always won, but by seventh grade it was clear Swin was developing into a formidable talent with a game honed by spirited games against eight male cousins. When Swin joined a basketball team at the local recreation center, she couldn't help standing out—she was the only girl in the entire league.

"I was not [just] the only female, but I also was an African American from a humble upbringing," she says.

Swin and her friends didn't have much money and often couldn't find an open basketball court, so they adjusted. Sometimes Swin cut the bottom of a milk carton and affixed it to the top of a garbage can to act as a makeshift backboard.

Before her freshman year of high school, Swin joined an Amateur Athletic Union (AAU) summer league to test her game against the best players in the region. On the first day of practice, Swin realized it was going to be hard for her to fit in. Her clothes and sneakers were older and less impressive than those of her teammates. Swin could sense the other players staring or whispering. She knew what they were saying.

"Kids could figure out how much my outfit cost," Swin says. "A lot of the kids had the best shoes and clothes . . . People had pity for me, I was a kid from the projects."

When she could, Swin's mother came to games and rooted hard from the sidelines. "Come on, Skee!" she screamed, using Swin's nickname.

Other times, though, Swin's mother missed games for work. Parents and teammates couldn't understand how Cynthia could miss her daughter's big games, especially since Swin had emerged as the team's star. Swin knew they were talking about her and her mother behind their backs. Parents sometimes approached Swin to ask if she wanted to go out to eat with them after a game. They meant well, but Swin wasn't sad.

"I looked around and knew people felt sorry for me," she says. "I could see how hard my mother was

working to make a better life for me . . . I was confident in who I was, even if people felt sorry for me."

Swin had a loving family, clothing on her back, and
enough food on the table. Others may have felt bad for
her, but Swin felt comfortable about herself.

"I didn't have a lot of things growing up, but I never
felt I had less. I was just growing up a different way,"
Swin says. "My mom was doing the best she could, I
was okay not having the Air Jordans that came out last
week, I never felt insecure."

Swin's mother emphasized how basketball might be
Swin's ticket to a better life—as long as Swin didn't
make mistakes off the court like she had. Cynthia never
managed to get the basketball scholarship she had
dreamed of, but through practice and discipline, maybe
Swin could.

"It was all about setting goals in life," Cynthia told
the *Hartford Courant*. "In Swin's case, it was a college
scholarship."

In high school, Swin's coach at McKeesport Area

High School, Gerald Grayson, quickly recognized Swin's developing talent. Coach Grayson emphasized a defense-first approach, and his players were relentless.

"Don't let anyone outwork you!" Coach Grayson often bellowed at his players.

Swin's teammates appreciated her work ethic, a grit and determination passed down by her mother, and defenders began to fear her. Searching for a way to stop her, rivals began overplaying her right-hand drive. Swin responded by going hard to her left, the heated games against her mother paying off.

By her sophomore year, Swin was on her way to a towering height of six foot one, and buzz about her potential reached nearby Pittsburgh and beyond. One day before her junior year of high school, as Swin played a pickup game with her AAU summer teammates, she noticed a short, older man in the gym watching the game carefully. Later, Swin found out it was Geno Auriemma, the famed coach of the University of Connecticut's basketball team. He was there to see if Swin might be good enough to play for his team, the perennial champions of women's college basketball.

Swin couldn't believe Coach Auriemma was there to scout her. "I began to realize that I was going to have an opportunity to do something special with basketball," she says.

After graduation, Swin enrolled at Connecticut and helped lead the Huskies to national championships in 2000 and 2002. In 2002, Swin was voted an All-American and the Most Outstanding Player in the Final Four, posting 20 points and thirteen rebounds in the national championship game, an 82–70 win over Oklahoma that completed Connecticut's undefeated 39–0 season.

When she graduated in 2002, Swin ended her college career as the storied Huskies program's seventh all-time leading scorer with 1,583 points. After graduation, she was selected by the Detroit Shock with the number two overall pick in the 2002 WNBA draft. Swin had achieved the goal her mother had set out for her. Walking onto the draft-day stage, she could see that the woman who'd always believed in her was filled with pride.

But Swin's professional career got off to a rocky

start. Her team, the Detroit Shock, began the 2002 season on a thirteen-game losing streak. Within a matter of two weeks, morale sank and management scrambled for solutions. The team switched coaches, hiring former NBA center Bill Laimbeer, who almost immediately named Swin the team's captain, making it clear the Shock would rebuild around Swin.

The move stunned her teammates, fans, and the media. Yes, Swin had won two national titles, but she was still a *rookie*, they kept saying. Rookies are expected to earn the respect of peers and rivals in the pro game; they're not asked to lead veteran teammates just *ten* games into their debut season.

It's hard enough adjusting to the pro game—it's even more difficult when teammates grumble about you in the locker room. Some of Swin's teammates even began to isolate Swin, refusing to speak to her. Sometimes they went out for dinner by themselves, leaving Swin to fend for herself.

"There was real resentment," Swin says. "It was a very difficult situation."

Swin tried to ignore the criticism and work even

harder on her game, setting a new goal for herself: prove to her teammates that she deserved to be the team's captain.

"I just kept plugging away," Swin says. "I came from a college program that drilled into me the need to be selfless." It had also taught her to not worry about criticism.

Swin even sympathized with her teammates, despite their harsh treatment of her. After all, there was so much attention and excitement surrounding her, but Swin's career had barely even begun.

"I was getting crowned as the 'next thing' without proving anything yet," she says.

It turned out that Swin Cash would meet the hype and then some.

Just a year later, the Shock won twenty-five games and lost nine, winning their first WNBA title. Swin and her teammates upset the defending champion, the Los Angeles Sparks, in a final game that drew the largest crowd in WNBA history. She led the team in scoring and made the All-Star game, cementing her position as one of the league's top players. Just as important, her team finally embraced her, accepting Swin as their true captain.

Over the next three years, Swin made the US Olympic basketball team and helped lead the squad to a gold medal in Athens, Greece.

Swin seemed on top of the world. She traveled home to McKeesport as the city rededicated Harrison Village's recreation center in her name, painting Olympic rings on the building's front.

Swin had no idea how quickly things would change.

Disaster struck a few weeks before the 2004 playoffs when Swin fell during a game, tearing her anterior cruciate ligament (ACL), one of the knee's four main ligaments. Just when it felt like she was on top of the world, Swin had taken a huge fall both literally and figuratively.

Without Swin—who had posted a career-high field goal percentage of 46.9 percent that year and close to 17 points a game—Detroit was eliminated in the first round against the New York Liberty.

After surgery, Swin lost both weight and muscle. She dedicated herself to rehabilitating her knee, but the effects of the injury lasted longer than she expected. Swin scored under 6 points per game in the 2005 season and just 10.5 points per game in 2006, though the Shock did win the championship that year. By 2007, Swin had developed back pain due to the impact of the injury. She barely told anyone about the herniated disc in her back, afraid fans and the media would think she was giving an excuse for her poor play. Swin still remembered when she'd been on the receiving end of whispered insults all those years back at her first AAU summer league practice. She thought it best to keep her head down and push through the injury.

"At the time, all I remember was the pain," Swin recalls. "I wasn't playing my best . . . I felt isolated and alone. My body wasn't the same. My game wasn't the same."

Swin's relationship with Coach Laimbeer quickly deteriorated. He was a demanding coach who wanted more from Swin. She managed to boost her scoring to a respectable 11.1 points per game that season, with over six rebounds a game, but it wasn't nearly Swin's best. Her coach let her know it on a regular basis.

"Imagine playing a basketball game with a hundred-pound jacket on your back and a myriad of thoughts running through your mind," Swin wrote in her book, *Humble Journey*. "It hurt to sit, to walk, and to run, basically to do anything."

Looking for an explanation for the pain, Swin had an MRI procedure that allowed doctors to view the body in finer detail. The doctor called with the results—and Swin wasn't prepared for what she was about to hear.

"I saw something on your kidney," the doctor said. "It's a tumor. You have to come in immediately so we can determine if it's cancerous."

Suddenly, Swin couldn't hear a thing. Her entire world went silent. She was so stunned—so scared—that the doctor asked if she was still on the phone. In that moment, all Swin could think about was her aunt who had died of cancer. Now Swin worried the disease might claim her, as well.

After a series of tests, doctors determined that

Swin's tumor was malignant. If the cancer wasn't removed, it could spread through her body and her life would be at risk, they said. But there was good news—doctors said they were confident they could remove the cancer. In fact, she was lucky—if it hadn't been for the back pain, the cancer might have continued to grow and spread, doctors told her.

Swin rejoined her team, prepared to remove the tumor after the season. She was determined to keep her diagnosis a secret, telling only Coach Laimbeer and Detroit's team trainer.

"I wasn't comfortable talking about it; I was going through a difficult time," Swin says. "I was nervous and trying to process it myself, and I didn't want anyone to feel sorry for me."

Despite her health issues, Coach Laimbeer didn't treat her any differently—he continued to ride her and tell Swin how disappointed he was in her performance. She tried to stay positive and trust that she would fully recover after the cancer was removed, as her doctors promised. But sometimes Swin couldn't fully concentrate. In the second game of the Eastern

Conference Finals, Coach Laimbeer benched Swin, claiming she wasn't playing hard enough, a final insult in an awful year. In front of twenty-thousand fans in Detroit, Swin and her teammates were blown out by 19 points, ousted from the playoffs on their home court.

Two days after the season ended, still feeling the sting of that painful loss, a terrified Swin drove to the hospital for surgery to remove the tumor on her kidney.

Thankfully, the operation went well, but Swin knew she had to focus on recovering from surgery, once again, and also would have to deal with her continued back pain. She also concluded that her relationship with Coach Laimbeer couldn't be salvaged. She had felt hurt when he'd benched her and questioned her hustle, even though he knew about all the pain and problems Swin was dealing with.

Detroit was a perennial championship contender, but if the locker room continued to be a dark place for Swin, she decided it would be too hard for her to stay with the team while dealing with her continued health challenges.

"I'd rather have peace of mind and happiness more than another [championship] ring," Swin says. "I realized that my health would not improve if my professional life did not change."

Swin requested a trade, and in early 2008 she was sent to the Seattle Storm for the draft rights to the number four pick in the 2008 WNBA draft. Swin was certain she could help her new team and prove she was worthy of making the US roster for the 2008 Olympics that summer.

Severe back pain persisted, though, affecting her play.

"Sharp movements would feel like someone was stabbing me with a steak knife," she says.

Swin turned to painkillers and injections, hoping to avoid surgery that would eliminate her from consideration for the Olympic team. But she started losing muscle mass. Pain led to stress. Stress led to more weight loss.

"Weight loss just caused more pain, mentally and physically," Swin says.

One day that season, she received a phone call she wasn't expecting.

"I'm calling to inform you that the committee has made their decisions about the US Olympic team," Carol Callan, head of the women's national team, said, Swin recalls. "Unfortunately, you weren't chosen as one of our twelve players."

Swin was crushed. She wasn't even chosen as an alternate to replace a player in case of injury.

"I felt like I had swallowed a bomb that exploded," Swin recalls. "I couldn't speak."

For days, Swin sat in her apartment crying. She was angry and in pain and felt very much alone. Swin was twenty-eight years old and for the first time in her life felt like an utter failure. It was the lowest point in her life, she says.

"There were a lot of times when my face was planted on the floor in tears," Swin told the *New York Times*. "You cry out to God and you're trying to understand, 'Why is this happening to me?'"

Slowly, Swin began dealing with her difficulties, trying to get past them.

"It was a lot of prayer, a lot of family, and a reevaluation of my life," she says.

Swin's Olympic dream had been crushed, but sometimes from disappointment comes opportunity. Swin was asked to be a television analyst for NBC for the Olympic Games. It gave Swin valuable experience for a future career in broadcasting and allowed her to take a step back from the daily game.

She gained perspective and became more "grounded," she says.

"I learned that things aren't always as bad as they seem, and they're also not as good," she says.

At an event in New York, Swin met Teresa Edwards, a former star basketball player who was a member of the US Olympic Committee. Swin opened up about her frustrations, and Edwards offered encouragement, promising to work with Swin to help her recapture her former level of play.

"Hearing myself talk it out with Tee was just the form of therapy that I needed," Swin says.

Swin decided to change her perspective. Yes, she had gone through a tough time and was still dealing with challenges, but she wasn't going to feel sorry for herself. She'd set new goals, just as her mother had taught her, and work to reach them by working even harder on and off the court.

"I had a revelation," Swin says. "I wouldn't be a victim any longer . . . I had to look within myself and make things happen."

Her biggest goal: make the 2012 Olympic team and prove the skeptics wrong.

"I had a chip on my shoulder that I used for motivation," Swin says. "The naysayers drove me."

Swin found happiness returning to McKeesport, a city that was facing economic challenges. She established a charity, Cash for Kids, that empowers children to lead healthier lifestyles and become leaders in their communities. The charity sponsors activities in health and fitness, provides mentors, and uses sports to motivate and educate children. Sometimes young people traveled to visit Swin. They joined her at museums and other cultural institutions and then watched her play.

Before the 2009 season, Swin finally had surgery to repair her ailing back, embracing a grueling routine in subsequent months to rehabilitate her body. A year later, the Seattle Storm enjoyed one of the most dominant seasons in WNBA history, posting a league-best 28–6 record as Swin scored nearly fourteen points a game along with six rebounds to cap off one of her best years in the league.

In the playoffs, Seattle went on a 7–0 run, sweeping Atlanta for the title, with Swin making critical plays in many games, more proof to the doubters of how well she could play when healthy.

After the game, as fans cheered wildly and teammates embraced, Swin took a moment to remember the lowest moment of her life, just two years earlier, when she'd cried on her couch, alone and despondent, after being told she had been left off the 2008 Olympic team.

"It all flashed in that moment and felt so good," Swin says.

Swin continued to return to Western Pennsylvania to attend camps and leagues run by her nonprofit, announcing games on a loudspeaker and cheering for the kids. Swin gave children her e-mail address, allowed them to be her Facebook friend, and forged bonds with girls and boys going through their own tough times.

In 2012, on a visit to her hometown, Swin heard her cell phone ring—it was a call from a representative of the US Olympic basketball team.

Swin broke down, tears of joy falling down her face. She had made the women's basketball squad for that year's Olympics, becoming the second-oldest member of the team. But the celebration was only beginning—that summer, Swin and her teammates brought home the gold once again.

It was a lesson, Swin says, in how life's lowest moments can make us stronger.

"I wouldn't change anything that's happened to me," she told the *New York Times*. "Whenever it's raining, when it stops, you get to the other side, and you see this rainbow, and you see this sunshine, and then that's when you're just smiling."

In June 2016, after four more years of play in the WNBA, Swin, the winner of two titles in Detroit, one in Seattle and two Olympic gold medals, was named by the league as one of the twenty greatest players in its history.

When she announced her retirement that year, the *New York Times* said, "few players have matched [her] influence and accomplishments."

Swin says young people have their own unique challenges they need to deal with, some of which rival those she overcame.

"Today, kids have so much pressure from their peers."

She urges children and teens "to seek out knowledge and wisdom from people older and even peers . . . young people expect to have it all together but it's important to put time into education and sports, to become a better person *and* athlete."

Be kind to each other. The girl next to you is likely going through the same things you are, Swin says.

"Women are being rated by society all the time," Swin says. "We need to pay less attention to that and have more compassion [for] each other."

Most of all, Swin emphasizes that even those who come from "humble beginnings," can find success, just as she did.

Yet Swin says there's something that brings her more joy than her medals and victories ever could. "It's how I can share the victories with my mother," she says. "Every time I see her, I can see her pride."

In 2015, when Swin married her longtime boyfriend and the band played the traditional father-daughter dance at her wedding, Swin brought her mother onto the floor. They danced to Celine Dion's "Because You Loved Me."

On that day, Swin's heart was full. All of the sacrifices her mother had made, all of the hard work and dedication, paved a road to success for Swin.

KERRI STRUG

The US team's shot at winning the Olympic gold medal wasn't supposed to come down to Kerri Strug. She knew it, her coaches knew it, and all the fans in the Olympic stadium knew it.

Dominique Moceanu was the prodigy of the American gymnastics team. Shannon Miller and Dominique Dawes were the acknowledged emerging stars, commanding most of the attention and accolades.

Then there was Kerri, the quiet and sometimes overlooked member of the 1996 women's Olympic team. Sure, in 1992, at age fourteen, Kerri had been a solid contributor and the youngest member of a 1992 Olympic squad that won a bronze medal at the Barcelona Olympics. In fact, Kerri had been one of the top female gymnasts in the country for several years and a member of the American gymnastics team from 1991 to 1995.

But some experts questioned her abilities, potential, and dedication. A four-foot-nine gymnast from Tucson, Arizona, Kerri didn't seem to have the fearlessness or threshold for pain of some of her teammates. She spent a few years in high school living at home without a dedicated coach. She also didn't seem to have the same level of talent as the other girls. The American team was nicknamed "the Magnificent Seven," but everyone knew Kerri wasn't the team's most important gymnast.

"Mentally, I wasn't as tough as other competitors," Kerri acknowledges. "I was always great in training but my competitions weren't as good."

A US women's gymnastics team had never won an Olympic team gold medal, but 1996 was the year they had been waiting for. The nation had spent four years counting down to these games, when the American women finally would outlast fierce rivals, including Russia. At one point in the team competition, the US lead seemed so insurmountable that some Russian gymnasts, who had dominated the sport for years, were close to tears.

Then everything changed. Moceanu fell twice, stunning fans. A comfortable US lead quickly evaporated. Suddenly, the US team's chances of winning gold rested solely on Kerri's shoulders as she began the vault exercise. Most of the thirty-two thousand in the crowd were on their feet as Kerri took a deep breath and sprinted down a seventy-five-foot runway. She launched herself into a challenging vault, carrying the hopes of the nation along with her.

The fans had no idea they were about to see one of the greatest and most dramatic moments in Olympics history.

From age three, Kerri had participated in gymnastics, enrolling in a Mom and Tot's class, following in the footsteps of her older sister, Lisa.

By eight, Kerri was working with a local coach and winning competitions.

"Until twelve, I just loved it," Kerri says.

It seemed clear that Kerri had a shot at the Olympics if she kept improving, though there were trade-offs in her decision to focus on the sport.

"It was a big sacrifice," Kerri says. "I didn't have a normal social life and I had a strict diet."

In January 1991, at age thirteen, Kerri joined the US national team and moved to Houston to train with legendary coach Bela Karolyi.

"If you're going to leave home, you might as well come to the best [coach]," Kerri says, explaining the move.

The youngest of three children, Kerri was close to her parents, and it was difficult to be hundreds of miles away from them. Kerri, who lived with host families while training in Houston, says she never felt so alone. Many nights, she called her family crying, saying she wanted to come home. Kerri's parents said she could return any time she wanted, hoping to relax her. She decided to try to get through the experience one day at a time.

"Let me wait a bit and see," Kerri told her parents, hoping the situation would get better.

Kerri's mother flew out to Houston to comfort her daughter, but the trip was long and she couldn't visit frequently.

At one point, the relationship between Kerri and gymnastics was pure love. Now, with Kerri deeply homesick and frustrated, it was "love-hate," she says.

Is it all worth it? Kerri wondered some days.

Kerri knew that the career of a female gymnast generally is short and most peak in their teenage years, so if she decided to continue training, she would need to go all out to have a chance at making the Olympic team. After doing some soul-searching, she decided to stick with the sport she'd loved for most of her life.

"If I was going to make the sacrifice I wanted to do it 100 percent," she says. "I didn't want to look back and say, if only I had trained harder and with the very best I would have done better, so I gave it my full commitment."

Kerri worked out as many as seven days a week, eight hours a day. Coach Bela and his wife, Martha, scrutinized everything Kerri and her teammates ate and even dictated when they went to sleep each night.

They had little free time. Munching on frozen strawberries or staying up late on Saturday night to watch the comedy show *Saturday Night Live* was one of the few indulgences Kerri was allowed. She rarely ate pizza, but when she did on a special occasion, she had to pick the cheese off the slice.

Over time, Kerri says she developed "eating issues."

"I was muscular and back then everyone looked like ballet dancers, with clean lines; my coach was into thin and graceful and tiny," Kerri says. "I was eating good food but you get desperate and you begin eliminating caloric intake and doing more cardio."

Beyond the challenge of following a strict diet, Kerri also had to withstand constant, and often harsh, criticism. Sometimes Coach Bela screamed at Kerri, especially if she performed poorly in a competition or had a bad workout.

"You know he's just trying to motivate you, but months and weeks of hearing it is hard," she says. "The coaches didn't coddle me. I was in a lot of pain all the time and I used to ask why he's making me do fifteen vaults, not just ten."

Having already decided to keep training, Kerri continued to improve and her chances of making the 1992 Barcelona Olympics seemed good. But on the final rotation on the last day of the Olympic trials in Baltimore in June of that year, Kerri fell while competing in one of her strongest events, the floor exercise, putting her Olympics participation in jeopardy. Kerri managed to make the team, though she didn't participate in individual competitions, and earned a team bronze medal. All in all, it was a bittersweet competition—though she'd won a team medal, she hadn't had a chance to show off her true potential as an individual.

That year, Coach Bela retired and Kerri considered giving up the sport. She didn't think she'd be able to make the 1996 Olympics and looked forward to a new life with different hobbies, old friends, and none of the pressures of competition.

In the end, Kerri decided to give gymnastics a bit more time to see if she could win another medal. Kerri spent three years bouncing between gyms, cities, and coaches, losing confidence along the way, partly because she didn't have Coach Bela to guide her. Kerri also had her share of bad luck, tearing a stomach muscle in a European meet, forcing her to endure six months of recuperation. Kerri decided to go home and spend time with her family.

That decision allowed her to finish high school with old friends. Kerri enjoyed her classes and got top grades, managing to squeeze in her gymnastic training before and after school.

Finally a normal teenager and living with her family again, and with a less brutal training schedule, Kerri seemed to thrive. Then came another setback—in a meet in 1994, Kerri was on the uneven bars when her grip slipped and she swung backward off the bar. She hit the mat painfully, hurting her back muscles, an injury that required another six months of recovery.

For most of her career, Kerri earned silver and bronze medals, often failing to win gold by just a fraction of a point, as if there were a mental barrier holding her back. She had been part of the 1992 Olympic team but it ended in frustration when she barely missed out on the chance to compete in the individual All-Around competition, losing to a competitor by .001 point. Now she was dealing with her second serious injury and she began to lose faith in her abilities.

"For so long, I put so much pressure on myself and it wasn't working," she says.

Kerri began meeting with sport psychologists, discussing her fears and goals. Over time, she started to see results from her therapy sessions.

"I became more confident," she says. "I finally learned that focusing on everyone else's performance— and what could go wrong for me—was not beneficial."

In 1995, Kerri graduated from her hometown high school in Tucson, Arizona. It likely helped that she was in a comfortable environment near supportive friends and family.

Enjoying her newfound focus and poise, Kerri won some competitions, including the America's Cup title in March 1996, returning her to the ranks of the elite members of the sport. Kerri put off starting college at UCLA to resume training with Coach Bela, who had ended his brief retirement. A shot at an Olympic medal seemed within reach. The big difference: She finally believed in herself.

"Everyone can tell you things, but until you believe it, it's not the same," she says. "I also knew it was my last year in competition, so I had everything to gain and nothing to lose . . . my goal was to make the Olympics but I realized life was going to go on either way. I had parents who loved me and I was going to college."

At the Olympic trials in Boston, Kerri earned a spot on the team with an impressive performance in all her rotations, taking the highest score in the vault and floor exercises.

As the Olympics approached, Kerri saw an individual medal as the one thing that could prove her ability and dedication once and for all. Skeptics worried she wasn't up to the challenge, but Kerri felt more confident than ever before, partly due to her conversations with her therapist.

As Dominique Moceanu, one of the team's golden girls, began the vault on July 23, 1996, Kerri wasn't even watching. It was the last apparatus left in the competition and the team's lead over Russia was so enormous their victory seemed assured.

"I was focused and in my zone, keeping my muscles loose and preparing," she says.

Then Kerri heard gasps from the crowd. Moceanu had fallen. Kerri stopped her preparations to watch Moceanu on the Georgia Dome's Jumbotron. Shockingly, she fell again.

"Dom was the darling of the Olympic games, she had never fallen on the vault," Kerri says, still amazed by the turn of events.

Most of the US's lead had evaporated. The gold medal would come down to Kerri's performance.

"The Americans could lose the gold medal," the television announcer said.

Referring to Kerri, he said: "She's the last to go, she's the only one who can do it."

In the stands, Kerri's parents looked tense as their daughter took a few last deep breaths.

"I didn't look at the scoreboard, but I thought, 'I can do this, I've done it all year, there's a reason I'm here,'" Kerri recalls. "I knew what to do."

She took off, launching a challenging routine that included a headspring and a twisting dismount as the crowd rose to its feet. As Kerri made her landing, however, she fell short, slipping and then falling on her backside. Kerri couldn't stick the landing.

She also heard a snap in her left ankle.

"Oh no!" the announcer exclaimed. "Three falls in a row for the Americans!"

It was Kerri's nightmare unfolding in the full glare of the world.

"I don't know the last time Kerri Strug did something like that," the announcer said. "This is her event."

"I was seriously embarrassed," Kerri says. "This was supposed to clinch it for us and I vaulted tens of thousands of times, and now I'm thinking, 'Here we go again.'"

Kerri didn't grimace or show signs of pain. But she began to limp as she walked off the mat. It was clear she was badly injured. Pain shot through Kerri's leg. She didn't realize it at the time, but she had suffered two torn ligaments in her ankle.

"This is scary," the television announcer said.

Kerri remembered how she had seriously hurt her

back just a few years earlier and began to think a gold medal wasn't meant to be.

"I'm the type of person who is 'Woe is me,'" she says. "I thought 'Is this a sign from the man upstairs?'"

When Kerri's score, a weak 9.162, flashed on the Jumbotron it seemed the US gold medal was in serious jeopardy. Kerri still had her second vault ahead, but it wasn't clear she could go on. Kerri's parents covered their faces.

"It hurt and felt out of place, and it was scary not knowing what was wrong," she says.

Kerri's supporters rose to the occasion, trying to give her a boost. The US coaches encouraged her, as did her teammates.

"You can do it!" Coach Bela yelled out.

Kerri's head ached, her ankle throbbed, and it wasn't even clear if she could run. But Kerri made a decision. She'd push forward and do one more vault.

"I didn't want to go out like that," Kerri says. "I didn't want to be remembered for being injured."

She also didn't want the US team to be known as the squad that fell three times and blew a huge lead to lose the gold. Kerri's experience dealing with a grueling training regimen began to pay off, she says.

"All those injuries and competing in pain earlier in my career helped," she says. Coaches had "always pushed me past the point where I thought I could go, but it was a blessing in disguise."

Kerri had dreamed of winning an Olympic medal since she was five years old. She wasn't going to give up now.

"I was really hurt but I was just thinking about the gold medal," Kerri says. "I didn't think about quitting."

American team medics helped Kerri get to her feet as the crowd cheered wildly. The Russian team stopped to watch. Kerri began running down the runway on her damaged ankle for her second and final vault.

She realized she was in trouble right away.

"I felt pain and my ankle wasn't stable," Kerri says. "It felt like I was going to fall on my face [and] I felt slower. It just didn't feel right."

Somehow, Kerri remained on her feet and raced forward, picking up speed and launching herself high in the air. Relying on muscle memory and ignoring her pain, she pulled off a perfect back handspring onto the vault, descending toward the ground as many in the crowd held their breath. They knew how painful it would be when Kerri landed.

Improbably, Kerri landed on both feet without a stumble and raised her hands over her head to finish the vault with proper form. Just then, she heard another crack in her damaged left ankle. Instinctively, Kerri lifted her injured left leg, moving it behind her right as she hopped and shifted her weight to her healthy right leg. She even forced a smile on her face in the traditional post-performance pose.

Kerri held the pose long enough for the judges to give their marks. She then crumbled to the ground in agony as her coaches raced over to help her get off the mat.

A few minutes later, her score flashed for all to see.

"A 9.712, she has done it!" the announcer screamed. "Kerri Strug has won the gold medal for the American team!"

Kerri was carried off on a stretcher to seek medical

assistance as her teammates jumped for joy and the Russian gymnasts broke down in tears.

"The Georgia Dome is all at once in pandemonium and everyone is worried about Kerri Strug," the announcer said.

Before leaving for X-rays, Coach Bela scooped Kerri up, carrying her to the medal podium where she and the team received gold medals, as the crowd exploded in cheers.

Kerri's heroics brought fans to their feet and wowed television audiences around the world. Even as Kerri smiled for the cameras, inside she was dealing with mixed emotions, however.

She was thrilled to have won a gold medal, of course. That was her life's dream. But she was in a lot of pain. She also was dealing with deep disappointment. Kerri had expected to compete in individual events at the Olympics. Even after her fall, Kerri figured some rest, massage, and icing would enable her to go on. But it became clear that her injury was too severe for her to participate in more events. Her Olympic career likely was over.

"I shouldn't have fallen in the first place, this is what I spent my life preparing for," Kerri says. "I accomplished one goal, the team gold, but I was really upset I couldn't pursue my individual goals . . . I was really down."

Kerri worried she'd be known as the girl who fell in the Olympics. At the time, she didn't realize that she would instead be remembered as the brave young gymnast who refused to stay down.

Indeed, Kerri and her teammates were in the secluded Olympic Village and she didn't know the entire nation was cheering her, rather than focusing on her fall. A US Olympic official brought her a copy of the *USA Today* newspaper, pointing to the cover.

"You'll want to keep this," he said.

Kerri and her feat of courage were featured on the cover of the paper.

"It was a good feeling," she says.

Still, at the time, Kerri didn't fully grasp the significance of what she had done. Instead of taking pride in her amazing accomplishment, she continued to criticize herself even as she received acclaim from all over the world. Few had seen such a young person with so much mettle. Kerri became a national sports hero. She visited President Bill Clinton, appeared on television talk shows, and was on the cover of *Sports Illustrated* magazine, and, in the great tradition of star athletes, her face was plastered on the front of a Wheaties cereal box.

It took a while before Kerri could truly be proud of what she had accomplished.

"I was so focused on what was next and winning," she says. "I wish I had enjoyed the Olympics more than I did."

Eventually, after much self-reflection, Kerri learned some valuable lessons. She was so caught up in achieving her goals that she didn't understand that the journey to get to a certain destination can be even more valuable than the final result. Over time, she learned to treat herself with kindness. After all, very few people are ever in a position to compete in the Olympics. Falling or even failing in the Olympics should be a point of pride, not embarrassment, especially if the end result is winning a gold medal.

"Now I'm more thankful and appreciate that people mess up," she says.

Kerri also realized that had she and her teammates cruised to victory or if she had captured several individual gold medals, Kerri wouldn't have been able to inspire so many around the world with her resilience.

"Perseverance is a valuable characteristic," she acknowledges.

It's a trait Kerri finally appreciated about herself, and one she hopes others can learn from.

"I fell down but if this young girl can be tough and recover, so can others," she says.

Other life lessons also emerged from her experience.

"I gained an understanding that life doesn't always give you want you want. You think you know the path you want to take and how things will go." Yet, as Kerri discovered, it's rare that life doesn't take twists and turns that require grit and determination.

After the Olympics, Kerri graduated from Stanford University. Today, she lives in the Washington, D.C., area and gives motivational speeches around the country, sharing her experiences at the Olympics and more.

But she spends most of her time working and helping young people try to overcome their own challenges. In addition to being a mom to two young children, Kerri works as a program manager for the Office of Juvenile Justice and Delinquency Prevention, a division of the Department of Justice. She works with and advises programs for high-risk youth that receive federal funding, among other forms of aid.

"I spent most of my adolescence focused on me and my goals," she says. "I wanted to help others and serve in some capacity."

Just as with the Olympics, she says, she and others at the Department of Justice, "different people with different roles, work together to make America better."

When she speaks with young people, Kerri reminds them that success and accomplishment require practice, dedication, and perseverance.

"When you sacrifice so much and you finally do well, it feels really good," she says.

As Kerri learned after her moment of triumph, it's often our toughest setbacks that lead to our greatest victories.

AFTERWORD

As we spoke with the remarkable women featured in *Rising Above* it became clear that their athleticism and natural talent hadn't been enough to help them achieve greatness. Each star had overcome imposing obstacles at some point in their careers, a reminder that almost every life is filled with serious tests and challenges. In many ways, more than their abilities, it was those character-building moments that set them apart and allowed the women to develop into superstars.

Many of the athletes, including Serena and Venus Williams, confronted serious medical issues. Simone Biles, Ronda Rousey, and others faced humiliation due to their unique body types. Wilma Rudolph dealt with racism and Elena Delle Donne was impacted by the needs of a family member. Skeptics said Carli Lloyd and Kerri Strug, among others, wouldn't accomplish greatness. Bethany Hamilton and other athletes faced serious setbacks so sudden they had no time to prepare or adjust to their new circumstances. Yet, each of the women managed to rise above their difficult circumstances to excel in gymnastics, tennis, basketball, soccer, and more.

As we spoke with the stars and heard their life stories, some common themes emerged. The athletes often turned to others for help. Simone Biles worked with a psychologist, Carli Lloyd found a coach she trusted, while Swin Cash confided in an older mentor. The lesson: Turning to a friend, parent, therapist, or other person for help or guidance isn't a sign of weakness. Instead, it can be the best way to deal with life's trials.

The stars also shared an unwillingness to blame others for their difficulties. In fact, some said they began to become both better people and players when they stopped pointing the finger at others and accepted responsibility for their successes and failures.

"I had a revelation," Swin Cash told us. "I wouldn't

be a victim any longer . . . I had to look within myself and make things happen."

Simone Biles and others emphasized the importance of developing life goals and keeping them in focus, no matter how distracted one can get.

"Write them down," Simone told us. "And don't give up on them!"

Most of all, the stars emphasized the importance of believing in oneself and ignoring inevitable critics and skeptics.

"Always bet on yourself," Venus said to us. "Don't let outsiders bring negativity into your mind and your life."

Keep in mind what Kerri Strug, Wilma Rudolph, Bethany Hamilton and others discovered: Misfortune and sudden disappointments that appear to be blows can actually turn into big breaks.

It's our belief that everyone has a difference of some kind. Most of us will have to deal with huge disappointments at some point. But setbacks don't have to be roadblocks. Sometimes, they're even opportunities. We hope the stories from *Rising Above* can serve as useful life lessons for those facing their own challenges.

Gregory, Gabriel and Elijah Zuckerman

West Orange, NJ

May 2017

ACKNOWLEDGMENTS

We'd like to thank Venus Williams, Simone Biles, Carli Lloyd, Swin Cash, Kerri Strug, Bethany Hamilton and Mo'ne Davis all of whom generously took time to share thoughts, stories and lessons.

Brian Geffen is truly a remarkable editor. Supportive, enthusiastic and full of insight and wisdom. We thank you for the huge role you play in all our work. Our publisher, Michael Green, believed in this project from day one and we appreciate your continued support.

Susie, Hannah, Rebecca, Nathan (P.T.) and Liora cheer us from the sidelines and we love you guys. Josh Marcus provided necessary comic relief. Thanks as well to Monica for your hard work and being there for us.

Michelle, you're the true superstar of the family. Thank you for your love, wit, and kindness. Go, Yankees!

BIBLIOGRAPHY

Simone Biles

Simone Biles with Michelle Burford, *Courage to Soar: A Body in Motion, A Life in Balance*, Zondervan, 2016

Nick Zaccardi, "Simone Biles Recalls Being Called 'Too Fat' at Her Worst Meet," NBC Sports, November 16, 2016

Rose Minutaglio, "Simone Biles on Overcoming Body-Shaming from Coach," *People*, November 16, 2016

Pritha Sarkar, "Gymnastics: Bullies Are Tormenting Douglas, Says Mother," Reuters, August 14, 2016

Dvora Meyers, "Simone Biles' Mental Gymnastics," BuzzFeed, July 8, 2016

Linley Sanders, *Teen Vogue*, September 15, 2016

Alice Park, "The Olympic Gymnast Who Overcame a Drug-Addicted Mother," *Time*, June 3, 2016

Susan Rinkunas, "Gymnastics Star Simone Biles on Rio and Embracing Her Muscles," *New York*, July 13, 2016

Louise Radnofsky and Ben Cohen, "Simone Biles Wins Third Gold With Women's Vault Triumph," *Wall Street Journal*, August 14, 2016

Chelsea Hirsch, "Inside Gymnast Simone Biles' Tragic Early Days: Bio Mom Arrested for Stealing Baby Formula," Radar Online, August 11, 2016

Lonnae O'Neal, "The Difficulty of Being Simone Biles," *ESPN The Magazine*, July 6, 2016

Nicole Pelletiere, "Simone Biles Says 'Final Five' Will Take Vacation Together," ABC News, August 19, 2016, http://abcnews.go.com/Entertainment/simone-biles-return-rio/story?id=41509433

Elena Delle Donne

Sean Morrison, "Chicago Trades Elena Delle Donne for No. 2 Overall Pick, 2 Players," ABC Sports, https://abc7.com/sports /chicago-trades-elena-delle-donne-for-no-2-overall-pick-2 -players/1733605/

Jere Longman, "At Pinnacle, Stepping Away from Basketball," *New York Times*, October 18, 2008

Graham Hays, "Finding Her Way Back Home," ESPN, December 7, 2012, http://espn.go.com/espn/eticket/story?page=elenaDonne

Taffy Brodesser-Akner, "The Audacity of Height," *ESPN The Magazine*, November 22, 2016

Serena and Venus Williams

Serena Williams with Daniel Paisner, *My Life: Queen of the Court*, Simon & Schuster, 2009

James Masters and Pat Cash, "Venus Williams: The Champion Trying to Slam Sjögren's Syndrome, CNN, March 21, 2014, http://edition.cnn.com/2014/03/20/sport/tennis /venus-williams-sjogrens-syndrome/

Dayna Evans, "Serena Williams Prefers to Be Known as One of the Greatest Athletes of All Time," *New York*, July 7, 2016, http:// nymag.com/thecut/2016/07/serena-williams-best-female -athlete.html

"Serena Williams Sits Down with Common to Talk about Race and Identity," *The Undefeated*, December 19, 2016, http://theundefeated.com/features/serena-williams-sits-down -with-common-to-talk-about-race-and-identity/

Zoe Henry, "Venus Williams: Here's When It's OK to Fail," *Inc.*, November 3, 2016

Jordan Crucchiola, "Serena Williams' Mom Gives Great Advice on How to Handle Body Shamers," Good, July 11, 2016, https://www.good.is/articles/serena-williams-wimbledon-body-shaming

Mo'ne Davis

Kimberly Richards, "South Philly Girl, 10, Excels in Several Sports," *Philadelphia Tribune*, December 14, 2011

Bethany Hamilton

Bethany Hamilton, *Soul Surfer*, MTV Books, 2004

Michael Lee, "The Great Escape," *Washington Post*, February 17, 2008

Victor Mather, "Bethany Hamilton, a Shark-Attack Survivor, Reaches an Unlikely Crest," *New York Times*, May 31, 2016

Carli Lloyd

Carli Lloyd with Wayne Coffey, *When Nobody Was Watching*, Houghton Mifflin Harcourt, 2016

Jose de Jesus Ortiz, "Lloyd's Quest for World Cup Title Forged by 2011 Setback," *Houston Chronicle*, June 6, 2015

Jeff Carlisle, "How Getting Cut Helped Carli Lloyd Refocus and Find Her Spot on The USWNT," ESPN.com, June 3, 2015

Wilma Rudolph

Wilma Rudolph, *Wilma*, Signet, 1977

Kathleen Krull, *Wilma Unlimited*, Voyager, 2000

Ronda Rousey

Ramona Shelburne, "In Her Quest for Revenge and Pride, Ronda Rousey Lost Her Own Way," ESPN, January 2, 2017

Gabrielle Olya, "Ronda Rousey Gets in Fighting Shape with 6-Hour Gym Sessions! Her Trainer Breaks Down Her Intense

Workout," *People*, July 26, 2016, http://www.people.com/
article/ronda-rousey-boxing-workout

Ronda Rousey, *My Fight/Your Fight*, Regan Arts 2015

Brian Martin, "Ronda Rousey: Pro Fight No. 3—Defeated Sarah
D'Alelio via Technical Submission (Armbar), 0:25, First
Round," *Los Angeles Daily News*, July 29 2015

Swin Cash

Swin Cash, *Humble Journey: More Precious Than Gold*, Empower-
ing You, 2013

Jeff Jacobs, "Mom's The Word," *Hartford Courant*, March 24, 2001

J. Brad McCollough, "At Olympics, Swin Cash has McKeesport on
Her Mind," Pittsburgh Post-Gazette, July 22, 2012

Nina Mandel, "WNBA veteran Swin Cash Draws Inspiration,
Toughness from Her Mom," *USA Today*, May 10, 2015

Seth Berman, "Swin Cash Leaving Her Mark on Liberty in Her
Last WNBA Season," *New York Times*, September 6, 2016

Kerri Strug

Rick Weinberg, "51: Kerri Strug Fights Off Pain, Helps US Win
Gold," ESPN, July 19, 2004, http://www.espn.com/espn
/espn25/story?page=moments/51

Kerri Strug: Official Web Site of Olympic Gold Medal Gymnast,
http://www.kerristrug.info/

INDEX

ALSO BY
GREGORY ZUCKERMAN
with Elijah and Gabriel Zuckerman

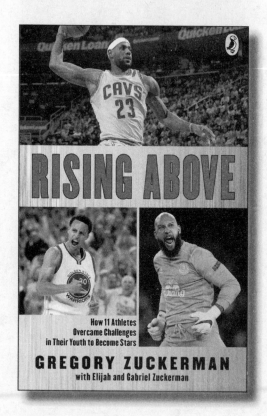

The Lāmībe of Fombina

A Political History of Adamawa
1809–1901

SA'AD ABUBAKAR, B.A., Ph.D.

Senior Lecturer in History,
Ahmadu Bello University, Zaria

AHMADU BELLO UNIVERSITY PRESS
OXFORD UNIVERSITY PRESS

AHMADU BELLO UNIVERSITY PRESS
and
OXFORD UNIVERSITY PRESS

© Ahmadu Bello University Press, 1977

ISBN 0 19 575452 2 (OUP)
ISBN 978 125 011 9 (ABUP)

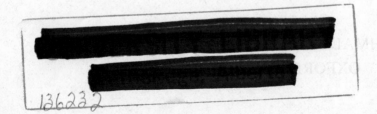

Contents

Maps

In memory of Chubado, my mother,
and Abubakar bin Saleh, my grandfather

Foreword

by Professor Iya Abubakar

It gives me great pleasure to introduce to the general public this major contribution to historical knowledge. The publication of this work will mark an important step in development both of Ahmadu Bello University and the society that it serves. Dr Abubakar's doctorate was the first awarded by Ahmadu Bello University and it is appropriate that this new version of the dissertation that gained him that honour should have been among the first titles to have been accepted for publication by the University's new Publishing House.

In many respects Dr Abubakar's is a pioneering study. Seventeen years ago Professor Abdullahi Smith described the Jihad movements that burst across West Africa in the early years of the nineteenth century as a 'neglected theme' in West-African history. The story of the Jihad in Fombina and of the state to which it gave rise has been a neglected theme within that neglected theme. The fragmentation of the political entity that followed upon the onset of colonial rule and partition has left the people who belonged to it under different governments, in Nigeria and the Republic of Cameroun and, as its historical continuity has been broken, it is easy to lose sight of the conjoint part of the original political creation, similar to, but in many respects entirely different from its fellow emirates that emerged under the auspices of Sokoto. Dr Abubakar has most convincingly brought back to life in these pages the world of the Fombina Emirate, the special problems that it faced as a society, itself segmentary, seeking by persuasion and conquest to draw into a harmonious unity the people of an area, tenacious of their secular separateness.

While Dr Abubakar's presentation of this topic is truly a pioneering effort one must note that it is also firmly rooted in the highly developed sense of history and historical consciousness of the people whose story he tells. He has listened carefully to those with traditions to relate about the events of the past. He has collected these traditions far and wide seeking to amalgamate and add a new dimension to the data he has gathered. In doing so he has fulfilled a role which is indeed that of Ahmadu Bello University as a whole – not to confront or stand in opposition to the society that it serves but to develop, enlarge and generalize the flow of thought already present among the scholars and wise elders in the society. His account is richly peopled with warriors and traders, scholars and administrators, men whose names have been known and revered for generations. Those figures now appear to us within a more closely defined historical pattern, indicating the stages through which the Emirate of Fombina passed as each group set the tone for a period, as institutions broadly matured, as the initial period of conquest and commercial change gave place to a questioning among intellectual leaders of how a right order could be forged out of the military achievements of their predecessors. In doing this, and in his broad sympathy for all the personalities and groups that enter into his historical picture, Dr Abubakar has provided us with a model that will not be without lessons for modern statesmen grappling with the problems of nation-building, among whose number indeed Dr Abubakar is temporarily numbered at the moment.

This publication must certainly add in a most important and valuable fashion to the development of modern African historiography and I congratulate Ahmadu Bello University Press for having presented it to the public as a foretaste of what may be expected in the future from our Publishing House.

IYA ABUBAKAR
Vice Chancellor of
Ahmadu Bello University

Preface

This book is addressed to the following classes of readers: students in Universities, Colleges of Arts and Science, and Advanced Teachers Colleges, where there are courses relating to the history of Africa, nineteenth-century trade and politics, and the jihad movements in West Africa; second, to all students of the social, economic and political background of Nigerian societies; and finally, the increasing number of intelligent Nigerians who are keen to know more about our rich cultural heritage, which forms the solid base for the growth of an authentic black nation.

In writing this book I have benefited from people in all walks of life, too numerous to mention in this restricted space. I am very grateful to all of them. I would however like to record my thanks to Professor Abdullahi Smith of Arewa House, Ahmadu Bello University, who supervised the doctoral work on which this book is based and helped me with the Arabic, German, and French documents. I am particularly grateful for his untiring encouragement which is the main motivation behind the publication of this book. I also thank the authorities of Ahmadu Bello University for the scholarship which enabled me to undertake this study, and the UNESCO Centre for the Collection and Documentation of Oral Traditions, Niamey, for sponsoring my second visit to the Republic of Cameroun in 1969. In Cameroun, I am grateful to Mr Eldridge Mohammadou for placing his papers at my disposal; Father Engelbert Mveng and the entire staff of the Cultural and Linguistic Centre, Ya'ounde, for their willing co-operation. My thanks also go to the staff of the Kashim Ibrahim Library, ABU, and of the National Archives, Kaduna; to Professor R. J. Gavin of the History Department, ABU, who read the thesis and the revised volume for publication and made valuable suggestions; to Professor O. S. A. Ismail, Director of the Northern History Research Scheme, ABU, for his useful comments, and Professor Michael Crowder of Lagos University. Finally, I thank Barka Mshelthlila and Bala Malgwi of the Faculty of Arts and Social Sciences, Ahmadu Bello University, Zaria, and Emmanuel E. Ebobe of the Ministry of Education, Yola, for typing the manuscript.
SA'AD ABUBAKAR
Ministry of Education,
Yola,
Gongola State, Nigeria

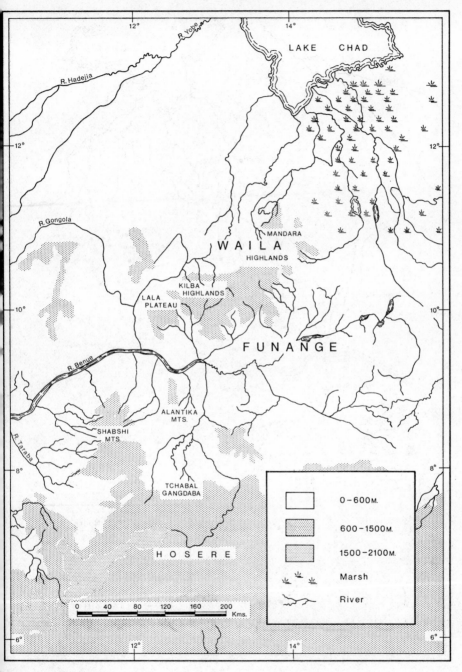

LAKE CHAD

R. Yobe

R. Hadejia

R. Gongola

W A I L A
HIGHLANDS

MANDARA

KILBA
HIGHLANDS

LALA
PLATEAU

F U N A N G E

R. Benue

ALANTIKA
MTS.

R. Taraba

SHABSHI
MTS

TCHABAL
GANGDABA

H O S E R E

	0–600M.
	600–1500M.
	1500–2100M.
⚶ ⚶ ⚶	Marsh
	River

0   40   80   120   160   200
Kms.

Map 1. Fombina Relief

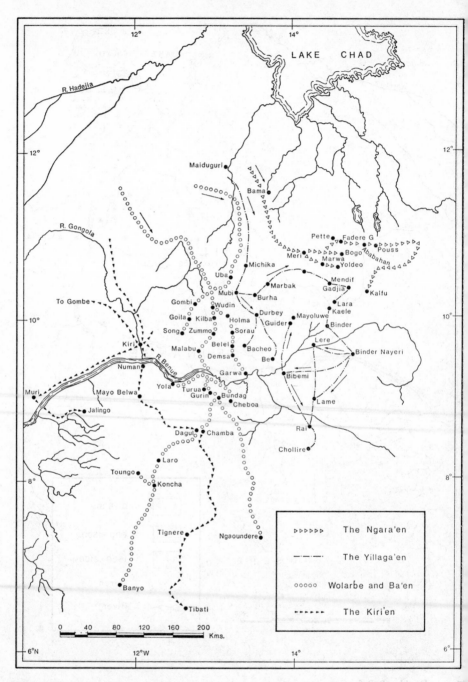

LAKE CHAD

R. Hadejia

R. Gongola

12°

Maiduguri

Bama

Pette · Fadere G · Pouss
Meri · Bogo Ababahan
Marwa · Yoldeo
Michika
Mendif
Uba
Marbak · Gadjia
Mubi · Burha
Gombi
Wudin
Goila · Kilba
Holma · Durbey · Mayoluwe
Song · Zummo · Sorau · Guider
Belel · Bacheo
Malabu · Be
Demsa
Garwa
Yola
Turua
Gurin · Bundag
Cheboa

Kalfu
Lara
Kaele
Binder
Lere
Binder Nayeri
Bibemi
Lame

To Gombe

Kiri
R. Benue
Numan
Muri
Mayo Belwa
Jalingo

Dagul · Chamba

Rai

Chollire

Laro
Toungo
Koncha

Tignere
Ngaoundere

Banyo

Tibati

▷▷▷▷▷▷	The Ngara'en
-·-·-·-	The Yillaga'en
ooooo	Wolarbe and Ba'en
▸▸▸▸▸▸	The Kiri'en

0 40 80 120 160 200
Kms.

6°N   12°W   14°   6°

Map 2. Movements of the Early Clans into Fombina Before the Nineteenth Century

Introduction

The study of the Sokoto Caliphate has, in recent years, seriously engaged the attention of history students and scholars. Unfortunately emphasis was generally on the metropolis of the Caliphate, and the whole political and administrative set-up of the system was viewed from the point of view of Sokoto. The component emirates of the Caliphate, numbering over three dozen, have not been studied in full and until this is done the reconstruction of a comprehensive history of the Sokoto Caliphate will not be possible. This book, therefore, is designed towards achieving the latter objective. It is a study of the way in which decentralized, almost segmentalized, units came together to form a large-scale centralized system in the early years of the nineteenth century and how that system finally disintegrated in the course of that century.

The region lying to the south of the Chad basin to as far as the northern limit of the rain forest, was for long known as Fombina, a Fulfulde word for 'south'. Inhabited by diverse ethnic groups claiming to have migrated into it, the region witnessed several successive attempts at political centralization on a large scale. The Jukun followed by the Chamba and the Bata had, one after the other, attempted to bring the whole region under their authority. Whether they succeeded or failed is not clear, but by the end of the eighteenth century the different ethnic groups lived not under one polity but in varying scales of political organization. Some chiefdoms (the Chamba, Mbum, Kilba and Gude) were territorially extensive, while the Bata, Tikar, Higgi, Verre, and Mbula, though limited, were effective and held the various clans under a single sway. The political situation of the region changed dramatically in the nineteenth century when the last of the immigrants, the Ful6e, succeeded in ending the political fragmentation of the region. Thus, the various ethnic states (chiefdoms) gave way to an extensive multi-ethnic polity under the leadership of people who hitherto were not only politically segmented but also culturally different from the vast majority of the region's inhabitants.

The first Ful6e to have entered Fombina did so as a result of their usual nomadic migratory drifts perhaps as early as the eighteenth century. By the beginning of the nineteenth century, the good pasturage conditions in the region attracted a large body of Ful6e from Borno and the Hausa states; and on entering Fombina they accepted the social, economic, and political conditions which prevailed in the region. In short, they were subject to non-Ful6e authorities to whom they paid tribute and grazing dues to ensure their rights and liberties.

Outside Fombina the nineteenth century opened with the *jihad*, and that from Borno had great consequences for the south. Firstly, a much larger body of Fulɓe moved from Borno into Fombina so as to avoid being involved in the fighting. Secondly, following the resurgence of Borno under al-Kanemi, virtually all the Fulɓe had to escape from Borno to safer places, one of which was certainly Fombina. The entry of refugees from Borno was the turning point in the history of relations between the Fulɓe and their autochthonous hosts. While the earlier immigrants were 'half-way' Muslims, the later were militant Jihadists, and so were less prepared to accept the conditions under which the former had lived for centuries. The Fulɓe population increased greatly, and having fled from the Kanuri, they were not prepared to accept the overlordship of the less advanced autochthons. Thus, relations deteriorated and ultimately jihad was resorted to so that the Fulɓe could achieve independence (*maral hōre*) and end the hardship (*bone*) associated with the authority of the non-Fulɓe.

The jihad in the region started in about 1809 with Mōdibbo Adama leading his supporters in the valley of the river Faro. Other kindred leaders followed suit in the outlying districts with the blessing of the Mōdibbo and by the eighteen thirties the military position of the Fulɓe was so much strengthened that they were able to invade *Hōsēre* (the plateau) in the south. With the jihad virtually over, consolidation and expansion continued till the end of the nineteenth century.

However, the main problem for the Fulɓe was the maintenance of the system they had established. Politically the Fulɓe lived in small units led by *Ardo'en* (kindred leaders) whose authority was strongly supported by a code of conduct, *Pulāku*. Unlike the Kanuri and Hausa systems, the Fulɓe political system was inadequate for Fombina. The emirate type of government which they were expected to operate was derived from Islam modified by the Hausa-Kanuri system under which the Fulɓe lived before their entry into Fombina. Indeed, an emirate did emerge, with Mōdibbo Adama as its head and Yola as its capital, but the operation of the system was far from smooth.

Fombina was quite different from most of the emirates in that it contained diverse ethnic groups, was extensive in area and supported several Fulɓe clans. The cultural homogeneity which prevailed in Hausaland was lacking in Fombina as was the large body of Muslims necessary for the successful functioning of an Islamic system. Above all, the establishment of the emirate was not through a combined military effort under a single leadership but through independent conquests by numerous armies, each led by a separate leader. Each unit was therefore subsequently unwilling to acknowledge a superior authority or accept outside interference in the day-to-day handling of its affairs. Apart from the emirate government in Yola there were over forty other units – sub-emirates or *lamidats* – each with its *Lamdo* (chief; pl. *Lamɓe*), and a congerie of officials similar to those in Yola. Each chief could declare war, arrange for peace and enter into alliances with outside bodies without reference to Yola.

Mōdibbo Adama, by virtue of the flag from the Shehu in Sokoto and his Islamic learning, was committed to establishing an emirate administration under his leadership, but the old Fulɓe clan jealousies and the basic desire for autonomy stood in the way of political fusion of the various groups. The non-Fulɓe in various localities had at no time permanently acknowledged Fulɓe hegemony, therefore they constantly sought for ways of maintaining their independence. The history of their relations with the Fulɓe was marked by conflicts, the latter struggling to maintain their hegemony while the non-Fulɓe fought to remain free. Conflicts also marked the relations between Yola and the sub-emirates, the former in its continuous bid to exercise paramountcy and the latter to preserve their autonomy and separate identity.

The political position of the Lāmīɓe in Yola varied from one part of the emirate to the other. In the north and north-east, the fear of Borno and Mandara made the petty sub-emirates more dependent upon Yola for protection against external threats. In the south the situation was different: there was no Mandara or Borno to force them to rally around Yola and they therefore posed more serious problems to the Lāmīɓe Fombina. This apparent internal weakness provided good ground for the spread of Mahdism in the emirate. That Hayat b. Sa'id had entered Fombina and succeeded in establishing himself at the expense of the Lāmīɓe in Yola is an indication of the degree of internal weakness and the lack of an effective central leadership in the emirate.

In a bid to bring about greater internal unity and to check the menace of Mahdism, the administration in Yola relaxed its policy of checking the activities of Europeans (*Nasāra'en*) in Yola. Certainly, the need for arms and not the fostering of greater commerce was uppermost in the mind of the Lāmīɓe at the time. Not that the Europeans, even if checked, would not have eventually conquered the emirate, but by welcoming all the major powers – British, French, and Germans – the Lāmīɗo exposed himself and his domain to international attention and a subsequent carve-up. Certainly, the forces of colonialism were too strong for Fombina to withstand, but it might have survived as an entity if the Lāmīɓe had been more cautious and judicious in their relations with the Europeans.

1. The Region and its Inhabitants

Fombina, a Fulfulde term meaning 'the southlands', is the region lying to the south of the Chad basin and not, as Barth would have it, a great pagan kingdom on the Benue.[1] From the Chad basin, the region extends southwards to the equatorial forest zone. Its western border is marked by the Hawal river and the Lala plateau in the north and by the Cameroun mountain system in the south. In the east, the region is bounded by the Logone river to the northeast, and by the limit of the southern plateau – Hōsēre[2] – to the south-east. Thus Fombina was neither a truly geographical nor political entity, but a region which contained diverse physical and human environments and which became the south-eastern border-state of the Sokoto Caliphate in the nineteenth century.

THE INHABITANTS

Long before the nineteenth century, the peoples of the region lived in groups of different sizes, speaking different languages, and having various customs and traditions. The two dominant language families are the Bata-Margi of the Afro-Asiatic group and the Adamawa eastern dialect of the Niger-Congo.[3] It is not my intention to consider all the ethnic groups in Fombina. But an attempt will be made to study the origins and socio-political organization of the major groups, starting from the inhabitants of the southern plateau.

The Mbum

Before the nineteenth century, the Mbum inhabited the south-eastern corner of Fombina, an area extending from the headwaters of the Logone up to the environs of Tibati in the west. They are believed to have originated from Borno,[4] in the region of Maifoni – a village near what is now Maiduguri – as subjects to the legendary So people. Eventually, they migrated south to Mulgwe, possibly to escape So control, where they came into contact with the Margi. But even in Mulgwe, the Mbum did not become free, because they were subjugated by the Gadzama kindred. However, other groups moved away southwards to the lands of Rai on the headwaters of the Benue river. The assertion that the Mbum were at one time in Borno can only be justified by the argument that the Niger-Congo language speaking peoples were at one time located further north of their present-day habitat. The Mbum, as their socio-political institutions indicate, are more akin to the Jukun who, their traditions claim, had in the past settled in the region of the Mandara highlands.[5] The southward movements of the Jukun and related groups were perhaps a result of incursions by Afro-Asiatic language speaking peoples. The latter were probably also forced to move by the infiltrations and invasions of the superior Nilo-Saharan language speaking group represented by the Kanuri.[6] At the beginning of the nineteenth century, the Mbum were settled on the watershed separating the headwaters of the rivers Logone, Benue, and Faro from the south-flowing tributaries of the Sanaga river. The area of the headwaters of the Logone was occupied by the Mbum-Mbere while the Mbum-ganha were found along the rivers Nbere and Vina. The third group, the Mbum-njwi, were found to the north-east of Ngaundere and along the river Djerem near Tibati.

The Mbum were organized in chieftaincies, the leading ones being Ngawkor and Ganha, each headed by a *Belaka* (chief). However, the most powerful Mbum ruler was the Belaka of Ngawkor, said to be divine and surrounded with taboos. He was the 'custodian of cults', and so he was held to be the repository of life and the prosperity of the whole people. He was also intimately associated with birth, the rains, and the health of the people. The seed for the corn cultivated annually was kept by the Belaka – in short, life revolved around his person. Misfortunes, such as epidemics, bad harvests, or drought were usually attributed to the Belaka's failure to observe rituals or taboos. Such an accusation usually resulted in the deposition of the incumbent.

Like the Jukun, the Mbum segregated menstruating women. They believed that the Belaka lived without eating so that his food had to be prepared in secret by virgins, carefully supervised by eunuchs, to protect him from being poisoned. The virgin cooks were usually confined to the palace and prevented from contacting the chief's wives to maintain the secrecy surrounding the Belaka's feeding.

The Mbum kingship institutions were similar to those of the Jukun. One tradition has it that the Mbum were subject to the Jukun during the latter's period of hegemony.[7] However, since the nineteenth century, the two groups have not even been neighbours. While the Jukun are mainly found along the middle Benue valley in the west, the Mbum are separated from them by a number of ethnic groups to the east. Thus, it may have been that either the two ethnic groups were descended from the same stock, or that the similarities were due to prolonged contacts and intercourse in the past. Alternatively, the Mbum and Jukun institutions may have developed independently. The concept of divine kingship was not confined to the Jukun; it was a common phenomenon among the ancient non-Muslim states of West Africa.

The Tikar

The immediate neighbours of the Mbum are the Tikar. Indeed, according to
Dugast, the two are of the same stock, having separated between Ngaundere
and Tibati several generations ago, the Tikar thereafter settling on the vast
plains watered by the river Mbum and its tributaries.[8] Linguistic evidence
suggests however, that the Tikar are of the same stock as the Dama, Mundang,
Lakka and other small groups of the Māyo-Kebbi–Logone region and Percival claims that only the Tikar ruling group traced their origin from Mbum.[9]
As to traditions of origin, according to McCulloch the Tikar have come from
no further than the Tibati, Ndobo, and Kimi region to the north and south-
east of their present-day habitat.[10] Their south and south-westward movement
could have been the consequence of Chamba and particularly nineteenth
century Fulɓe pressure. While the traditions collected by McCulloch do not
indicate long-distance migration, Percival's earlier account mentioned Tikar
migration from Borno;[11] also, according to Jibu traditions, they came from
the east to the edge of Lake Chad along with the Jukun and Jibu and turned
southward while the Jukun entered Borno proper.[12] Similarly, the Mbula
claim that the Tikar were among the groups brought to the Benue in their
mythical 'iron canoe' from the east.[13] While too much reliance should not be
placed on these and similar traditions, they nevertheless point the way to
further investigations.

Like the Mbum, the Tikar lived in chieftaincies. The three chieftaincies of
Ditam, Ngambe, and Bamkin in the Mbum river basin were established by
migrants coming south from the Faro river region where they had been in
contact with the Chamba.

The Tikar rulers are called *Fon* and they exercised political and spiritual
authority over their subjects.[14] Each Fon was surrounded by a highly-
structured body of officials performing various functions. The palace officials
were called *Atanto* and those governing conquered districts were known as the
Afon. There were also priests, the *Tawong* and the *Yewung* – the 'father' and
'mother' of the country respectively. Each chieftaincy had an inner council
the members of which were called *Vibai*. Its orders were executed by the
Ngwirong, a sort of police force. They also acted as personal attendants or
messengers of the Fon under the control of the *Fai-o-ndendzef*. The members
of the Ngwirong were selected from among the *Nshilif* (slaves) and not from
among the near kin of the Fon.

Among the Nsaw group of western Tikarland, there were three important
social classes defined in terms of the relationship of each to the Fon. The
highest class was the *Wiri-e-Fon* made up of the 'royalty', the paternal and
maternal relatives of the Fon down to the sixth generation. The next class
was the *M'tar* and the last was the Nshilif, freeborn and slaves respectively.
The three classes were socially inter-related. The M'tar, for example, were
men who became voluntary allies of the Fon. The Nshilif on the other hand
provided him with daughters (these were either made wives of the Fon or

were given to his officials, to consolidate his hold upon them). Thus, ethnic solidarity, which also meant the solidarity of the chieftaincy, was secured by marriage alliances. Among the Tikar of Kon, for example, all conquered villages had to send wives to the Fon, or his chieftains, each year. The daughters of such marriages would become the wives of village heads or of heads of lineage groups.

The Chamba

To the north of the Mbum and the Tikar are the Chamba whose main base was initially along the lower Faro valley. But by the beginning of the nine-teenth century, they had spread westwards to the Shabshi highlands, and southwards down to the Bamenda plateau. The Chamba of Donga claim that they migrated from Deng – a chieftaincy to the east of Yola.[15] The migration was attributed to hunger. According to Garbosa, the Chamba were invaded by alien elements, first the Bata and then the Ful6e. Consequently, there was famine and a shortage of land which compelled the Chamba to migrate to new lands in the south. There are some inconsistencies in the Chamba of Donga tradition. Firstly, the immigration of the Bata into the Upper Benue valley was not simultaneous with that of the Ful6e. While the former entered the Benue valley in the eighteenth century, the Chamba, according to one account, started to migrate when the Bata began to encroach upon their settlements, Mapeo, Sapeo, and Zolba, in the Faro valley.[16] Secondly, when the Ful6e entered the Benue valley they found the Bata – and not the Chamba – in the dominant position. However, it cannot be doubted that Ful6e activi-ties in the nineteenth century led to further Chamba migrations, such as those of Bali in the present-day Cameroun Republic.

The Chamba of Daka, now in the region to the south of the Shabshi high-lands and to the north of the river Kam, claim to have migrated at the same time as the Donga group. Led by their leader Ganyana, they moved first to the environs of Koncha in the south and later moved north, up to Māyo Danaba.[17] From thence they eventually moved westwards to establish them-selves in Daka. However, most of the Chamba are still located in the region to the west of the Faro river and to the south of the Alantika mountains. The northern Chamba groups have different traditions of origin. The Chamba of Sugu, for example, claim migration from Kona – a Jukun settlement in the west.[18] Thus, from Kona they moved eastwards to Māyo Loru and then north to Yelli where they joined the main body of the Chamba. It was from Yelli that they moved and founded the Sugu chieftaincy. The traditions of the Donga, Daka, and Sugu Chamba indicate that they were for a long time established in the southern Benue area. Moreover, the Sugu tradition tends to make them a Jukun offshoot or at least Jukun-influenced. Kona, their claimed ancestral home, was a very powerful Jukun chieftaincy before the nineteenth century, exercising control over the Mumuye and other neighbour-ing groups. The Chamba of Yebbi and Gurumpawo on the other hand claim origin outside Fombina, having migrated into it from the shores of Lake Chad. From the Chad basin, they moved to the south and settled on the western slopes of the Mandara highlands near modern Madagali. Eventually they migrated to the Benue valley and settled in the Bagale area, and expanded along the Benue and the lower Faro valleys where their stronghold is said to have been Yelli. Thus, while the traditions of the southern Chamba groups speak of migration southwards from the Benue, those of the northern groups speak of entry into the region. It appears in fact that there may have been two distinct migrations of the Chamba.

The history of the Chamba before the nineteenth century falls into two periods. The first was the time when they were a smaller group under a much more centralized chieftaincy, but little is known about this early period. Traditions speak of three chiefs, one reigning when they were in the Chad region, the second after they migrated to the region between the Chad and the Benue valley, and the third at Yelli.[19] It may have been that the three chiefs represent separate dynasties or dynastic houses in the three places. The second period of Chamba history was one of dispersal, and the establishment of a number of small chieftaincies. It has been suggested that the Chamba developed chieftaincy institutions after they had come into contact with the Jukun,[20] but this is not very likely. The Sugu Chamba group claims some connection with the Jukun who had, at one time, very considerable influence in the middle Benue basin. But it is not known if the Sugu Chamba were originally Jukun, Jukun-influenced, or enslaved by the Jukun but regained their liberty after the decline of the Jukun. Alternatively, the Sugu may have been Jukun who married into the Chamba and introduced kingship institutions of the Jukun type. This is derived from the tradition that, at Yelli, there was a very serious dynastic dispute after the reign of Gang Barubi.[21] It was not just a dynastic dispute between the leading titled princes but one which centred on whether the paternal or maternal claimants should succeed. The only realistic speculation is that the Nyakanyare who had migrated from the Jukun settlement in the west vied for succession, basing their claims on the matrilineal side. Thus they may have had some marriage connections with the Yelli ruling house.

Gurumpawo and Yebbi were, according to the traditions, founded by the patrilineal faction that migrated from Yelli.[22] Gang Kingking and his brother, Gang Bunjiganko, led their supporters to the west and settled among the Jangani and Kpenyienbu inhabitants of the Shabshi highlands. Through mutual contact and assimilation, the immigrants established their hegemony over the few early inhabitants of the area. While the original inhabitants remained in the mountains, the Chamba immigrants expanded to the plains and had their centre at Yebbi. At a later period, Gurumpawo was founded and it too developed into a chieftaincy under the younger brother of the Yebbi chief, Gang Kingking. The third chieftaincy, Sugu, was established by the matrilineal group from Yelli. According to tradition, they were the first to migrate to the Jangani area.[23] Then they attacked DaDubbu, an earlier Chamba settlement, and conquered the Jangani inhabitants. The Sugu chieftaincy has a longer king-list, which would support its claim to seniority, but the kingship institutions of the three chieftaincies were very dissimilar, and this makes it difficult to endorse the theory of common derivation. The only common feature in the three chieftaincies was that while at Yelli, the *Gang* was a priest-chief and he had no officials around him. However, after their dispersal, the kingship institutions became more elaborate and the Gang became a secular ruler. Also, all the northern chieftaincies acknowledged the spiritual over-lordship of the priest who remained at Yelli.

The last chieftaincies to be established, towards the end of the eighteenth century, were Binyeri and Dakka in the Shabshi and Mumuye highlands. The founding groups, led by Damashi, Shabshi, and Binywa, are said to have migrated from the main body of the Chamba.[24] The group under Damashi settled among the Mumuye and eventually established its hegemony through conquest. Damashi established Binyeri as his base and in the ninteeenth century it developed as the most powerful Chamba chieftaincy, its leader described as the 'King of all the Chamba'. The chieftaincy of Dakka was established by Binywa as a result of military activities against the Kwarami inhabitants of the region.

The kingship institutions among the Chamba chieftaincies were strikingly different.[25] In Gurumpāwo, for example, the political set-up consisted of religious, administrative, judicial, and propaganda officials. The Gang was surrounded by two types of officials: the *Mban* (advisers), headed by the *Kaigama-ishi*, and the *Kamen* (executive), headed by the *Mbanshem* (vizier). The advisers were the *Ganta* (chief priest), *Mbanvaso* (in charge of royal burials), the *Mbanbengi* (head of the *Jangani* cults), and the *Mbanshi* (priest). The administrative officials included, apart from the Mbanshem, the *Kuni* (judge), the *Mbantem* (the intermediary between the Gang and village heads), and the *Mbansoro* (royal proclaimer). Thus, the Gang of Gurumpawo was anything but a dictator. In Sugu on the other hand, the Gang had full executive power. He had no advisers, but war leaders, *Ganguramen* and the *Nyagang*; a regent, the *Gangtoma*; a collector of tributes and taxes, the *Kamandimen*; and a chief priest, the *Mbangaji*. While Gurumpawo was orientated towards religious matters and the mediation of disputes, Sugu was orientated towards war, taxation, plunder, and discipline. The third chieftaincy, Yebbi, stood between the two: there, the Gang was surrounded by a body of officials under the *Banjeano* (vizier). In both Sugu and Yebbi, the officials, except the priests, were appointees of the Gang. But in Gurumpawo, the Gang's right to appoint men of his choice was limited by the fact that each clan had the right of occupancy of certain posts. The Gang-ship belonged to the Gurumba clan, the Kaigama-ishi was the preserve of the Nyasikwai clan, and the Mbanshem that of the Kpenyienbu, who also had the right of succession to the Gang-ship whenever there was no member from the ruling kindred eligible by age or sex. However, as a guard against possible usurpation of the succession, a Kpienyienbu Gang was prohibited by taboo from residing in the capital which would be under the control of a Gang-toma.

The inhabitants of the three northern Chamba chieftaincies were heterogeneous and each chieftaincy was basically autonomous. In spiritual matters, the overlordship of the priest at Yelli was acknowledged by all the Chamba. The Gangs of the three chieftaincies had to send their contributions through Sugu whenever religious rites were to be performed, although each chieftaincy had its own cults and priests. The northern Chamba had, culturally and linguistically, influenced the people they had conquered. The activities of the Binyeri and the Dakka groups had extended over the Mumuye. The Mumuye of Je, Zinna, Yakoko, and Yorro had for long been under Chamba influence while the Sagboro, the Lampo, the Sharo, and the Gongoro were under the control of Binyeri. Similarly, the Kotopo are said to have been driven further south by the northern Chamba groups. Undoubtedly, these developments began before the nineteenth century.

The Bata

The Bata constituted the largest language group in Fombina before the nineteenth century even though they are not today a homogeneous people. They fall into such tribal groups as the Bachama, Gisiga, Gudu, Malabu, Njai, Zummo, and Holma, all speaking the Bata language or one of its dialects.[26] The group that still calls itself Bata traces its origin to Gobir in Hausaland and claims that they entered the upper Benue valley by way of Herwa and Zum. While the claim of origin from Gobir is far-fetched, it cannot be disputed that the Bata entered the Benue region from the Chad Basin. Their peopling of the Benue valley took the form of an invasion in two waves. The first took place in the seventeenth century and it came through the Mandara region to Bazza in the upper Yedseram river valley.[27] After pausing for a generation, the migrants then moved southwards, spreading eventually down to the Benue river. This wave comprised the Bata speaking peoples of Zummo, Holma, Bulai, Kofa, Mulon, and Njai groups of Koboshi, Nzangi, and Zany. The second wave, while coming from the north, followed the eastern piedmont of the Mandara hills and then down to the Benue valley through the valleys of the Tiel and the Māyo Kebbi. Eventually, they spread along the Benue valley westwards to the Bagale hill.

There is reason to believe that the Bata are related to the Margi. Firstly, according to Barth and later Meek, the Bata language bears close resemblance to Margi.[28] This view is still maintained, and the two languages form a subgroup of Greenberg's Afro-Asiatic family of languages.[29] Secondly, the Bata traditions of origin indicate that their leading strongholds during their southward migration were Herwa and Zum. The former was the Margi's stronghold, also known as Maifoni, in the Chad basin. Zum, on the other hand, might be the Hōsēre Zum in Kilbaland which lies on the way to the Benue. A possible conclusion, therefore, is that the Bata were either proto-Margi or an offshoot. Another tenable conclusion is that the two waves of migrants represent the migration of two distinct language groups from which the modern Bata emerged. The Gudu, for example, claim origin from Mandara together with the Gabin and Hona peoples.[30] Similarly, the various Njai groups do not trace their migration from beyond Mandara.

Thus it can be said that the first wave of migrants consisted of the Mandara people and the second of the Margi. The latter, greater by far in numbers, eventually emerged as the ruling group over the earlier immigrants. For example, it is pointed out that the ruling kindred of the Njai groups, Zummo, Bulai, Malabu, Kofa, Mulon, and Bolki, 'still speak a different dialect and in some cases observe a different custom'[31] from the rest of the people.

The establishment of the Bata in the upper Benue valley was at the expense of the Chamba. The Chamba stronghold, Lāmorde Njongum, to the east of the Māyo Faro was broken up as a result of Bata pressure. In fact, according to Meek, the Chamba were forced to abandon the upper Faro valley in order to escape conquest.[32] However in the region north of the Benue, Bata traditions make no mention of the Chamba. That region came under the occupation of the earlier stratum of migrants, the Jirai, who spread from Song in the west to Holma in the east. Being the earliest Bata immigrants, they established their hegemony in the north Benue plains. But there had never existed a single centralized polity; they seem to have lived in separate, small communities, each under its kindred leader. What is certain is that societies were originally present, and over these the immigrants established their hegemony. The chieftaincies of Mulon, Mboi, Bolki, and Mulke developed in areas formerly inhabited by the Yungur. Some of the last-named, under Bata pressure, are said to have migrated through the valley of the Māyo Loko to the Pirgambe hills.[33] According to tradition this was in the seventeenth or eighteenth century. Similarly, the chieftancies of Zummo, Holma, and Kopa may have been established at the expense of the Fali.

The hegemony of the first wave of immigrants was replaced by that of the second towards the end of the eighteenth century. The Bazza group, probably Margi, had two advantages. First, they were hunters and so they possessed superior weapons. Second, they were greater in number. In the Song region, the Bazza led by Njakabarau settled at first near Mulke.[34] Here, Njakabarau became friendly with Mulke and on the death of its chief, he acceded to power. From Mulke, he moved to Du-Voi, near Song, and began to threaten the position of Bolki, the greatest Jirai centre in the region. The chief of Bolki, Benti, probably realizing the futility of fighting against a very large body of invaders, is said to have concluded a treaty of alliance and friendship with Njakabarau. Here too, after the death of Benti, the immigrants' leader became the chief. At about the same time, other Bazza immigrants were active in the region to the east of Mulke and Bolki. One group led by Nenkenu established the chieftaincy of Mboi and others came to power at Holma, Zommo, and Maiha. Further east, along the lower Tiel valley, another group had been established at Demsa-pwa (this is the group that bears the name 'Bata' today).

Unlike the other groups, their traditions do not indicate that there were inhabitants either on the Tiel or along the upper Benue valley at the time of their arrival.[35] The implication is that the establishment of their chieftancies was not a result of conquest or conflicts, but this cannot be accepted as it stands. It has been shown that Chamba had hitherto occupied the upper Benue and the lower Faro river valleys, and their traditions speak of conflicts with the Bata immigrants. Also the various ethnic groups to the south, east, and west of the Bata are linguistically and culturally different. While the Bata belong to the Bata Margi sub-group of the Afro-Asiatic family of languages, their neighbours speak the Adamawa eastern dialect of the Niger-Congo. The available evidence tends to indicate that the Bata must have displaced the Chamba to occupy the rich and fertile upper Benue valley.

From Demsa-pwa, splinter Bata groups (Bundang, Pema, Turua, Kokumi, Njobolio, and Bagale) moved away to establish themselves elsewhere along the Faro and the Benue rivers, all recognizing the paramountcy of the chief of Demsa-pwa. Among the various kindred chieftaincies, according to Barth, Kokumi, which occupied the country on the middle course of the Benue and extending along the Faro up to the Alantika mountains, was the 'chief and central place of the Bata'.[36] The next powerful chieftaincy was Bagale, whose chief 'exercised paramount authority over the neighbouring tribes and is said to have even claimed the "jus primae noctis" '[37] at the height of his power.

Unfortunately, there is little information about the organization and structure of the early Bata chieftaincies. Such information as there is relates to Demsa-Mosu, established by the Bata after their nineteenth-century conflicts with the Fulбe. The *Hemen* (chief) was surrounded by about 24 titled officials headed by the *Kpana*, the commander of the army, the right hand man of the Hemen, as well as the custodian and the administrator of the latter's wealth. Then, there was the *Zumoto*, the head courtier and the intermediary between the people and the chief. The other officials were the *Zomodogbaki* and the *Guva* (counsellors). The remaining 20 officials were merely clients of one or the other of the four leading functionaries. The Hemen had various functions and was normally selected from the house of Nzoswod, the legendary leader of the Bata during their immigrations.

The Bata and the Chamba dominated the upper Benue valley before the nineteenth century, although there were a number of other ethnic groups who lived there independently. These include the Vere, and the Mbula and related groups. The latter claim migration from the region to the south-east of the Benue headwaters – probably from what is now the Republic of Zaire.[38] Certainly, by the eighteenth century, they were located on the Māyo Kebbi. Linguistically, the Mbula are related to the Mundang and the Nagumi of the Cameroun Republic, both located in the Māyo Kebbi region. From there, they spread along the Benue to the Tanbo area in the west and then northwards into Kilbaland and the Song region. From the Benue region, other Mbula groups such as the Bambur, Bununu, and the Dass moved further west onto the Bauchi Plateau. However, in the Benue region, the Mbula developed a close relationship with the Bata and this ultimately affected some of their institutions, though their language still remains of Bantu origin.

Politically the clans were the largest units. The symbol of their unity remained religion. The priest of the *Ngeylu* cults at Tanbo were their spiritual overlord and his prayers were considered necessary to avert impending dangers such as drought and epidemics. The Mbula were also very warlike and this quality was responsible for their survival in the face of Bata onslaught in the eighteenth century and the Ful6e attack in the nineteenth.

The Kilba

To the north of the Bata lived the Kilba, a term employed to describe the various heterogeneous elements who inhabit the region bounded in the north by the Tum, in the west by the Hawal, and in the east by the Kilenge rivers respectively. The present-day Kilba people emerged out of an ethnic inter-mixture which includes Mbula Bata, Pabur Margi, and Mandara elements.[39] The earliest inhabitants of the region are generally regarded as the Girhuba who occupied the prominent mountain sites, Pella, Hong, Kudinyi, Zedinyi, Mukavi, Gederi, Garaha, Mijili, Wuto, Mukwahi, Bashikbi, Za, Munga, Giging, and Gambi. Certainly, these were strategic positions which afforded natural protection to the people. Each mountain community was headed by a *Till-Krama* (chief of mountain) discharging politico-religious functions. However, probably in the eighteenth century, new immigrants entered the region from the north-east and the south-east. The former, entered Kilbaland from Mandara. They probably belonged to the same stream of immigrants who had established priestly chieftaincies at Sukur, Gulak, Kafa-Miya, and Mokule among the Margi. Other immigrants entered the region from the west, including the group that claim that they originate from Birni Gazargamo and that they had entered the Gongola-Hawal Plateau region via Mandara;[40] then, under a leader named Furkudil, they entered Kilbaland at Mitil. Furkudil, according to tradition, was a brother of Yamta Wala, the founder of the Pabur dynasty of Kuthli-Viyu. The last wave of immigrants were the Mbula who had migrated either from the Māyo Kebbi region or from Tanbo on the Benue to the south of Kilbaland.

Prior to the coming of the new immigrants, the *Krama* communities in Kilbaland had been very restive. Their relations were soured by conflicts and struggles between the Tills, mainly over political and religious issues. The two leading personalities were the Till Batari and the Bulama in the region of Hong; both had been attracting new immigrants to their communities. Eventually however, Batari's support was strengthened when the Mandara elements led by Furkudil and the Mbula from the south allied with him. Both the Mandara and the Mbula immigrants were hunters and warriors, so with his new support, Batari attacked and routed his rival, but then he too was defeated by the aliens who took control of affairs in Hong.

The leader of the Mandara group, Furkudil, became the Till Hong and the leader of the Mbula, Birura Dirsuba, became the *Hedima* (chief adviser). However, the authority of the new rulers was limited to Hong and the numerous Till-Krama had to be overthrown or forced to recognize the superiority of the new rulers. In a bid to extend their control, the Mandara and the Mbula elements associated themselves with the powerful religious cults in Hong. This gained for them the support of some of the mountain inhabitants. Those that had submitted continued to live under their Till-Krama but as subjects of the Till Hong. Also, the spiritual positions of the local rulers were maintained and their aid, advice, and consent were sought on all issues affecting the chieftaincy. But some communities did not submit peacefully and this necessitated military intervention. The immigrants had the advantage of being the largest and strongest organized group in Kilbaland, and this enabled them to extend their control over the various recalcitrant groups. Eventually local subordinate rulers were appointed by the Till Hong.

The system of government established by the new rulers of Kilbaland was very elaborate and highly organized.[41] The Till Hong was surrounded by a body of officials discharging executive, judicial, and court functions. The executive consisted of the Hedima, *Birawol Kadagimi, Batari, Zarma* and *Midala*. The Judicial officials were the priest of Duba-Dabu, the *Tali'i, Dubukuma*, and the *Dainyatil*. The palace officials or courtiers were the *Kadalla, Sunoma, Biratada, Barguma*, and *Kadakaliya*.

What was remarkable in the Hong government was its reflection of the ethnic heterogeneity of Kilbaland. Each major kindred-group had certain offices as its preserve. The Till Hong, for example, belonged to the Kabu group and the important posts of Hedima, Birawol, and Kadagimi alternated between the Mbula and the Mudaku kindred-groups. The Till Hong appointed the Hedima who in turn had to select all the other officials except district rulers and advisers on royal issues. The selection of the Till Hong was the prerogative of the Hong officials who had also the power to depose him.

The Kilba lived in kindred villages each headed by a local Till and groups of villages formed districts under royal princes (*Shells*). The appointment of the royal members as district rulers had started when, according to tradition, Furkudil appointed his sons, Gongpella and Kwatankiliya, as the Shells of the west and east respectively. With the expansion and consolidation of the chieftaincy the system developed that whenever a new Till was appointed, all members of Kabu had to leave the capital and live in the districts either as Shells or as mere princes (*Yerima*). This gave rise to the foundation of villages under the control of royal members. New immigrants continued to enter Kilbaland, but such people were not subject to the Tills or the Shells. In all cases, they lived as autonomous communities under their leaders but subject to the Till Hong. The growth of the dynasty gave rise to a very serious dynastic dispute in the nineteenth century, but this was resolved by adopting a rotating system of succession whereby the Till-ship alternated between the two leading royal houses, Arabiu and Mininga, and stability was thus maintained.

The Kilba chieftaincy extended by conquest over the Margi groups of Dille and Gulak in the north. Its western limit was Garkida and Gojofa while to the south and east, the chieftaincy bordered with Mubi and Zummo respectively. The most important unifying factor had been religion. The Till Hong was not 'divine', but he and two of his leading officials, the Hedima and the Kadagimi, were the heads of the *Katashawa*, *Kurndasu*, and the *Shantaru* cults respectively. Also, the other priests of cults outside Hong were either members of the judicial council or district rulers. The unity of the chieftaincy was also ensured by the representation of the different kindred-groups in the Hong government. Harmony and understanding between the different groups were maintained in this way, and by the beginning of the nineteenth century, the various culture-groups, Bata, Margi, Mandara, and the Mbula, became mutually assimilated by intermarriage, political solidarity, common beliefs and attendance at the Hong shrines. These factors, coupled with the physical nature of Kilbaland, were responsible for the survival of the Kilba chieftaincy during the jihad in Fombina.

The Margi

Another large ethnic group in the northern part of Fombina was the Margi. Even though their origins are obscure, there are reasons to believe that they had for long been living within the confines of the Chad basin. Probably they formed, like the Mbum, part of the So peoples of central Borno. As Schulze points out, Maifoni, a settlement which was near modern Maiduguri, was the former stronghold of the Margi.[42] Thus, from about the fourteenth century, the Margi appear to have lived in the region of their present habitat. Probably before the consolidation of the Borno empire, they occupied a more northerly position. But following the expansion and consolidation of Borno under the Sefuwa, some Margi were 'Kanuri-ized' while a large number of others drifted gradually to the south and inhabited the regions they now occupy. Politically, the Margi within Fombina lived under the control of non-Margi chieftaincies as can be seen below.

The Gudur

The various ethnic groups north of the Chad-Benue watershed claim to have drifted to their present abode from Gudur in Mandara. The circumstances that gave rise to their migration are various. The Baza group, for example, attribute their migration to a conflict which developed between the Gudur ruling kindred.[43] Five brothers (presumably five clans) moved westwards and established themselves on the western slopes of the Mandara highlands, from Magar in the north to Mokule in the south. While the Baza attribute their migration to dynastic dispute, the Michika group say that theirs was largely in search of open and unoccupied lands.[44] Certainly the mountainous Mandara area could only support a limited number of people. Thus, even to alleviate population pressure, people had to migrate from time to time. It may have been that both factors gave rise to population movements from Mandara – indeed, two waves of immigrants have been identified. The first consisted of the plains inhabitants, Kopa Higi, who were at first based at Za. Then they split into three groups, Kopa, Michika, and Baza, which eventually expanded onto the plains. The Kopa split into Kafa-Miya, Kesara and Garka groups, the Baza into Jigelambu, Lapiri, Koma, Mokule, Laba, and Gire. The second wave of immigrants were the Kapsiki, who now inhabit the mountains eastwards to Mandara. The Sukur and the other inhabitants of the northern parts of the Magar mountains also claim to have come from Gudur.

Mandara had occasional periods of political turmoil. There must have been conflicts during the establishment of the Mandara ruling dynasty, conflicts that may have given rise to large scale migration.[45] At the beginning of the eighteenth century, the Mandara rulers embraced Islam,[46] and in subsequent years, they made attempts to spread their new faith, which may also have caused some people to move away. Today the majority of the people in the northern half of the upper Benue basin speak of migration from Mandara.

As regards political organization, the Gudur people lived under fairly centralized policies which acknowledged the spiritual paramountcy of the priest of Gudur, but the leading political influence in the region was Sukur which had been under the *Duwa* (blacksmiths) dynasty since the eighteenth century.[47] The circumstances leading to its emergence are obscure. It is said that the immigrants from Gudur possessed superior magico-religious powers and this enabled them to seize power at Sukur and then at Wula and Gulak. The Sukur ruling class was closely associated with the blacksmiths of Sukur, thus, magico-religious power coupled with the possession of iron – used for making war weapons – was of great significance in the ascendancy of the immigrants. Moreover, the warriors were mounted, so it can be assumed that Sukur possessed a fairly strong cavalry.

With its cavalry and effective iron weapons, Sukur extended its control eastwards to Gudur and westwards along the Yedseram basin. Eventually, the Matakam inhabiting the northern and eastern slopes of the Mandara highlands and the Margi groups of the Yedseram basin were subdued. Mijili, the Yedseram stronghold, was overshadowed and Sukur princes were stationed at Gulak and Wula to administer the inhabitants of the plains.

The *Llidi* Sukur was 'divine' and he owed his power and prestige to his position in the ethnic religion. He was the representative of *Mboi*, the priest of Gudur, in the west and south and therefore could confer religious orders from Gudur and perform the affixing of the sacred lock of hair on other Gudur chiefs on behalf of the Mboi. The Llidi was also a priest in his own right, issued his own religious orders and supplied 'cults' to the Gudur chiefs at Kafa-Miya, Gulak, Palm, Mildu, Wula, and Kamale. As the vicar of the gods, the Llidi enjoyed unrivalled political and religious eminence in the Chad-Benue watershed region. His power was such that he even enjoyed the right of 'jus primae noctis'. He was surrounded by a body of officials who acted in religious, civil, and palace matters. The leading civil official was the *Lluffu* and under him were *Makarama, Medella, Llagama, Barguma,* and *Fate-Llidi.* The last-named official was regarded as the titular 'father' of the incumbent for, according to tradition, no man can be made a Llidi while his father is alive.[48] The Fate-Llidi was therefore a father-substitute whose main function was to check, through paternal reproach, undesirable tendencies or despotism of the Llidi. The religious officials were the *Ndallata, Lli*-Sukur, *Mbosofui, Disku,* and *Darakiras,* the servitors of the leading cults concerned with the day-to-day affairs of state. The palace officials comprised the *Birma, Tdif, Lligun,* and *Zarma.* All the officers of the government had direct approach to the Llidi, but commoners had to go through the Makarama.

The other Gudur chieftaincies were Kafa-Miya and Mokule, in the region to the south of Sukur.[49] Among the early clans which migrated from Gudur, the leaders of the clans (*Mbuga*) were the most senior political leaders. However, the clans had common cults. Eventually the two leading priests of the more powerful cults began to influence other clans and the various Mbuga came to look either to Kafa-Miya or Mokule for spiritual guidance and leadership. Like Sukur, Mokule and Kafa-Miya were theocratic chieftaincies; the power of the chiefs was supported and maintained by bonds of common origins and common religious beliefs. In each chieftaincy the clans were basically autonomous, headed by a Mbuga, who had to be installed by the priest-chief. On such occasions, the Mbuga had to appear before the priest-chief with presents, such as goats, corn, salt, and cotton cloth (*daura*).

At the beginning of the rains, the priests had to perform rites before the sowing, and before harvest he had to taste the new crops. After the harvest, each man who had farmed was expected to take a portion of the produce to the priest for these prayers, which they considered as affecting the rains and the good harvest. The priest, as a 'divine' ruler, was prohibited from eating fresh vegetables and crops in the dry season or dried ones in the wet season.

The priest-chief of Mokule exercised authority over a number of Margi groups, and unlike the Kafa-Miya which recognized the Llidi Sukur as overlord, he was independent. It is not known when the Margi moved on to the plains west of the Mandara highlands. It may have been that while the Higi were moving to the east, the Margi were advancing from the west. In the eighteenth century, for example, there was a Pabur exodus from Viyu into the Mokule region.[50] They founded settlements centred upon four hills – Huyum, Dille, Musa and Multafu – which provided the essentials for organized habitation, first as a refuge for fugitives and then as a sanctuary for their cults. As immigrant settlements, these four centres were too small and ill-equipped to defend themselves against such attacks as were launched from time to time by the Mandara and the Kanuri. Thus, they looked to Mokule for protection and paid tribute in return. Two Pabur kindred-groups among the migrants, the Mamza and Woba, proceeded to the piedmont of the Mokule massif. The Mamza leader secured from the priest-chief 'the agency general for the plains Margi'[51] and was invested as a prince of Mokule with the title of Till with his base near Baza. The Mamza Till provided *Chiduma* for the outlying Margi settlements – Huyum, Multafu, Musa, and Dille. The Mokule chief was the protector of the plains Margi.

The Mokule government was not as sophisticated as that of Sukur. The chief was assisted by court officials known as *Tulli*, drawn from the various clans. There were also the Mbuga of the clans who maintained contact with Mokule through their own servants (*rigi*). The relationship with the Margi Chiduma was contractual in nature. It was this system of government by contract that held the Margi, Pabir and Higi together under a common political structure.

The Gude, Chekke, and Fali

The upper reaches of the Yedseram and Māyo-Luwe are inhabited by the Gude, Chekke, and Fali. The first two are found mainly on the plains due south of the Mandara mountains. The Fali fall into two groups: northern and southern, the former in the mountains, and the latter east of the river Kilenge. There are grounds to believe that the Gude-Chekka moved into their present habitation at a much later date than the Fali. The Gude formed part of the 'Mandara' migrants who had established chieftaincies among the Pabur, Margi, and the Hirhuba of the Kilba area. Others are the Gudu and the Holma-Zummo all in the north Benue plains. The Gudu, for example, claim to have come from Borno by way of Mandara and to have settled among the Imshi and Fali as hunters.[52] They possessed horses as well as very powerful religious cults, and eventually usurped power from the autochthons. This is said to have taken place at Manja, an Imshi stronghold, and Kanara, the leader of the immigrants, became the *de facto* ruler with the aid of some Fali groups. In this way, the Muvya chieftaincy came into being.

Under the Kanara dynasty. Muvya entered a period of expansion and consolidation. The latter was effected largely through the spread of 'Mandara' religious institutions. Another centre of the Imshi, Mijili, fell to the immigrants and became a leading religious centre as well as the capital of the new kingdom. It was here that the first three rulers, Kanara, Dewa, and Kobakoba, reigned, and later Kadalla and Birma. The *Barkuma* was the chief official of the government, the intermediary between the Muvya chief and the other officials as well as for the district rulers. Like the *Aku* of the Jukuns, the Muvya chief was secluded.

The various Fombina chieftaincies considered above had much in common. The chiefs were, in most cases, the political and religious heads of their communities; their authority was supported by religious sanctions. The system of appointing chiefs and vassal rulers, and the procedure for burial of dead chiefs were strikingly similar. Where the chieftaincies comprised different peoples, such as Mokule, Kafa-Miya, and Sukur, the authority of the chief was indirectly exercised through clan leaders or heads of lineage groups. Finally, the titles and functions of officials were similar, especially among the

c

chieftaincies north of the Benue. This indicates contact and intercourse between the peoples.

In the majority of the chieftaincies, a number of factors, such as kinship relations, language, religion, land and the need for security, bound together the heterogeneous inhabitants. In Sukut for example, the Margi, Higi, and other Gudur elements were bound and held in authority not through kinship but by the magico-religious powers of the Llidi, the custodian of the cults from which his powers were derived. His orders were respected because not to do so meant incurring the displeasure of the gods (e.g. crop failure or epidemic). He performed religious rites before the beginning of the rainy season and before the harvest, and in return for these duties, the Llidi received gifts, tribute, and the respect of the people.

In Muvya, Kafa-Miya, and Mokule, religion was used for the same purpose. The Higi, though they lived in clans each with its own chief, had a common religion derived from Gudur. The religious head belonged to the 'senior kindred' and so came to exercise political authority. He was the focus of Higi unity and through his religious performances, successful harvests were obtained, childbirth promoted, and epidemics averted. To offend him was to offend the gods. Among the Bata on the other hand, exogamous social groups had common cults and these were associated with the *Homon*, through the priests or officials appointed by him to act as servitors. Thus, the Homon was the focus of ethnic and religious unity. Among the Kilba, the principal cults, *Vidigal, Garga, Ngau*, and *Jagurni*, were centred on the royal family. The Till Hong and his most senior officials, the *Yedima*, were, in fact, the priests of Vidigal and Garga, both regarded as custodians of health and prosperity. The attendants of the two cults were also members of the government, the Dubu-kuma and the *Tali-ihi*. Thus, the directives of the Till Hong were obeyed in order to avert drought, crop failure, and epidemics.

The need for land and security also bound together different ethnic groups within some chieftaincies. In Mokule, for example, the Higı, Margi, and Pabur were connected partly by the need for protection against periodic military expeditions from their more powerful neighbours, Borno and Mandara. Moreover, the Margi and Pabur as newcomers into the areas regarded the Higi as 'landlords'. It may have been for this reason that the newcomers acknowledged the authority of the Mokule chief.

Some chieftaincies had little centralization of authority, power being distributed among their component ethnic groups. The Chamba chieftaincies and Kilba are examples of this. In the latter, the Jirhuba lived under their Till Krama while other groups had their Shells; so the control of the central authority was limited. Furthermore, the different kindred-groups were entitled to office in the government, as in the case of the Chamba chieftaincies. No doubt this practice went a long way towards maintaining unity and harmony between the different elements of the chieftaincies.

POPULATION DISTRIBUTION AND ECONOMIC ACTIVITIES

The physical features of Fombina vary from plains to mountains and govern the distribution of the population. Another important factor is climate. In general, the mountains were sparsely populated and people resorted to them only in time of danger or invasion by more powerful groups or neighbouring states. Thus, the highlands of the north were centres of refuge before the nineteenth century. Generally the plains were preferred especially where these were crossed by rivers and provided good farm land.

There was a substantial population along the Yedseram and on the plains to the east and west of the Mandara highlands. Other areas of fairly high population were the basin of Kilenge, and the plains west of the Kilba mountains, and east of the Hawal river valley. But the Lala plateau was sparsely populated. The majority of the inhabitants of Fombina tended to settle where continuous availability of water for drinking and agriculture was assured. Settlements were generally sited along river valleys or near the flood plains.

The Benue plains had a denser population because of its rich alluvial deposits creating good farming land. For the same reason, there was a substantial population along the lower Faro valley and on the Nasarawo, Beti and Māyo-Ine plains. The low-lying Benue plain was the most densely populated region in Fombina. All the tributaries of the Benue river have broad flood plains in their lower courses which attracted immigrants from the north. However, the population decreases to the south probably because of the mountain ranges there, and for this reason Hōsēre was the most sparsely peopled region of Fombina.

For the majority of the people of Fombina, farming was the most important occupation, especially subsistence farming, and explains the importance of the seasons in the lives of the various communities. The onset of the rains was of religious significance; clearing the bush, hoeing and sowing were all preceded by priestly rites, and harvest commenced only after religious rites had been performed. All the major groups had rain-cults and among some groups the priests of those cults were members of the ruling élite.

The duration of the rainy season varies from the north to the south. In the Benue plains it lasts only for five months and this is the farming season. However, preparation for farming was lengthy. Long before the first rains, fields had to be cleared and in the case of new farms, trees had to be felled before sowing. At the end of the rains, the harvest period lasted approximately three months, making an agricultural year of about nine months. The crops grown in the north were mainly guinea-corn and millet, with some cassava, cotton, and tiger-nuts.

On the Benue plains, farming was subsidiary to fishing which was the principal occupation of the Bata. The environs of the riverain Bata villages abounded in farms producing such crops as rice and millet. In the dry season, the Bata also farmed on the damp marshes producing maize, banana, and plantains. The crops grown in the southern Benue area were basically similar to those of the north, except that those of the south were better because the rainfall was heavier. On the southern plateau only maize was grown. Crops such as guinea-corn, millet, and the like do not flourish owing to the high rainfall, but because of the length of the rainy season, maize was cultivated twice.

In the dry season, farming was not possible and so a number of groups pursued other activities. The most common was hunting. Traditions are full of accounts of hunters migrating to the south and eventually establishing control over extensive areas, such as the Kilba, Gude, and the western Bata. Among the Chamba and the Bata, it was the practice to organize hunting expeditions in the dry season. Such expeditions, led by warriors, used to venture into the jungle. Subsequently all large animals killed, such as lions, leopards, and elephants, had to be presented to the chiefs. Small animals, such as gazelles, rabbits, and rats, were kept by the common folk. Other dry season activities were bee-keeping and honey-collecting, both very common among the Chamba.

The Fulɓe had brought vast herds of fine cattle into Fombina but they did not actually introduce cattle to its people. The Kilba and the Lala owned cattle, the humpless type (*muturu*), long before the coming of the Fulɓe,[53] but these were not herded in the manner of the Fulɓe, nor were they kept for meat, but for milk. However, following the advent of the Fulɓe, more and more of the autochthons acquired cattle in various ways. Chiefs and the leaders of clans were given cattle by Fulɓe groups wishing to acquire favour and graze on their lands. Even though a number of the autochthons had acquired cattle, they remained settled agriculturalists and the Fulɓe undertook herding on their behalf, as among the Maiha and Lala,[54] in return for the right to graze their herds on their lands.

The pre-nineteenth century Fombina society was concerned purely with agriculture. It is therefore not easy to talk of industrial activities. Nevertheless, both farming and hunting require tools, no matter how rudimentary. The making of hoes, arrows, and knives necessary for successful farming and hunting was an important industry among a number of ethnic groups. Among the Vere, Lala, and Dama, iron-smelting was an important enterprise. The ore, in the form of a fine black sand, was usually gathered by panning after heavy rains. Then the ore was smelted and the metal made into short iron bars (*tāje*) used as currency and for making implements. Iron smelting was a common industry among the majority of the ethnic groups in Fombina. Traditions are full of accounts of kindred groups who specialized in iron production, such as the Duwa among the Sukur and the Killa among the Kilba. Among the Sukur, the Duwa because of their importance, was the only group from which the Llidi could marry and in Kilbaland the Killa were subservient to the Gidigal and Garga cults.[55] During drought or epidemic the Killa had to perform appeasement rites to both deities.

Apart from iron-making, textile-weaving was another widespread industry. The making of cotton cloth is still an important activity among the Bata, Higi, and Gude in the region north of the Benue. The leading textile centres were Holma and Zummo. The cloth was manufactured and dyed locally, using local cotton. It was widely used among the Kilba for payment of dowry and among other groups for the burial of chiefs and local dignitaries. On the southern plateau, cloth-making was not known and the people used bark-cloth. However, in the nineteenth century, following the development of long distance trade, the stencilled Benue cloths began to appear in the south and eventually superseded bark-cloth.[56] Until quite recently, daura was regarded as having more prestige and beauty than most European cloths, and its use was restricted to men of high status.

The various peoples of Fombina may have been in contact with one another through trade, but there is little available material on pre-nineteenth century internal and external trade. Nonetheless, it cannot be assumed that trade was unimportant. Fombina is not isolated geographically from the peoples of the northern savanna and the southern equatorial forest regions; the river Benue runs through it, from its heartland down to the Niger in the west and then down to the sea. Also from the Benue valley the rivers Kilenge and Tiel provide access up to the Chad basin, while the Māyo Kebbi links the Benue to that of the Logone. The Faro and its tributaries serve as the links with the people of the southern plateau who had contact with those of the coastal region.

As regards the region north of the Benue, it is said that there was a colony of Kanuri hunters in the region of Song before the Fulɓe reached it.[57] They specialized in hunting elephants. The Kanuri were interested in ivory and a flourishing trade could have existed between Borno and Fombina in ivory and hunting implements. Also in the Song region, the Gudu people claim that it was through trading activities that their prince became Muslim in the eighteenth century and then he 'islamized' his people.[58] The Higi have a similar tradition relating to dry season communications with Borno. From these traditions it can be concluded that the peoples bordering Borno to the south had been trading with their Kanuri neighbours to the north. When the Fulɓe entered Fombina in the eighteenth century, they looked to Borno for the supply of potash used in the watering of their herds. This may have given rise to increased Kanuri trading centures into Fombina. Also, the Benue cotton cloths which in the nineteenth century made a name among the peoples of the Bamenda grassfield, may have been exported to the markets of Borno and Hausaland long before they became available in southern Fombina. That region had been visited by the Jukun or (Jukunized) traders long before the Hausa reached it. The Jukun were the leading producers of salt in the Benue regions, and the leading salt centres were Akwana, Jebjeb, and Bomanda.[59] From these areas, salt was exported south on to the Bamenda plateau and eastwards to Fombina which had no local centre of salt production.

NOTES

1. H. Barth, *Travels and Discoveries in North and Central Africa*, (5 vols., London, 1857), vol. II.
2. Hōsēre is Fulfulde for mountain, but it is applied to the mountains of the present Département d'Adamaoua of the Cameroun Republic. The exact borders of Fombina cannot be precisely determined because of the diversity of its physical features and ethnic groups. In 1915, at the time of the first world war against Germany, the Lāmīdo and his council attempted to define the limits of Fombina in terms of those accepted in the nineteenth century. They pointed out that in the north, it bordered Borno at Waloji; in the north-east with Bagarmi at Māyo Bori, Babare, and Wudaka; in the east with Laka at Lame and Hōsēre Chollire; in the south with the Baya at Bertua, Kunde, Delele, and Durmu, with the Tikar at Manjogolo and Jitam, and with the Bute at Majum and Tigom; in the south-west with the emirate of Muri at Garbabi. S. H. P. Vereker, 'Cameroun War Campaigns', 1915-17, NNAK, SNP, K.2, p. 10.
3. J. Greenberg, *The Languages of Africa*, (The Hague, 1963).
4. According to the Gadzama chronicles in possession of the Mai Kabama of the Margi District, Borno Province (trans. in R. J. Patterson, 'Special Report on Uje District', Ethnology Mbum, NNAK, 2700).
5. Ibid.
6. Greenberg, *Languages*.
7. Patterson.
8. R. Dugast, 'Essai sur le peuplement du Cameroun', *Et. Cam.*, 1, 21/2 (1948), 19-33.
9. D. A. Percival, 'Notes on the Tikar Tribe', 1938, NNAK, Adamprof.
10. M. McCulloch, 'The Tikar' in *Peoples of the Central Cameroun*, (London, 1954), p. 20.
11. Percival, 'Notes on the Tikar Tribe', p. 22.
12. Ibid.
13. Ibid., p. 23.
14. The information below is largely based upon the work of P. M. Kaberry, 'Notes on Nsaw History and social categories', *Africa*, 22, 1 (1952), 72-5, see pp. 72-3. See also McCulloch, pp. 36-41.
15. Garbosa II, 'Labarun Chamba da Alamuransu', NHRS, p. 8. M. D W. Jeffreys, 'Some notes on the customs of the grassfield Bali of Northwest Cameroons', *Afr. u. Übersee*, 46, 3 (May 1963), 161-8, suggests 1780 as being about the time the Chamba left Dindi.
16. H. S. Berkeley, 'The Chamba', 1905, extracts from provincial correspondence jacket, PCJ. 345/1922, MAJ, file no. 34.
17. H. S. Berkeley, 'Chamba District Notes', 1907, MAJ, file no. 48.
18. C. K. Meek, 'The Kona', 1928, MAJ, file no. 34.
19. Chamba traditions, collected by the author at Ganye, Sugu, and Yelwa in September 1968.
20. Logan, Percival and Shaw, Notes in Sugu District Notebook, Local Authority Office, Ganye, and also G. M. Clifford, 'Chamba Area Reorganisation', 1933-40, Vol. 1, NNAK, Adamprof, p. 70.
21. Chamba traditions.
22. Gurumpawo and Yebbi informants, September, 1968.
23. Sugu informants, September, 1968.
24. Clifford.
25. The information below is derived from Chamba Traditions; Logan, Percival and Shaw; and Berkeley.
26. C. K. Meek, *The Northern Tribes of Nigeria*, (2 vols., London, 1925), vol. I, p. 70.
27. Ibid.
28. Barth, p. 482, and Meek, *Northern Tribes*, pp. 4-5.
29. Greenberg, *Languages*.
30. J. Skelly, 'Ethnology Gudu', 1928, NNAK, SNP, 2710H.
31. W. R. Shirley, 'Malabu and Belel District Miscellaneous Papers', 1917-46, NNAK, Adamprof, p. 2.
32. Berkeley, 'The Chamba'; Meek, *Northern Tribes*, vol. 2, p. 329.

The Region and its Inhabitants   25

33. W. O. P. Rosedale, 'Yungur District Miscellaneous Papers', 1923-29, NNAK, G.19; also J. H. Shaw, 'Yungur District Miscellaneous Papers', 1935-40, NNAK, G.20.
34. Song traditions, collected by the author, August, 1968.
35. Bata traditions, collected by the author, August, 1968.
36. Barth, p. 501.
37. Ibid, p. 479.
38. R. M. Maiyaki, 'The emergence of chieftainship among the Mbula', unpublished B.A. research essay, Ahmadu Bello University, June 1972; also Mbula traditions, collected by the author, August 1968.
39. Kilba traditions, collected by the author, August 1968.
40. Yerima Balla, 'Tarihin Kilba', Secondary School, Hong; see also G. Chaskda, 'The establishment of a Goverment-General among the Kilba', unpublished B.A. research essay, ABU, June, 1972, pp. 13-26.
41. Chaskda, pp. 41-8. It should be pointed out that some of the Kilba political titles are Kanuri or Kanuri-derived, *viz. Zarma, Medalla* and *Bulama*. There are reasons to suppose a strong Kanuri influence in the formation and subsequent development of some of the chieftaincies in Fombina.
42. A. Schultze, *The Sultanate of Bornu*, trans. P. A. Benton, (London, 1913), p. 57.
43. Baza traditions, collected by the author, August 1968.
44. Michika traditions, collected by the author, August 1968.
45. Ibrahim Dodo, 'Tarihin Maiha', NHRS, Zaria, indicated that the Maiha and Holma groups moved out from Mandara following a dynastic dispute.
46. J. Vossart, 'Histoire du Sultanat du Mandara', *Et. Cam.*, 35/36 (1952), 19-52.
47. Barth, pp. 397-8; see also C. K. Meek, *Tribal Studies in Northern Nigeria*, (2 vols., London, 1931), pp. 312-13, and A. H. M. Kirk-Greene, 'The Kingdom of Sukur', *Nigeria Field*, 25, 2 (1960), 67-96, see pp. 68ff.
48. Kirk-Greene, *Nigeria Field*, 25, 2 (1960), 93.
49. Information for the section following is derived from Michika and Baza traditions.
50. D. F. H. McBride, 'Report on Northern Margi Area', 1936, in Uba DNB.
51. Ibid.
52. Lamorde traditions, collected by the author, August 1968.
53. According to C. O. Migeod, *Gazeteer of Yola Province*, (Lagos, 1927), p. II, though the Fulani brought with them vast herds of fine cattle to these regions, for it seems that they found a breed of rather small or dwarf cattle in the country.
54. Ibid. p. 10; Ibrahim Dodo.
55. Meek, *Tribal Studies*, vol. 1, p. 187.
56. E. M. Chilver, 'Nineteenth century trade in the Bamenda Grassfields, southern Cameroons', *Afr. U. Übersee*, 45, 4 (1962), 233-58, see pp. 245-6.
57. Song traditions, and Song DNB, C.D.'s office, Yola.
58. Skelly.
59. J. M. Fremantle, *Gazeteer of Muri Province*, (London, 1922), p. 53.

2. The Fulɓe of Fombina and their Jihad

The earliest centre of the Fulɓe in the Western Sudan was the region of the Senegal basin. But today they are found as far east as the Sudan and Ethiopia, although it is only in Nigeria that they number over a million.[1] Their origin is a matter of controversy; and many theories have been advanced to explain their emergence.[2] Their own tradition, however, claims descent from the famous Arab, Uqba b. Amir b. Nafi.[3] Briefly, the tradition is that Uqba left Arabia at the time of the prophet because it was predicted that he was going to have a non-Arab son. Coming to the western Sudan, he married a 'black' wife, Bajemango.[4] Their children were the ancestors of all the Fulɓe apart from the Mbororo'en: Deita, ancestor of Songhai Fulɓe; Woya, of Fulɓe Woya; Roroba, of the Wolaba'en; and Nasi, of Baowina and the Wolarɓe. According to tradition, the Mbororo'en were descendants of the son delivered by Bajemango after she was ravished by a water spirit or by Uqba's slave.

The Fulɓe tradition of origin should be understood as a legend, just like those of the Hausa (the Bayajidda legend), Yoruba (Oduduwa), Nupe (Tsoede), and the Kanuri (Saif b. Dhi Yazan). Uqba b. Nafi, who was associated with the Arab conquest of North Africa, had never been to the western Sudan. However, the significance of the legend is that, following the activities of this Arab general in North Africa, a number of Berber groups migrated to the south probably to escape Arab conquest, and they came into contact with the 'black' peoples. Some of the Berbers were nomadic and began to infiltrate into the south. Consequently, the Berbers may have intermarried with the negro farmers. It has been shown that the whole Senegal valley functioned as a 'permeable membrane' which the Berber nomads crossed from the north to pasture their herds on the Ferlo plateau.[5] Having found good pasture, the Berber immigrants tended to become culturally isolated from the northern groups whom they had little motive for rejoining. Thus, they intermarried with their darker, southern neighbours and the products of such unions may have been the Fulɓe.

Long before the migration of the Fulɓe into Fombina, developments within their society had produced three groups distinguished by the degree of the attachment of each to pastoral nomadism. These were the nomadic Mbororo'en, the semi-settled Fulɓe Na'i, and the settled Fulɓe-Shi'e. Originally all three groups belonged to the Mbororo'en group but for a number of reasons their nomadic society began to diversify. In the course of migrations in search of better grazing lands, some groups were left behind either as a result of cattle decline through disease and other misfortunes, or because of good pasturage, they preferred not to migrate. Those who no longer migrated because of the decline in the size of their herds had to adopt other occupations to supplement their resources, usually farming. In the event of the herds disappearing totally, the Fulɓe became settled agriculturalists, but where they still had some cattle, though not sufficient for their sole reliance upon them, they became semi-settled, tending cattle and doing small-scale farming. The latter, called Fulɓe Na'i, represented those Fulɓe who were partly changed through cattle decline and through the adoption of other occupations for subsistence. They occupied a transitional position. When the cattle were recouped, pastoral nomadism was reverted to, but failing that they became settled peasants, Fulɓe Shi'e, the last category of changed Fulɓe.

Apart from the decline in the size of herds, contact and prolonged intercourse with the peasant communities also encouraged the emergence of semi-settled and settled Fulɓe groups. Following the coming of Islam in West Africa in the eleventh century, the Fulɓe were the first people to accept it, and eventually became its most dedicated disseminators.[6] Islam is not merely a religion but a complete culture, and those nomadic Fulɓe who embraced it tended to devote more of their time to Islamic observances and less to cattle husbandry. They moved from one malam to another in search of education till they themselves became 'learned' (*mōdiɓɓe*). Then they settled down with their dependants, as teachers, judges, advisers to local rulers, or simply as worshippers (*Torōɓe*).[7] Those who did not take Islam so seriously continued as pastoral nomads, practising their traditional customs.

Since the eleventh century, therefore, more and more Fulɓe had been settling down as peasants. Because of the nature of their new society, the pattern of settled and semi-settled agriculturalist Fulɓe having socio-economic intercourse with their non-Fulɓe counterparts was established. In time the Fulɓe began to exchange cultural mores with their hosts and neighbours. They had also begun to intermarry, intensifying the move towards sedentarism.

The term Mbororo'en refers to the Fulɓe parent stock who, being less Islamized, had no permanent abode, but wandered from place to place according to the dictates of the seasons. Socially cohesive, they practised various forms of their inherited customs (*alfālūji*) in order to protect their herds and bring about their multiplication.[8] Having escaped intermarriage and culture-contacts with the non-Fulɓe, the Mbororo'en remained, and remain to this day, a distinct group with different customs, values, and way of life, adhering to nomadic ways and ideals. While the Fulɓe Na'i and the Fulɓe Shi'e looked down upon them, the Mbororo'en in turn regarded them (the Na'i and the Shi'e) as degenerates whose culture and outlook had been debased by contacts and intermarriage with the Hāɓe (non-Fulɓe). The Mbororo'en lived as a sequestered society and had a strong sense of solidarity, intensified by their relative independence which they were at all times prepared to defend, by force if need be, but more often by emigration. They believed that their continued survival depended upon remaining nomads and 'pure Fulɓe'.

THE FUL'BE MIGRATION TO FOMBINA

The trend of Fulɓe migration was eastwards, within the Savanna belt. To its north lies the desert, and to the south equatorial forest, making nomadic movements outside the belt difficult. From the scanty evidence available, it would appear that the Fulɓe had been emigrating from the Senegal basin, following political and social developments in that region. Apart from the Almoravid invasion in the eleventh century, the rise and decline of states – Tekrur, Ghana, Mali, and Songhai – spanned five centuries during which peaceful and disturbed conditions alternated.

By the beginning of the fourteenth century, advance parties of immigrant Fulɓe reached Hausaland and by the sixteenth century they had moved as far east as Bargami.[9] By the beginning of the seventeenth century, there was a substantial number of Fulɓe in the Hausa states and the empire of Borno, where since the mid-sixteenth century, the Muslim Mai Idris Alooma had patronized and protected the Fulɓe. His numerous campaigns against the Tuareg and the Ngizim were aimed at eliminating their threat to the Fulɓe.[10] Similarly, Alooma's attack on the Gamargu, the scattering of the So peoples, and the defeat of Mandara encouraged the free movement of pastoral Fulɓe within the Borno empire. The westwards expansion of Borno under the Galadimas based at Nguru since the seventeenth century was also of considerable significance,[11] and a large number of Fulɓe were brought under the authority of the Mai of Borno.

The first Fulɓe groups to have entered Fombina were the Mbororo'en who had no Muslim leaders (arɗo'en) who could gain for them the recognition of the Sefuwa Mais. Consequently, they avoided Borno altogether. From Hausaland they moved south-eastwards until they reached the Gongola valley in the seventeenth century.[12] The migrations of the Fulɓe from Borno into Fombina took place by stages and at first through nomadic wanderings (*eggol*) – a movement which involved the displacement of regular grazing orbits due to deteriorating pasture conditions or increased incursion by other nomads. The nomads in Borno moved to the south in the dry season and north in the wet. As a result of this seasonal migration, the Fulɓe began to drift into Fombina from southern Borno. Migration into Fombina increased when their eastward passage was blocked by the hostility of the Bagarmi.[13] Moreover, the land bordering Lake Chad to as far south as Mandara was characterized by a boggy loam (*firki*) which became waterlogged in the rains. In the dry season, the surface was split by gaping cracks, very difficult for men and animals to cross. The whole region between the Logone river and Matia is liable to flood at the height of the rainy season, and renders cattle susceptible to foot-and-mouth disease and foot-rot disease. Thus, the region near Lake Chad was unsuitable for cattle grazing and was an impediment to the eastward migratory drift of the Fulɓe. It has also been suggested that they ran into the westbound movements of Shuwa Arab herdsmen.[14] Consequently, the movements of the less numerous Shuwa were halted and the Fulɓe began to migrate, in ever increasing numbers, to the south.

Fombina, unlike Borno, was a very fertile area which contained regions of perennial pasture. Thus, nomadic groups tended to remain behind whenever the region was visited. The Wolarɓe, for example, had long been in the Daya region and then, through eggol, had spread eastwards to the Yedseram valley pasturing their herds among the Margi. Their eastwards migration was halted partly because the Mandara highlands were impenetrable, and partly due to the factors outlined above. For a long time, the Wolarɓe grazed their herds along the tributaries of the Yedseram in the dry season and on the western plains in the wet, but as more and more nomads entered the region, a shortage of grazing lands developed. There was also an outbreak of a fly-borne epizootic disease. The Fulɓe had to emigrate also because of the pressure exerted by Mandara. According to Lemoigne, the Wolarɓe in the Yedseram basin had acquired considerable influence over the Margi and because Mandara regarded the area as falling within its sphere of influence, the presence of the Fulɓe and their growing influence over the Margi of the region were viewed with apprehension.[15] Thus, as a result of pressure from Mandara, the Wolarɓe began to drift southwards towards the Higi and Kilba communities.

A number of Wolarɓe groups established their camps at Moda, Duhu, and Kopa while others settled among the Wula and the Sukur of the Magar mountains, although the main body of the Wolarɓe and related groups, led by Arɗo'en Ba-Sambo, Jaunde, and Hamman Julde, entered Kilbaland and settled at Kwabaktina.[16] The position of the Wolarɓe in the Yedseram basin was taken over by new immigrants, the Yillaga'en from the west. They subsequently spread up to the Chad-Benue watershed region and settled among the Chekke, Gude, and Fali. To the north and north-east of the Yillaga'en were the Ngara Fulɓe (so called because they had adopted Kanuri facial marks;[17] this suggests long residence in the Borno empire and close association with the Kanuri). They were probably the first Fulɓe group to have entered into Mandara, for in that Kingdom they had enjoyed the patronage of the sultans to the exclusion of all other groups. From Mandara, the Ngara subsequently spread to the east and south-east towards the Logone river.

Other Fulɓe clans were in other parts of Fombina. For example, the Mbororo'en had been present on the Gongola since the seventeenth century and by the beginning of the eighteenth century some of them had developed intimate relations with the non-Muslim autochthons of the region. The Bewe'en, because they had good relations with the Pabir, accompanied them during their northward exodus in the eighteenth century.[18] While the Pabir settled at Huyum, Musa, Dille, and Multafu, the Bewe'en founded Wobare in the same region. Another group, the Kiri'en, who had been in the lower

Gongola region, were evenly spread among the communities of the middle Benue region by the middle of the eighteenth century.[19] Finally, on the Lala plateau, the Kitijen Fulɓe settled among the Lala, Hona, Ga'anda, and Bura.

By the middle of the eighteenth century, there were a number of Fulɓe groups in Fombina, but mainly in the region to the north of the Benue. The two major clans, the Wolarɓe and the Yillaga'en, were concentrated in Kilba-land and the Chad-Benue watershed region respectively. However, before the end of the century, these two clans dispersed, probably due to the growth in the size of their herds and their own increasing numbers, neither problem as Stenning points out, being easily solved 'by cattle raiding, feud or war' but only by migration.[20] Apart from these two possible reasons, it may have been that the Wolarɓe and Yillaga'en dispersed because they had learnt about grazing regions elsewhere in Fombina. The Wolarɓe, after settling for some years, had found that Kilbaland had limited dry season pasturage and the herds were being affected. Another reason for their dispersal was that the region had been an area of cultural fusion and the Kilba had emerged out of an intermixture of heterogeneous elements through intermarriage. The Wolarɓe were being increasingly compelled to socialize, which aided their absorption into Kilba society. The alternatives were expulsion from Kilbaland or payment of exorbitant tribute and grazing dues, conditions which also led to some emigration.[21]

Arɗo Neowa, leading his group southwards, crossed the Benue at Tepe and settled among the Bata of Kokumi. From here, Arɗo Ju'a proceeded to Djongum, and after his death, his son, Arɗo Umaru, moved into the Bata of Baronga. Similarly, following the death of Arɗo Neowa, his son, Arɗo Siddiki, moved further south and settled at Cheboa. Shehu Muhammadu led his group from Kilbaland to Zummo, Arɗo Hamman Julde moved to the Benue, and Hamman Yero Biri settled among the Bata along the valley of the Tiel river. Finally, while Arɗo Dembo moved to Geweke and Jauro Dagurma entered Holma, Ba Dau's group remained within Kilbaland, centred at Mbilla-Kilba.

The Yillaga'en also dispersed from the Chad-Benue watershed region. This may have been as a result of shortage of grazing lands consequent upon clan expansion, or because through transhumance, they had discovered the more fertile Gawaza plains to the east of their habitat. Consequently, a number of groups crossed the Poppologosum pass into the fertile plains.

In the Marba area, however, the Yillaga'en were compelled to emigrate by the Ngara who had preceded them.[22] The main body of the Yillaga'en led by Arɗo Bondi La Malle moved south, crossed the Māyo Kebbi, and settled at Lame. Then Bondi La Malle's son, Arɗo Yajo, moved to Liporo among the Mono Mundang. Another group moved north-east and established itself at Bibemi. However, a number of Yillaga groups remained in the region north of the Māyo Kebbi. After the expulsion from Marba, Arɗo Buba b. Hamman moved across Sumealands to Mendif, then southwards across the

Tuburi into the lands of the Mundang, and from the north, one group moved to Mayeso, Golembe, and Gider, while Ardo Manga led his supporters and settled with them among the Niam-Niam at Deo.

The migrations of the Fulɓe from Borno into Fombina and their dispersal there went on till the nineteenth century. However, more Fulɓe had emigrated from Borno during the last quarter of the eighteenth century. Unlike the early migrations, the later ones were provoked by the political conditions in the Borno empire. The Fulɓe, a politically segmented people, hated strict political control and oppression, which they avoided either by emigration (*perol*) or by force of arms. They also tended to emigrate in time of famine, epidemic, conflict with their hosts, or natural crisis.

The eighteenth century was a period of unstable political conditions in the Borno empire.[23] The traditions established by the Mai Idris Alooma had been lost and the dynasty and the empire had begun to decline. The Mais no longer concerned themselves with government and military campaigns, and consequently, dependent provinces became autonomous or independent. Thus, the Borno government became unable to give the protection against the sedentary autochthons which the Fulɓe so much desired. Hence, they were exposed to the authority and influence of the Hāɓe in southern Borno. Apart from deteriorating political conditions, eighteenth century Borno was also characterized by serious famine which affected the Fulɓe and their cattle.[24] These conditions were responsible for the continued migrations of the Fulɓe into Fombina down to the nineteenth century.

THE SOCIO-POLITICAL AND ECONOMIC CONDITIONS OF FOMBINA FUL'BE

Fulɓe society in pre-nineteenth century Fombina was essentially nomadic, and socio-political organization was geared towards the perpetuation of the Fulɓe way of life. The largest social group among the Fulɓe was the clan (*lenyol*); the smallest was the single lineage family, a basically independent group whose cohesion was dependent on possession of sufficient cattle. Sons and parents, wives and husbands, were bound together by interest in the herd. The sons, as dependants, were cattle herdsmen while the womenfolk marketed the bovine products and built huts when they migrated. The head of the family was respected by his sons and the wider community according to the size of his herds. As far as his family was concerned, he was Ardo (leader) and so long as the cattle remained under his control, the cohesion of the family was assured. His sons would render their services in order to be rewarded with sufficient cattle to begin their own independent lives. Ownership of cattle began at birth, usually as gifts from relatives, emphasizing the importance of cattle in the society. These gifts (*sukkulki*) would be repeated on important occasions, and by the time the child had grown up, he possessed some cattle within the family herd. Finally, on marriage, he received more cattle from his father to support his family. From then on he had two alternatives: either to settle alone as an independent herd-owner or continue to live with his parents in a large lineage family. This was determined by the size of the family herds; where the cattle were few, reliance upon parents and relatives was continued.

The two major classes in Fulɓe society were the *Bikkoi* and *Mauɓe* (youths and elders, respectively). Children below the age of puberty were called *Bacci*, boys above *Sukāɓe* and mature girls *Iwaiɓe*. In Mbororo'en society, another important social group was the *Kori'en* which was above the *Sukāɓe* class. While the latter embraced all the unmarried youth, the former was a sort of association of the newly-wed. After marriage, usually in the twenty-fifth year, the hair was shaved and after three years, the Kori'en formally joined the Mauɓe class. The Mauɓe was divided into two categories, those below the mid-forties and those above. The latter were called *Naye'en* or *Ndotti'en*, each social group looking to its immediate senior for guidance and leadership. The senior class, the Ndotti'en, enjoyed the respect and obedience of every individual in the society.

Another important social unit was the *Wāldēru*, age group association, whose members addressed one another as *Ngorgi*, or *Sappa* in the case of females. Age-mates usually played together, grew together, and paired during the *Sharo* festival. Wāldēru was of profound importance. Apart from generating love, brotherhood, and the sense of belonging in the youths, it fostered strong kinship ties which were essential for the continued existence of Fulɓe society in its original form.

The Mbororo'en called the settled Fulɓe *ndowi'en* or *huya'en* (those who do not know the life of the bush). To them such Fulɓe were no longer true Fulɓe because they had lost their cattle as well as their 'Fulɓe-ism' through intermarriage with the Hāɓe. The Mbororo'en neither intermarried nor maintained much social intercourse with the settled or semi-settled Fulɓe. Such Fulɓe, on their part, looked at the Mbororo'en with envy (because while the latter had plenty of cattle they had none) and contempt as they believed that their way of life was much better and so they regarded themselves as the élite and the spokesmen of the pastoral nomads in matters affecting the Fulɓe in general. Though the way of life of the Mbororo'en was different from the settled and the semi-settled groups, they did not regard each other as aliens. They would co-operate and unite when faced with common problems and threats. There had never been conflicts between the various Fulɓe groups even over grazing tracts because they recognized the principle of 'first come first served'. Moreover, in all parts of Fombina, the Fulɓe, irrespective of group, lived as aliens. Consequently, the sense of brotherhood (*banndirāgu*) was well developed among the different groups.

An important social code which regulated the day-to-day life of the Fulɓe was *Pulāku*. Its essential elements were shyness (*semtēnde*), patience (*munyal*), care and forethought (*hakkīlo*), obedience (*doutāre*), respect for elders (*mangingo*), trust (*yerduye*), courage (*chūsu*), and strict observance of religion (*ainol dīna*).[25] All these were regarded as important especially when dealing with relatives, parents, and elders. Strict adherence to the code was essential so that everybody could enjoy 'the material and moral benefits of living with his clansmen'.[26] The flouting of any element of the code had serious repercussions, the offender being liable to ostracism (*hombondu*), or a fine payable in cattle (*nyamtol*). Partly because of this and partly because the principles of the code were inculcated in the minds of children from birth, the code was rarely flouted. Traditionally, Pulāku was said to have been found in Pullo of pure Fulɓe descent, because its characteristics are inherited from generations of Fulɓe parents. It was also held that an Arɗo was an embodiment of Pulāku – he was thus its head (*Maudo*) and guardian.[27] It was his duty to order hombondu and nyamtol in the event of breaches of the code. Undoubtedly, the code of Pulāku was the main agency behind the support and respect enjoyed by the Mauɓe and the Arɗo'en. It could be described as the Fulɓe law.

Fulɓe society was an exclusive one, retained even when living among non-Fulɓe, and the exercise of authority by the chief in whose land they resided was through the Fulɓe Arɗo'en. The major political units among the Fulɓe were the family and the lenyol. In the former, its head, (normally the father) exercised full authority. The lenyol, on the other hand, was headed by a single leader when its members resided in the same place, or by the various family heads when they were dispersed. Basically, 'arɗo' was a kinship term in the sense that the incumbent was either the father of his dependants or the most senior man of a closely related group. In the latter, the Arɗo had little influence; actual authority was exercised over families by their respective heads. However, the Arɗo'en were the foci of clan or group unity, and performed important functions in the group. They officiated at ceremonies such as the Sharo, namings, and marriages. In addition, they had judicial and political functions. In the event of conflicts between Fulɓe and non-Fulɓe, the Arɗo'en usually resolved them by meeting their non-Fulɓe counterparts. Similarly, in the event of conflicts between Fulɓe groups, the Arɗo'en would meet together to resolve them. They also acted as judges for their groups. Civil cases such as fights or conflicts over women were settled by the council of elders, the common punishment in civil cases, such as breaches of customs and traditions, being hombondu whereby the offender was ostracized by his age-mates, other friends, and relatives. The offender became an outlaw, and, during the period of his ostracism, he would be outside the sphere of the clan's collective responsibility, security, and protection. Re-integration was only possible through repentance before the Mauɓe of the lenyol.

The Arɗo'en administered their groups with the assistance of the Mauɓe. They collectively acted as spokesmen for their groups to the ruler of the area in which they lived and grazed their herds. They were also spokesmen to other groups of clans (*Le'i*). But decisions affecting the whole group were not made by the Arɗo alone. For example, before migrating, the Mauɓe had to meet, and arrive at decisions collectively. Such decisions, however, had no binding effect; each family had the right to go along or stay behind.

After migrating the leaders of the Fulɓe played more important roles. Before they entered and settled in a new area, the authorities had to be consulted and their consent obtained. The Arɗo'en and their Mauɓe would present themselves before the ruler of the area and request permission for the Fulɓe to settle and pasture in his domain. There would be serious negotiations, sometimes necessitating some form of agreement such as yearly payment of tribute, grazing dues, and herding the non-Fulɓe's cattle along with their own.[28] When an agreement was arrived at, the ruler of the land would inform all his subjects of the Fulɓe presence. This then guaranteed the Fulɓe the right to graze freely within the domain and also the right of protest, should they be attacked or molested by the local populace. Subsequently, they lived as a distinct community under the direct authority of their Mauɓe. In Fulɓe society, the individual owed allegiance not to an arɗo – a nominal leader – but to the group or lenyol to which he belonged, for it was from them that he expected the protection of his rights and interests.

The Fulɓe in pre-nineteenth century Fombina were pastoralists, and cattle husbandry was their most important economic activity. Families were basically independent economically – the herds provided for their daily needs. Milk was part of the diet, but in the wet season when milk was plentiful, it was marketed or bartered to the non-Fulɓe by the womenfolk for foodstuff. It was cattle 'that united the Fulɓe as a group within the plural society and with a degree of solidarity which transcended both kinship and clanship'.[29] The cultural and ethnic identity of the Fulɓe, as well as their socio-economic structure, depended upon possession of cattle.

Pastoralism is defined as a mode of life 'in which a human community is enabled through its control of domestic animals, and also through its own dependence on them, to dispense with the cultivation or even the necessary collection of plant or plant food, or any deliberate interference with the natural vegetation of a region'.[30] But the majority of the Fulɓe in Fombina had never been pastoralists in the strict sense of the definition above. In fact, there were a number of settled and semi-settled Fulɓe in the region before the nineteenth century. They fell into two categories, those whose cattle were insufficient for a nomadic life, and those whose habitat was so favourable that the Mauɓe lived permanently in one place. Where cattle were insufficient, the Fulɓe had to seek other means to supplement their meagre resources. To continue to rely on the cattle for food would eventually lead to the total disappearance of the cattle, and the solution of combining cattle husbandry with farming was unpopular because the Fulɓe had no pride in farming. Similarly, those Fulɓe who moved their cattle according to the dictates of the season, themselves remaining settled in one place, had to seek other means of subsistence whenever the cattle moved. Thus, there are reasons to believe that the majority of the Fombina Fulɓe were not, before the nineteenth century, entirely independent in their basic economic needs. To avoid farming and to preserve the herds from dwindling, they looked to the non-Fulɓe peoples for foodstuff, either in the dry or the wet season. Consequently, they acknow-

D

ledged the political overlordship of the non-Ful6e and developed close relations with some of them.

Finally the Ful6e, irrespective of whether they were settled or nomadic,
were dependent upon the lands of the non-Ful6e. The right to use land, for
grazing, farming, or settlement, was acquired in return for tribute and grazing
dues. For those with few cattle, farming land was obtained only after strong
relations had been developed with the non-Ful6e. All the Ful6e had to
acknowledge the authority of local rulers and in some areas they had also to
abide by customs which were against the Ful6e way of life (*lāwol pulāku*),
such as the marriage customs. To ignore these was to face the possibility of
being expelled from the chieftaincies, or the hostility of the rulers and people.

THE EVENTS LEADING TO THE JIHAD IN FOMBINA

Jihad has been defined as 'the fighting of a Muslim against an unbeliever who
has no covenant (with the Muslims) to uphold God's law'.[31] In short, it is a
Muslim holy war in the interest of Islam. It might therefore be assumed that
prior to the nineteenth century, the majority of the Fombina Ful6e, the protagonists of the jihad, were Muslims. However, evidence so far available
tends to indicate that the Muslims among the Ful6e in Fombina before their
jihad were very few. Undoubtedly, before the nineteenth century, Fombina
was a non-Muslim region and Islam did not penetrate into it, probably
because of the limited contact between it and the Islamized areas of the north,
Borno, Mandara, and Bagarmi. Borno had been an important terminus of
the trans-Saharan trade routes and it had for long been in contact with
Islamic North Africa as well as with the other Muslim centres of the Western
Sudan. This also applied to Bagarmi and Mandara which were also visited
by pilgrims to and from the holy lands. The rulers of the latter became
Muslims at the beginning of the eighteenth century, but down to the begin-
ning of the nineteenth century, Islam was not widely spread even within the
Mandara kingdom.[32]

Islam has been defined as a religion of trade,[33] no doubt because trade and
traders were instrumental in its spread. But Fombina had only very limited
trade connections with both Borno and Hausaland. Slave raiders and hunters
had been visiting Fombina from Borno, and their activities would have
encouraged trade in slaves and ivory.[34] Nevertheless, the trade was certainly
not well organized and there is no evidence that the Kanuri slave raiders and
traders did proselytize. Moreover, their activities covered only the northern
parts of Fombina. The bulk of the region was, by and large, closed to the
penetration of the influence of Islam, and its inhabitants remained pagans
until after the Ful6e jihad in the nineteenth century.

Undoubtedly, the number of Muslims increased following the advent of the
Ful6e, who had been entering Fombina not as traders, teachers, or conquerors,
but simply as pastoral nomads. But, even among them, the Muslims were

initially very few. Both nomadism and Islam as ways of life embodied certain forms of organization, sets of rules, and ways of living. Thus, the acceptance of Islam by the pastoral nomads depended upon whether or not it could fit into the Fulɓe way of life. While the Fulɓe had professed themselves to be Muslims, yet on closer examination, it appears that the position of Islam varied from one group to another. Among the Mbororo'en, the Fulɓe parent stock, Islam had no place in the social organization, customs, and traditions. Those below the age of Korāku received no religious restrictions or training. They neither prayed nor fasted during Ramaḍān and some had never seen the Qur'ān much less read it. The Mbororo'en believed that only the Mauɓe needed to devote their time to dīna and that was enough for the different groups. The youths spent their time on Sukāku and Sharo till they became Kori'en in their twenty-fifth year. Then their attitude to life and Islam would change. Their previous laxity in behaviour would disappear and they would become careful and devout Muslims. Among the Ba'en, Mallamanko'en, Wodāɓe and Gerōji, the youths on becoming Kori'en would start to read the Qur'ān and learn the rituals of prayer; at times a Mōdibbo was recruited for that purpose. But among other groups even after the age of Korāku, the youths continue as nominal Muslims, ignorant of the teachings of the faith.

The semi-settled and settled Fulɓe regarded the Mbororo'en as pagans (*heferɓe*) essentially because the life of the Mbororo'en was full of fetish practices (*tsa'afi*). They lived according to lāwol pulāku observing their ancient customs and traditions. Boys had to undergo the '*yarnol*, an initiation ceremony preparing them for adult life, girls the *jantinirdu*. The ceremonies, of great religious significance, took place when the youths reached the age of thirteen, and were considered necessary so that the cattle would multiply as the youths grew up. Other significant practices included the Wodāɓe custom of wearing black cloth and owning only 'red' cattle. The Danēji, on the other hand, believed in owning only 'white' cattle. These customs were superstitiously adhered to, and there are strong indications that the pre-Islamic religion of the Fulɓe had some connection with propitiation of evil and the fertility of cattle.

Islam was not strong among the Fombina Fulɓe because its acceptance and strict observance meant less attention to cattle husbandry. Even among the settled and semi-settled Fulɓe groups, those concerned with the herding of cattle paid less attention to Islamic pursuits. The Mauɓe, having little to do with the cattle, had more time to devote to Islamic worship and scholarship, or at least to perform the daily prayers regularly. The latter, and fasting during Ramaḍān, are two of the five 'pillars of Islam'; but neither was well practised by the pastoral nomadic Fulɓe. The Mbororo'en, for example, prayed irregularly, and during Ramaḍān they selected thirty Nauɓe to fast for one day. This was held by them to be equivalent to fasting for the whole thirty days. They believed that regular prayers and the fast would distract their attention from the task of caring for the cattle which were their livelihood. *Zakat* (obligatory alms), another 'pillar of Islam', was also unpopular among the nomadic Fulɓe because it would ultimately lead to decline in the size of the herd. Stenning noted that the Woɗaɓe had a system of alms,[35] probably the sukkulki, whereby poor relatives and those who had lost their cattle were given some to build new herds. But it should not be equated with the zakat which is obligatory upon all Muslims.

The Muslim law of inheritance was also not strictly observed by the Fulɓe. They would divide the cattle long before the owner died, and the owner used to give his cattle to his children from birth onwards. When sons married, they received enough cattle to enable them to start life, and daughters received a limited number, enough to help to maintain their husbands. Direct inheritance was only possible where the father was survived by unmarried children or when he had more than enough cattle for all his children. The share of the unmarried would then be deducted and the remainder divided equally between the married sons. However, where a man died childless, all his paternal male relatives would inherit. The main factors that hindered the spread of Islam and militated against strict adherence to its doctrine by the nomadic Fulɓe were the need to continue their way of life, the need to preserve their system of ownership and distribution of cattle among children, the need to preserve their ethnic identity, and the exclusiveness of their society.

The spread of Islam among the Fulɓe was slow. At first, prayers were performed irregularly. As time went on, selected youths were taught the Qur'ān and they in turn instructed others. Gradually the religion gained ground and prayers became more regular and fasting was observed when convenient. But the detailed prescriptions of the Shari'a on marriage, inheritance, and the zakat were either rejected outright or modified, and embodied within existing concepts. The semi-settled Fulɓe were by far the most Islamized group in Fombina before the nineteenth century. They had succeeded in synthesizing their nomadic pastoral life with Islamic interests. Because they possessed few cattle, their Mauɓe and Sukāɓe had ample time to pursue the study of the Qur'ān and the Islamic sciences. Some of the leading Arɗo'en of the semi-settled Fulɓe in Fombina were described as mōdiɓɓe (sing. mōdibbo; scholar), such as Mōdibbo He, Mōdibbo Hamman Gurin, and Mōdibbo Jam, all in the upper Benue valley.[36] There were also the Mōdibbo Da'u among the Kilba, Mōdibbo Hamman Song among the Bata, Mōdibbo Yajo among the Gude-Fali, Mōdibbo Hamman Jūnde among the Holma-Zummo, Mōdibbo Hamman Selbe and Mōdibbo Damraka in the Gazawa plains, east of Mandara.[37] But it is doubtful whether all these men were learned scholars of the calibre of Shehu Usman 'Dan Fodio, Abdullahi 'Dan Fodio or Muhammad Bello in north-western Hausaland. The mōdiɓɓe in pre-nineteenth century Fombina may have been glorified Quranic teachers who had very limited knowledge of the Islamic sciences. By and large, the torōɓe class such as existed among the pre-nineteenth century Fulɓe in Hausaland and Borno had not developed among those in Fombina.

It would seem that by the beginning of the nineteenth century, the number of Muslims among the Fombina Fulɓe was small. So it cannot be claimed that their jihad was motivated by the desire to spread the Islamic faith. Similarly, the jihad in Fombina cannot be described as the culmination of Muslim-pagan conflicts over religious issues. It is true that in the Song region, the Muslims among the Wolarɓe dared not pray or fast openly because of the hostility of the Bata rulers. In most areas, the Fulbe provided the animals needed for sacrifices during local religious festivals and in the Faro valley they were made to partake in the festivals as well. In spite of this, it cannot be said that the Muslims in Fombina were denied freedom of worship or that they were forced to practise the pagan religion of the non-Fulɓe. The jihad in the upper Benue region arose out of the social, economic, and political conditions under which the Fulɓe had been living.

RELATIONS BETWEEN THE FUL'BE AND THE AUTOCHTHONS

The peoples of Fombina lived under various different political systems. The dominant power was Mandara and its authority is said to have extended to the Māyo Kebbi in the south.[38] There were innumerable chieftaincies and communities into which the Fulɓe had entered and settled. Their main concern in any area was to obtain a guarantee (*yerduye*) of their rights (*hakke*) from the local authorities. The greatest need of the Fulɓe was land for cattle grazing, and to acquire this they tended to ally themselves with local rulers, communities, or clans. In Mandara, for example, the Ngara Fulɓe were accorded all hospitality including a monopoly of grazing land.[39] They had similar rights among the Gisiga and these were defended by the local chiefs. Thus, when the Yillaga'en arrived, they were compelled to re-migrate, leaving the Ngara'en to enjoy their privileges.

Acknowledgement of autochthonous authority was necessary to enable the Fulɓe to graze their herds without fear of theft or molestation, and in certain areas they had also to abide by customs which were against pulāku, such as the custom of 'jus primae noctis'.[40] The alternative to accepting these conditions was conflict. The Fulɓe on the plain west of Mandara had never accepted Mandara's overlordship. The plains were important to Mandara as a source of food and were in fact peopled by Mandara immigrants. The presence of the Fulɓe was unwelcome and they were subject to pressure and raids from Mandara, although the autochthons of the region remained on good terms with the Fulɓe.

Among the Higi, for example, the Fulɓe lived not as aliens but as clan members and accorded all the rights and privileges due to a Higi member; neither were they required to pay the grazing dues paid by groups elsewhere. In like manner, the Fulɓe who settled among the Margi lived as a community with their hosts, although subject to the authority of the chief of Mokule. While they did not pay tribute and grazing dues, it was the custom to give all dead cattle to the people on whose land they lived and grazed their herds.[41] Also, during ritual performances, it was customary for the Fulɓe to supply the sacrificial animal, usually black bulls. Thus, in the region west of Mandara, the Fulɓe co-operated with local groups and rulers to obtain unhindered pastoral exploitation. They also looked to the chieftaincies of Sukur, Kafa-Miya, and Mokule for protection against Mandara's periodic military expeditions.[42] Eventually, the Fulɓe became fully integrated and the role of protecting the western lowlands passed into their hands.

The position of the Fulɓe further to the south was markedly different. In the wet season, they utilized Kilbaland and then moved to the lands of the Ga'anda and Bura in the dry. The Kilba maintain that their relations with the Fulɓe had been cordial, the latter paying tribute and grazing dues to the Till Hong and to the local clans, such as at Wudin and Mijili. The Arɗo'en of the Fulɓe acknowledged the authority of the Till Hong. Similar conditions prevailed in the Chad Benue watershed region except that Arɗo Yajo, by befriending the Muvya chief, had obtained free grazing rights for his group. All the other Yillaga groups paid dues in addition to tax (*jomol*), tribute, acknowledgement of 'jus primae noctis' and other customs. One of the last was that ultimate ownership of property and wealth, including that of individuals, belonged to the gods, and the chief had certain rights over them. The exercise of this custom over the cattle of the Fulɓe led to very serious conflicts which culminated in the devastation of the chieftaincy at the beginning of the nineteenth century.[43] Similar conditions were imposed on the Fulɓe by the Bata.

By the beginning of the nineteenth century, the Fulɓe in the various regions of Fombina lived under the authority of the Hāɓe. The conditions under which the Fulɓe lived among the autochthons were basically similar, since they had no authority and no control over land. The initial policy of some Fulɓe groups was to develop close relations with their hosts and local rulers so as to receive better treatment and free rights of pasturage. In Holma, for example, Arɗo Dagurma established good relations with Dimitilli, the local chief, and eventually became his son-in-law.[44] This improved the conditions and status of his people. Similarly, Arɗo Yajo acquired considerable influence to the advantage of the Yillaga'en when he married the daughter of the Dama chief.[45] Other Fulɓe groups, such as those under the Arɗo'en Dembo and Hassan, among the Gewe, developed strong affinities for their non-Fulɓe hosts.[46] The best example are the Kitijen found among the Lala and other groups in the Gongola-Hawal confluence region. These Fulɓe remained pagans even after the jihad and for a long time had not been living according to lāwol pulāku. Being the first group that had migrated into Fombina and having been long associated with the non-Fulɓe, isolated and far removed from the other Fulɓe groups, their ethnic consciousness declined. Hence, they accepted the Hāɓe, lived within their settlements, and intermarried with them. They also practised pagan rites and other customs, such as non-circumcision and beer drinking.[47] It appears that the Kitijen were constrained by their physical and socio-economic environment to adapt to the Hāɓe in order to live in peace.

A number of other Fulɓe groups lived under conditions which they described as entailing hardship. Consequently, uneasy situations developed between them and their hosts. Traditions in the Benue valley speak of the arbitrary exercise of power and exactions by the Bata chiefs. Kuso of Bolki, for example, in addition to the tribute and grazing dues paid to him by the Fulɓe, used to demand cattle from them every week,[48] so the majority of the Wolarɓe abandoned his chieftaincy. Similarly, in Bagale and Bagda, the Bata chiefs resorted to raids against the Fulɓe in order to acquire more cattle.[49] Thus, there was a general lack of security for the Fulɓe and conflicts between them and the Bata became common. Another source of conflict was over the problem of farmer-nomad relations. Even though in most areas the Fulɓe exchanged milk for grain, and their cattle manured the Bata farms, there had always been the problem of cattle straying into farms and spoiling crops. This would result either in open fights between the Bata and the Fulɓe or in heavy fines, paid in cattle. Finally, the 'jus primae noctis' exercised over the Fulɓe by the Bata and others was against lāwol pulāku and a slight upon Fulɓe ethnic pride.

The initial response of the Fulɓe to the hardship of living among the Hāɓe was to migrate, but towards the end of the eighteenth century, this was no longer a solution because conditions were similar throughout Fombina. Instead, the Fulɓe among the Bata resorted to total boycott of any community that maltreated them. They then negotiated more favourable terms with other communities to enter their lands. Because the Bata had realized the advantages of admitting the Fulɓe, the boycott system adopted by the latter produced two results: conflicts among the Bata themselves over the movements of the nomads, and cattle raids by boycotted Bata groups such as the Bagda and Bagale. As a result of continued hardships, the Fulɓe began to form larger groups and to establish bigger settlements in order to be in a much stronger position to oppose the Bata. Thus, large Fulɓe villages emerged: Bundang, Guriga, Gurin Nyanyare, Gurin Nati, Hosere Beltunde, and Wuro Chekke. However, what prevented an armed Fulɓe uprising on a large scale was the fear of the possible outcome, since they were a minority. Nonetheless, there was a series of armed conflicts in various parts of Fombina involving local Fulɓe groups. In Wuro Chekke, for example, conflicts arose over the Bata marriage custom which required any newly married Pullo to feast the Bata and allow a local prince to spend the first night with the bride. When Seyi b. Arɗo Jalo married, he feasted the Bata prince of Bagale and later killed him rather than allow him to sleep with his bride.[50] This led to an expedition against Wuro Chekke which resulted in the defeat of the Bata Bagale. Eventually, the Bata decided to end the ancient custom, so peace was maintained.

Another armed conflict developed at Bundang when Arɗo Njobdi slew his daughter who was demanded in marriage by the chief of Bundang and later slew the chief also,[51] an episode illustrating the dilemma of the Fulɓe at that time. It eventually led to war. The result was that the Fulɓe crossed the Faro

to Gurin Nyanyare on the west bank of the river. The conflict at Bundang
has been described as the first Fulɓe move for independence.[52] It was, however, the culmination of the various responses of the Fulɓe to the changing
socio-political situation of the Benue plains before the jihad itself. As new
situations developed, new responses were found, and the conflict at Bundang
was the last before the Fulɓe 'struggle for independence' took the form of
a jihad.

The natural habitat of the Fulɓe was the more northerly areas of the
Savanna where there were large centralized states and societies where they
lived together satisfactorily. The states maintained security but did not interfere with the details of Fulɓe social life. The Fulɓe, in turn, paid tribute, sold
bovine products to the urban inhabitants, and their cattle manured the farms
of the peasants. But the situation within Fombina was different. Large
centralized states and urban communities did not exist and so there were no
regular markets for milk, sheep, goats, and cattle. Manure was less needed,
as the region was much more fertile than the north, and there was a general
lack of interest in what the Fulɓe had to market. In some areas the cattle were
needed but in others interest centred on the beautiful Fulɓe women. The cattle
were needed for sacrifices though, in some areas, pretty Fulɓe girls were
demanded in return for rights of grazing. Nothing could be more galling and
devastating to Fulɓe self respect than such a system. It is not surprising
therefore that the system gave rise to serious tension and armed conflicts
before the jihad.

The jihad started in the Benue-Faro valley, a region which was the major
habitat of the Fulɓe at the beginning of the nineteenth century, Unlike other
areas, it contained differing groups from different clans, but because they had
been grazing within the same areas, the various Fulɓe groups remained in
close contact with one another. They had also common social, political, and
economic systems. Nevertheless, each group remained basically independent
and their Arɗo'en lived as equals. A single political leader, with authority
over the various groups, did not emerge, but news and information circulated
among the groups, and by the beginning of the nineteenth century, a common
attitude towards the problem confronting them had developed. However, as
the Fulɓe were not united, it was difficult to mount a concerted effort against
the political overlordship and economic exploitation of the non-Fulɓe. The
various Fulɓe groups continued to live under the authority of the Hāɓe,
paying the levies imposed by the local rulers. Some groups maintained friendly
relations with the local political élite and its subjects; they even intermarried
to obtain better conditions for themselves and their cattle. Thus, some of the
Fulɓe groups within Fombina were in a very serious economic situation. The
semi-settled Fulɓe, for example, maintained a dual mode of living – pastoralism and farming – neither sufficient to sustain them. Their position was in
fact more precarious in the dry season because milk was scarce (they had
limited cattle) and so they depended upon the non-Fulɓe for foodstuff in
exchange for a precious calf.

THE JIHAD IN FOMBINA

In 1804 the jihad, under the leadership of Shehu Usman'Dan Fodio, started in the Hausa state of Gobir.[53] By 1809, not only were all the Hausa states conquered, but the movement of rebellion had extended to the neighbouring regions of Borno, Bauchi, and Nupeland.[54] Although in all these areas, there was social, economic, and political discontent among the Fulɓe, it was the early military successes of the movement in Hausaland that catalyzed their uprisings. Thus, the jihad outside Hausaland was a series of sympathetic risings. Right from the beginning of the jihad in Gobir, Borno was threatened by the Felata (the Fulɓe in Borno). Following the conflicts in Hausaland, the ruler of Daura fled towards Borno and the Emir of Kano, Alwali, appealed to the Mai, Ahmed, for military assistance against the Fulɓe.[55] In response to the appeal, the Mai sent a token contingent under the Galadima Dunama. But in 1805, the Borno and Kano forces were defeated at the battle of Dan Yahaya. Thus, Borno was drawn into the conflict with the jihadists.[56] The Felata, long resident in the southern and western dependencies, in sympathy with the Fulɓe in revolt in the Hausa states, came into active conflict with the Kanuri government for the first time. In the dry season of 1804-5, the Arɗo Abduwa took up arms against the Galadima.[57] When Arɗo Abduwa died in 1805, his activities were continued by his sons, Umaru and Sambo Digimsa. After they had obtained a flag from the Shehu, they conquered Auyo and left it under the control of their younger brother, Yusuf. Eventually, Umaru and Sambo Digimsa conquered the districts around Machena and established Hadejia as their stronghold.[58] Thus, the emirate of Hadejia emerged in 1809.

In 1806, Arɗo Lerlima, a native of Kaburi and the son-in-law of the Galadima Dunama, declared his support for Usman'Dan Fodio. He was reluctant to take up arms against his father-in-law, who had appointed him the *Cimajilibe* for the environs of Nguru, but Lerlima's open support for the Shehu meant that he had renounced his allegiance to the Galadima and Mai Ahmed of Borno, who attacked and defeated him in 1806.[59] The Fulɓe leaders operating independently in the region, Umaru and Sambo Digimsa of the Machena region and Ibrahim Zaki of Shira, were alarmed. They quickly mobilized their forces and went to the aid of their defeated colleague. In the subsequent fighting, Nguru was sacked, Mai Ahmed fled, and Galadima Dunama and the Kaigama lost their lives. The fall of Nguru and the death of the Galadima, the most powerful imperial official, emboldened the Felata, who then turned their attention to overthrowing the Kanuri government at Gazargamo.

The Felata in the southern dependencies also joined the rebellion against the Borno government. Their risings started when Mai Ahmed wanted to subdue his rebellious vassal Lafia, the chief of Daya.[60] Eventually, he was deposed in favour of Salgami, his younger brother. But the new chief was not favourably disposed towards the Felata. It may have been that, following the risings around Nguru, Salgami became apprehensive and started to oppress

4

4

The Lāmībe of Fombina

the Fulɓe. He ordered 'all the people of the towns to kill the Phula'.[61] Consequently, the Fulɓe migrated to Gujba and then began to attack the Daya people. This may have been in about 1807. In that year, the Felata leader, Gwoni Mukhtar, had received the Shehu's flag and was probably at the head of the immigrants who founded Gujba. Following the break-down of law and order in Daya, Mai Ahmed intervened. He first sent an expedition under Kaigama Made, then a second one under Kaigama Ali Marema, and a third under Kaigama Dunama. But none achieved any success; each of these expeditions ended in disaster for the Borno government. The Felata of the south led by Gwoni Mukhtar then advanced into metropolitan Borno and eventually captured Gazargamo in 1808. With the fall of the imperial capital, Mai Ahmed retreated eastwards and the Borno government collapsed. The Mai, however, appealed to the noted scholar, Muhammad al-Amin al-Kanemi, for assistance and support. Al-Kanemi mobilized his supporters, the Shuwa Arabs and the Kanembu, and faced the Felata, driving them out of Gazargamo in 1809, after their leader, Gwoni Mukhtar, was killed. Thus the Felata threat came to a temporary halt.

The Felata attacks upon Borno were resumed under the leadership of Ibrahim Zaki who had established the emirate of Katagum in the former *kasar* (land) Shira in *c*. 1809.[62] Like Gwoni Mukhtar before him, Ibrahim Zaki led the western Felata and sacked Gazargamo during the dry season of 1811-12. Again, the Mai was forced to abandon his seat of power only to be restored once more by al-Kanemi. He forced Ibrahim Zaki to retreat to Katagum. Gazargamo was captured a third and fourth time by Muhammad Manga b. Gwoni Mukhtar. But he too was driven out. Thus the emergence of al-Kanemi in Borno politics checked the aims of the Felata within metropolitan Borno. The jihad failed to conquer the Kanuri empire and for the first time in Borno history, the Felata became the enemy. The various groups within the empire were subjected to attacks and victimization and, as a consequence migrated. While a number of groups moved westwards and established the emirates of Katagum, Hadejia, Misau, and Jama'āre, others moved south into Gombe under Buba Yero. Others yet migrated into Fombina.

Following the outbreak of the jihad in the Daya region, Arɗo Chappa b. Mōdibbo Bebe left Damaturu, a leading centre of Islamic learning, and travelled with his group towards the Gongola valley. Eventually, he entered Kilbaland from across the Hawal river and settled at Pella-Chiroma.[63] Similarly, the Bewe'en had to emigrate out of Borno because of their involvement in the risings. While they were in the 'great forest' the leading Arɗo'en of the clan allied to the jihad leaders in the west and south of Borno. Arɗo Buba, the senior leader of the Bewe'en, formed an alliance with Buba Yero of Gombe and was appointed the Lamɗo of Balala in the upper Hawal river basin.[64] Arɗo Dembo led another group, allied himself with Arɗo Lerlima in the Nguru region, and was appointed the chief of Muni.[65] Following the death of Arɗo Lerlima in war against Mai Ahmed, Arɗo Dembo moved to the south and joined Gwoni Mukhtar. He played an important role in the capture of Gazargamo in 1808. However, when the Borno army under al-Kanemi re-entered the imperial capital and forced the Felata to retreat, Arɗo Dembo led his group southwards to Balala where he rejoined the main body of the Bewe'en. After the death of Arɗo Buba, his son Likali became the chief of Balala while Arɗo Dembo's son, Uzuri, became the chief of Duhu in Margiland. They subsequently moved to the upper Benue valley as the Arɗo'en of Ribadu and Dawari respectively. Other immigrants from Borno, following the failure of the jihad, were the Fulɓe of Njobolio, Beti, and a large body of pastoral nomads.[66] These last had migrated into Fombina to escape the unsettled conditions in Borno and to avoid the fighting there. Thus by the end of the first decade of the nineteenth century, a considerable number of refugees (*perĩɓe*) had entered Fombina from Borno.

The entry of the Fulɓe refugees into Fombina from Borno swelled the population of the Fulɓe and gave rise to increased strife. Certainly, a need for more grazing lands was created especially in the upper Benue valley, the southernmost habitat of the Fombina Fulɓe. Furthermore, grazing dues were increased, and the Fulɓe squatters were placed in a very serious position. The perĩɓe were also different from the earlier migrants into Fombina. They were mainly semi-settled people, who, as a result of their long stay in Hausaland and Borno, had come to know and appreciate the value of a centralized political system. Their risings in Borno were motivated by the desire to end their hardship and to participate in government.

Throughout their long stay in Borno, the Felata had remained socially isolated and politically powerless even though their society contained highly talented scholars capable of holding responsible positions in the government. The best known was Muhammed al-Mahir at-Tahir b. Ibrahim who lived in Gazargamo towards the end of the eighteenth century.[67] Though he was a friend of Mai Ali, at-Tahir b. Ibrahim was excluded from the court and ostracized for fear that his teaching might subvert the Kanuri regime. The tension that had been growing between the Felata and the Kanuri towards the end of the eighteenth century culminated in the unsuccessful risings of the former. Frustrated by their failure to take over the government in Gazargamo, the Felata, it appears, became very determined to establish independent domains in the regions neighbouring Borno. Undoubtedly, their presence in the upper Benue valley acted as a catalyst to the events that led to the meeting of the Arɗo'en to deliberate on the need for jihad to end the subservience of the Fulɓe.

The jihad in Borno gave rise to unprecedented developments in Fombina. In Mandara, the Fulɓe began to menace their neighbours following the news of the Felata risings in the Nguru region. The Ngara Fulɓe, who had long resided in the kingdom, attempted to incite Borno to attack Mandara.[68] Consequently, they not only fell from the Sultan's favour, but were themselves attacked, and nearly wiped out at Eissa Harde. To the north-west of Mandara, the Fulɓe of Musfel and Kora, probably also Ngara'en, revolted and succeeded in gaining control of Mandara's Kerawa province.[69] The Fulɓe pressure against Mandara increased after the failure of the jihad in Borno, and as a result the capital of Mandara was transferred from Delow to Mora during the first decade of the nineteenth century. Sultan Bukar of Mandara also concluded a treaty of alliance with Borno to counter the Fulɓe threat,[70] and this brought to a temporary end the hostility of Borno towards Mandara which had developed after Borno's humiliating defeat in c. 1781. Consequently, the attention of Mandara was focused squarely on checking the menace of the Fulɓe within the kingdom and on its borders.

In the region east and south-east of Mandara, relations between Fulɓe and non-Fulɓe began to deteriorate. Following news of the risings of the Felata in Borno, the Yillaga decided no longer to tolerate the excesses of their hosts. The Fulɓe of Durbeleng and Gazawa revolted against the Gisiga and killed a number of cattle raiders.[71] This action aroused the hostility of the non-Fulɓe, and their chiefs mobilized themselves to deal with the various Fulɓe groups, who assembled at Hōsēre Miskin in order to defend themselves more effectively. Further south, the Yillaga'en under Arɗo Buba came into conflict with the Binder people, so the assembled Fulɓe groups in Hōsēre Miskin moved to Lara and teamed up with Arɗo Buba against the Binder. After Buba's victory, the northern Yillaga'en, led by Muhammadu Selbe, met and overwhelmed the combined force of Gisiga and Mandara at Marba.[72] In c. 1806, the Yillaga'en attacked Makabai and killed the chief of Gisiga, Jomkoy Leleng. He was succeeded by his son, Laeta, as the chief of Gisiga based at Marba, so the Fulɓe failed at that time to take over power in Makabai but the death of Jomkoy Leleng was followed by schism. The Gisiga in Kaliyau installed another son of Jomkoy Leleng, Bi Babarang, as their ruler. The Fulɓe contacted him and suggested the formation of an alliance against Laeta with a view to dethroning him. Bi Babarang, seeing an opportunity of becoming the chief of all the Gisiga, teamed up with the Fulɓe, and together they attacked Marba and expelled Laeta. Eventually, however, the Fulɓe expelled Bi Babarang also, and Marba fell under the control of the Yillaga'en.

In Bagarmi too, Arɗo Ali of the Ngara'en attempted to take over power from the Mbang, but was decisively defeated[73] and consequently migrated into the lands of the Binder. Here, as among the Gisiga, there were two rival chiefs, one in the north and the other in the south. The latter, called Gonjue, requested and obtained the aid of the Yillaga leader, Arɗo Buba,[74] and in c. 1806, they attacked and subdued the chief of north Binder. Then Arɗo Buba turned against Gonjue and took over power as the ruler of all the Binder. In the north, Arɗo Buba Biru also rebelled against Hāɓe rule and eventually established himself as the chief of Mendif. Finally, in the valley of the Māyo Kebbi, relations between the Yillaga'en and the Niam-Niam also deteriorated. The knowledge of the activities of the Fulɓe in the north aroused the hostility of the Niam-Niam and civil strife resulted. Two Arɗo'en, Jalige b. Wuri and later his brother Kaido b. Wuri, were killed in the conflicts with their hosts.[75] Thus, even though jihad was not formally declared in Fombina, the Fulɓe in the region north of the Benue had started fighting against their hosts just as their kith and kin were doing in Borno.

Another major effect of the jihad in Borno on Fombina was the extension of military activities into its northern parts by former commanders of the Borno campaigns, Sambo Sambabu, Bauchi Gordi, and Buba Yero.[76] The first, Sambo Sambabu, was a Damaturu Pullo who plagued and devastated the Musgu country. Bauchi Gordi, an associate of Buba Yero, appeared in northern Fombina following the Borno campaign; he crossed the Yedseram at Kopa and began a series of campaigns that took him as far east as Māyo Sancho. Then he turned south and laid waste the rich and populous plains of Mubi,[77] liberating the Yillaga'en from the yoke of the Gude. From Mubi, he proceeded to Uba where he defeated chief Use-Urnda of the Margi first at Burtil Ba and later at Mampia. With the destruction of the Uba Hāɓe, the Yillaga'en Arɗo Iliyasa gained the paramountcy over the Margi. From Uba, it is said that Bauchi Gordi marched south along the eastern edge of the Uba mountains to Belel. Then he turned west to the Lala plateau where he was killed in battle, possibly against the Yungur. Undoubtedly, Bauchi Gordi's defeat and destruction of Kopa, Moda, Michika, and Bazza prepared the ground for the emergence of Fulɓe hegemony in Waila.

Buba Yero's main theatre of military activity was the Gongola valley. But, again probably after the Borno campaign, he advanced to the Benue plains by way of Uba, Digil, and Mirnyi to Maiha.[78] He obtained the peaceful submission of the Maiha chief, Ahmadu, and that of Kirngabu. Then he conquered Timpil and destroyed Paka, the main centre of the Njai. From Maiha, Buba Yero moved to the valley of the Tiel river and conquered the Fali of Bulmi before deciding to attack the Bata of Demsa pwa. In the course of the campaigns, Buba Yero distributed subordinate flags to a number of Arɗo'en, such as Arɗo Tahiru b. Buba who was in the Gudu area north of the Benue, Arɗo Hamman Manga of the Kīri'en and also the Wolarɓe of Bundang.[79] The campaigns of Buba Yero came to an abrupt end because, it is said, he was recalled by the Shehu. Tradition indicates that Buba Yero was becoming too difficult for the Sokoto leaders to control, so when he was in Koboshi on the Māyo Tiel, he was recalled and directed to confine his activities to Gombe, which was nearer Sokoto. However, it appears that following the visit of Mōdibbo Adama to the Shehu and his investiture as the leader of the jihad in the east, some territorial readjustment was necessary for a new emirate to emerge. Hence the eventual limitation of Buba Yero's activities in the Gongola valley.

The early life of Mōdibbo Adama is obscure. But, as far as can be ascertained, he was born in *c.* 1779, probably in Wuro-Chekke in the upper Benue valley. The son of Arɗo Hassana, Mōdibbo Adama belonged to the Yillaga clan.[80] The group under his father had been moving between Song in the north and Beti to the south of the Benue. Adama started his education under his father and at the early age of eleven he finished the study of the Qur'ān. He was then sent away to further his education. Accompanied by Hamman

Song of the Wolarɓe, Adama went to Bagarmi where they became students of Shehu Muhammad Tahir.[81] Under him, Adama recited the Qur'ān, one of the prerequisites for Islamic studies in those days. From Bagarmi, Adama travelled westwards into Borno where he became a student of Kiyari in Birni Gazargamo. He stayed for ten years studying Islamic books (*Defte*) before returning to the upper Benue valley.

It is significant that Adama received his major Islamic education outside Fombina. This would indicate a lack of learned Muslim scholars among the Fombina Fulɓe. It also affirms the importance of Borno as a centre of learning and Islamic scholarship from early times down to the beginning of the nineteenth century. Adama was certainly in Borno at a time when tension was mounting between the Kanuri and the Felata, but he had returned to the Benue valley before the outbreak of the Felata risings in Borno. Back home he found that his father had died in the conflict with the Bata over the latter's marriage customs, so he left Wuro-Chekke for the Faro valley. At Guriga, Adama attached himself to the Ba'en under Arɗo Hamman whose sister he eventually married. Hamman was one of the most respected Arɗo'en in the Benue-Faro valley, and he was also a scholar. The two scholars intensified their Islamic activities, teaching and preaching among the Fulɓe of the Māyo Faro valley. Mōdibbo Adama emphasized the teaching of the Qur'ān not only to the children but also to the Mauɓe, the majority of whom were ignorant of the basic principles of the faith although they professed to be Muslims. Very soon he established a reputation for learning and piety in the upper Benue region, and the period between his return and the outbreak of jihad in the area was one of intense Islamization among the Fulɓe.

Described as 'lean and of tall stature, his features sharp and somewhat disfigured by small-pox, his nose slightly curved,'[82] Adama, though the son of an Arɗo, was never one himself and had never shown any interest in political power. The circumstances preceding his emergence as the leader of the jihad in Fombina are not clear. One account is that when Mōdibbo Adama returned from Borno, he brought authentic news of the jihad to the Fulɓe of the upper Benue valley and because of his religious fervour, he was elected leader and the various groups promised to combine for mutual support.[83] Another is that Mōdibbo Adama was delegated by the leading Arɗo'en, Gamawa of Rai, Njobdi of Bungang, Hamman Dandi, and Hamman Sambo, to visit Shehu Usman 'Dan Fodio in order to find out what was to be done.[84] However, the Yola tradition maintains that five years after the jihad of Usman 'Dan Fodio, Mōdibbo Adama requested Mōdibbo Hamman Gurin to visit the Shehu and receive a flag for them, but on reaching Gombe, Hamman obtained Buba Yero's flag which was eventually repudiated by Mōdibbo Adama. He then travelled to Sokoto and obtained one from the Shehu himself. There are grounds to believe that the second account was what happened. The jihad in Fombina started at a much later period. Moreover, the entry of militant Felata migrants following the failure of their risings in Borno and the activities of their commanders in the north Benue region influenced those in the Benue-Faro valley to resort to jihad in order to achieve independence (maral hōre). Before then, the rich, cattle-owning Arɗo'en who had news about the jihad under Shehu Usman'Dan Fodio were reluctant to fight a large scale war because they feared losing their cattle should it end in their defeat. However, the news of Fulɓe victories in Hausaland continued to reach them through the Felata immigrants and when the military activities of Bauchi Gordi and Buba Yero proved successful within Fombina, the Arɗo'en reluctantly decided to act.

At a meeting at Guriga in *c.* 1809, they decided to send a representative to the Shehu. Their choice fell on Mōdibbo Adama, an honest learned man, who had shown no interest in power (*baude*) or politics (*siyāsa*). Moreover, he was a *mērājo* (not concerned with cattle husbandry) and therefore the most suitable person to undertake the long journey to Sokoto. When he visited the Shehu, he was given a flag for the jihad 'in the lands in the east'[85] and was instructed to return to his people and seek their support. He was also empowered to give subordinate flags to the Arɓo'en to pursue jihad in their respective areas and was appointed intermediary between them and the Shehu in Sokoto.

When Mōdibbo Adama received the flag from Shehu Usman'Dan Fodio in *c.* 1809 he became a *Na'ib* or an *Emir*. This was in accordance with classical Islamic practice. The main political result of the Sokoto jihad was the establishment of a Caliphate, an Islamic political system under a Caliph who served as both political and religious leader.[86] In the early years of Islam, the prophet Muhammad, apart from being the leader of the faithful, was also the political head of the Muslim community. After his death, the political and religious leadership of the faithful passed to his close associates, Abubakar, Uthman, Umar, and Ali, one after the other. They were known as the *Khalifas* (successors to the prophet of God). Thus the Caliphate as a political system began to develop. The early Khalifas took over the secular functions of the prophet such as control of policy, the appointment of officials to collect taxes and tribute, the exercise of supreme authority in military matters, and the dispatch of military expeditions. They also served as supreme judges of the Shari'a (Muslim law). The early Caliphate was highly centralized, no doubt because the territory under Muslim control was limited. The office of Caliph was both secular and ecclesiastical. Khalifa Umar had adopted the title *āmir al-Muminin* (leader of the Muslims) thereby emphasizing the secular aspect of his office and in later years, the title *Imam* (leader) also came into use.

Following the expansion of Muslim dominion, the theory of the Caliphate underwent further development. Governing was no longer confined to limited territory. The acquisition of new lands far from the capital necessitated the appointment of provincial administrators to control affairs on behalf of the Caliph. This system started as early as the time of Khalifa Umar, but it was during the Abbasid period that the Caliphate saw its greatest developments. A leading jurist of the period, Abu al-Hassan Ali al-Mawardi, summed up the functions of a Caliph as the 'defence of religion and the administration of the state'.[87] The Caliphate system involved the delegation of authority to *nuwwāb* or *umarā* (competent lieutenants), but their authority, according to al-Mawardi, should extend only over a 'limited territory' and, as their power was delegated from the Caliph, they should not in turn delegate it to others. However, the umarā could appoint subordinate officials, and a *wazir* (executive) to help them execute their defined responsibilities.

The Sokoto Caliphate was patterned on the Abbasid's, no doubt because the Sokoto *ulama* (scholars) were guided in their understanding of the Caliphate system by the works of the Muslim jurists of the Abbasid period. Thus, when the jihad was starting at Gobir, Shehu Usman 'Dan Fodio was proclaimed the amir al-Muminin by the *jama'a* (community) and so became the political head and the religious leader of what later became the Sokoto Caliphate. When jihad wars started, commanders such as Ali Jedo, Abdullah 'Dan Fodio, and Muhammad Bello who led campaigns, were given the title *amir al-jaish* (leader of the armed forces). The title also applied to other leaders of jihad in Hausaland as well as to Buba Yero in the Gongola valley. However, following the division of responsibility by the Shehu Usman 'Dan Fodio in Sokoto in *c.* 1812, the position of the provincial commanders was altered.[88] They became umarā (emirs) with defined duties and responsibilities, and spheres of influence became known as *emirates*. An Emir had certain obligations towards the Caliph, his political head and religious leader. The latter should receive annually zakat, *kharaj, jizya*, inheritance money (*irth*), and one fifth of any booty (*khums*) from an Emir.[89] The appointment and deposition of Emirs were vested with the Caliph and the Emirs paid homage to him from time to time.

The appointment of Mōdibbo Adama as the jihad leader 'in the lands in the east' meant that he should establish an Islamic government and perform the functions of an Emir. These, according to Muhammad Bello, in his letter to Amir Ya'qub of Bauchi,[90] included the organization and deployment of the army. It was the duty of an Emir to conduct expeditions personally or through his lieutenants and to conclude agreements. Second, the Emir was in charge of the administration of justice in his domain. In this regard, he had to appoint *Qadis* (judges) and had also to ensure that Islamic law was enforced and the authority of the judges respected. It was also the responsibility of the Emir to see to the establishment of Islam in conquered territories. Third, he had to see to the collection of land tax and the obligatory poor rate and to ensure that these were distributed according to the laws. Fourth, the Emir had to protect the position of women, and to preserve Islam from adulteration and change. Fifth, punishment laid down by God's law should be meted out and the rights of common men protected. Sixth, the Emir should lead at prayers or appoint an Imam (deputy). Last, he should aid pilgrims, both native and foreign, on their way to the Holy Land.

An emirate is a political entity under a centralized government and judiciary.[91] The functions of the Emir could be discharged with the aid of officials and lieutenants outside the capital. The latter, called *Amils* (executive officers), could be appointed by the Emir with or without the approval of the Caliph. However, the Amils as representatives of the Emir had to abide by the directives of the emirate government. Thus, the Amils were vassals of the Emir as he was of the Caliph. As regards officials in the capital, their power should extend over the area under Amils. The maintenance of law and order, the enforcement of the Sharia, could be delegated to the Amils, but the over-all responsibility was the Emir's.

The emirate-type of government outlined above was what Mōdibbo Adama was expected to establish through jihad in a region that was non-Islamic and over people the majority of whom were politically segmented and culturally varied. The Fulɓe themselves were politically segmented. Thus, when Mōdibbo Adama returned to the Faro valley as the leader appointed by Sokoto, he was not well received. He had been sent merely to investigate, and so, the powerful Arɗo'en, Njobdi of Bundang, Sabana Zummo, Lawan Sule Holma, Gamawa of Rai, Hamman Sambo, and Hamman Dandi, refused to accept Mōdibbo Adama as their leader.[92] This delayed the beginning of the jihad. The Mō-dibbo's initial support among the Fulɓe was extremely limited. The group behind him, the Ba'en, was too small to undertake the jihad against the numerous and powerful non-Fulɓe communities. The largest clan was the Wolarɓe, but its Arɗo'en refused to throw in their lot with Mōdibbo Adama. The Ngara'en, a very powerful group, were outside the Benue valley and the Yillaga'en were mainly spread along the Māyo Kebbi. Those under Arɗo Gamawa in the Benue region also refused to support the Mōdibbo. At last when Mōdibbo Adama started wars against the Bata, the Arɗo'en who at first refused to support him became impressed by his victories. Consequently, they tendered their allegiance to him and received subordinate flags. Eventually, the task of establishing an emirate was started in earnest.

NOTES

1. The Fulɓe in Nigeria are found mainly in the northern states. They predominate in Sokoto, Kaduna, Kano, and Borno. But it is only in Adamawa that the Fulfulde language is widely spoken.

2. For example, that the Fulɓe were either Jews or Syrians was put forward by Guirandon, 1888, Morel 1902 and Delafosse 1912; Crozals 1883, Passarge 1895, and Meyer 1897 suggested that the Fulɓe were Berbers; Bayol 1887, Machet 1906, Palmer 1923 and Gautier 1935 suggested that they came from Ethiopia. Other theories include origin from Hindustan as advanced by Golbery 1805 and in 1892 by Binger; or Polynesia as suggested by D'Eichal in 1841.

3. See W. J. R. Haffenden, *The Red Men of Nigeria* (London, 1930), p. 97; E. A. Brackenbury, 'Notes on the "Bororo Fulbe" or nomad "Cattle Fulani" ', *JAS*, 23, 91 (1924), 208–17, see p. 211; and C. V. Boyle 'Historical notes on Yola Fulanis', *JAS*, 10, 37 (1910), 73–92, see p. 73. 'Uqba was the general who tried to put an end to Berber resistance during the Arab conquest of North Africa in the first century A.H.

4. A. M. Junaidu, *Tarihin Fulani*, (Zaria, 1957), p. 7.

5. R. G. Armstrong, *The Study of West African Languages* (Ibadan, 1964), p. 26.

6. J. S. Trimingham, *History of Islam in West Africa*, (London, 1962), pp. 160ff.

7. H. F. C. Smith, 'A neglected theme of West African history: the Islamic revolutions

E

of the 19th century', *JHSN*, II, 1 (1961), 169-85, see p. 172. The leading Torobe settlements in Hausaland and Borno were generally outside the big towns.

8. Brackenbury, *JAS*, 23, 92 (1924), 272-7; P. W. de St. Croix, *The Fulani of Northern Nigeria*, (Lagos, 1944), pp. 54ff.

9. Migeod, p. 9.

10. Ahmed ibn Fartua, *History of the First Twelve Years of the Reign of Mai Idris Alooma of Bornu (1571-83)*, trans. H. R. Palmer, (Lagos, 1926). Barth, *Travels and Discoveries in North and Central Africa*, (5 vols., London, 1857), pp. 650-69.

11. D. Stenning, *Savannah Nomads*, (London, 1959), pp. 29-30; and A. K. Benisheik, 'The Galadimas of Bornu', unpublished B.A. research essay, Ahmadu Bello University, June 1972.

12. H. R. Palmer's introduction to C. K. Meek, *A Sudanese Kingdom*, (London, 1931), p. xxiv.

13. Boyle, *JAS*, 10, 37 (1910), 73; Migeod, p. 9.

14. H. A. S. Johnston, *The Fulani Empire of Sokoto* (London 1967).

15. C. Lemoigne, 'Les pays conquis du Cameroun nord', *Rens. Coloniaux Bull. Com. Afrique Française*, XVII (1918), 130-53, see 134-45.

16. Yerima Balla, 'Tarihin Kilba', 1959, Secondary School, Hong.

17. 'Tarhin Rai-Buba' (Version Officiale), 1966. EMC.

18. D. F. M. McBride, Notes in Uba DNB.

19. Kona traditions, recorded by McAllister, ('The Kona', MAJ, file no. 34), indicate that the Fulɓe appeared in their midst in the reign of their twelfth chief, Taiku, whose reign started in *c.* 1756.

20. Stenning, *Savannah Nomads*, p. 22.

21. See K. Strumpell, *The History of Adamawa*, (Hamburg, 1912) being a trans., mimeo, NNAK, J.18, p. 43; Migeod, p. II.

22. Strumpell, *History*, p. 22.

23. H. R. Palmer, *The Bornu Sahara and Sudan*, (London, 1936), pp. 25ff.

24. Ibid., p. 251ff.

25. This may have been derived from the Arabic '*ayn al-dîn* (true religion).

26. Stenning, *Savannah Nomads*, p. 59.

27. Among present day Fulɓe, such as the Fulɓe Na'i in Gwandu, there is an *Alkali Fulfulde*, a judge for breaches of customs and traditions. But this is only for young people. See C. E. Hopen, 'Note on Alkali Fulfulde', *Africa*, 34, 1 (1964), 21-7. Similarly, among the Woɗaɓe of Borno there is a *maudo lawol pulāku*, the guardian of the code, Stenning, *Savannah Nomads*, pp. 55-6.

28. Ibrahim Dodo, 'Tarihin Maiha', 1934, NHRS.

29. C. E. Hopen, *The Pastoral Fulbe Family in Bwandu*, (London, 1958), p. 23.

30. J. L. Myres, 'Nomadism', *JRAI*, 71 (1941), 19-42, p. 20.

31. F. H. El Masri, *Bayān Wüjub Al-Hijra, by Uthman ibn Fūdi*, (Khartoum, 1977). See M. Khaddūri, *War and Peace in the Law of Islam* (Baltimore, 1955), pp. 55-74 for a discussion on various types of jihad.

32. J. Vossart, 'Histoire du Sultanat du Mandara', *Et. Cam.*, 35/36 (1952), 19-52. Islam in Mandara was essentially a religion of the dynasty and the capital; the great majority of the people remained pagan.

33. Trimingham.

34. Song D.N.B.

35. Stenning, *Savannah Nomads*, p. 62.

36. Yola traditions, collected by the author, July-August, 1968.

37. Garua traditions, collected by the author, June 1969.

38. Lemoigne, p. 136; Strumpell, *History*, p. 22.

39. Strumpell, *History*, p. 23.

40. Ibid, p. 7; this was the practice in Mandara, and among the Gude, Gisiga, and the Bata of the upper Benue valley. It required every newly-wed Pullo to permit a pagan prince to spend the first night with the bride.

41. Michika and Baza traditions.

42. J. H. Shaw, 'Madagali District', 1935, NNAK, 25073, p. 3.

43. Lamorde traditions.

44. Strumpell, *History*, p. 44; Vereker, 'The Kitijen', Fulani Collected Papers and Correspondence, 1910-34, NNAK, J.2, p. 15.

45. Ibid.; p. 67. But according to 'Tarihin Rai-Buba', it was Arɗo Yajo's son, Buba Njidda, who married Asta Nyale, a Dama princess.

46. Ibid., pp. 22-3.

47. Vereker, 'The Kitijen', p. 2.

48. Song traditions.

49. Ibid.

50. Yola traditions.

51. J. M. Fremantle, 'History of the Emirate of Yola', 1908, NNAK, J.I. p. 4; D. F. H. McBride, 'Wollarbe History', Pagan Administration, 1933-5, NNAK, F.4, p. 136.

52. Migeod, p. 12; Fremantle, 'History', p. 4.

53. D. M. Last, *The Sokoto Caliphate*, (London, 1967). R. A. Adeleye, *Power and Diplomacy in Northern Nigeria, 1804-1906* (London, 1971), p. 29.

54. See S. A. Balogun, 'Gwandu Emirates in the nineteenth century, with special reference to political relations: 1817-1903', unpublished Ph.D. thesis, Ibadan University, 1970, for the jihad in the south; M. Mason, 'The Nupe Kingdom in the nineteenth century: A Political History', unpublished Ph.D. thesis, Birmingham University, 1970; and Y. A. Aliyu, 'The establishment and development of Emirate government in Bauchi, 1805-1903', unpublished Ph.D. thesis, Ahmadu Bello University, 1974.

55. R. M. East, *Labarun Hausawa da Makwabatansu*, vol. ii, (Zaria, 1932).

56. Benisheik; L. Brenner, *The Shehus of Kukawa* (London, 1973), pp. 26ff.

57. Stenning, *Savannah Nomads*, p. 30.

58. W. F. Gowers, *Gazetteer of Kano Province*, (London, 1921), p. 35.

59. Brenner, p. 29.

60. S. E. Koelle (ed.), *African Native Literature*, (London, 1854), pp. 213-23, a story of the jihad in Bornu by an eye witness, Alli Eisami.

61. Ibid.

62. Gowers, *Gazetteer*, p. 8.

63. E. A. Brackenbury, 'History of Goila' (narrated by Arɗo Goila Zubairu in 1910), NNAK, G.2E.

64. W. O. P. Rosedale, 'History of Balala', 1926, NNAK, Acc.77.

65. Ibid.

66. Boyle, 'Historical Notes on Njobolio, Beti and Ribadu', 1909-10, NNAK, J.2, pp. 63-74.

67. Palmer, *Borni Sahara*, p. 271.

68. D. Denham, H. Clapperton and Dr. Oudney, *Narrative of Travels and Discoveries in Northern and Central Africa, in the years 1822, 1823 and 1824*, (London, 1826), p. 156.

69. Ibid., p. 159.

70. Ibid.

71. 'Tarihin Marua', EMC.

72. Ibid.

73. Strumpell, *History*, p. 12.

74. Ibid., p. 22.

75. 'Tarihin Bibemi', EMC.

76. For the activities of Bauchi Gordi see Strumpell, *History*, p. 13, and J. H. Shaw, Report on Uba, p. 14. For Sambo Sambabu, see Strumpell, *History*, p. 12, and for Buba Yero, p. 14; Ibrahim Dodo, 'Tarihin Maiha', p. 7; and Anon., 'Tabyin amr Buba Yero ma'a ummalihi wa-ashabihi', NHRS.

77. Strumpell, *History*, p. 13.

78. Ibrahim Dodo, p. 7.

79. D. R. Percival, 'History of Mayo Farang', 1907-13, NNAK, p. 25.

80. Yola Traditions.

81. Ibid. This view is expressed by Malam Ahmadu Marafa.

82. Strumpell, *History*, p. 19. His authority is not indicated.

83. Migeod, p. 13.

84. R. M. East, *Stories of Old Adamawa*, (Zaria, 1935), p. 19. Other versions are contained in E. Mohamadou, 'L'Histoire des lamidats de Tchamba et Tibati', *Abbia*, 6 (1964), 16-58, see pp. 19-29; A. H. M. Kirk-Greene, *Adamawa Past and Present* (London, 1958), p. 129; and S. J. Hogben and A. H. M. Kirk-Greene, *The Emirates of Northern Nigeria* (London, 1966), p. 432.

85. 'Abd al-Qādir b. Gidado, 'Majmu-'b'ad Rasa'il Amir al-Muminin Muhammad Bello NHRS, trans. Abdullahi Smith.
86. T. W. Arnold, *The Caliphate* (London, 1965), pp. 30-9.
87. A. A. M. Al-Māwardi, *Al-Ahkam al-Sultaniyya* (Bonn, 1853).
88. Last, *Sokoto Caliphate*, pp. 53ff.
89. Ibid., p. 102.
90. Muhammad Bello.
91. For detailed consideration see S. Abubakar, 'The Emirate type of Government in the 19th century Sokoto Caliphate', (paper submitted to a Social Sciences Seminar, Faculty of Arts and Social Sciences, 1970, ABU, Zaria).
92. Song Traditions.

3. The Foundation of an Emirate:
1809–47

Allah Chenīɗo Yāfo Seihu'en amin
Omtuɓe Adamawa, mbo'ini lesde amin.[1]

After Mōdibbo Adama's return from his visit to Shehu Usman 'Dan Fodio
in *c*. 1809, he was faced with the problem of how to start wars against the
Bata. The majority of the powerful Arɗo'en of the different groups refused
to accept his leadership. It was not until three years later that he was able to
start fighting in the lower Faro valley.[2] Although it is said that he merely
complied with 'Dan Fodio's injunction, it appears that the reason for the
delay stemmed from the unwillingness of the Arɗo'en to undertake fighting
under a centralized leadership. The Fombina Fulɓe of the time lived in independent groups each under its Arɗo. Without the support and co-operation
of all the Arɗo'en, Mōdibbo Adama was not in a position to start fighting.
The members of his clan, the Yillaga'en, were by then found outside the Faro
valley. Similarly, the Ba'en with whom he became closely associated after his
marriage to Yasebo, the sister of Mōdibbo Hamman Gurin, was too small a
group to undertake the difficult task of fighting the Bata. For this reason,
Mōdibbo Adama began to seek the support of some Arɗo'en among the
Wolarɓe – the largest clan along the Benue-Faro valley – and to seek the
peaceful submission of some Bata groups. He obtained the support of some
of the Wolarɓe groups north of the Benue, led by Mōdibbo Hamman Song
and Arɗo Dembo of Malabu, both Adama's friends, and that of the Wolarɓe
group under Mōdibbo Jam in the Bundang area. In consequence, the followers of the Arɗo'en migrated to the Faro valley, while those opposed to
Adama's leadership migrated up that valley, to the south,[3] thus solving the
problem of depopulation of the Faro valley by the infiltrations from the
north. There were also migrants from Borno,[4] mainly Fulɓe who had taken
part in the jihad against the Kanuri. Their arrival at that time was significant;
the support of Mōdibbo Adama not only increased, but he had at his disposal
people who were frustrated by their failure to overthrow the government of
Borno and who were determined to fight in order to establish their
authority.

Among the non-Fulɓe, Mōdibbo Adama gained the support of the Bata
of Kokumi when their leader embraced Islam,[5] and similarly, the Bata of

Kopa.[6] The early supporters of the movement rendered considerable assistance before and after the start of the jihad wars. Their early major help was in the making of weapons for the Ful6e. Apart from manpower, Mōdibbo Adama and his supporters needed horses, and donkeys for transporting food. The few the Ful6e possessed were mainly used during transhumance or in the course of emigration for carrying the sick and old, and oxen were mostly used for transportation. As for fighting equipment, the traditional weapons were bows and arrows, but for wars on a large scale they needed large quantities of such weapons and here the subjected Bata gave their help. As smiths, they made the much needed arrows and spears for the Ful6e. They were also horse-breeding people.[7] Apart from surrendering their horses, some of them were sent to exchange cattle for horses among other Bata communities. In this way, the Ful6e under Mōdibbo Adama established a formidable cavalry with ample weapons for their wars. Other important functions of the early Bata allies of the Ful6e were as guides for expeditions and, at times, as spies upon other Bata groups.

The appointment of Mōdibbo Adama as the leader of the jihad for Fombina was also not widely accepted in the north. It is said that when the Ful6e in that region heard of the jihad under 'Dan Fodio, the leading Ardo'en travelled to Sokoto to receive flags for their groups,[8] but because Mōdibbo Adama had already been appointed and also because the Shehu had empowered him to give subordinate flags, all those who went to Sokoto from the east were directed to contact him.[9] It was not until after his two Mandara expeditions that Adama obtained the wholehearted support of the Ardo'en in the east and the north. Their reluctance to support Mōdibbo Adama was because long before he received the flag from the Shehu, some Ful6e groups in those areas had already seized power from their erstwhile hosts. The Ngara and the Yillaga Ful6e were by that time powerful among the Gisiga and the Binder. Similarly, the Yillaga Ardo'en, Yajo and Yaya, gained considerable influence among the Gude of Muvi and the Margi of Uba respectively. They would not have liked to pay homage to Mōdibbo Adama and accept a subordinate flag of office from him.

While some of the Ardo'en migrated from the Faro valley and others attempted to obtain independent flags from Sokoto, other groups remained uncommitted; they were in support of neither the jihad nor Mōdibbo Adama. Ardo Hassana of the Gewe Wolar6e and the Yillaga Ardo of Kei'a refused to appear before him and, while the jihad was in progress, they remained loyal to their Hā6e hosts with whom they maintained normal intercourse and relations.[10] Thus, the decision to resort to jihad was painfully hard for some Ful6e. While some groups feared defeat, and the consequent loss of their cattle, others did not want to fight at all because it meant the end of the privileges they enjoyed.[11] Consequently, some Ful6e played a double role: they associated themselves with the jihad in order not to fall out with their Ful6e brethren, but their commitment was very limited. For example, the Wolar6e of Kilba participated in the fighting against their hosts only when forces from the Benue valley attacked Kilba. But once the attacks were over, they resumed normal contacts with the Kilba.[12]

On the whole, the process towards solidarity among the Fulɓe was a difficult one. The stumbling block was the question of leadership. In Sokoto, for example, at the beginning of the jihad, the Shehu, while being the Imam of the community, was less directly concerned with the wars. When the Caliphate was established, he remained a nominal leader and responsibilities were divided among leading members of the community, such as the commander of the army, Ali Jedo, and two viziers, the Shehu's brother Abdullahi, and his son Muhammad Bello, both of whom acted as commanders during campaigns. There were other commanders as well, such as Moijo the leader of the Kebbi Fulɓe, Muhammadu Namoda of the Alibawa Fulɓe of Zamfara, and Muhammadu Wara of the Sullebawa.[13] Within the Caliphate, local political power was delegated to Emirs. Similarly, after 1812, the supervision of the Caliphate was divided between the two main helpers of the Shehu, Abdullahi and Muhammad Bello. Thus, the unity of the community under a centralized leadership was maintained by this division of responsibility and by the delegation of power to the Emirs.

One fundamental difference between the Shehu's community and Fombina is that while the former was headed by intellectuals, the latter was headed by pastoral elders. The pastoral Fulɓe as a socially and politically segmented people lived in many small units, each independent in certain fundamental issues. Each determined its own action and future, and under the leadership of their Arɗo, they met other groups, not as subjects or dependants, but as equals.

Mōdibbo Adama's emergence did not change the situation overnight. Those Arɗo'en who refused to submit to Mōdibbo Adama led their people in the southwards migration, and those who attempted to obtain Sokoto's recognition were merely demonstrating their opposition to the idea of having an overall political leader. The majority of the Arɗo'en had a concept of a wider freedom for the whole Fulɓe. But instead of pursuing the jihad under a centralized command – which meant subjecting themselves and their groups to the leadership of Mōdibbo Adama – the various Arɗo'en preferred to remain as leaders of their groups. They also preferred to muster their men for the jihad wars as leaders with equal power and having direct relations with Sokoto. This was essentially a conflict of political concepts. On the one hand, Mōdibbo Adama – a scholar who studied in Borno – and his close associates wanted the establishment of a centralized Islamic polity under a single leader and government. On the other hand, some Arɗo'en preferred the establishment of a political structure in which the basis of Fulɓe society was reflected, i.e. a group of independent clan-emirates each headed by an Arɗo equal in status to any other and having direct relations with Sokoto. This conflict was not resolved by the Lāmīɓe of Fombina until the end of the nineteenth century.

THE EARLY CONFLICTS

The Fulɓe were not a military people, although fighting was not new to them. Throughout their migrations, they had encountered different problems among various peoples. In some places, political pressure or threats to their lives and wealth compelled them to resort to arms in order to defend themselves. As wandering herdsmen, they became used to the tough and hard life of the bush. To protect themselves and their herds from wild life, the Fulɓe were adequately armed and organized for their defence. They had bows, arrows, knives, and swords as weapons which they normally carried. Also, their cattle encampments were guarded by selected youths armed with bows and arrows.

The early military organization was of the simplest kind – the men under Mōdibbo Adama were a conglomeration of various groups. There was neither *Lamdo Konu* or *Sarki Yayi* (official commanders), nor was there a special class of warriors. It is said, however, that when Mōdibbo Adama was at Sokoto for the flag, he was given permission to recruit men for the jihad, and as he travelled back through Hausaland the forces at his disposal increased as people, fired by the prospect of booty and wealth in an unexplored region, joined his company.[14] Certainly, at a later period, non-Fulɓe people, especially Hausa, played leading roles in the jihad. Yola oral traditions maintain that the men under Mōdibbo Adama were Fulɓe and those Bata who had embraced Islam.

In the absence of a Sarki Yayi there was the *Daurōde* (a sort of war cabinet), composed of Mōdibbo Adama, Arɗo Dembo, Mōdibbo Hamman Song, and Mōdibbo Jam of Cheboa. They had no official titles and each led and commanded his own men under the direction of Mōdibbo Adama. The army was divided into cavalry and infantry. The former was initially very limited as horses were difficult to procure. The main bulk of the fighters were infantry, most of them archers who preceded the cavalry.

With a nucleus of voluntary fighters from outside Fombina, and together with his allies – groups of the Wolarɓe, Ngara'en, and Ba'en – the jihad wars were started in the Upper Benue valley in the dry season of *c.* 1811. According to tradition, in the early conflicts, Mōdibbo Adama adhered strictly to the laws governing the jihad.[15] The Hāɓe were given the option of accepting Islam or recognizing the authority of the Muslims through the payment of tribute (jizya). As regards fighting weapons, poisoned arrows, swords, spears, and knives were not permitted. Similarly, villages and communities were not attacked without due notice being given: normally, there were important dialogues between the Muslims and the non-Muslims before the outbreak of hostilities. First, they would be invited to accept Islam. Once this was accepted, they would be required to promise to observe the daily prayers and the Ramaḍan fast. Acceptance of Islam meant automatic acceptance of the Islamic political leadership under Mōdibbo Adama. Those who accepted

Islam were required to aid the Muslims by supplying men to take part in the jihad wars, and by payment of tribute to the Muslim ruler.

For their part, the Muslims were supposed to instruct these people in worship and the Qur'ān. This was done in two ways: either the Muslims supplied a learned man to live with them and instruct them, or the community sent their men to be instructed by the Muslims, to return to their people as instructors. Those who embraced Islam could not be enslaved, and in theory they were regarded as equals by the Fulɓe, although for people who refused to accept the invitation to embrace Islam or refused to enter into *Amāna* (friendship pact) with the Muslims, attack was inevitable.[16]

For Mōdibbo Adama and his subordinates, the cardinal point in the initial conflicts was Islam. Their sincerity and commitment need not be doubted, for their aim – at least initially – was the spread of Islam not only among the Hāɓe but also among the non-Muslim Fulɓe. During the jihad, it was not only Hāɓe that were attacked but recalcitrant Fulɓe groups as well.[17] Other Fulɓe, while professing Islam, refused to join the Muslims in the performance of that important obligation, the jihad.

CAMPAIGNS IN THE UPPER BENUE VALLEY, *c.* 1811–47

When the Fombina Fulɓe began their jihad wars, their first target was, naturally, the Bata who were the dominant ethnic group along the valley of the Benue. The Fulɓe community of Gurin was surrounded by petty Bata chieftaincies – Kokumi, Bundang, Pema, Turua, and Njobolio. When an invitation was sent to these groups inviting them to embrace Islam, it was rejected by most except those of Kokumi and Kopa who consequently became allies of the Fulɓe. The first expeditions were therefore directed against the Bata communities living around the Fulɓe centre. Within a few days, the Fulɓe sacked and destroyed Pema, Turua, and Tepe, thereby creating a nucleus for the Emirate of Fombina centred at Gurin.[18] From this base, conquests extended in all directions.

The campaigns in the Upper Benue plains fall into three parts, *c.* 1811–25, then 1827–34, and lastly 1835–47. The first phase was the period of attempts by the Muslims to establish and consolidate their position along the Faro valley. During the course of these years, the Bata of the region were either subdued or forced to migrate into the unconquered regions to the west and north of the Benue. With the weakening of the Bata, the Muslims turned their attention to the inhabitants of the Upper Faro valley and the Vere of the Alantika region. The latter submitted and accepted the Amāna offered them. To the east of the Faro, the Chamba of Lāmorde Njongum were attacked and conquered. After this victory, Mōdibbo Adama installed his friend Mōdibbo Jam as a flag bearer and vassal ruler of the region – the first flag bearer and 'sub-Emir' under Mōdibbo Adama. While the main body of the Muslim forces turned north, Mōdibbo Jam stayed behind to consolidate the victory. He was also charged with the responsibility of holding in check the various Bata and Chamba communities of the area.

Mōdibbo Adama then received a Fulɓe deputation led by Arɗo Hamman Manga of the Kiri'en at Pakorgel, and Jauro Nuhu Dakka of the Ba'en at Dagula.[19] The two Fulɓe leaders were given flags and were thus empowered to prosecute the jihad among the Chamba in the south-east. However, they achieved only limited military success, partly because they led only small groups; another reason was the timely submission of a Chamba chief. Perhaps realizing the intention of the Fulɓe, Gang Damashi left his base at Dirdiu, travelled to Gurin and paid homage to Mōdibbo Adama. As a reward for accepting an Amāna, Damashi, though not given a flag because he was not a Muslim, was empowered to make wars and extend his dominion over the Chamba and the Mumuye.[20] This Chamba ruler, whom Meek described as 'the greatest Chamba conqueror',[21] immediately began a career of conquest in the south-west and eventually founded the Chamba-Mumuye 'sub-emirate' of Binyeri.

By the appointments of Mōdibbo Jam, Jauro Nuhu, Hamman Manga, and Damashi, the southern areas bordering the newly-established emirate were held in check. There being no danger of invasion from the south, the Muslims turned their attention to the north and east. In the latter, the wars took place on two fronts: in the region of Garwa and along the Tiel valley north of the Benue. When the jihad was in progress along the valley of the Faro, the Wolarɓe, led by Arɗo'en Hamman Joda and Mōdibbo Demsa b. Hamman Gari, refused to pay the customary tribute and grazing dues to Yideng, the Bata chief of Demsa-Pwa.[22] This opened conflict between the Wolarɓe and the Bata in which the former were disastrously defeated. On the invitation of the Fulɓe, Adama came to their aid. He subdued Yideng and established, not the Arɗo, because he was not learned, but Mōdibbo Demsa as the ruler of the Tiel valley. With his hand strengthened, Mōdibbo Demsa gradually subdued the remaining Bata groups, the Fali and the Tengelin, on the northern banks of the Benue between c. 1820 and 1830.[23] From the Tiel valley, Mōdibbo Adama advanced with his forces eastwards to Bibemi where it is said he gave aid to the Yillaga'en under Arɗo Salatu b. Sambo.[24] He is also credited with resolving a conflict between the Yillaga'en of Binder and Mendif over a common claim to a border village.[25]

The second phase of the campaigns on the Benue plains was mainly directed against the Bata and Njai in the region north of the Benue and west of Māyo Tiel. In c. 1831, the base of the Emirate was transferred from Gurin to Ribadu on the southern bank of the Benue and up to c. 1839 this remained Mōdibbo Adama's base.[26] Before leaving Gurin, he appointed as his Khalifa there his brother-in-law, Mōdibbo Hamman, who, in the absence of Adama, was to be the Lamɗo of the Faro valley, but not a flag bearer.[27]

The region to which Mōdibbo Adama turned his attention from c. 1831 had a number of flag bearers who had already established Fulɓe rule. In Holma, for example, through marriage between the Arɗo and the daughter of the Holma chief Dimitilli, the Wolarɓe leader gained influence and later the chieftaincy.[28] After the death of Dimitilli, his grandson, Arɗo Dembo Dagurma, became the chief. Similarly, in Sorau, through association with the Njai and alliance with Holma, the Fulɓe under Arɗo Hamman Joda established their rule before 1831.[29] Between 1831 and 1839, the intention of the Fulɓe, therefore, was to consolidate their rule north of the Benue. In that region, as there were numerous autonomous Fulɓe groups, each under its Arɗo and keen to maintain its independence, a number of petty sub-emirates were established, such as Vokna under Arɗo Alhaji who received Adama's flag in c. 1839,[30] and Belel in c. 1830 after the migrant Shuwa Arabs from Waloji in Borno obtained the peaceful submission of the Bata communities.[31]

By far the most important development north of the Benue was the establishment of the sub-emirates of Malabu and Song. The Wolarɓe Arɗo'en of these areas, Mōdibbo Hamman Song and Arɗo Dembo of Malabu, were close friends of Mōdibbo Adama, and from the beginning of the jihad were his main support and strength. By 1830, the conquest in the Faro valley was over and Mōdibbo Adama, as a reward for the services they had rendered to him, turned his attention to the north to install them by conquest as the Lāmɓe of their former homes. In c. 1831, the Bata of the Malabu hills were conquered, and as those of Kopa had already submitted by accepting Islam, Arɗo Dembo was appointed ruler of Malabu.[32] The new ruler carried out the work of consolidating his rule with determined energy. He established border strongholds (*ribats*)[33] at Mutheli, Nantina, and Korka'e in the Kopa hills. Later, he founded the Malabu sub-emirate on the route to Borno as a military check-point against possible encroachment, especially from Borno.

The establishment of the sub-emirate of Song needed greater energy and strength because the area contained the powerful Bata chieftaincies of Bolki, Mulke, Handa, Bagda, and Mboi,[34] and the surrounding area was peopled by powerful groups, living in inaccessible regions. There were the Yungur of the Pirgambe hills, the Lala and Ga'anda of the Lala plateau, and the Kilba to the north. Eventually, three Fulɓe sub-emirates emerged, but of the three only Song was able to establish a firm footing. The other two, Goila and Mbilla-Kilba, were only sub-emirates in name: they succeeded in gaining independence from the Hāɓe but did not effect the real subjugation of the non-Fulɓe groups. In the case of Goila, this failure was partly due to the nature of the terrain inhabited by the Yungur and Lala. In that of Kilba, besides the terrain, it was also because relations between some Wolarɓe and the Kilba were on the whole cordial and friendly. Nevertheless, after he was given a flag by Mōdibbo Adama, Mōdibbo Da'u assembled the Wolarɓe kindred groups of Wudin and Mijili,[35] and led them from Mbilla-Kilba through the valley of Māyo Daguba, between Wudin and Duwa, to the plains east of the Lala plateau where he established the stronghold of Goila.[36] From this place, a section of the Wolarɓe under Hamman Njundi broke away and moved down to the Benue valley where they eventually established themselves at Garua-Winde. Mōdibbo Da'u also left Goila and founded a new settlement at Agorma. During his absence, the Wolar6e at Goila declared their independence from his control and installed a new leader.[37] Mōdibbo Da'u was discouraged from trying to repossess Goila and fighting an internecine war by his son Hajj Mumammadu. Instead he founded Mbillawa from Agorma as a base for occasional raids against Kilba villages.[38] By and large, the Wolar6e had failed to establish a sub-emirate over the Kilba. Mōdibbo Da'u continued as he had been, only an Arɗo of the Ful6e. The majority of the Ful6e Wolar6e maintained normal contacts with the Kilba, attending their markets and exchanging bovine products for foodstuffs.[39]

On the eastern border of Kilbaland, Arɗo Sabana had succeeded in establishing peaceful Ful6e rule over the Zummo people. Even though he had obtained a flag from Mōdibbo Adama, his emergence as a ruler was a result of the abdication, in his favour, of his grandfather, the pagan chief of Zummo.[40] To the south-west of Zummo is Song, and the campaign for the establishment of a sub-emirate there was begun in c. 1836. After the second Mandara campaign, Mōdibbo Adama led the Ful6e forces from Ribadu to Song where, with the aid of the established Kanuri elephant hunters, they attacked and subdued the several Bata communities one after the other. The first to be attacked was Hamairai of Bolki, who was defeated and his settlement burned down. With the defeat of Bolki – the most powerful Bata community in the area – the others, Mulke, Mboi, and Mulon, submitted without a struggle.[41] The last not only submitted but embraced Islam, while Mulke and Mboi became Amana'en. It was at this time that Gudu also surrendered and accepted Islam. Finally, with the fall of Girbisa in c. 1837, the settlement of Song was established and Mōdibbo Hamman was installed as ruler.

By 1837, Mōdibbo Adama had successfully created important military outposts both to the north and south of the Benue. The founding of Malabu was not only to hold in check the Bata and Jirai, but also to guard against infiltrations from Mandara and the north. The establishment of Song was aimed at checking the warlike Yungur and Lala, to the west and north-west. It was also to fight in co-operation with the small sub-emirate of Goila, whose leader was attacked in c. 1830 for his non-Islamic inclinations but later, in 1842, given a flag[42] against the Hona, Ga'anda, and Babur. These two sub-emirates, from their founding up to the coming of the British, were intermittently engaged in struggles with their various non-Ful6e neighbours.

With the completion of the establishment of Ful6e sub-emirates among the Bata in the east and the north, and having set in motion similar processes in the south among the Chamba, Mōdibbo Adama turned his attention to the west, a region where hitherto there were no Ful6e activities and whence therefore the displaced groups of Bata had retreated and re-established their political institutions. From their new centres of power, they began hostilities against Ful6e pastoralists, confiscating cattle. They were also a direct threat to the Ful6e territories in the east.

In order to begin an offensive against these Bata groups, the capital of the emirate was again shifted, from Ribadu to Njobolio, in *c.* 1839.[43] Ribadu, before it became Adama's base, was a centre of the Bewe'en Fulɓe who had entered Fombina after the failure of their Borno campaign under Gwoni Mukhtar of Damaturu, Mōdibbo Adama gave them a flag,[44] but their independence was overshadowed when the Mōdibbo made Ribadu his base in 1831. When Mōdibbo Adama moved to Njobolio, they regained their former status but with a somewhat peculiar position. Ribadu was their base, but the territory under their control was in Margiland where they had long been resident, and where the majority of the clan lived in the nineteenth century.[45] This unusual situation arose from the fact that Mōdibbo Adama mistrusted them, and when they obtained the peaceful submission of Musa-Dille Margi, requested their Arɗo'en to remain at Ribadu so that they could be under his surveillance.[46]

From their new centre of Njobolio, the Fulɓe attempted to subject the riverain Bata communities. However, despite a two-year stay at Njobolio, they could not subdue the Bata stronghold of Bagale though they succeeded in causing the further migration of Zaro Dungye,[47] a Bata chief who had been resident in the lower Faro valley before the jihad. Soon afterwards, Mōdibbo Adama migrated from Njobolio because it was not a good place – located as it is in the Benue marshes – and established himself on the rising ground ('*yōlde*) that was formerly occupied by Zaro Dungye. This place was renamed Yola in 1841 and it became the permanent headquarters of the Fombina Emirate. From 1841 until the end of the reign of Mōdibbo Adama in 1847 there were no major conquests, but occasional fighting with the western Bata continued, and the new capital was still vulnerable to their periodic incursions. The threat from the Bata was only partly removed in the reign of Lāmīɗo Lawal, and the struggles with them did not finally end until the beginning of this century.

THE MANDARA CAMPAIGNS AND THE JIHAD IN FUNĀNGE, *c.* 1825–35

The kingdom of Mandara occupied an important position in relation to the non-Fulɓe peoples of northern Fombina. Long before the jihad, there had been a tradition of hostility toward the Fulɓe in Mandara, and this became intensified with the outbreak of the jihad, especially after its extension to Borno. After the resurgence of Borno under al-Kanemi, Mandara concluded a treaty of alliance with her former master in order to check Fulɓe activities both within and without the kingdom.[48] The most important regions inhabited by the Fulɓe before the nineteenth century were the Yedseram basin in the west and the Gasawa plains in the east. The Fulɓe of these two areas were a direct threat to the kingdom. As Denham noted, Kerawa, Mandara's capital, was wrested from them by the Fulɓe of Musfea and Kora. It was Sultan Bukar of Mandara who saved the kingdom and moved the capital first to Dolo and later to Mora at the beginning of the nineteenth century.[49]

He also exerted pressure upon the Ful6e within the kingdom and upon those along the Yedseram basin. In the course of this, he attacked and defeated the Ful6e stronghold of Magadali,[50] but his expedition to Musfea and Kora was disastrous for Mandara.

Perhaps it was after failing to subdue these Ful6e groups that Sultan Bukar turned his attention to the Yedseram basin. At Gar-ire Tanne he expelled Ardo Dadi, and at Isa Hā6e he avenged his defeat and almost wiped out the Ful6e Ngara'en.[51] This was a turning point in the history of Mandara-Ful6e conflict. The Ful6e in Waila and Fūnānge were in danger. It was as a result of the Ful6e defeat at Isa Hā6e that Mōdibbo Adama was either invited or himself decided to aid his maternal relatives.[52] It seems also that Adama was stimulated to go to Mandara because it was the most powerful state to the north of Fombina and its influence extended far beyond its borders. The peoples of the north had been for a long time at the mercy of the might of Mandara. Therefore, before the Ful6e could establish their rule permanently, the influence and the myth of Mandara power would have to be eliminated. Undoubtedly, what hastened the expedition was Mandara's hostility and attacks upon the Ful6e populations of the Yedseram basin and the Gasawa plains.

In c. 1825, Mōdibbo Adama advanced northwards from the Benue valley. After a series of operations on the way, the Ful6e met and defeated Sultan Bukar near Guider.[53] Mōdibbo Adama drove home his victory by advancing and capturing the Mandara capital, Dolo. But it was not held for long; after a few days, the Ful6e retired and Sultan Bukar, who had taken refuge at Dikwa, returned.[54] The withdrawal of the Ful6e from Dolo, according to tradition, was because the Ful6e conquerors found so much booty – property, slaves, and women – that they became wholly absorbed in these luxuries. They forgot Islam and the fact that they were in occupation of enemy territory, and consequently, they neither attended the mosque for congregational prayers, nor cared for their own defence. After three days, Mandara forces attacked and routed them.[55] From Dolo, Mōdibbo Adama entered the Gasawa plains where the Ngara'en had acquired some form of political power over the Gisiga. At Mogassam, he met and subdued Laeta, the chief of Marba, and strengthened the position of the Marba Ful6e. Furthermore, before returning to the Benue valley, his activities in the Gasawa plains compelled Sultan Bukar to accept Mungabe as the border with Marwa[56] which, together with Mendif, became a sub-emirate of Fombina.

The expedition to Mandara was Mōdibbo Adama's most celebrated campaign and it remains alive in the minds of the Ful6e in general and their oral historians in particular. That the expedition was undertaken at all, considering the distance involved, is an indication that by c. 1825, the power of the Ful6e was firmly established on the Benue plains. By the defeat of Mandara, Mōdibbo Adama clearly demonstrated the strength of the forces at his command and what they could achieve. Before the encounter with Mandara, his leadership was only half-heartedly accepted by the Ful6e of Waila and

Fūnānge. However, as a result of his victorious encounter with Sultan Bukar, all the Fulɓe in these regions now gave him their support and loyalty. He had become the main bulwark against Mandara, the myth of whose invincibility was broken. Mōdibbo Adama had demonstrated that he was capable of protecting the Fulɓe of the region, and this first expedition paved the way for the establishment of Fulɓe hegemony in the Gasawa plains and the Yedseram basin.

In *c.* 1828, the long reign of Sultan Bukar came to an end, and Mandara under the vigorous reign of its young sultan, Iliyasu, renewed its hostility towards the Fulɓe. Their settlements were occasionally raided and their cattle taken.[57] Matters were brought to a head by the expulsion of Arɗo Njidda from his capital at Madagali by the forces of Mandara under Sultan Iliyasu.[58] Mōbiddo Adama hastened to his aid. Advancing through the valley of Māyo Tiel, he entered Gider, where the pagan ruler, Kenkelesso, surrendered and embraced Islam. Mōdibbo Adama renamed him Salisu and re-appointed him the Muslim ruler of Gider.[59] The Mōdibbo also conducted raids among the Musgu during this campaign. The second expedition of *c.* 1834 was, however, unsuccessful; the pressure from the young Sultan was so great that Mōdibbo Adama was compelled to abandon the assault upon the capital, although in the ensuing battle, the Fulɓe turned and faced the Mandara forces and eventually drove them back. Thus, Mandara's victory was inconclusive. Subsequently, Mōdibbo Adama and Sultan Iliyasu concluded a treaty of friendship and mutual non-aggression.[60] Thus, while the first expedition brought about Mandara's recognition of the Fulba's conquests in the east, the second prepared the ground for the emergence of their sub-emirates in the Yedseram basin.

The Fulɓe of the Yedseram basin had gained ascendancy as a result of Bauchi Gordi's activities, but up to *c.* 1834, with the exception of Madagali whose Arɗo received Adama's flag in *c.* 1811, they had neither made extensive conquests, nor completely gained power in the areas where they were influential. But following the conclusion of the treaty with Mandara, Mōdibbo Adama conducted Arɗo Njidda from Bungel, where he had been living since his expulsion twelve years before, to Madagali, his headquarters. He also promised aid and support against all future Mandara attacks.[61] Then four Fulɓe Arɗo'en, Mōdibbo Hamman Mubi, Hamman Chibuni of Michika, Yaya of Uba, and Buba Njitti of Moda, received his flags for the jihad wars in their respective areas.[62] Eventually, they established sub-emirates and Fulɓe administration over the Gude, Fali, Margi, and the Sukur of the Yedseram basin.

Despite two expeditions, the kingdom of Mandara was not conquered and incorporated into the Fombina Emirate. Even so, as a result of the expeditions and other Fulɓe activities in Waila and Funānge, Mandara's influence was considerably reduced and some of her possessions wrested from her. Most of the fertile plains which hitherto supported the kingdom were conquered and a number of sub-emirates emerged under the control of the Fulɓe, restricting

Mandara's possessions to the mountains. Fulɓe relations with Mandara after *c.* 1835 were on the basis of equality even though the latter used to send occasional raiding parties to the plains.[63] After *c.* 1835 there were no further expeditions to Mandara by the Lāmīɓe of Fombina.[64] But one may say that after 1835 the foundation of Fulɓe conquest and expansion was firmly laid down in the regions north of the Benue valley.

CAMPAIGNS IN HŌSĒRE

One contrast between the jihad in the Benue valley northwards up to Mandara and that in the south, is that in the former it was declared and undertaken by resident Fulɓe. In the southern regions, the jihad was an invasion by some of the Fulɓe groups who formerly lived along the valleys of the Benue and Faro rivers. The three most important of these groups were the Wolarɓe under Hamman Njobdi and Arɗo Hamman Gabdo (also called Hamman Dandi) and the Kiri'en under Arɗo Hamman Sambo. Each of the three Arɗo'en had considerable wealth and following. When Mōdibbo Adama was appointed the flag bearer, they refused to support him at first because they regarded themselves as powerful Fulɓe leaders and thought that the jihad leader should have been selected from among them. However, when Adama started to wage war successfully against the Bata, it is said that they tendered their submission and received subordinate flags from him.[65] However, even after they had tendered their allegiance and received flags from Mōdibbo Adama, they refused to remain near him to pool their forces. Rather than stay in the Faro valley where they could be under Adama's actual leadership and control, the three Arɗo'en moved further away to areas where they could live and lead their people without undue supervision and interference.[66] Thus, it was their spirit of independence that set them on the move and when they established sub-emirates, they made several attempts to be independent rulers with the same status as Mōdibbo Adama, i.e. having direct relations with the Caliph.

It is true that in Waila and Funānge, Adama's leadership was also not wholly accepted at first, but as a consequence of his victorious campaigns against Mandara, he obtained the support and loyalty of all the Arɗo'en in those regions. In the case of the Arɗo'en of the south, there was no Mandara to rally them behind Mōdibbo Adama. Similarly, in the north, Adama was in one way or another closely connected with the establishment of the sub-emirates. This was not the case in the south. The conquests and the subsequent establishment of Fulɓe administration were carried out by those groups under the three Arɗo'en without Adama's participation or aid.

The southernmost point of Adama's direct activity was the Bata chieftaincy of Lāmorde Njongum which he subdued and placed under Mōdibbo Jam.[67] But the activities of Buba Jam did not reach the confluence of the Faro and Deo rivers. It was in this region that the three Arɗo'en, Njobdi, Sambo, and

Gabdo, established themselves after they had received Mōdibbo Adama's flags. In the 1830s ,they started to advance to the south.

Mōdibbo Adama's position had become so strong that the Arɗo'en in the Faro-Deo confluence felt they were being overshadowed. The successful expeditions which he undertook to Mandara, his success in clearing the Bata from the Faro valley and in establishing sub-emirates in the north gained him the support of various Fulɓe groups. Consequently, the Arɗo'en of the south began to feel uneasy and they feared that Mōdibbo Adama might extend his control over them. There also appears to have been little room for the three Arɗo'en to establish separate sub-emirates at the Faro-Deo confluence, except to the south. To the north was Gurin, the former base of Mōdibbo Adama, and to the north-east the sub-emirate of Cheboa under Mōdibbo Jam was already established. To the east, the Yillaga'en were busy with their conquests and the establishment of Rai-Buba and Bibemi. To the west lay the Alantika and the Shebshi mountains extending as far as the Cameroun mountains in the south. Their only alternative was to remain as petty rulers of small sub-emirates under the surveillance of Mōdibbo Adama. A further reason for their advance southwards was the need to explore the south with a view to acquiring better grazing lands. The adventurous nomads who had ventured to the south reported that the Hōsēre (the region south of the Benue plains, beyond the Faro-Deo confluence, now known as the Adamawa Plateau, in Cameroun) was well suited for cattle grazing.[68] Thus, the invasion of the south was only partly motivated by the desire of the Wolarɓe and the Kiri'en to remove themselves further from Adama's sphere of activity and controlling influence.

The invasion of Hōsēre by the Kiri'en and Wolarɓe was one of the most spectacular developments of the jihad in Fombina. The region was practically unknown to the Fulɓe. It is not known when the Fulɓe conquerors began their advance onto the plateau, except that the Kiri'en had founded Tibati nineteen years before their Arɗo died in 1849.[69] From this we may conclude that the invasion took place between *c.* 1825 and *c.* 1830.

The Fulɓe advance was on two fronts, by way of the Faro valley and up the valley of Māyo Deo. In the former, Arɗo'en Hamman Sambo and Hamman Njobdi combined their forces. They subdued the Voko, conquered Bantaji, and moved south till they reached the base of the plateau where they also subdued the Manna, a northern sub-group of the Mbum.[70] The two leaders concluded a treaty of alliance with the Mbum centred at Lauboro. There was therefore no need to establish a permanent residency among the conquered groups; they merely stationed a representative at Bakane and returned to their bases in the north. Their representative later moved from Bakane to Delbe, still among the Mbum, but there he was attacked by the Mbum of Lauboro. This breach of treaty hastened Arɗo Njobdi and Hamman Sambo to the scene. Passing near Chabbal Gangdaba, they attacked Koya, the Belaka (chief of) Mbum, and expelled him from his seat of power.[71] This area was renamed 'Ngaundere' and became the seat of Arɗo Njobdi. With the subjection of Koya, Arɗo Njobdi gradually established his authority over the Mbum, mainly by diplomacy and not by wars.[72]

From Ngaundere, Arɗo Hamman Sambo led the Kiri'en westwards and conquered the western Mbum, the Wokka, the Suga, and the Kotopo in the region of Tinger. Eventually he reached Yagure, a settlement he had previously established.[73] From this point, Hamman Sambo and his men moved south and conquered the Baya. Without establishing a base, the expedition proceeded into the land of the Wute, whose stronghold of Tibati was conquered in *c.* 1830.[74] This became the new centre of the Kiri'en sub-emirate of that name.

The second wave of invasion of the plateau was led by two brothers, Arɗo Ja'imu and Arɗo Hamman Gabdo (or Hamman Dandi), sons of Arɗo Asamatu of the Wolarɓe. They had left Wassandu in *c.* 1825 and began their southward advance along the valley of Māyo Deo.[75] The Wolarɓe advance in this region was by distinct stages. The first was the Banglang campaign after which they established a fortified base on a ridge overlooking the Deo river. The base, known as Laro, was left in the charge of Jauro Hamman Joda, also of the Kiri'en Fulɓe, after the southward move of the two Arɗo'en. The second stage of the advance was the capture of Koncha, the stronghold of the Kotopo, whose chief, Tidajalli, was defeated.[76] Koncha was made the capital of Hamman Gabdo in *c.* 1835.[77] The third stage of the advance took place after Mōdibbo Adama empowered him to continue his conquest down to the sea. [78] From Koncha, Hamman Gabdo advanced through the Genderu pass (5,500 feet) and entered the country of the Wute where he fought one of the greatest battles in the south. The Wute people had united their forces with the Tikar in order to halt the Fulɓe invaders; Hamman Gabdo, however, was unaided – he received no aid from Mōdibbo Adama or from the Arɗo'en of Tibati and Ngaundere. With only the forces under his own command, he attacked and completely routed the combined forces of the Wute and the Tikar at Sambolabu. Then he advanced and captured the Wute stronghold of Banyo, which became his new and final base.[79] By *c.* 1835, three sub-emirates, Banyo, Tibati, and Ngaundere, were firmly established on the plateau under the Wolarɓe and Kiri'en Fulɓe.

To the north-east of these sub-emirates were the Dama people who inhabited the headwaters of the Benue river. Among them the Yillaga'en were actively engaged in the establishment of their domain. Long before the jihad, their Arɗo, Buba Joda b. Bondi la Malle, gained considerable influence among the Dama when he married Na'ade, the daughter of Asama, the chief of the Dama of Godi.[80] When the jihad began, because not all the Dama were on good terms with the Yillaga'en, Arɗo Buba Joda sent his son to Sokoto to receive on his behalf a flag from the Shehu for the jihad. But it is said that Buba Njidda met Mōdibbo Adama at Malabu and received a subordinate flag with which he returned to his base at Ba'ajari.[81] Not long afterwards his father died and Buba Njidda became the Arɗo of the Yillaga'en.

The opportunity for war came one year after he had received the flag. The chief of Arai revolted against Sigra, the chief of Ndoro, who was perhaps the overall chief of the Dama people.[82] Arɗo Buba, uninvited, intervened by attacking the chief of Arai, and when he defeated him, established himself in the Arai's stronghold which he renamed 'Nasarāwo' (the victory town). Then he advanced and conquered Hulmai, the chief of Arai-Manga, who had refused to embrace Islam when called upon to do so by Arɗo Njidda.[83] Thereafter, he extended his conquests up to Chollire and the Djapa mountains, subduing the Pani people. To the south, he advanced up to the headwaters of the Benue and conquered the Dui and the mountain-dwelling Mbum. His conquest in the east extended over the Laka peoples and beyond. Buba Njidda thus succeeded in founding one of the most powerful sub-emirates of nineteenth century Fombina.

Apart from Buba Njidda, other Yillaga Arɗo'en in this region also received flags from Mōdibbo Adama. These included the Arɗo'en of Balda, Wuro Māyo-Jarendi, and Mbere.[84] But they neither became powerful nor were they able to establish large domains. They were more or less subject to the will of the powerful Buba Njidda of Rai, whose conquest overshadowed their own and who acted as their overlord. In fact their domains were only Fulɓe 'city states' dependent upon Rai-Buba for their defence and survival.

By *c.* 1840, the various Fulɓe groups had established themselves as the ruling class of the sub-emirates. Mōdibbo Adama, as the man to whom command was delegated, played the role of the Shehu in the distribution of flags to his subordinates. His example unleashed an unprecedented era of conquests which extended from Mandara in the north to Tibati in the south. The Fulɓe take-over of power in Fombina was peaceful in some places and bloody in others; in certain areas, the non-Fulɓe submitted without conflict and their chiefs surrendered power to the Fulɓe. This was not only to avoid bloodshed but because of the blood-ties between the Fulɓe leader and the chief of the area they had replaced. Unlike the jihad in Hausaland, that of Fombina was an all Fulɓe affair. But it was to the credit of Mōdibbo Adama that non-Fulɓe chiefs who had accepted his invitation and embraced Islam were recognized as rulers of dependent sub-emirates.

Considering the numerical inferiority of the Muslims within Fombina, the success of their conquest is remarkable. That the task was accomplished at all is surprising. It is essential therefore to examine the factors that brought victory to them. The current view among the Fulɓe is that the victory came about because they were fighting for Islam and therefore Allah was on their side. But a more detailed explanation is required for our purpose. The Fombina jihad was not very successful in spreading Islam among the Hāɓe. As a matter of fact, the true Islamization of the conquered Hāɓe came not during the conquests, but well after the emirate was established and only when the Fulɓe/non-Fulɓe relationship had returned to normal. In the nineteenth century, the majority of the Fombina Fulɓe became Muslims, and religion became a most important element in their organization – an element which overcame the isolation of Fulɓe groups, organized and united them as a single force in the region. On the other hand, the majority of the non-Fulɓe peoples lacked this element in their organization. Along the Benue valley, for example, the Bata people lived not as a homogeneous political or social unit, but under petty chieftaincies often in conflict with one another. Before the jihad, the Fulɓe policy of playing off one chief against another created animosity between the various chiefs, with the result that when the Fulɓe began their wars, the Bata were divided. There was no united Bata force to confront the Fulɓe and so one Bata chieftaincy after the other could be conquered separately. Had the Bata been united, the situation would have been different and the task for the Fulɓe more difficult. This is aptly proved in the case of the Kilba where the jihad made little inroad. In southern Fombina, the Tikar were disunited and remained in small groups prior to the Fulɓe invasion, and like the Bata, they were attacked one group after the other. But unlike the Bata, instead of further migration, they formed alliances, built fortified towns, and were eventually able to hold off further Fulɓe advance till the German conquest.[85]

With the exception of the Kilba and the Tikar, the situation in other parts of Fombina was generally the same: there were either disunited groups of people or petty chieftaincies usually in conflict with one another. This made conquest easier for the Fulɓe who were determined to achieve, among other things, the free exploitation of grazing lands for their cattle. They had what can be regarded as three common objectives: to get rid of Hāɓe oppressors, to end their hardship (bone), and to establish an Islamic Fulɓe administration in Fombina. Nowhere was the need for grazing exploitation so important as in the invasion of the plateau. Arɗo'en Hamman Sambo and Njobdi, after the establishment of Bakane as their base, realized that Hōsēre was admirably suited to cattle grazing. The realization speeded up their determination for the conquest of the fertile plateau.[86]

Again the Fulɓe were victorious because of the way they organized themselves and conducted their conquests. Realizing that they were a minority, and a socially segmented people, their differences were put aside and they began their wars not in separate groups but in massive alliances. In the Benue valley, Mōdibbo Adama fought not as head of a clan but as leader of an alliance of Wolarɓe, Ba'en, and Yillaga'en. There were also some Ngara'en, Kiri'en, and Bewe'en Fulɓe supporting him. The various groups led by their Arɗo'en returned to the areas assigned to them and which the alliance had conquered for each. Similarly, the two expeditions to Mandara were not undertaken by Mōdibbo Adama alone, but by all the Fulɓe Arɗo'en in the areas north of the Benue valley.

On the southern plateau, a similar understanding and co-operation existed. The expeditions that led to the establishment of the sub-emirates of Ngaundere and Tibati were jointly undertaken by the Kiri'en and Wolarɓe under Arɗo'en Sambo and Njobdi respectively. After the sub-emirates were established, the co-operation and alliance continued. It was the only way they could sustain themselves and hold their conquered lands. This spirit of alliance and co-operation was displayed when Arɗo Njobdi of Ngaundere suffered a reverse at Ngauka at the hands of Belaka Nganha. Buba Njidda of Rai and Hamman Sambo of Tibati came to his aid, and after a combined siege of three weeks, Ngauka fell.[87] In later years when the sub-emirates became fully established and operative, the earlier spirit of co-operation and understanding declined. This was partly responsible for the decline of Fulɓe hegemony in Fombina. Instead of co-operation, local conflicts, mainly nurtured by jealousies between the sub-emirates, became intense.

THE EARLY EMIRATE GOVERNMENT OF FOMBINA, 1809–47

The nineteenth century jihad was not a movement of disgruntled and destructive people. As the writings of the time show, the leaders had firm plans to follow.[88] In Fombina, the leaders either wrote no political tracts or what they wrote is yet to be recovered. Nevertheless, because the Fombina jihad was part of that of Sokoto and judging from the libraries inherited by malams of the present day, it can be inferred that the Fombina leaders may have used the political tracts of the Sokoto triumvirate. Similarly, because the jihad in the area started rather late, when it was practically over in Hausaland, the Fombina leaders in setting up their government had more than one place from which they could draw examples.

The task of establishing a government was beset by many problems. The inhabitants of Fombina were diverse; they lived under petty chieftaincies or in small groups headed by kindred elders. In Hausaland, the population was much more homogeneous; there were pre-existing large states with fully established governments. After the jihad, the new ruling groups had a basic framework upon which they could establish their administration. In fact, the post-jihad government of Hausaland developed on the pattern of the pre-jihad Haɓe governments.[89] In Fombina, the situation was different. The Fulɓe had to undertake not merely the conquest of numerous states over a large and geographically difficult area, but also the task of establishing a wholly new system of government to embrace a large number of heterogeneous peoples.

In Gobir and other Hausa states, the aim of the Muslims was to take over the Hausa governments so as to conduct the affairs of the states according to the injunctions of the Qur'ān and the Sunna. In Fombina, the Muslims were in a minority. The basic aim of the Fulɓe was to establish a government to cater for their interests. Such a government was to protect the minority Muslim community and to secure certain fundamental rights for them in a country that was predominantly non-Islamic. Thus, because the Fulɓe had to conquer the Haɓe before they could establish a government, up to the founding of Yola in *c.* 1841 there had not existed a proper emirate government.

While Mōdibbo Adama pursued the conquest of the Bata with the support of the Arɗo'en loyal to him, in other parts of Fombina other Arɗo'en who had received flags pursued the conquest of the non-Fulɓe. In the region where the Mōdibbo was active, he was the commander (Emir) and the Arɗo'en under him were his officials. Outside Adama's sphere of activity the Arɗo'en who led their kindred groups were the *de facto* commanders and their officials were the Mauɓe of the groups. The Mōdibbo regarded them as subordinates, but they only recognized him as a leader because he had given them flags. This, as we shall see, was the genesis of the conflict between the Emirs of Fombina and the local Arɗo'en, who commanded their men and established their domains.

Between 1809 and 1831, Mōdibbo Adama had his base at Gurin. In this period the Mōdibbo acted as the Imam of the Muslim community. The only appointment he made was that of the Qadi and it is said that he appointed Mōdibbo Hamman Gurin,[90] perhaps as a recognition of his seniority. However, Mōdibbo Adama had a number of close advisers. There were the three Arɗo'en who formed the backbone of his support – Hamman Song, Dembo of Malabu, and Buba Jam. In addition, there were his close associates such as Alkasum of the Ngara'en, his former herder who had accompanied him during his journey to Sokoto as a carrier. Another close associate was Sambo Holma. But none of them was appointed to any office; they were only warriors of the jihad.

Mōdibbo Adama did not appoint a large body of officials, perhaps because there were not enough capable men sufficiently well-grounded in Islamic scholarship to occupy the type of posts recommended by the Shehu. In 'Kitab al-Farq', the Shehu recommends the appointment of at least four officials – a vizier, a judge, a chief of police, and a collector of land tax (kharaj).[91] Unlike the Shehu's community at Degel, those in Gurin were not intellectuals but a community of pastoral elders. Before 1840, knowing that the problem facing him was the lack of learned men, Mōdibbo Adama used to try to attract scholars whenever he visited Sokoto or whenever scholars visited him on their way to the holy land. Men such as Mōdibbo Hassan and Mōdibbo Tongude were encouraged to remain in Fombina.[92]

It is true that when the Sokoto jihad started, members of the Shehu's family and his relatives, such as his son Bello and his brother Abdullahi, played important roles in the early government of the Caliphate. But the family of Mōdibbo Adama was comparatively small. He had neither brothers nor sisters, and his children were not of an age to play an active role. Adama was himself quite a young man – he was only thirty-three when he became the leader of the jihad, and he had married only after his return from Borno in *c.* 1798/9.[93] His eldest son, Muhammadu Lawal, was born only in *c.* 1814.

In the last years of Mōdibbo Adama's reign, his children began to play their part in the jihad and government. His eldest son, Muhammadu Lawal, and Lawal's younger brother, Hamidu, began to command minor expeditions.

In *c.* 1831, after the capital was shifted from Gurin to Ribadu, Mōdibbo Hamman Gurin was left behind as Adama's Khalifa. The post of Qadi became vacant, and Mōdibbo Adama appointed the migrant scholar, Mōdibbo Tongude, who held the post up to the reign of Muhammadu Lawal.[94] Up until 1841, Tongude was the only titled officer of the government and his function was purely religious. After 1841, the need for civil officials increased. First, Mōdibbo Adama had decided to make Yola his permanent base and the headquarters of the emirate. Second, his lieutenants and friends had all returned to their respective pre-jihad localities as Lamɓe (chiefs) of sub-emirates. In *c.* 1812 Mōdibbo Jam returned to Cheboa; in *c.* 1831 Arɗo Dembo moved to his base at Malabu; and in *c.* 1837 Mōdibbo Hamman moved to Song. Even though the sub-emirates of these leading aides of Mōdibbo Adama lay within the Benue plains and they could still be consulted, the new capital needed men to direct its affairs. Also, the Mōdibbo needed lieutenants within his immediate reach. Consequently, he appointed two civil officials – the Galadima and the Kaigama, both Bornoan titles.[95] The Kaigama performed the functions of the *wali-al-shurta* (chief of police). He was also responsible for the preliminary organization of local expeditions, especially against the western Bata. Thus, the defence of the new capital was under his charge.

Mōdibbo Adama was by inclination a religious man. He established a Quranic school in his house to teach children in particular how to read and write the Qur'ān. He also taught religious sciences (defte) to adult pupils. As a preacher, he occasionally went on tours in the neighbouring districts of Song, Holma, Gurin, and Malabu.[96] In the course of such tours, converts were made, teachers assigned to them and mosques built. In addition to his functions as Emir and Imam, he was also a judge for cases referred to him by the Qadi or for those involving capital punishment. The life of Mōdibbo Adama was, on the whole, of the simplest kind. Dependent not upon the booty of war, he earned his living by making rope which was sold to obtain food for his family. Throughout his forty years' reign, he had only his four permitted wives and he had neither slaves nor concubines to help his wives in their domestic pursuits. When he died, he left behind only his books and the mule he was fond of using during his preaching tours.

By and large, the early Fombina government was simple. It was *ad hoc* in nature – established to serve the purpose of a community that was engaged in wars and undergoing transformation. It reflected a nomadic Fulɓe society where government rested with the Mauɓe and the Arɗo. In a sense, Mōdibbo Adama was the Arɗo, and the Mauɓe were his officials and the subordinate Lamɓe of the sub-emirates on the Benue plains. The composition and nature of the early government eventually changed with the expansion and consolidation of the Emirate.

The Mōdibbo's faithful friends were rewarded not by appointment but by uniting them with his daughters in marriage.[97] He married his eldest daughter, Adda Gurin, to Mōdibbo Hamman Song, and his daughter, Hawa'u, to Arɗo Dembo of Malabu. Similarly, he rewarded his former servant and warrior of the jihad, Alkasum, by marrying him to his third daughter, Yaya. This, more than anything else, further strengthened Mōdibbo Adama's position as the 'Emir' of Fombina. The sense of relationship between him and his neighbouring northern vassals passed the formal stage of friendship to that of in-laws. The Mōdibbo was gradually entrenching his position as Emir and protecting the metropolitan lands. He was surrounded to the north and east by Lam6e who were related to his family through marriage.

With the establishment of a permanent base at Yola in *c.* 1841, the attention of Mōdibbo Adama was turned towards the western Bata who had been of the greatest trouble to the capital and the Ful6e communities of the Benue valley. The campaigns of Mōdibbo Adama while at Njobolio succeeded only in scattering the Bata who eventually established themselves at Wuroheme, seventeen miles west of Yola. Other scattered Bata groups found safety in the Bagale hills, opposite Yola across the Benue river, and this became their second centre in the Benue valley. Neither stronghold was subdued in the lifetime of Mōdibbo Adama. The advance of the Ful6e to the west and southwest was very slow. In the latter, as already indicated, the Arɗo'en of the Kiri'en and Ba'en Ful6e had obtained flags from Mōdibbo Adama, and a Chamba chief, Damashi, was commissioned to make wars in the area. Damashi proved to be the most successful conqueror when he subdued the Mumuye, expelled the Tolla Chamba, and established a tributary pagan state of Binyeri on the plains formerly occupied by the Dindi Mumuye.

The progress of Arɗo Hamman Manga of Pakorgel and Jauro Nuhu of Dagula was very limited, and for this reason, Mōdibbo Adama intervened to protect the metropolitan lands from the hostility of the Chamba and the Vere. Subsequently, he assigned the region to two of his sons – Hamidu and Bakari – presumably as fiefs.[98] These were the only sons of Mōdibbo Adama who held any appointments during his lifetime. His eldest son, Muhammadu Lawal, never held any office of fiefdom. This was not because he was less loved, but because he was the eldest son and first born; his father, according to pulāku, was not supposed to show him love openly.[99] Nevertheless, Lawal was regarded as the Yerima – prince, another Bornoan title – even though he was not formally so designated. The Yerima played his part in campaigns especially against the western Bata.

Hamidu and Bakari – both children of Yasebo – took possession of their fiefs. Hamidu began to pacify the Chamba area and eventually succeeded in gaining full control of the Nasarawo plains, another fertile grazing area. Then he established himself as ruler with his temporary base at Nyibango, which after the death of his father became his permanent base. The conquests of Hamidu never extended into the heartland of the Chamba country – a most difficult region to penetrate, as it is mountainous – but the Chamba of Yebbi and Matiya were subjected to periodic raids.[100] As a result of Hamidu's activities in that region, the former Ful6e Lam6e of the area – Pakorgel and Dagula – were overshadowed and they continued as Jauro'en under him.[101] Bakari, whose fief was Vere, did not undertake similar activities because the inhabitants had peacefully accepted the Amāna offered by the Ful6e.

THE PROBLEMS IN ESTABLISHING A CENTRALIZED GOVERNMENT

The Shehu's Emir in Fombina was Mōdibbo Adama, but from the time he received the flag from the Shehu, his leadership was questioned by a number of Arɗo'en. Apart from the reasons already outlined some Arɗo'en did not wish to be subservient to Mōdibbo Adama because before the jihad they had been men of authority. It is true that they received flags from the Mōdibbo, but they were merely his lieutenants. The Arɗo'en, with the exception of those on the Benue plains, were not aided by the Mōdibbo in the campaigns which preceded the establishment of their domains. Consequently they had no sense of obligation towards Mōdibbo Adama, a factor which made the establishment of a centralized emirate with a single government and judiciary impossible until the European invasion. Other equally important factors which made the centralization of power under Mōdibbo Adama impossible were the vastness of the emirate and the nature of the Fulɓe and non-Fulɓe societies.

Geographically, Fombina was a large and extensive region which comprised heterogeneous peoples living under varying political systems. The Fulɓe who had conquered the region belonged to different groups, each under its Arɗo. Socially and politically they were segmented people, and centralization of power was foreign to them. The various groups which conquered the region were, before the nineteenth century, independent of one another in the management of their affairs. To expect each group to renounce its independence at once was too much. The Arɗo'en who toiled and fought unaided by Mōdibbo Adama could not all of a sudden turn and give allegiance to him on account of his having given them flags.

The jihad in Fombina started amidst opposition to Mōdibbo Adama's leadership. Eventually, he built up his support from the Wolarɓe groups under his friends and it was with this support that he began to evoke the loyalty of the other Fulɓe groups. The Mōdibbo proved himself capable of protecting the Fulɓe of the north and north-east from Mandara's depredations. Similarly, the aid he rendered to some Fulɓe groups of Fūnānge gained him the loyalty of their Arɗo'en. Moreover, the emergence of his children as warriors – Lawal and Hamidu whose efforts led to the establishment of the metropolis – meant that Adama had emerged as a powerful figure over the pre-nineteenth century Fulɓe Arɗo'en. It may have been around that time that the Arɗo'en who established the sub-emirates of Ngaundere, Tibati, and Banyo moved from the Faro valley.[102] With the growing power of Mōdibbo Adama, it appears, the southern Arɗo'en had no alternative other than to recognize the nominal overlordship of the Mōdibbo so that he would not interfere with their activities further south. Nevertheless, there were challenges to Mōdibbo Adama's leadership by those Arɗo'en.

The structure of the emirate of Fombina was a replica in miniature of the Caliphate. The Lāmɓe of the sub-emirates were Mōdibbo Adama's flag-bearers and the majority of them established the sub-emirates they governed through conquest, with themselves as local commanders. While Mōdibbo Adama was busy in the Benue-Faro valleys conquering the Bata and establishing an administration, the Arɗo'en were doing the same in their localities. By the time a permanent base was created by the Mōdibbo and a government established, the Arɗo'en had also established their governments with themselves as Lāmɓe. Thus, the Yola government found its authority truly effective only in the areas which Mōdibbo Adama had conquered. All the sub-emirates had Lāmɓe and a similar structure of officials to those of the Yola government.

Most Arɗo'en preferred to regard as their overlord not Mōdibbo Adama, but the Caliph at Sokoto. Mōdibbo Adama was merely regarded as their senior, the intermediary between them and the Caliph. On the other hand Mōdibbo Adama, by virtue of the Shehu's appointment, considered the Arɗo'en as vassals in the same way as other Emirs considered their Amils. He considered the appointment and deposition of Lāmɓe as his prerogative. Similarly, as the Emir he expected, as of right, the participation of all the Lāmɓe in all major wars, or their contribution for such. Moreover, in addition to tribute, the Lāmɓe had to tender their allegiance to him at Yola from time to time, and to abide by the directives of the Yola government. Thus the conflicts between Mōdibbo Adama and the Lāmɓe of the sub-emirates developed not only over the unwillingness of the Arɗo'en to pursue the jihad under a centralized leadership but also because even after some of them had established themselves independently they were expected by Yola to recognize the Emir as their overlord.

Conflicts between Mōdibbo Adama and the Arɗo'en began in the early years of the jihad. When Mōdibbo Adama returned to the Benue valley with a flag from the Shehu, Arɗo Hamman Njundi of the Kilba Wolarɓe refused to submit to him.[103] With the support of his group, he subsequently declared jihad in the Kilenge valley and began fighting. Within a very short time he conquered Maiha, Holma, and other settlements of the Bata and Njanyi.[104] By so doing, Hamman Njundi had exceeded his powers. Alarmed by the victories of his lieutenant, Mōdibbo Adama appealed to the Caliph at Sokoto, and as a result, Hamman Njundi who was engaged in the conquest of Kōsēje Njai was summoned to Sokoto where eventually he was detained for seven years.[105] The case of Hamman Njundi represented the first rupture between the new administration and a vassal ruler. After the period of his detention, Hamman Njundi returned to Fombina and in *c.* 1845, Mōdibbo Adama allowed him once again to lead his group.[106] Thereupon, he conquered the Bata and the Fali to establish his stronghold at Garwa on the Benue. From then until the European conquest, the rulers of Garwa remained loyal to the Lāmīɓe of Fombina.

Another Arɗo not only questioned the leadership of Mōdibbo Adama, but even tried to eliminate him. This was Sabana of Zummo, also of the Wolarɓe clan.[107] He was one of those Arɗo'en who had risen to power without conflict or aid from Mōdibbo Adama and the other Arɗo'en. Perhaps he was secretly nursing the idea of being the leader of the jihad. Thus, he conceived a plan to et Adama killed during the expedition to Yungur, and at the Konu Monde, Modibbo Adama nearly fell into the hands of the enemy by Sabana's design. He took no action against Sabana because, as an act of repentance, Sabana gave four of his daughters in marriage to four sons of Modibbo Adama.

Further threats to Adama's leadership came from Bundang, an important centre of the Wolarɓe south of the Benue river. Like the other Wolarɓe, they resented the idea of being led by a non-Bolaro Pullo. Moreover, they possessed another subsidiary flag for the jihad which was given to them by Buba Yero of Gombe.[108] In the early years of the jihad, the Wolarɓe constituted the main support in the wars of Modibbo Adama. But during the campaign to establish Buba Jam at Cheboa, the Wolarɓe of Bundang deserted the battle-field *en loc*. This was a calculated plan to jeopardise the Fulɓe chances of victory. Desertion from battle is a serious offence especially in a Holy War,[109] and when Adama emerged victorious, he arrested the leading Bundang Fulɓe for trial and punishment. But on the intervention of Arɗo Njobdi, the patriarch of the Wolarɓe, the Bundang Mauɓe were released.[110] There was further Bundang opposition to the central government of Fombina in the reign of Emir Lawal.

There were similar challenges to the leadership of Modibbo Adama in other parts of Fombina. In the early years of the jihad, Arɗo Buba Biru of the north-eastern Yillaga'en, after he had established himself at Mendif, sent an embassy to Sokoto to request a flag and appointment for a new emirate of Funānge.[111] This request was rejected and he was advised to follow and support Modibbo Adama whom the Shehu had already appointed. A similar request by the Yillaga Arɗo of Mubi was rejected, but that of the Ngara'en further east was granted.

These attempts by the northern Arɗo'en to be independent of Modibbo Adama may not, strictly speaking, have been rebellious. After all, they were not aware of the developments in the Benue valley and none of them had taken any part in the deliberations of the Arɗo'en at Gurin.[112] Therefore, they were ignorant of the emergence of Modibbo Adama as the Shehu's commander in Fombina and the east. The activities of Modibbo Adama had not by then extended to the far north, and when they did, in the two Mandara campaigns, practically all the Arɗo'en in the region rallied behind him.

The most serious challenge to Adama's leadership came from the Yillaga'en of Rai-Buba. The struggle between the Modibbo and Buba Njidda had its root in the circumstances surrounding the emergence of the latter as the ruler of the Dama and the Yillaga'en. While the Wolarɓe clan was the largest in Fombina, the Yillaga'en were the wealthiest. Moreover, those of Rai-Buba belonged to Bondi la Malle's group, which claimed kinship with the family of Shehu Usman 'Dan Fodio,[113] and therefore superiority over all the other Fulɓe clans and groups. Above all, as their tradition says, their association with Modibbo Adama came about by accident. In the course of the jihad, Buba Njidda built up a powerful Yillaga sub-emirate mainly with the support of his maternal relatives, the Dama. In his domain, his word was law and he was regarded as the father of his subjects.[114] He was perhaps the most powerful Arɗo in Fombina with a strong non-Fulɓe military force at his command. For these reasons, Arɗo Buba Njidda bore with reluctance the overlordship of Mōdibbo Adama. Their relationship became increasingly strained, and reached a crisis when Buba Njidda subjected the rulers of the petty Fulɓe sub-emirates of Balda, Wuro-Māyo Jarendi, and Mbere. What brought matters to a head was Buba's refusal to participate in the expedition against Namshi in which the Mōdibbo was defeated. As if to emphasize his strength compared with that of the Yola army, Arɗo Buba Njidda then led out his forces, subdued the Namshi, and sent captives to Mōdibbo Adama.[115] Mōdibbo Adama became jealous of the growing military strength and expansion of Rai-Buba which was becoming too dangerous. Buba Njidda was therefore summoned to Yola where a plan was made to eliminate him, but both this and a subsequent one at the Faro failed.

On his return to Rai-Buba, Buba Njidda declared his independence, promised never to set foot in Yola again, and rejected the overtures of peace and reconciliation which the Mōdibbo offered.[116] Finding no other alternative, Mōdibbo Adama with the aid of his other vassals, both Yillaga and Wolarɓe, led an expedition against Rai-Buba. Adama's expedition was a failure and after a siege of four months, he had to withdraw, because from the beginning of the expedition, the Yillaga'en and the Wolarɓe groups among Adama's grand army accompanied him without the slightest intention of fighting. They feared that once Rai-Buba was defeated and brought under control, their own domains would be regarded as fiefs. During the siege, the Arɗo'en of the two groups assured Buba Njidda of their moral support and sympathy. Eventually Mōdibbo Adama had to call off the siege because of the approaching farming season.

Further open conflict with Rai-Buba was avoided through the mediation of Yerima Halilu,[117] Adama's son, as a result of which Buba Njidda renounced his secession and recognized the autonomy of the Arɗo'en he had subjected. He also conceded the lands north of Māyo-Shina to the Arɗo of Bibemi. But it appears that Buba Njidda was not altogether willing; he had accepted it in order to avoid fighting with Yola. Consequently, his tribute to Yola grew less and less and in the third year after Mōdibbo Adama's expedition, he stopped sending it.[118] This provoked another expedition from Yola. But before the expedition reached Rai-Buba, Buba Njidda, accompanied by his devoted non-Fulɓe soldiers (the Dama, Arei, Godi, and Ndoro), had taken refuge at his Chollire base. The majority of the Fulɓe refused to accompany him. Instead they remained at Rai, which Mōdibbo Adama entered peacefully.[119] He declared Buba Njidda deposed and appointed Jauro Salihu, a son of Buba Njidda, as the new Lāmɗo of Rai-Buba. The new ruler did not reign for long, for as soon as the forces that installed him went away, his father returned and regained power.[120] So ended the conflict. But from then until the end of the reigns of Adama and Buba Njidda, Rai-Buba remained virtually independent, although further attempts to re-integrate it with the Emirate were made by the Lāmīɗo Lawal.

While Rai-Buba adopted non-co-operation as a means of gaining independence from Mōdibbo Adama's leadership, Lāmɗo Hamman Sambo of Tibati followed the 'constitutional' way. Realizing that the power lay with the Caliph, he sent a magnificent gift of slaves and horses to Caliph Atiku in *c.* 1842 and requested a separate flag of office and recognition as an independent ruler, and it is said that Atiku granted this request. As a result, Mōdibbo Adama who realized that it was futile to fight Hamman Sambo, as he was duly recognized by the Caliph, decided to embark upon a pilgrimage journey to the Holy Land. But after reaching the eastern limit of the Caliphate, a petition from some of his loyal vassals[121] and the news of Atiku's death reached him. The journey was abandoned and Mōdibbo Adama returned to Yola. Subsequently, at a meeting of all the Lāmɓe of the Emirate at Beka,[122] Mōdibbo Adama was reconciled with Hamman Sambo, who returned in person the flag given him by the Caliph. This was the last conflict in the reign of Mōdibbo Adama.

NOTES

1. Fulfulde poem, 'Artinadum', recorded by R. M. East, *Stories of Old Adamawa*, (Zaria, 1935), p. 16. It reads,
    'May Allah, the Holy One, forgive our learned men,
        Who opened Adamawa and reformed our lands.'
2. Yola traditions.
3. Garua traditions.
4. Yola traditions.
5. Ibid.
6. W. C. Moore, 'Balala District Ass. Report', 1917, NNAK, G.3, Y.
7. H. B. Ryan, 'Report on Yola Province', 1911, Yola Collected Histories, NNAK, J.2, p. 96.
8. Yawa, Mubi, and Lamorde traditions.
9. Of the arɗo'en who went to Sokoto from Fombina, only the Arɗo of the Ngara'en obtained a flag. But it was meant for jihad in Bagarmi; see D. M. Last, *The Sokoto Caliphate*, (London, 1967), p. 54. The name of the flag bearer is given as Muhammad al-Hajj al-Amin. However, in the reign of al-Seyyid, who succeeded Abdullah in *c.* 1825, the Caliph Muhammad Bello subordinated al-Seyyid to Mōdibbo Adama. See Gidado Dan Laima, 'Majmu Ashab Muhammad Bello . . .', NHRS.
10. D. F. H. McBride, 'Wollarbe History', Pagan Administration, vol. ii, 1933-5, NNAK, F.4, p. 137.
11. Such as free grazing on clan and tribal lands which the majority of the Wolarɓe enjoyed among the Kilba, Njanyi, and Zummo peoples.
12. McBride, 'Wollarbe History'.
13. Last, *Sokoto Caliphate*, p. 52.
14. Migeod, p. 14; S. J. Hogben and A. H. M. Kirke-Greene, *The Emirates of Northern Nigeria*, (London, 1966), p. 432.
15. Yola traditions. For the laws governing the conduct of jihad wars, see F. H. El-Masri, *Bayān Wūjub Al-Hijra, by Uthman ibn Fūdi*, (Khartoum, 1977).
16. On Amāna, see M. Khadduri, *War and Peace in the Law of Islam*, (Baltimore, 1955), pp. 107, 115, and 163.
17. Among the Fulɓe groups attacked were those under Arɗo Hassan and Arɗo Dembo among the Gewe pagans (by Mōdibbo Jam of Cheboa); K. Strumpell, *A History of Adam-*

80 *The Lāmīɓe of Fombina*

awa, (Hamburg, 1912), mimeo trans., NNAK, J.18, p. 49. Similarly, Mōdibbo Adama attacked Ardo Umaru of Goila in *c*. 1830 for his non-Muslim inclinations.

18. Yola traditions.
19. Jada traditions, September 1968.
20. Anon., 'Nasarawo District Misc. Papers', 1925-7, NNAK, G.2, 2, p. 122; D. A. Percival, 'Mayo-Balwa, Mayo-Farang, Yendang-Waka District Misc. Papers', 1907-47, NNAK G.2, 2F., pp. 25.6; Binyeri DNB, Divisional Office, Yola. Also, Yola traditions, August 1968. By this arrangement, Damashi secured protection from Fulɓe attack for the Binyer Chamba, and the Fulɓe were free to pursue the jihad elsewhere without fear of attack from the south-east.
21. C. K. Meek, *Tribal Studies in Northern Nigeria*, (2 vols., London, 1931), vol. II, p. 500
22. Migeod, p. 17.
23. Strumpell, p. 46.
24. 'Tarihi Bibemi', EMC.
25. Strumpell, p. 74.
26. C. V. Boyle, 'Historical notes on Yola Fulanis', *JAS*, 10, 37 (1910), 73-92, p. 74. Yola traditions. August 1968. The early bases were war camps, the size of a modern village. Their inhabitants included the families of the Mōdibbo, his advisers, and soldiers – both Fulɓe and their allies – as well as slaves. They depended upon food brought from the tributary districts as well as booty captured during campaigns. The bases were founded on new sites and were centres of organisation – by virtue of the presence of the jihad leader. Apart from Yola which had a mud wall built at the time of the Mōdibbo, the various bases had no strong fortifications. In Gurin, for example, the mosque was built with corn stalks.
27. Yola traditions.
28. Strumpell, p. 43; S. H. P. Vereker, 'Précis of Yola Local History', Partition of the Cameroun, 1919-30, NNAK, K.5, p. 2.
29. Strumpell, p. 43; Vereker, 'Précis', p. 2. Both sources point out that Ardo Hamman Joda was a former flag bearer of Buba Yero.
30. Dossier, the Chief's Book, Divisional Office Yola.
31. Belel DNB: A. C. Talbor 'Belel and Malabu Districts Misc. Papers', 1917-46, NNAK, G.2, H, p. 5.
32. Talbor; see also Belel DNB.
33. The ribats in most parts of the Emirate were camps where slaves and a few Fulɓe were stationed as permanent war camps. The inhabitants lived in constant readiness for war. None of the ribats had wall fortifications but some, like Takkande, were surrounded with thorn entanglements similar to the *zariba* system of the Kanuri.
34. Song traditions.
35. McBride, p. 136.
36. Ibid., p. 122.
37. Ibid.
38. Ibid.
39. McBride, p. 137; Jauro Goila, 'History of the origin of Kilba District', May 1950, Kilba DNB. According to Kilba traditions, up to the coming of the British, the Kilba were never subject to the Lāmīɓe of Fombina. They said only Kilba's peripheral lands were attacked from time to time.
40. Zummo DNB. Sabana obtained a flag from Mōdibbo Adama in *c*. 1811 and power was surrendered to him two years later. He was the son of Asta Yale, daughter of Dampale, the pagan chief of Zummo. See Strumpell, p. 45.
41. Song traditions.
42. E. A. Brackenbury, 'Goila District Miscellaneous Papers', 1910-36, NNAK, G.2, p. 1.
43. Yola traditions.
44. Dossier, the Chief's Book, Divisional Office, Yola; W. O. P. Rosedale, 'Notes on Balala History', Balala DNB.
45. Uba DNB.
46. G. B. Webster, 'Historical Notes on Ribadu District', Pagan Administration, Vol. I, 1910-27, NNAK, F.3.
47. Bata traditions. Bagale was subdued in the reign of the Emir Lawal.
48. D. Denham, H. Clapperton and Dr. Oudney, *Narrative of Travels and Discoveries in Northern and Central Africa in the years 1822, 1823 and 1824*, (London, 1826), p. 159.
49. Denham et al., pp. 155-6.

50. J. H. Shaw, 'Report on Madagali District', 1935, NNAK, 25073.
51. Strumpell, p. 23.
52. East, *Stories of Old Adamawa*, (Zaria, 1935), p. 23.
53. Strumpell, p. 23.
54. Migeod, p. 16.
55. East, p. 26. Yola and Song traditions, collected by East. The Mōdibbo had prayed for the return of the Mandara people.
56. 'Tarihi Marwa', a translation of an Arabic text, in the possession of Mōdibbo Nasuru Goni Bello.
57. East, *Stories*, p. 29.
58. Madagali traditions, collected by the author, August 1968.
59. Strumpell, p. 64.
60. 'Tarihi Marwa'; Yola traditions.
61. Strumpell, p. 58.
62. Vereker, pp. 1-3; Migeod, p. 16.
63. 'Tarihi Marwa'.
64. Yola traditions. After these expeditions, the Emirs of Fombina and the Sultans of Mandara used to exchange gifts. But according to Marwa traditions, Mandara used to send occasional tribute to Lamße Marwa.
65. Yola traditions.
66. Garua traditions.
67. Strumpell, p. 50.
68. Liman Ngaundere Isa, 'Tarihi Ngaundere', May 1967, EMC.
69. E. Mohamadou, 'L'Histoire des lamidats de Tchamba et Tibati', *Abbia*, 6 (August 1964), 16-58, see p. 44.
70. Mohamadou, *Abbia*, 6 (1964).
71. Strumpell, p. 51.
72. Liman Ngaundere Isa.
73. Mohamadou, *Abbia*, 6 (1964), 38.
74. Ibid., p. 144.
75. S. H. P. Vereker, 'Notes on the History of Koncha and Banyo', Partition of the Cameroun, 1919-30, NNAK, K.5, p. 50.
76. Ibrahim Hammawa, 'Tarihi Koncha e Banyo', June 1967, ELM.
77. Migeod, p. 15.
78. J. M. Fremantle, 'The Fulani: Collected Papers & Correspondence', 1910-34, NNAK, J.2, p. 4.
79. Migeod, pp. 15-16.
80. 'Tarihi Rai Buba', version officiale, EMC.
81. Ibid.
82. Strumpell, p. 68.
83. 'Tarihi Rai Buba'.
84. Migeod, p. 17.
85. M. McCulloch, 'The Tikar', *The Peoples of Central Cameroun*, (London, 1954), p. 24.
86. Liman Ngaundere Isa, see also Strumpell, p. 28.
87. Strumpell, p. 51.
88. See bibliography in Last, *Caliphate*, p. 23ff.
89. See M. G. Smith, *Government in Zazzau 1800-1950*, (London, 1960) for an insight into the nature of the Fulße government in Zaria and the Häße one which it replaced, but which continued to function at Abuja.
90. Yola and Song traditions.
91. M. Hiskett, 'Kitab al-Farq: a work on the Habe kingdoms attributed to Uthman dan Fodio', *BSOAS*, 23, 3 (1960), 558-79.
92. For the role of the Mōdibbo in the government of Fombina, see S. Abubakar, 'The foundation of an Islamic scholastic community in Yola', *Kashim Ibrahim Library Bulletin* (ABU), 5, 2, (Dec. 1972), 2-16, see pp. 9-12.
93. Yola traditions.
94. Yola traditions. See also D. M. Last, 'Notes' in Adamawa File, NHRS.
95. See D. Stenning, *Savannah Nomads*, (London, 1959), p. 28.
96. Ibrahim Dodo, 'Tarihin Maiha', NHRS.
97. Yola traditions.

98. Various Nasarawo Misc. Papers, 1925-37, NNAK, G.2, 2, p. 123.

99. In Fulɓe society, a father has as little as possible to do with his first born (*Afo* or *Arano*), neither calling him by name or sitting with him. If he wishes to give him something it has to be through a third party. This avoidance is complex and coupled with 'a strong sense of obligation'. East, *Stories*, p. 128.

100. Nasarawo Misc. Papers, p. 123; Chamba traditions.

101. Jada traditions.

102. Garwa traditions.

103. H. Bassoro, 'Un manuscrit peul sur *L'Histoire de Garou*', *Abbia*, 8 (Feb./Mar. 1965), 45-75, see p. 55.

104. Ibid., p. 59.

105. Garwa traditions, June 1969.

106. Bassoro, p. 59.

107. Strumpell, p. 45.

108. Boyle, p. 53.

109. See El-Masri, *Bayān Wūjub*, on the law concerning running away in the face of the enemy in jihad.

110. Boyle.

111. Strumpell, p. 18.

112. Mubi, Yawa, and Uba traditions.

113. Migeod, p. 17.

114. According to Brackenbury, 'Cameroun: Assumption of Administration', 1915-17 NNAK, K.2, p. 3, the chief of Rai-Buba 'wields a kind of paternal despotism which appears to be most efficient and successful'.

115. Migeod, p. 17.

116. 'Tarihi Rai-Buba'.

117. Strumpell, p. 70.

118. 'Tarihi Rai-Buba'.

119. Ibid.; Migeod, p. 18.

120. Migeod.

121. According to Song traditions, these were Lamɗo Hamman Song, Arɗo Dembo of Malabu, Lamɗo Cheboa Atiku, and Lamɗo Marwa.

122. Migeod, p. 14: Yola traditions.

4. Expansion, Consolidation, and Conflicts: 1847–72

Following the death of Mōdibbo Adama in 1847, his eldest son, Muhammad Lawal, became the Lāmīɗo. In his time, the early *ad hoc* administration established by the Mōdibbo was developed through the creation of new offices for entirely new tasks. The emirate government became more and more elaborate as clients and kinsmen were appointed to key positions. The reign of the Lāmīɗo Muhammad Lawal was marked by territorial expansion by conquest and the extension of Fulɓe influence through friendly contacts. This period was also remarkable for the spread of Islam and the growth of an Islamic scholastic community. Nevertheless, the basic problem, that of establishing a strong centralized administration based in Yola, remained. The Lamɓe of the sub-emirates remained basically loyal to the Lāmīɗo, but the more powerful ones in the south continued to challenge his overlordship from time to time.

Economic problems also arose. The destruction of the old symbiosis between Fulɓe nomads and non-Fulɓe farmers meant that the Fulɓe had to seek new means of existence. This was also a cultural problem in the sense that the code of Pulāku was not suited to the new political, social, and economic position of the Fulɓe. Undoubtedly, Fulɓe society was undergoing a revolution, and, as in all revolutions, there were bound to be problems and difficulties in its way.

Relations between the Lāmīɗo and the Lamɓe of the sub-emirates began to take shape in the reign of Muhammad Lawal. Similarly, relations with Sokoto, the suzerain, became more defined. Contact with outside regions, which was hitherto limited, was followed by a phenomenal development in commerce with Borno and Hausaland. Prospects for trade, settlement, and grazing facilities in turn led to an unprecedented migration of nomadic Fulɓe, and Hausa and Kanuri traders into the emirate. By the beginning of the third quarter of the nineteenth century, a complex society had developed in Yola.

THE ACCESSION OF MUHAMMAD LAWAL

One of the problems posed by the death of Mōdibbo Adama in 1847 was the question of selecting a new leader. There were two groups among whom a

G

possible successor could be found: the children of the Mōdibbo and the Arɗo'en of the sub-emirates. The two groups had equal rights to succession. According to the principles of leadership inheritance among the Ful6e, only the Mau6e had the right to select a suitable candidate to succeed as an Arɗo. The successor could be from among the Mau6e or from among the children of the deceased. Mōdibbo Adama was the first Emir of Fombina, and the principle of hereditary succession was not established, thus his successor could either be from among the Mau6e, in this case the Arɗo'en of the sub-emirates, or from his children.

Among the Arɗo'en of the sub-emirates, those loyal to Mōdibbo Adama had the best claim to succession. These included Mōdibbo Hamman Gurin, Mōdibbo Hamman Song, Arɗo Dembo of Malabu, and Mōdibbo Jam of Cheboa. They had rendered considerable assistance to the Mōdibbo during the establishment of the nucleus for the emirate and they all belonged to the Wolar6e, the largest Ful6e clan in Fombina. Some of them were learned Muslim scholars and were widely respected. Of the four, Mōdibbo Hamman Gurin was the most eligible leader. Long before the jihad, he had been the most influential Arɗo in the Faro valley. He had studied and lived with Mōdibbo Adama, who eventually married his younger sister. However, the greatest disqualification for Mōdibbo Hamman Gurin was his age; he was over eighty at the time of Mōdibbo Adama's death.[1]

The two most likely successors among the eleven sons of Mōdibbo Adama were his eldest, Muhammad Lawal, and the second, Hamidu. Hamidu was the son of Yasebo, the sister to Mōdibbo Hamman Gurin, and had the advantage of support from his rich and powerful maternal relatives. Moreover, he was the most courageous and best educated of the brothers.[2] Muhammad Lawal's maternal background could not be compared to that of his brother, but he had the advantage of age and the honour of being the first-born of Mōdibbo Adama's children. Above all, he was the only son of Mōdibbo Adama who could easily obtain the support of the neighbouring sub-emirates and the small circle of officials in Yola. By forging matrimonial connections, Mōdibbo Adama had allied himself with powerful Ful6e groups of the Benue plains, probably to perpetuate the solidarity and understanding between his family and the Wolar6e leaders surrounding Yola. The three daughters of Mōdibbo Adama who were married to the leading notables were all full junior sisters of Muhammad Lawal. He could therefore count on the support of his powerful brothers-in-law in the event of a contest for leadership between him and his younger brother, Hamidu.

Fortunately, there was no open contest either between the Arɗo'en and the children of Mōdibbo Adama, or between the two brothers. It is said that Mōdibbo Adama, long before his death, had advised Hamidu not to stand in the way of his elder brother's succession.[3] Another source has it that Mōdibbo Adama had stipulated the order of succession by his children as a last wish. He indicated that Muhammad Lawal was to succeed him, then Umaru Sanda and Zubairu.[4] The omission of the second eldest son, Hamidu and his full younger brother, Bakari, is strange, although it has been suggested that it was a punishment for their mother's infidelity to the Mōdibbo.[5]

When the Mōdibbo died, Muhammad Lawal was away leading an expedition in the north,[6] so the Galadima and the Kaigama together with the other Yola notables appointed Hamidu as the interim leader pending his return and that of the other dignitaries, when a full meeting of Mauɓe would deliberate on the successor to the jihad leader. For three months Hamidu acted as Lāmīɗo, and on the day of his elder brother's return, he led a large contingent of horses and men in a military fashion to welcome the man whom his father wanted to succeed. It was an alarming sight. Muhammad Lawal thought at first that it was an expedition against him, but as the two groups were about to meet, Hamidu, holding a white flag, advanced to his elder brother and tendered his allegiance. The other officials and the Yola Mauɓe had no alternative but to do the same. Thus, Muhammad Lawal became the new leader of the Fulɓe and the Lāmīɗo of Fombina.

The accession of Muhammad Lawal was peaceful and smooth. Because of his brother's open allegiance, he had obtained the support of the leading Yola personalities. His appointment was significant; it marked the real beginning of a Ba'en dynasty for the emirate. Unlike his father, Muhammad Lawal was to become the Emir, not remain merely Mōdibbo and leader. Until 1847, Mōdibbo Adama was, in the eyes of the sub-emirate rulers, only a leader whose role was limited to being an intermediary between them and Sokoto. The concept of Emir embodies political leadership and authority over all clans and groups. The immediate problem confronting Muhammad Lawal was to gain the recognition of the Arɗo'en, the rulers of the sub-emirates, and that of the Caliph in Sokoto. The last was by far the most important. Without sanction from the Caliph, some sub-emirate Lamɓe would certainly challenge his accession to the leadership. So, when the Yola notables accepted Muhammad Lawal as Lāmīɗo, they wrote and informed the Caliph Ali b. Bello.[7] The following year, 1848, Muhammad Lawal visited Sokoto for his formal installation. Whereas in the case of Zaria, the Waziri normally represented the Caliph for formal installation itself, in Fombina a precedent had been set by Mōdibbo Adama, who had been installed by the Shehu in Sokoto, and subsequently, going to Sokoto for the installation of the newly appointed Lāmīɓe of Fombina became necessary to legitimize the succession. Muhammad Lawal also presented gifts (*kofnol*) to the Caliph before his installation and this too became the tradition for subsequent Lāmīɓe of Fombina. The gift from Fombina was set at the value of one hundred slaves.[8] In return, the new Lāmīɗo would be provided with a gown and a turban by the Caliph. So in 1848, Muhammad Lawal was installed *Amir al-Yaman* (Lāmīɗo of Fombina) by Caliph Ali b. Bello.

On his return to Yola, Muhammad Lawal faced the problem of obtaining the support of the sub-emirate rulers. The majority of them came of their own accord and tendered their allegiance, and others were invited to come and do so. But Arɗo Buba Njidda of Rai refused to come to Yola or swear allegiance to the new Lāmīɗo, although he 'maintained an otherwise friendly attitude'.[9] The new Lāmīɗo, apparently not satisfied, dispatched an expedition under Hamman Gabdo against Buba Njidda. But it is said that war was avoided because the Yola men were outnumbered.[10] Thus the independent attitude of Rai continued and the Lāmīɗo Muhammad Lawal had to content himself with Rai's friendliness, occasional deputations, and presents of slaves.

THE CONSOLIDATION OF FUL'BE AUTHORITY IN THE BENUE VALLEY

Lāmīɗo Muhammad Lawal inherited a reasonably secure emirate. The numerous petty chieftaincies had been overthrown and replaced by large and small sub-emirates. The fertile plains and plateaux, much prized by the Fulɓe as pasture lands, had been conquered and their non-Fulɓe inhabitants subdued or driven to the mountains. The most important task for Muhammad Lawal was the final subjugation of the remaining independent groups within the emirate, especially those in the districts neighbouring the capital. One such group was the Bata to the west of Yola. The Bata chief of the area, Zaro Dungye, had been forced to abandon the valley of Māyo Chochi when Mōdibbo Adama established Yola in 1841,[11] and to re-establish himself and his people in Wuroheme on the banks of the Māyo Ine, west of Yola. Mōdibbo Adama had also failed to subdue the Bata of Bagale. The Bata of Wuroheme and Bagale together with the Mbula were the greatest menace to Yola as well as to the nomadic Fulɓe. The region they inhabited was the country through which the vital trade route to the western emirates passed. But due to the increasing migration and settlement of the Bata, who were basically hostile to the Fulɓe, it became more and more difficult for caravans to use the trade routes without military escorts.

The area to the west of Yola was also important because it contained fertile regions suitable for grazing and farming, although as a result of Bata hostilities neither farming nor grazing of cattle was practicable for the Fulɓe. The Bata of Bagale under their chief, Geloye, resisted the assaults of the Fulɓe for many years. According to Barth, the Bata of Bagale 'protected by the inaccessible character of their strongholds, and their formidable double spears, have not only been able hitherto to repulse all attacks' which the Fulɓe had been making against them, 'but descending from their haunts, commit almost daily depredations upon the cattle of their enemies'.[12] Lāmīɗo Muhammad Lawal's first concern was therefore the consolidation of the position of the Fulɓe in the upper Benue plains.

In 1853, Muhammad Lawal led an expedition against Bagale, the third undertaken by the Fulɓe. The previous two had failed woefully because it was difficult for the Yola cavalry to penetrate into the mountainous region. The third campaign differed from the others; this time, Lāmīɗo Muhammad Lawal was determined on a long siege, until Bagale either surrendered or was conquered. In fact, Lawal had promised not to return to Yola until Bagale was subdued.[13] So he established the war camp (*sangēre*) called Takkande where he concentrated his forces. He also founded Girei as a base for the duration of the siege. While in Girei, prayers for the subjugation of Bagale, were conducted daily, a common practice on campaigns.

According to Yola traditions, after a siege of two months Allah answered their prayers and Bagale was at last conquered. The conquest appears to have been, in reality, the outcome of new military tactics. Barth attributed it to firearms which the Ful6e acquired.[14] This may have been so, but traditions indicate that prior to 1853 the inaccessible nature of the Bagale area was the most important factor in the Bata resistance; cavalry was useless and the infantry were not familiar with the routes leading into the mountains. In 1853 the situation changed due to the assistance of a Bagale woman who came to the Ful6e in search of vengeance against Geloye, who had abducted her daughter.[15] She was used as a guide for a night attack upon Bagale. A selected number of Ful6e warriors attacked and killed Geloye, routed the inhabitants, and set fire to the stronghold. In this way, the Bata of Bagale were subdued.

The conquest of Bagale by Muhammad Lawal was one of the most spectacular campaigns of the Fombina Ful6e, and is still recounted with pride by Yola historians. The victory was of profound importance. It marked the beginning of a new era in the western Benue plains, an era of Ful6e settlement and colonization. The environs of Bagale which abound in good grazing tracts were opened to the Ful6e nomads, and grazing camps emerged. Similarly, as more and more land became available, Ful6e settlements started to develop. In fact, Ful6e settlements in the area were encouraged by the Lāmīd̄o as a means of controlling the subdued Bagale Bata. The Sangēje, Takkande, and Girei, which were founded during the siege, were developed as ribats to protect the new Ful6e villages and grazing settlements against Bagale's future hostility and reprisals. Another ribat for the same purpose was established at Wuro dole.[16] The whole Bagale area was transformed into a district owned by the Lāmīd̄o but administered by his personal servants. The first administrator appointed was Lawan'Dan Goba, who was given authority over all the inhabitants of the plains north of the Benue river. Towards the end of the reign of Lāmīd̄o Muhammad Lawal, the Girei region became important as a centre for those learned men who had entered Fombina from other parts of the Sokoto Caliphate.

After the fall of Bagale in 1853, the Ful6e of Yola directed their energies towards eliminating the menace of the Bata along the valley of the Māyo Ine. Unlike those of Bagale, the Bata of the Māyo Ine valley relied not upon natural defences, but upon their ponies and double spears.[17] Their last encounter with the Ful6e was in *c.* 1841 when they were scattered from their bases along the Māyo Chochi. Retreating westwards, the various Bata groups re-grouped, regenerated their strength, and initiated a series of hostilities against nomads and isolated Ful6e groups. They plundered the Ful6e-inhabited areas and abducted cattle in organized bands.[18] Lāmīdo Muhammad Lawal was forced to act, and during his reign he conducted five campaigns in the region. Ultimately, he succeeded in clearing the Bata from the region east of the Māyo Ine valley.

The first target of the Yola forces was Wuroheme, the headquarters of the Bata, and it was conquered relatively easily, probably because of the dynastic dispute which developed within the family of the Homon. The Bata were divided into two factions: one was in support of Zaro Dungye, the chief in Wuroheme, and the other of his brother, Zaro Palami. The dynastic dispute led to the migration of the Palami faction towards the Benue in the west and the fall of Wuroheme to the Fulɓe. Following their defeat, Zaro Dungye and his supporters also migrated from Wuroheme to the south-west and founded a new settlement at Bawo. This too was abandoned because it was still vulnerable to Yola raids. Thus, the Bata moved to a new place they called Gabalwa. Their former stronghold, Wuroheme, was converted to a ribat called Ngurore.

The second stage of the campaigns for the clearance of the fertile plains was directed against the new Bata stronghold of Gabalwa. This too was taken and established as a ribat known as Māyo balwa. The Bata, in search of a more secure dwelling-place, moved to Kikan, then Nwamo and under a new chief, Dunama, they moved to Deniyobusa (Demsa-Mosu) which has been their main centre to this day. With the foundation of Demsa-Mosu, the Bata were able to withstand Fulɓe attacks up until the end of the nineteenth century. This was possible because of a number of factors. First, the Demsa-Mosu area is an extensive undulating region, and the new settlement was located in a commanding position – on a ridge seven miles from the Benue river. It was therefore possible to see all advancing Fulɓe raiders, so that they could prepare for any attack. Second, the Bata would scout for Fulɓe raiders. The third and probably the most important factor was their alliance with the Mbula, the riverain inhabitants of the area. The two ethnic groups combined their forces for defence against Fulɓe invasion. Nevertheless, Muhammad Lawal's incessant raids against them obliged the rulers of Demsa-Mosu to become tributaries to Yola, and up to the end of his reign, the Bata never failed to send their tribute of spears and horses to Yola.[19]

The military activities of Yola in the west extended to the banks of the Māyo Balwa. The two most important campaigns were against Bille and Gereng. During the Konu Bille, a Bata migrant from Njongum, Mai Kwodda, defeated the forces of Lāmīd'o Muhammad Lawal, but very shortly afterwards the Fulɓe re-mobilized and scattered the Bille forces.[20] Thus, the temporary setback was overcome. The only serious opponent whom the Lāmīd'o Muhammad Lawal failed to subdue despite several encounters was Mboima, the chief of the riverain Mbula.[21] Nevertheless, the Bata were cleared from the valley of the Māyo Ine and forced to retreat further west. The border of the emirate was extended to as far west as Gereng, Māyo-Balwa, Bille, and Deniyobusa. However, the Bata continued to disturb the lives of nomads and were regarded as a thorn in the side of the dynasty. Lāmīd'o Muhammad Lawal began to devise solutions to some of these problems and he did this by repopulating the fertile western plains for military, political, and economic reasons. The conquered areas in the west were distributed by the Lāmīɗo to his clients and brothers as fiefs. He also established a number of ribats manned by slaves. Jibiro-Wafango became the Lāmīɗo's personal *rumnde* (agrarian slave settlement), but the overall responsibility for the region was entrusted to his brother, Yerima Bakari, and his client, Lamɗo Kebbi Muhammadu. These two were to pacify the region and establish themselves as fief holders. Lāmɗo Kebbi Muhammadu was one of the leading warriors in the reign of the Lāmīɗo Muhammad Lawal. Little is known about his background, except that he was perhaps an immigrant from Kebbi who had entered the emirate during the beginning of the jihad.[22] He played an important role in the campaigns against the western Bata, either as the commander or in the company of the Lāmīɗo. During one such campaign commanded jointly by him and Yerima Bakari, Wafango was conquered. Yerima Bakari became the district ruler and Māyo-Ine served as the district headquarters.[23] From Māyo-Ine, the two commanders extended their conquest down to Māyo-Balwa which also formed part of the district. Lamɗo Kebbi Muhammadu became the administrator of both Māyo-Ine and Māyo-Balwa but subordinate to the Yerima Bakari.

Other important outposts established were Namtari and Ngurore. The former was governed by Rabiu, a client of Lāmīɗo Lawal, from *c.* 1858.[24] The other district, Ngurore, was entrusted to Buba Māyo Sudi, one of the warriors (*barāde*) of the Yola army. It served as a ribat against Bata infiltrations from their stronghold of Demsa-Mosu, ten miles away. Another district was established in *c.* 1857 by Jauro Dahiru, leader of a Worarɓe group formerly resident in Gudu, said to be the last holder of a flag given by Mōdibbo Adama. When Yola was founded in 1841, he migrated to the southern Benue plains and settled there with the aim of prosecuting the jihad among the Daka Chamba. But for three years he was badly harassed by the Chamba, and was forced to move to Jambutu and then to Paja in the Mumuye country. Here, he collected a large following and then returned to pursue the conquest of the Daka Chamba. He established Daka as his stronghold and began his campaigns, but for eight years he succeeded only in holding his ground.[25] Having failed to conquer the Chamba, Jauro Dahiru retreated to Silkan and then to Gijiro where, with the support of his Mumuye followers, he established by conquest the district of Māyo-Farang. He remained its ruler up to his death in *c.* 1863.

The districts of Māyo-Ine, Namtari, and Māyo-Farang were in reality created as a buffer between the regions occupied by the Fulɓe in the east and those inhabited by the unconquered non-Fulɓe groups in the west. Similarly, the settlements, Wafango, Gijiro, Ngurore, Namtari, Māyo-Balwa, Māyo-Ine, and Māyo-Farang, were military ribats, established for the purpose of checking the non-Fulɓe groups and protecting Yola from their menace. The clearance of the Bata from these new districts was followed by the establishment of grazing camps (*dumɗe*) and villages (*nguron*). Immigrant Fulɓe who had been moving into the Benue plains from the north were normally directed to settle in the western districts. As early as *c.* 1831, Mōdibbo Adama directed new Fulɓe immigrants to settle at Njobolio. In 1841, after Yola was established, the leader of the immigrants, Arɗo Buba, was appointed the chief (*lawan* – a Kanuri usage). Another local Pullo leader, Arɗo Halliru, was appointed the Lawan of Beti by the Mōdibbo. Finally, in 1843 when Arɗo Chuti migrated into Fombina from Borno, Mōdibbo Adama directed him to move from Yola to Gawi as the Lawan.[26] Lāmīɗo Muhammad Lawal adopted the same policy in order to consolidate the authority and position of the Fulɓe in the Benue valley. Thus, when Arɗo Tobi of the Bewe'en migrated from Madagali in the north, the Lāmīɗo directed him to settle at Namtari and he eventually became its Arɗo.[27]

By 1872, the western Benue plains became peopled by both Fulɓe and non-Fulɓe immigrants. The former belonged to different clans.[28] Those surrounding Yola were principally Ba'en and Ngara'en, while those in Namtari district were Yillaga'en and Kesu'en. In Māyo-Ine they were mainly Ba'en with some Kiri'en in the south-west. Māyo-Balwa district was predominantly inhabited by the Bewe'en. The non-Fulbe inhabitants were in two categories: free men and slaves. The former, mainly Hausa and Kanuri, were resident along the river valleys as irrigation farmers. Some of them were traders. One important immigrant group that came to Fombina was a large body of Hausa who had left Hadejia in order to escape the turmoil associated with the activities of the Emir, Buhari, who had rebelled against Sokoto.[29] Lāmīɗo Muhammad Lawal welcomed this group and allowed it to settle on the marshlands to the east of Dasin hill. The immigrants established their community at Hausare Dasin on the shores of *Wēndu* (lake) Gerwede.

The largest group of peoples in the western districts were slaves of the leading officials, members of the dynasty, and warriors. After the expulsion of the Bata, enslaved peoples from other parts of Fombina were settled in the west because it would have been dangerous to keep Bata slaves at work in their own country. The slaves were mainly Fali, Laka, Dama, and other captured inhabitants of the region south of Bagarmi and east of Mandara.[30] Once in the west, the slaves were settled in slave villages (dumɗe) and they served dual functions, military and economic. The latter, mainly farming, was for the benefit of their masters. In regard to their military function, the slaves lived in the ribats to combat and check the eastward incursion of the Bata. Similarly, during campaigns elsewhere, the dumɗe slaves were mobilized as infantry under the command of their masters.

THE EXPANSION AND POLITICAL DEVELOPMENT OF THE EMIRATE

By the mid-nineteenth century, the emirate of Fombina had entered a new period in its development. It was a period for the creation of security, the removal of other populations, the installation of dumɗe, the establishment of Hausa and Kanuri traders, and the exploitation of grazing lands. This was a period of real jihad and expansion of the territory of the emirate. In effect, the emirate consisted of a scattering of strongholds. These were of two types, of which the most important were the large ones serving as key points for general defence, protection of trade routes, and as points from which slaving sorties were made. In some areas they also served as points for protecting important grazing areas for the Fulɓe nomads. These larger strongholds were surrounded by unsubdued or semi-subdued farming communities, whose relationship with the Fulɓe strongholds varied from one area to another. The relationship with the stronger farming communities was war on an equal footing, the weaker ones were subject to periodic plundering for slaves. For the latter, the alternative to plunder was to accept Amāna thereby becoming tribute-paying communities, who provided foodstuffs for the Fulɓe centres and strongholds.

During the 1850s, an important change occurred – the number of food-producing slave farms was augmented. As a result, less tribute was needed but slaves were increasingly in demand. The development of exchange and long-distance trade speeded up as slaves were transferred from one end of the emirate to the other. The distance of movement enhanced the value of the slaves, and some of them were transferred out of the emirate altogether. The intensification of exchange attracted Hausa brokers skilled at this business, and the increase in the number of Hausa traders opened up new trading opportunities. As wealth increased within the Fulɓe system, the government of the emirate started to become more and more complex. It was no longer a loose organization stretching out to tributary groups which had to be handled with diplomacy. The main exploitable wealth of the emirate was increasingly coming under the direct control of the Fulɓe; hence, relations between the various Fulɓe groups became of increasing importance. Fief holders had to be accommodated, officers (*Sarki'en*) had to be appointed to control and conciliate, and above all, the whole process of rapid augmentation of Fulɓe wealth, whether by the Arɗo'en or sub-emirates, had to be balanced and controlled to prevent the whole system getting out of hand. In fact, one of the major areas of conflict was over who should be permitted to gather the ever more vital slaves from this or that area. Before the reign of Lāmīɗo Muhammad Lawal, the whole system was closely bound to the trade and grazing routes. The strongholds were strung like beads along a necklace of routes, with only here and there a stronghold with a large circle of slave farms around it.

By *c*. 1860 Lāmīɗo Muhammad Lawal had succeeded in consolidating the position and authority of the Fulɓe in the upper Benue valley. He then turned his attention to the region south of the Alantika mountains. The Vere and the Chamba inhabitants of the area had not been conquered in the reign of Mōdibbo Adama. The Vere of the north Alantika area had accepted the amāna offered by the Fulɓe. In the Chamba area, the jihad made little progress, even though the Arɗo'en of Dagula and Pakorgel had received flags from Mōdibbo Adama. The third Pullo leader, Jauro Dahiru, had also failed to subdue the Chamba Daka. Following the failure of the Arɗo'en to success-fully prosecute jihad in Chambaland, Mōdibbo Adama had appointed his son, Yerima Hamidu to conquer the region.[31] But he too was unsuccessful; he succeeded only in bringing the inhabitants of the fertile Nasarāwo plains under his authority.[32] Even then, a number of communities had retreated to the Alantika and Shebshi mountains in the east and south. From their new positions, they continued to raid Fulɓe settlements and nomad groups.

The intensive campaigns by the Lāmīɗo Muhammad Lawal, first in the west and then in the south, were motivated by the desire to establish districts for the members of the dynasty to administer. In the reign of Mōdibbo Adama, the Emir, while being the overall governor of Fombina, had little territory under his direct authority. For a long time, the territory under the control of the Emir was around the lower Faro valley and the regions immedi-ately surrounding Yola. Moreover, the territory was surrounded by the hostile and unsubdued Bata and Chamba. Thus, while Lāmīɗo Muhammad Lawal was consolidating the control of the Fulɓe in the west, his brother Hamidu was active in the south. the latter was aided by his nephews, Hammawa Alikura and Jauro Hamman Bello. Eventually, the Lāmīɗo came to their aid after the clearance of the western plains.

During his first expedition, Lāmīɗo Muhammad Lawal obtained the sub-mission of the Vere in the Gijiro area.[33] He led a second expedition against the Chamba stronghold of Limadi in the Alantika area. The campaign for Limadi was the toughest in the south because, as in Bagale, the stronghold was protected by mountains. After a long siege, the Fulɓe forces led by Yerima Sudi, the eldest son of Lāmīɗo Muhammad Lawal, attacked Limadi under the cover of night and burnt it to ashes.[34] The conquest of Limadi paved the way for the establishment of new districts under the control of the Fulɓe. Yerima Hamidu b. Mōdibbo Adama founded Nyibango which became the centre of the Nasarawo district. It comprised the lowlands north of the Shebshi highlands and west of the Alantika mountains.

The subsequent history of the area after the Konu Limadi is not clear. It is said that Hamidu's subsequent attempts to extend his conquest over the Chamba of Yebbi and Gurumpāwo were unsuccessful.[35] Nevertheless, some of the Chamba eventually came to regard the Fulɓe as overlords; this applied especially to the Chamba within the districts of Nasarāwo and the area surrounding it.[36] Those in the mountainous region were never conquered up to the beginning of this century. Thus, by about 1860 enormous territories were brought under the direct administration of the family of Mōdibbo Adama. The hostile and warlike inhabitants of the fertile Benue and Nasa-rāwo plains were either reduced to submission or moved to places where their threats were little felt. Above all, ribats were established to check their menace and contain them in the areas they inhabited. This enabled the Lāmīɗo to direct his attention to other problems, such as those concerned with governing and the expansion of the sub-emirates.

One of the great achievements of Lāmīɗo Muhammad Lawal was the firm establishment of Fulɓe authority in the Benue plains. Subsequently, he became more concerned with the jihad elsewhere within the emirate. He led campaigns against unconquered groups. Similarly, he sent aid to the Lamɓe of the sub-emirates engaged in the conquest of difficult regions. Certainly, this was in keeping with the functions of an Emir. But more important, by rendering military aid, Lāmīɗo Muhammad Lawal was showing the capability of the army under his command. The earliest example of this was directed against the Mundang of Lere who had threatened the authority of the Lamɗo Binder.[37] According to Strumpell, Mundangland was the home of Yerima Sudi's mother, the Lāmīɗo's wife, and so when the country was conquered Yerima Sudi was declared its ruler.[38] However, his appointment was only titular for he was not left behind as an Arɗo. It may have been that the territory was given to him as a fief.

From Mundang, the Lāmīɗo's brother, Umaru Sanda, advanced against some groups of the Dui, the inhabitants of the upper reaches of the Benue within the sub-emirate of Rai-Buba. The Dui had revolted against the authority of Rai-Buba, but Yola was not contacted for military aid. Thus the campaign by Umaru Sanda may have been a calculated political manoeuvre meant to normalize relations. After all, the allegiance of this powerful sub-emirate had never been strong. Alternatively, the campaign may have been a demonstration by the Lāmīɗo that he was in a position to aid his lieutenants no matter how weak or strong. Whatever the case, the main importance of the Mundang and Dui campaigns was that for the first time Yola had become militarily autonomous. She was no longer directly dependent upon the sub-emirates for military assistance during major campaigns.

Military aid and assistance were also rendered to the sub-emirates in Waila and Fūnānge, especially those bordering the Mandara kingdom. In the north, despite their initial successes, the Fulɓe found it difficult to extend their hegemony over the inhabitants of such mountainous areas as Sukur, Fali, Kilba, and Gude. In 1851, for example, the Yillaga'en Fulɓe of Uba had been in conflict with the Kilba of Gaya.[39] Similarly, the Yillaga'en in the Mubi area were hemmed in in the lowlands by their hostile mountain-dwelling neighbours to the east and north. Barth says that prior to his visit, Lāmīɗo Muhammad Lawal had sent his brother, Yerima Bakari, as the leader of a large expedition for the conquest and subjugation of the restless ethnic groups of the region.[40] In the late 1860s, the Lāmīɗo led another expedition to the same region. Advancing by way of Song, he subdued some Kilba groups in the west and reached Uba where he helped them subdue parts of the northern Kilba country.[41] From Uba, he proceeded to Mubi, where after a long siege, he subdued the Yawa and the Ba peoples. He appointed Arɗo Usmana as their ruler with his base in Yawa to consolidate the victory he had achieved.[42] He had also subdued the Fali who had been menacing the Yillaga'en of Mubi. However, the Lāmīɗo's greatest victory in the north was the destruction of Hina, the stronghold of the Matakam, the most warlike people south of Mandara.[43]

New sub-emirates were also established in Waila during the reign of the Lāmīɗo Muhammad Lawal. These included Burha, Basheo, and Dembo which were established by Yillaga Arɗo'en.[44] Others were Gasawa, which was founded by Arɗo Sambo but as a vassalage of Marua, then Bogo and Māyo-Luwe. The last, according to tradition, was founded after a conflict between Lawan Bakari and Buba Njidda of Rai-Buba. The Yillaga'en under the former appealed to Yola for autonomy and Lāmīɗo Muhammad Lawal directed them to settle at Hōsēre Bijal.[45] But because of the pressure from Lere, Tirene, Tupuri, and Jasing, they moved to Bantaji from whence they crossed the Māyo Kebbi to Lake Goptikere. The hostility of the Fulɓe in Binder compelled Arɗo Bakari to appeal to Yola for aid. Eventually, with the aid of an expedition from Yola they established the sub-emirate of Māyo-Luwe.[46] In the north-east, the Badua'en and Ngara'en Fulɓe were also extending their conquests at the expense of Mandara and Bagarmi. Eventually, the sub-emirates of Pette, Yoldeo, and Faddere emerged.[47]

In Hōsēre, expansion and consolidation were simultaneous. The main aim of the Wolarɓe in the 1850s was to consolidate their victories in the region between them and the other sub-emirates in the north, so that contact between them could be maintained. The continued survival of the Fulɓe regimes depended, *inter alia*, upon the flow of fellow immigrants from the north; once this contact ceased, Fulɓe authority was bound to collapse. The routes linking the north and south were also vital for trade which was becoming very important; if trade was to prosper, the routes had to be protected. Another aim of the Fulɓe was to expand to the south and east, so that eventually they could gain full control of the fertile plateau. By *c.* 1860, the Wolarɓe of Ngaundere began their southward expansion when they captured Yambaka.[48] By 1870 the border of their domain was extended from Yambaka to the pinnacle that separates the basins of the rivers Shari and Sanaga in the east. When the Laka of Uhom were subdued, the border of Ngaundere reached as far east as Māyo Kadei and Māyo Bori, with the southern border at Bertua.[49]

In the 1870s, the Baya who had been tolerating the passage of caravans through their territory began plundering along the trade routes between the Sanaga and Ngaundere. Alarmed by this new development, Lamɗo Abbo moved to protect the trade routes since trade was an important source of income. He decided to bring the Baya under his control and dispatched an expedition under Yerima Hamman Bello. The campaign lasted five years during which the extensive Baya country was thrown into disorder but was eventually subdued. Subsequently, the Wolarɓe encountered little resistance and so they advanced to the south through the valley of Libumbi and established a stronghold at Gaza.[50] It was from there that they advanced to the region of the Māyo Kadei.

To the west of Ngaundere the Kiri'en of Tibati and the Wolarɓe of Banyo were equally active in extending their domains. The dominion of Banyo extended well into Mbafum lands, beyond Māyo Liddi in the south. To the west, the border was Garbabi and the whole of the Mambila plateau region was considered part of the Banyo sub-emirate.[51] The expansion of Tibati was to the south. Barth claims that in c. 1848 Haman Sambo extended his expeditions as far as Mbafu and the Ibo country, and that at the time of his death in c. 1849, the influence of the Fulɓe and their dominion extended as far as the Bight of Benin.[52] It is true that the Kiri'en undertook many expeditions in the southern regions and that their rulers achieved power and fame as a result. Nevertheless, we know that the conquests of the Fulɓe never penetrated very far into the equatorial south. When Hamman Dandi of Banyo crossed the Mbam river and undertook campaigns against the Tikar, Bamum, and Banso, he was unable to obtain a firm foothold.[53] It was only among the Bamum that Fulɓe influence made some inroads, but this was not as a result of conquest and subjugation. The chief of Funbam, Njoya, appealed to Lamɗo Umaru of Banyo for military aid against a rival chief. The Wolarɓe of Banyo subsequently led an expedition, subdued the rival, and returned.[54] Thus, friendly relations developed between Funbam and Banyo. Njoya was so impressed with the discipline of the Fulɓe army and with the conduct of the Muslims that he embraced Islam and styled himself 'Sultan of Funbam'.

The conquest of the Fulɓe in the south stopped short of the equatorial forest for a number of reasons. Geographically, the extreme south differs from the area where the Fulɓe had established themselves. The rivers of the south, such as the Djerem, Mbam, and their tributaries, flow through forest land, with many islands which served as refuge centres for the local people because the muddy rivers formed effective barriers against the Fulɓe. The military strength of the Fulɓe depended upon their cavalry. They were able to advance in the Kadei and the Sanaga areas because their horses could tolerate the climate. Beyond these areas, their cavalry became less effective as the climate becomes harsher and movement difficult because of dense vegetation. Third, the Fulɓe, used to cereal food crops,[55] could not live on the resources of the forests such as cassava, bananas and other fruits. The main problem was that because of tsetse-borne diseases, the cattle could not survive in the forest region, and in any case the Fulɓe could not live on meat alone. The fourth and perhaps most important factor was the military situation of the southern peoples. They had for a long time been in contact with the Europeans on the coast and as a result they had acquired weapons with which they checked the southward advance of the Fulɓe who mainly used traditional weapons such as bows and arrows, spears and swords. According to Chilver, guns and gunpowder began to reach the southern parts of Fombina from the coast, mainly from the direction of Mamfe and the Banyang market as well as from the Bamilike markets, especially Bagam.[56] By the middle of the nineteenth century, the Banso had acquired guns.[57] Thus, the Kiri'en of Tibati were prevented from advancing beyond the banks of the Djerem river into the south.[58]

In another way, the Fulɓe inroad was blocked by changes in the political conditions of some of the people they had been conquering and forcing to migrate. The case of the Tikar is an excellent example. Before the Fulɓe invasion they existed in small independent groups, usually in mutual conflict. Fulɓe conquest in the mid-nineteenth century unleashed an unprecedented era of migration to the south and west but the Tikar, as a result of continued raids and pressure, instead of further migrations, united themselves, built fortified villages and with the aid of some Bamum groups, resisted further Fulɓe conquest.[59] The siege of Gambe, one of their strongholds, lasted seven years, and it was finally lifted when the Germans forced Muhammadu Lamu of Tibati to withdraw in 1899.[60]

Undoubtedly, the borders of the Emirate were extended very considerably during the reign of Lāmīɗo Muhammad Lawal. From north to south, the Emirate embraced the regions between the Chad basin and the northern limit of the equatorial forest. From west to east, the border extended from the Hawal to the Logone rivers, in the north, and from the Shebshi-Mambila plateau to the country of the Laka in the south. Apart from territorial expansion there were remarkable economic and political developments during the same period.

The Yola government inherited by Lāmīɗo Muhammad Lawal was a very small body, which was not really capable of administering the most extensive emirate in the Sokoto Caliphate. The expansion in dominion was therefore accompanied by an enlargement of the government. New offices were created for new responsibilities, and in effecting this, Lawal borrowed from the older emirates in the west as well as from Borno. One of his early appointments was that of a treasurer (*Ajia*).[61] As a result of flourishing economic activity in the emirate, it became increasingly necessary for the Lāmīɗo to appoint a custodian of wealth derived from tribute, gifts and taxes on trade. Thus, the Ajia was the officer in charge of the wealth of the government, and was normally a trusted and favourite slave of the Lāmīɗo.

Another important new office was that of *Shamaki*.[62] This was in response to the growth of the palace and the Lāmīɗo's estate. This office too was normally held by a palace slave. Among other things, his function was to supervise the supply of provisions produced by the numerous dumɗe slaves of the Lāmīɗo or sent as tribute from non-Fulɓe subjects, and to supervise the provisions transported along with the army during campaigns.

In the military field, there had never existed a standing army either in Yola or in the sub-emirates until towards the end of the nineteenth century. Rather there were a number of 'war lords' drawn from the officials and other notables. Each notable was a commander in his own right. Whenever an expedition was decided upon, the slaves in the farmsteads became soldiers. However, the most important military official in Yola was the Kaigama, who, like those of Borno under the Sefuwa, wielded tremendous power and influence. There were also leading warriors who were slaves of the Lāmīɗo, such as Madi Dakau, Kulangu, and Bakari.[63] Each of the military officials was in a position to command local expeditions. The major campaigns were commanded by the Lāmīɗo or by a senior official. For example, during a punitive expedition to Tibati, the command was entrusted to Hamman Njobdi, and during the campaigns in the western Benue plains, the army was jointly led by Yerima Bakari and Lamďo Kebbi Muhammadu. The control of the army during the reign of the Lāmīďo Muhammad Lawal was never entrusted to a permanent Lamďo Konu (better known as Sarki Yayi).

The emirate government of Fombina became more elaborate in the reign of Lāmīďo Muhammad Lawal and that of his successors. This may have been because the Lāmīɓe wanted to be real rulers and not just leaders as among the Fulɓe prior to the jihad. Even though the Lāmīɓe in Yola were Emirs in the eyes of the Sokoto Caliph, their authority was not fully recognized by all the Lamɓe of the sub-emirates. Outside the Benue plains and Waila, the Lāmīɓe in Yola were not able to break down the loyalty of the Fulɓe to the kindred leadership. Clearly the administration in Yola was not effective. Thus, the creation of new offices was designed to remedy this apparent defect. Apart from the Ajia and the Shamaki, Lāmīďo Muhammad Lawal established new offices in the Yola Emirate government including those of *Baraya* and *Majidadi*.[64] To the former, Lawal appointed one of his favourite slaves, Hamayel. A Bata by descent, he was the official closest to the Lāmīďo and therefore his confidential adviser on personal and palace matters.

Writing on the composition of the Yola government in the mid-nineteenth century, Barth indicated that there were a Qadi, Mōdibbo Hassan, a 'secretary of state', Mōdibbo Abdullahi, and a commander of troops, Arďo Ghamawa. Other officials were the Kaigama, Sarkin Gobir, Magaji Adar, and Mai Konama.[65] Undoubtedly, the increasing use of Hausa political titles was a result of closer contact with the western emirates of the Sokoto Caliphate, especially those in Hausaland. Mōdibbo Adama in his time had designated his officials in Borno fashion because of its influence upon the Fulɓe in pre-jihad times, and also because the Fulɓe, as segmented people, had limited political terminology to designate their officials. The tendency was therefore either to adopt Kanuri or Hausa titles for officials.

The government of the Emirate was decentralized not by design, but partly because of its size and basic structure. The Emirate was vast and its inhabitants comprised heterogeneous ethnic groups ruled by Fulɓe also of different clan groups. It was therefore not possible for the Lāmīďo to exercise real control over his 'vassals', the Lamɓe of the sub-emirates. In fact, some of the Lamɓe were more powerful than the Lāmīďo of Fombina himself. In the mid-nineteenth century, the three most powerful local rulers in Fombina were the chiefs of Koncha, Tibati, and Rai-Buba. Barth indicated that the last was in a state of quasi-independence and having failed to achieve total independence from the Lāmīďo in Yola, became opposed to both Yola and Sokoto.[66] Thus, up to the end of the nineteenth century, the Lamɓe of the southern sub-emirates, Banyo, Tibati, Rai-Buba, and Ngaundere, were in reality more powerful than the Lāmīďo Muhammad Lawal of Fombina, and only nominally dependant upon Yola.[67]

Structurally, the Yola government was headed by the Lāmīďo. By virtue of his wealth and the slaves around him, he was the most powerful person in the capital. He was surrounded by a large body of officials of different sorts. The first of these were the Lamɓe who resided in their respective sub-emirate capitals. By protocol, they were senior to all other officials. The second group were the officials of the Yola government (the Sarāki'en), in four classes: civil, religious, palace, and military officials. The civil and military functions were interwoven, and the officials performing these functions constituted the most important group in the government. Broadly speaking the officials of the Emirate government were divided into two groups: those who were members of the dynasty and those of Fulɓe descent. The former were collectively called *Yerima'en* (princes),[68] and they comprised the sons of the reigning Lāmīɗo, his brothers and their children. Each member of the dynasty was colloquially known as Yerima although only one of them was officially so designated, usually the Lāmīɗo's eldest son or immediate younger brother. The Yerima'en enjoyed the respect of the other officials and the generality of the people because of their royal descent and because of the possibility of their becoming Lāmīɗo in the future.

Muhammadu Lawal had eight grown-up brothers who were active in military campaigns and expeditions. They served as commanders during expeditions and punitive raids. Each of them had supporters and contingents of slaves in dumɗe from among whom they drew the men required for expeditions. The support and loyalty of the Yerima class to the Lāmīɗo were therefore essential. They could either be a source of power to him or a threat to his position, depending upon the Lāmīɗo's relations with them. During the reign of Lāmīɗo Muhammad Lawal, conflict within the dynasty did not occur. This may have been because its members were more concerned with establishing their position as the only legitimate body entitled to succession. Some Yerima'en held territorial titles. The Lāmīɗo's eldest son, Yerima Sudi, was appointed the ruler of Mundang after the campaign in the Māyo Kebbi valley.[69] Similarly, Muhammadu Lawal's half brothers, Hamidu and Bakari, maintained their positions as rulers of Chamba and Vere respectively. After the consolidation of the Lāmīɗo's authority in the western Benue plains, Yerima Bakari became its ruler with his base in Māyo-Ine. His elder brother, Hamidu, continued as the governor of Nasarāwo. Thus, the Yerima'en in Yola formed an important and powerful group behind the Lāmīɗo.

The officials of Fulɓe descent were appointees of the Lāmīɗo who had also the power to remove them. The two most important posts, the Galadima and Kaigama, were usually filled by men who had rendered loyal service to the Lāmīɗo. The two officials could be dismissed when they became sufficiently powerful to threaten the dynasty. Mōdibbo Adama appointed men who had not only rendered services to him but who were also his loyal supporters. Loyalty, being so crucial, became the main criterion for appointment in later years. One way by which the dynasty ensured that officials continued to be loyal was to appoint men who had some family relation with it. After the death of the Galadima, Buba Bamoi, Lāmīɗo Muhammad Lawal appointed the eldest son of Alkasum as his replacement.[70] Alkasum was a former servant of the Mōdibbo and a brother-in-law to Lāmīɗo Muhammad Lawal. Thus the loyalty of his children would never be questioned. The tenure of this post has remained hereditary up to this day. The two posts had both military and civil functions and their occupants became very powerful and influential in Yola.

The religious officials were the Imam and the Qadi. Unlike other offices, appointment to these was strictly based upon Islamic qualifications. The various Qadis in the reigns of Mōdibbo Adama and Lāmīɗo Muhammad Lawal were, with the exception of Mōdibbo Hamman Gurin, immigrants from the western emirates. Mōdibbo Hamman Gurin was relieved of the Qadiship when, following the pregnancy of his daughter outside matrimony, he sentenced many suspects to death. He was succeeded by Tongude who remained Qadi till the reign of Lāmīɗo Lawal, when he retired. He was succeeded by Mōdibbo Hassan, an immigrant scholar from Massina who, following one of Mōdibbo Adama's visits to Sokoto, accompanied him back to Fombina. He had stayed with Mōdibbo Adama in Gurin, Ribadu, Njobolio, and Yola, possibly as an adviser. After the death of the Qadi Hassan in *c.* 1855, Muhammad Lawal appointed another immigrant scholar, Muhammadu, nicknamed 'Bilkījo',[71] who continued in office until the reign of Lāmīɗo Umaru Sanda.

In the judicial system, the Lāmīɗo occupied a very high position. Each sub-emirate had its Qadi appointed by its Lamɗo, but the Qadi's court in Yola served as one for appeal (*wullitol*) in cases from the sub-emirates, especially on matters relating to inheritance, land, and capital offences.[72] The Lāmīɗo's court in Yola was the final one for all appeals, either from the sub-emirates or from the Qadi's court in the capital. It was also the only court that could pass death sentences after cases had been tried by the Qadi. Similarly, land disputes and conflicts among the Lamɓe were normally considered, and finally settled, by the Lāmīɗo's court at Yola. This also applied to land cases inside the sub-emirates but as there is no example of any such case having been referred to the Lāmīɗo, it was only a theoretical power. The power to sentence people to death was in accordance with the status of Emir, the only one duly recognized to do so by the Caliph. The court of final appeal was headed by the Lāmīɗo and comprised the Qadi and some selected mōdiɓɓe in Yola.[73] Once tried and sentenced by this court, there was no further appeal. But in a case where there was no consensus in the interpretation and application of the shari'a among the court members, Sokoto had to be consulted either for clarification or for its own opinion. In judicial matters, the sub-emirates recognized the Lāmīɗo's primacy because such matters pertained to religion (dīna).

The governing of the emirate was on feudal lines. The Lāmīɗo as the descendant of the flag holder, was its over-all head. However, the Lāmīɗo exercised real authority only over the district around Yola and the sub-emirates of the Benue plains. In the former, the rulers were either Lamɓe, such as those of Nasarāwo and Māyo-Ine, or Jauro'en, in the case of Pakorgel,

Dagula and Māyo Farang. Other local leaders were called *Lawan'en*. All were direct vassals and appointees of the Lāmīɗo who had the right to appoint men of his choice. Other important districts were Gurin and Girei: both were regarded as the Lāmīɗo's fiefs. The former was administered by his Khalifa and the latter by servants or slaves. In each district there were Fulɓe and non-Fulɓe residents; the latter lived as vassals either under their traditional chief or under an *Arnāɗo* (non-Pullo chief) appointed by the Lamɗo of the district. On the other hand, those Fulɓe who were nomads were governed by their traditionally appointed Arɗo'en who had to acknowledge the authority of the Pullo district ruler. The pastoral Fulɓe Na'i and the Fulɓe Shi'e were headed by Arɗo'en and Jauro'en or Lowan'en respectively, appointed by and directly responsible to the Lamɗo of the district they lived in. This general situation also obtained in the sub-emirates. The lowest men in the political hierarchy were Lowan'en, Jauro'en, Arɗo'en and *Arnāɓe*. They were responsible for their groups to the Lamɓe. Part of their functions was to collect tribute or jizya, as the case may be, from their subjects. After retaining their proportion, they sent the rest to their Lamɗo who in turn, after retaining his share, would send it to the Lāmīɗo.

THE ECONOMIC DEVELOPMENT OF THE EMIRATE

Before the nineteenth century, the external trade of the region was on a very limited scale, but Fulɓe conquest of the area and the subsequent establishment of an emirate with dependent sub-emirates changed the situation. Fombina became an integral part of an extensive Caliphate. Consequently, intercourse with its neighbours was accelerated. As Dr Barth pointed out, the Fulɓe in Fombina 'succeeded in giving to distant regions a certain bond of unity, . . . making the land more accessible to trade'.[74] Certainly the establishment of a single authority over the heterogeneous Fombina peoples facilitated the entry of outsiders. The Kanuri from the north and the Hausa from the north-west began to enter the emirate in large numbers in the nineteenth century and eventually dominated its trade.

The emirate was linked to Borno and the other western emirates of the Sokoto Caliphate by trade routes which also linked various sub-emirates. The route to Borno, which Barth followed to Yola, was through Sorau and the Margi country to Kukawa. It was Fombina's highway to the north and during the early years of the jihad it was well protected. During the conflict between the Felata and the Kanuri, there was a general fear in Fombina of a possible attack from Borno, and to guard against this, ribats were established in the northern Benue plains.

By the mid-nineteenth century, the importance of the route was purely commercial as trade with Borno had become fully established. Potash used by the Fulɓe for watering cattle was imported from Borno and in return, slaves, cattle, and ivory were exported northwards.

Trade in ivory became very important in Fombina in the nineteenth century. It was the leading producer of ivory in the Sokoto Caliphate and in 1885 alone, the amount of ivory exported to Germany was about 80,000 kilograms.[75] In the region north of the Benue, exports from Fatawel went not only to Borno but as far west as Hausaland.[76] However, the southern part of the emirate was the biggest exporter of ivory, and the sub-emirate of Banyo, situated between the watershed of the Sanaga and the Benue basins, acquired considerable commercial importance due to this trade. According to Ferryman, the ivory trade was in the hands of Hausa merchants, who bought it from hunters in the big markets of Banyo and Ngaundere.[77] Ngila on the river Sanaga was also an important ivory market in the south.[78] Other leading centres for ivory hunters were the valleys of the rivers Sanaga, Shari, and Logone.

Southern Fombina was linked to the west by a trade route which went by way of the Taraba through Gashaka, Bali, and Bakundi down to the Benue. The capital of Fombina, Yola, was linked to the neighbouring emirates, Muri, Gombe, and Bauchi. The route to Bauchi went through the Bata country, then along the valley of the Gongola to Gombe.[79] From there the route went via Gwaram to Kano. There were two routes to the emirate of Muri: the Mumuye and the Bachama roads. The former went *via* Māyo Ine and Chukkol to the river port of Lau on the Benue. The Bachama route, which was through Ngurore, was rarely used because of the hostility of the Bata and the Bachama of the western Māyo Ine plains. The most important trade commodity was salt, especially the brown salt of Bomanda which Muri exported.

The routes linking the northern and the southern parts of Fombina converged at Yola. The main link between the capital and the southern sub-emirates of Banyo, Tibati, and Ngaundere, was the Daka route. The Funānge route linked Yola with the sub-emirates of Marua, Guider, Binder, and Kalfu. From Marua, other routes led to Bagarmi in the east, and Borno and Mandara in the west. The other most important route was the river Benue, the natural highway that linked the emirate to the river Niger. Before the nineteenth century, the river was rarely used as a means of transport, but after the establishment of Fulɓe administration, it became a major highway for the Nupe who engaged in the slave trade, and the Kakanda who were fishermen and traders in fish. They travelled up the Benue to Garua fishing and acquiring smoked fish from the riverain inhabitants, the Djen, Bachama, Mbula, and Bata. The smoked fish was then exported down the river to markets in Nupeland and the Igbo country.

The rulers of Fombina, the Lāmīɗo and the Lamɓe of the sub-emirates, were particularly concerned with the trade between the emirate and the other parts of the Sokoto Caliphate. The trade routes were vital not only for trade but as a means of contact and communication within the emirate and with its neighbours. In most sub-emirates, there were local officials responsible for commercial activities. In Yola, for example, there was an official responsible for the collection of caravan tolls (the *sarkin karo*). There were also a number of market officials such as the market chief (*sarkin kasuwa*), chief hawker (*sarkin dillalai*) and chief butcher (*sarkin pawa*).[80] The sarkin kasuwa was responsible for the general control of the market, for maintaining law and order there. The chief of hawkers was normally appointed by the sarkin kasuwa and he was responsible for the upkeep of market stalls and booths. It was also his duty to collect a small weekly tax from peddlars and occupiers of booths and stalls. The sarkin pawa was entitled to a small portion of each animal slaughtered, and money from this went either towards market improvement or to the emirate. All canoes which were used for ferry purposes belonged to the Lāmīdo, and the proceeds from them were shared equally between him and the ferrymen.

Trade with Europeans (*Nasāra'en*) became important towards the end of the reign of the Lāmīɗo Muhammad Lawal, although European goods such as *turkudi*, striped Manchester cloth, beads, and salt had always been available. The first two were sold to the wealthier people in the emirate by Hausa traders[81] who dominated the commercial activity of Fombina.

Trade in the emirate was conducted on an advanced exchange system, *chēde* (cowrie shells), turkudi, and *leppi* (hand-woven cloth) being used interchangeably as currency. One turkudi was equivalent to 500 chēde, the cost of a medium sized elephant tusk. Two thousand chēde or four turkudi was the cost of a slave. However, the chēde were less acceptable than the leppi which was the Fulɓe currency of exchange.

Slavery and the slave trade in nineteenth century Fombina were portrayed by Europeans as the worst of their kind in the Sokoto Caliphate. In fact, it has been suggested that Fombina 'was looked upon by the Hausa states and particularly by Sokoto as the eldorado of the slave trade'.[82] There was certainly slave trading on a large scale in the nineteenth century. The emirate of Fombina was founded in a wholly non-Muslim region by a religious war aimed at establishing an Islamic polity by conquest. In Islam there is religious sanction for fighting those who refused either to accept Islam or to live in peace with Muslims, and a by-product of this fighting was prisoners of war who, according to Islamic law, could be enslaved.[83]

In Hausaland, the Muslim Fulɓe took over established Hausa states with highly developed economic systems of traders and merchants, and a monetary system. The situation was different in Fombina. When the emirate and sub-emirate governments were established they had very limited sources of income. The Fulɓe were not farmers and could not farm conquered land without changing their way of life. The jihad had created hostility between them and their previous suppliers of agricultural goods so they founded slave settlements to produce for them. Thus, the prevalence of slavery in the emirate of Fombina arose from economic necessity.

In the early years of the jihad, captives were put to economic and military uses, and they played important roles in the economic, political, and military life of the emirate. The Lāmīɗo acquired slaves in two ways: either by the conquest of pagans and rebellious *amāna'en*, or as tribute and gifts (*shāhu*) from the Lam6e of sub-emirates. The bulk of this tribute came from the large and powerful eastern and southern sub-emirates – Rai-Buba, Bibemi, Ngaundere, Tibati, and Banyo-Koncha.[84] The sub-emirates of Marua and Madagali in the north also sent some slaves. Barth estimated that the Lāmīɗo's tribute from the sub-emirates amounted to about five thousand slaves annually. The Lāmīɗo also acquired slaves through his expeditions and those of his leading lieutenants and brothers.

It was customary for the Lāmīɗo to send a tribute of one thousand slaves annually to the Caliph. A large number of slaves was also retained for the palace, the females either as concubines or domestic servants, and the males as personal servants, courtiers, and soldiers. Some slaves were given to the leading officials either as rewards for services or as gifts designed to obligate them to the Lāmīɗo. Ownership of slaves was not limited to the Lāmīɗo, the Lam6e, and their officials; warriors also acquired slaves during raids and expeditions in which they had taken part.

While slavery was prevalent in the emirate, slave trading was on a limited scale. The vast majority of slaves were not sold because it was in the owner's interest to keep them in permanent employment in the slave farmsteads (dumɗe); usually only unsatisfactory slaves were sold at the slave markets of the emirate. The Ful6e ruling class – the Lāmīɗo, Lam6e, and their officials – sold slaves in order to obtain luxury items brought into the emirate by Hausa and Kanuri traders.[85]

In all the sub-emirates, slaves were used by the ruling class. In the households of officials, the female slaves (*hor6e*) performed domestic jobs such as grinding corn to make flour, and the preparation of daily meals, thereby lightening the burden of the legally married women (*reu6e tēle*) who were superior to the concubines (*sulā6e*). Each of the reu6e tēle had a number of hor6e who did other jobs such as sweeping, spinning cotton, and plaiting hair. The male slaves (*maccu6e*) performed heavier household jobs, such as fetching water and firewood, but their real importance lay in the military and economic fields. Each member of the ruling class had farmsteads where slaves were settled to farm. In the environs of Yola, Chomyel Abba, Doulabi, Golomba, Langui, Wuro dole, Kirngabu, Konkol, Pette, and Yolel started as dumɗe, as did nearly all the villages in Namtari, Girei, and Gurin districts.[86]

The dumɗe produced most of the food consumed by the families of the Ful6e ruling group. Part of the food was obtained from the villages of the free non-Ful6e either as tribute or jizya. The agrarian slave settlers lived under a sort of contract with their masters. The latter owned the land and in this capacity they received the produce of the dumɗe. However, where a master was responsible for the upkeep of the slaves, he received all the produce of the farms. Alternatively, the slaves lived as tenants and they laboured in return for their occupancy, or gave part of the farm produce to the land owner. An alternative contractual relation was for the slaves to maintain two farms, one belonging to their master which they cultivated in the mornings and evenings, and the other, which was their own, they cultivated in their spare time.[87]

In the military field, slaves were the basis of the power of the Lāmīɗo, the Lamɓe and their officials. Even though a slave officer class such as had existed in Borno did not emerge, there were a number of notable slave warriors. The power of each official was determined by the number of slaves at his disposal. Thus the dumɗe were seen as the military garrisons of the leading officials of the emirate. The Lāmīɗo relied upon his officials to raise the necessary personnel for expeditions whenever required. At such times, each one had to lead his slaves from the farmsteads into the field as soldiers. Barth has indicated that many individuals in Yola possessed more than one thousand slaves and when occasion demanded they were sent into the battlefield. Thus, the dumɗe slaves served a dual function: they were farmers in the wet season, and soldiers in the dry. They also maintained their powerful masters in office, for the more slaves an official had the greater was his influence. The Lāmīɗo and the Lamɓe of the sub-emirates had the greatest number of slaves, necessary not only for their security but also for the enforcement of their orders.

Slavery in Fombina and the Sokoto Caliphate has been described as evil generally because the European understanding of it was associated with the American type – an advanced and sophisticated type of human exploitation unparalleled in history. In Fombina, indeed in the whole of the Sokoto Caliphate, the case had never been 'once a slave always a slave'. Long before the advent of the Nasāra'en it was possible for slaves to acquire freedom, wealth, prestige, and power. In Yola, for example, such offices as Baraya, Ajia, Shamaki, and Dan Rimi were held by slaves. Slaves were indeed put to work, but the forms of economic exploitation of the time were limited to farming, domestic jobs, and participation in campaigns; such duties were also performed by free men. The exploitation was not of the plantation type geared towards profit-making on a large scale. Non-Muslims were not enslaved arbitrarily, but either because they had rejected Islam or refused to submit to Muslim rule. After enslavement, the conditions and status of slaves gradually changed whenever they embraced Islam. Slaves occupied the lowest status in the social hierarchy of the nineteenth century but emergence from that status had always been possible.

THE SPREAD OF ISLAM

The reign of the Lāmīɗo Muhammad Lawal was remarkable for the spread of Islam and the growth of an Islamic scholastic community.[88] Islam was not widely practised by the Fulɓe and the autochthons of Fombina till the nineteenth century,[89] and there were very few scholars among the Fulɓe as the leading scholars had moved away from the Benue valley to lead the local jihad. During his reign, Mōdibbo Adama encouraged scholars including

Mōdi6e Tongude and Hassan to migrate into Fombina from the western emirates. Mōdibbo Tongude became Alkali during the time of Mōdibbo Adama, but Hassan refused any post. When Muhammad Lawal became the Lāmīd̃o, Mōdobbi Hassan was compelled to accept the post of Alkali. He was a noted scholar, probably a Tijjani, who after the conquest of Bagale in 1853, settled at Modire,[90] which subsequently became the centre for immigrant Malle Ful6e in the Yola area. As an Alkali, Hassan is said to have been exceptionally honest; he is remembered as the Alkali who, after a complaint from a poor man, tried and sentenced the Lāmīd̃o Muhammad Lawal. He was a noted Islamic teacher, but was unable to spread the Tijjaniyya because of its prohibition by the Lāmīd̃o Muhammad Lawal.

After *c.* 1840, the number of scholars migrating into Fombina increased considerably. This may have been in connection with the expectation of the emergence of the Mahdi as the thirteenth century after Hijra was coming to an end and the minds of scholars turned to the advent of the 'expected' generally believed to be in the east. Fombina was the easternmost emirate of the Sokoto Caliphate and one of the functions of its Emir was to keep the road to the east open for the emigration to the Mahdi when the time should come.[91] The Mahdist idea was so strong in the early years of the jihad that the Shehu Usman 'Dan Fodio and the Caliphs after him were concerned about the possibility of a mass exodus of the faithful to the east, especially because these were led by Muslim intellectuals and their students. The Caliph Abubakar Atiku (1837–42), in a bid to stop the drift of people eastwards, declared that the time of the emigration to the east had not yet come 'since there was still some good remaining among us'.[92] The other emirs in the Caliphate were also reluctant to allow scholars and their supporters to emigrate to the east. The Lāmī6e of Fombina not only prevented the emigration of scholars but were also not willing to allow those who had entered the emirate to proceed eastwards. Thus, in *c.* 1855, following the death of the Alkali Hassan, Lāmīd̃o Muhammad Lawal prevented the Massina scholar, Mōdibbo Muhammadu, from proceeding to the east and appointed him the new Alkali.[93]

The most notable scholar ever to have entered Fombina was Mōdibbo Raji b. Ali b. Abubakar. His father, Ali, is said to have been associated with the Shehu Usman'Dan Fodio a long time before the jihad. Migrating from Zinder, Ali had joined the Jama'a (community) of the Shehu at Marata.[94] He eventually married Rabi'a, the Shehu's niece, who in *c.* 1790 gave birth to Raji. Thus, Mōdibbo Raji grew up within the Jama'a first at Marata, then Degel, and finally Gwandu. He was taught first by his father and then by the Shehu before finally attaching himself to Abdullahi'Dan Fodio to specialize in *tafsir*. Raji developed closer relations with his last teacher with whom he settled permanently in Gwandu. The early activities of Mōdibbo Raji and his role in the Gwandu administration are not known, but in the reign of the Emir Khalil (1835–60) he became the chief Alkali and Na'ib, acting as the Imam of the Emir's mosque whenever the Emir was out of town.

Mōdibbo Raji decided to emigrate to the east in the reign of the Emir Khalil, a decision which may have emanated from his acceptance of the Tijjaniyya. When Hajj Umar b. Sa'id Tal visited the Sokoto-Gwandu area on his way home from his long pilgrimage, Raji and a number of men were initiated into the new sect.[95] For ten years he remained a secret convert, then in an open letter he declared his acceptance of the new sect and began initiating converts openly. The Tijjaniyya brotherhood was of an exclusivist nature and its doctrine was one of moral superiority over the other Islamic sects. The Caliph in Sokoto and the Emir of Gwandu, with their officials and leading supporters, belonged to the Qadiriyya. Thus Raji's adherence to the new and much more militant sect was an important break with the Sokoto-Gwandu intellectual tradition. After openly acknowledging the Tijjaniyya, Mōdibbo Raji sought permission from the Emir Khalil to migrate. His intention was to move to the east, perform the Hajj, and eventually settle on the banks of the Nile. Khalil was opposed to his emigration, but after the Emir and three of his leading officials had a similar dream on the same night, Mōdibbo Raji was at last permitted to leave.

In c. 1855, Mōdibbo Raji left Gwandu for the east. He was accompanied by most of his family, his students and their families. Travelling through Kano he reached Yola three months after the death of the Alkali Hassan.[96] He was warmly welcomed by the Lāmīɗo Muhammad Lawal who subsequently attempted, in vain, to discourage him from proceeding to the east. Raji left Yola in c. 1857 but was unable to continue his journey when he reached the eastern border of the emirate because of the trouble in Bagarmi. He remained in the sub-emirate of Kalfu and founded the town of Dinawo (religious town), waiting for peace in Bagarmi to continue his journey.

Four years later, Mōdibbo Raji is said to have declared himself the 'chosen of God' (the Mahdi) and eventually seized the 'temporal power from the hands of the Lamɗo Koiranga of Kalfu'.[97] It is unlikely that this interpretation is correct. The authority for the assertion is not indicated and a contemporary source indicates that Raji's emigration was not connected with the search for the Mahdi.[98] Moreover, it was common knowledge that the Mahdi would emerge in the east, the Holy Land, which the emirate of Fombina had never been. Similarly, the Mahdi's name shall be Muhammed and his father's Abdullah, just like the Prophet Muhammad. These basic facts were known by all Muslims and, as a Muslim scholar, Mōdibbo Raji must have known more than this in connection with the Mahdi.

In the nineteenth century, Muslim scholars were respected personalities. They attracted personal followers distinct from those of the rulers in whose territory they settled. Mōdibbo Raji was not an exception. The town that he had founded in the Kalfu sub-emirate and the community that developed in it were distinct by virtue of their Tijjaniyya inclination. Lamɗo Koiranga of Kalfu appealed to the Lāmīɗo Muhammad Lawal as he found the Mōdibbo too powerful for his control and too influential.[99] Muhammad Lawal moved to Dinawo in c. 1862 and prevailed upon Raji to return to

Yola. Mōdibbo Raji died there seven months later at the age of seventy two.[100]

Undoubtedly, Mōdibbo Raji was one of the greatest scholars in Fombina, and his arrival in Yola at a time when scholars were lacking opened an era of Islamic scholarship and laid down the foundation for a real Islamic scholastic community.[101] As a teacher, his most notable student was his son, Usman, who became Alkali Girei in the reign of Lāmīɗo Sanda. Other students were Hamma Joda and Mōdibbo Sufuyanu, a Katsina man, partly educated in Kano, but who eventually followed Mōdibbo Raji to Yola along with thirty of his own students. Thus, Raji was also instrumental in the migration of other leading scholars from the west to Yola. When he came to Kano on his way to the east, Raji stayed with Nakashiri, who, in *c*. 1857, also decided to migrate, and followed Raji to Yola.

Another notable scholar who entered Fombina in the reign of the Lāmīɗo Muhammad Lawal was Muhammadu Tan Moililal. He too was an immigrant from Gwandu but he had migrated before Mōdibbo Raji. As his name Moililal (literally: of the flags) implies, his father may have been a flag bearer, possibly, as Last suggests, the Sa'id b. Muhammad who died at Tsuntsua in 1805.[102] Following the arrival of Mōdibbo Raji, Moililal was initiated into the Tijjaniyya and subsequently became Raji's most devoted student. After Raji's death, he became famous for his *hadith, Tauhid,* and poetry. Described as an ascetic, 'a strangely austere, solitary man' who led a life of celibacy,[103] Moililal was a critic of people in authority for their love of power, pomp and ceremony. Another famous Raji student was Usman Badadi who migrated with the Mōdibbo from Gwandu.

By the end of the reign of the Lāmīɗo Muhammad Lawal, Yola had a flourishing community of immigrant (*wariwari'en*) scholars. Islamic schools catered for both adults and children under the encouragement of the Lāmīɗo. The scholars led independent lives; they shunned luxury and were not dependent upon the palace for their livelihood. Mōdibbo Raji never accompanied the Lāmīɗo on campaigns and he used to free the slaves given to him by the Lāmīɗo and his leading officials. The learned scholars owned farms where they lived with their students during the rainy season. Though the Lāmīɗo Muhammad Lawal welcomed scholars, he curtailed their activities. They conducted no preaching tours for conversion because it was feared they might spread the Tijjaniyya. He was also reluctant to allow the scholars to live outside Yola.

The Lāmīɗo's apprehension may have been due to the 'Agana affair'. After the death of Mōdibbo Adama, an indigenous scholar, Mōdibbo Adama Agana, renounced his allegiance to Ngaundere.[104] With the support of the Wolarɓe he declared himself Lamɗo Bundang, and Ngaundere failed to subdue him. He then raised a standard of revolt against Yola under Lawal, who reacted by leading a successful expedition against Bundang. Adama Agana was subdued and brought to Yola as a prisoner. Muhammad Lawal forbade the teaching of the Islamic political sciences (*Furu'a*) 'because it might enlighten the public by teaching them their rights and responsibilities'.[105] This aspect of Islamic education was seen as dangerous to the Yola establishment because it might lead to disrespect for constituted authority.

The spread of Islam in Fombina in the nineteenth century does not seem to have resulted from missionary activities by the Ful6e.[106] The study of Islam among the Ful6e, the protagonists of the jihad, became intensified as their power became more firmly established. In various sub-emirates, schools and mosques were established to disseminate the faith, and travel abroad for learning became the fashion. The foundation of an Islamic scholastic community in Yola attracted students from different parts of the emirate, who eventually moved to Sokoto and Zaria in the west or to the east to further their knowledge. By and large, however, the Ful6e identified themselves with Islam because it gave legitimacy to their wars and regimes. Where the autochthons were concerned, the cardinal point for the Ful6e was acceptance of their overlordship, whether by embracing Islam, or submission by the payment of tribute.

The first generation of Ful6e rulers showed greater interest in the dissemination of Islam among the peoples of the regions they governed, but later rulers showed little concern, probably, as Lacroix suggests, because of social, political, and economic reasons.[107] Certainly, Islamization by force would fail because it would breed hatred of Islam in the hearts of the conquered and subjected peoples. Nevertheless, Islamization was not totally neglected. The enslaved virtually accepted Islam while the conquered and those who had surrendered often embraced the religion. On the whole, however, the Ful6e rulers pursued a policy of religious toleration which allowed non-Muslims to pursue their religion and live according to their custom under their traditional rulers, but as vassals. Undoubtedly, this minimized the possibility of conflict between them and the non-Ful6e peoples. In some sub-emirates, the Lam6e drew their greatest support from the non-Ful6e peoples who, as allies or slaves, comprised the bulk of their armies. Similarly, the Ful6e rulers drew their concubines from non-Muslim groups. In Rai-Buba, Lamɗo Buba Njidda relied for support not upon the Yillaga Ful6e but upon his maternal relatives, the Dama.[108]

The Dama regarded Buba Njidda as divine, replacing their traditional deity. Even though Buba was a Muslim, he dared not refute the Dama belief that he was a god who would never die since the basis of his power and authority would have been undermined. How the various Ful6e chiefs regarded the non-Muslim peoples varied from one region to another, but generally, where the latter were loyal it was because they believed that the Lamɗo had supernatural power and ought therefore to be supported in order to avert misfortune and calamities. Lacroix suggests 'the pagan peoples of certain chiefdoms have regarded the Ful6e chiefs as divine intermediaries with the supernatural world, in a way so frequently encountered in the African societies of the region'.[109] Islamization of the non-Muslims might have led to an entirely new situation. The Lam6e had wide powers and spiritual hold over the local people without converting them to Islam.

EXTERNAL AND INTERNAL RELATIONS

The emirate of Fombina was within the Waziri of Sokoto's sphere of super-vision, but throughout the nineteenth century neither the Waziri nor any other leading official ever visited the emirate. Instead the Waziri had an agent who visited the emirate annually for the collection of tribute. Contact with Sokoto was also maintained by letters and periodic visits by the Lāmī6e. Mōdibbo Adama is said to have made up to eleven visits to Sokoto, each time carrying tribute and gifts to the Caliph. In subsequent reigns, it became cus-tomary for the Lāmīɗo of Fombina to visit Sokoto and pay homage after a new Caliph was appointed. The Lāmīɗo also went to Sokoto for turbanning on accession to office. (The selection of the Lāmīɗo was the prerogative of the officials in Yola, however, and whoever was nominated was accepted by Sokoto.)

Contact between the emirate and Sokoto was infrequent, due to distance and the poor means of communication. Thus, the Lāmī6e were free to manage their affairs without undue direction or interference from the Caliph. Fombina was politically isolated from the rest of the Caliphate, and geographically separated from the emirates of Muri and Gombe by the unconquered Bachama, Kanakuru, Lunguda, and the other inhabitants of the lower Gongola valley. Traditions do not speak of the emirate participating in the co-operative defence system of the Caliphate. When al-Kanemi was invading eastern Kano and the Borno marches, it was a joint army led by the major emirs that checked the aggression against the Caliphate,[110] and similarly, in the conflict with Bukhari of Hadejia, it was the active support of the leading emirs that contained the rebellion. In neither of these serious threats to the Caliphate did the Lāmīɗo Muhammad Lawal participate or send military aid.

There is no evidence of Sokoto's interference in the development of Fom-bina, and the Lāmīɗo Muhammad Lawal could have refused to pay tribute to the Caliph, thereby throwing off the overlordship of Sokoto. Muhammad Lawal, however, had nothing to lose by accepting Sokoto's theoretical con-trol. The majority of the emirs regarded Usman'Dan Fodio as an embodiment of Ful6e achievement, the man who had prayed and fought for religion (*dīna*) and in the end vindicated the superiority of Islam and its protagonists, and his descendants, the Caliphs, inherited this respect. Muhammad Lawal and his successors also had to maintain good relations with the Caliphs to obtain their moral support for containing the various Lam6e of the sub-emirates under Yola's control. Mōdibbo Adama had continued as the commander in the east with Sokoto's support against various moves by some Arɗo'en to obtain recognition as independent rulers of their domains. The loyalty of the

Lāmīɓe Fombina to the Caliphs continued undaunted throughout the nine-teenth century.

The main problem confronting the Lāmīɗo Muhammad Lawal was how to get his overlordship fully accepted, especially by the Lamɓe of the more powerful Rai-Buba, Ngaundere, Tibati, and Banyo all on the Hōsēre in the south. Structurally, Fombina comprised large and small sub-emirates, the majority of which were established through conquest by the leading Arɗo'en. The Arɗo'en were appointees of Mōdibbo Adama in that they were confirmed in the leadership of their groups and empowered by the Mōdibbo's flags to make jihad in their areas of residence. Relations between the sub-emirates and Yola had never been clearly defined. The Emir in Yola regarded the sub-emirs as dependent rulers whom he could appoint and depose, who had to send him yearly tribute and who had to render their allegiance from time to time through gifts and personal visits to Yola. Yola also claimed military levies from all sub-emirates for major expeditions and the right to send its forces to aid the Lamɓe in need of such. But the sub-emirs regarded the Emir in Yola as a mere leader and not sovereign. They had a free hand in the administration of their domains; they appointed local officials, made con-quests for the expansion of their territories, levied taxes and collected tribute from their vassals.

The Lāmīɓe of Fombina never enjoyed absolute political control over the sub-emirates. One reason for this was the military strength of Yola *vis-à-vis* the sub-emirates. Each sub-emirate was basically independent militarily. Thus, in order to exercise full authority, the Lāmīɗo in Yola had to command a strong military force capable of dealing with his sub-emirs otherwise his claim to ascendancy would be challenged by a powerful Lamɗo or a combination of Lamɓe. A second factor was the kindred differences of the Fulɓe. Those in the extreme north of the emirate were Bewe'en, and those in the north-east Ngara'en and Badu'en. The ruling groups to the south of these as far as the headwaters of the Benue were the Yillaga'en (to the east) and the Wolarɓe (to the west). There were also the Kiri'en and the Kesu'en, but the domains of the former were located in the extreme south of the emirate.

The main advantage of the kindred divisions was that it was impossible for all the groups to unite against the overlordship of Yola at a given time. It was equally impossible for Yola to impose its authority or exert its influence over all the different ruling kindred groups. Thus, against this background of Fulɓe kindred division, it was difficult for an effective centralized government to emerge unless it was constituted to reflect the basic kindred groupings. Even though the emirate government in Yola comprised officials from a number of kindred groups, a number of other groups were not represented.[111] Moreover, the leading officials in Yola were common men prior to the jihad; they had never been Arɗo'en among their kindreds. The powerful pre-jihad Arɗo'en were not retained around the dynasty in Yola. Even the main sup-porters of the Mōdibbo eventually moved away as rulers of sub-emirates, just like the other Arɗo'en who had received flags from Gurin.

Thus, when Muhammad Lawal became the Emir in Yola, the most powerful men in the emirate were the Fulɓe chiefs of Tibati, Chamba, and Rai-Buba.[112] The ruling group in each of these sub-emirates, and in others as well, belonged to a common kindred and the dynasties sprang from the pre-jihad leadership of each kindred. Therefore, the various Fulɓe groups within the sub-emirates recognized and accepted the authority of the Lamɓe because they had been in authority long before the jihad. In most sub-emirates, after the jihad, while the Arɗo became the Lamɗo, the Mauɓe became the officials, and the rank and file as a conquering group became socially superior to the conquered non-Fulɓe peoples. In Yola, however, neither the Mōdibbo nor his leading officials were Arɗo'en prior to the jihad, but the various Fulɓe groups had recognized no central authority. Thus, Muhammad Lawal had no strong legitimate claim to the loyalty of his sub-emirs and their followers.

The main political problem for the central administration of Fombina was that of replacing kindred group leadership among the Fulɓe by government of territory under the Yola dynasty. Muhammad Lawal was very much concerned with making his authority effective in all the sub-emirates and early in his reign he pressed for the sub-emirs to visit Yola to pay their homage.

Buba Njidda of Rai-Buba neither came to Yola nor swore an oath of loyalty to Muhammad Lawal; he showed complete indifference towards his overlord, and only obeyed the Emir's commands when it was in his interest. The Lāmīɗo Muhammad Lawal tolerated Buba Njidda's behaviour, but in *c.* 1865 when Buba Njidda died, he attempted to bring Rai-Buba under control. Lamɗo Buba Jurum, Buba Njidda's successor, was requested to pay homage to Yola as was customary when a new sub-emir assumed office. He refused, despite repeated invitations, and so an expedition, led by Hamman Gabdo, was sent against Rai-Buba. Fighting was avoided, however, and Hamman Gabdo returned to Yola.[113] From then till the end of the nineteenth century, Rai-Buba remained merely a nominal dependency of Yola, independent in all respects.

The rulers of the sub-emirates in Hōsēre, especially that of Tibati, began to emulate the example of Rai-Buba. Unfortunately for Tibati, however, the Lamɗo Hamman Sambo died in *c.* 1849 and a succession dispute followed which the Lāmīɗo Muhammad Lawal exploited to his advantage. Hamman Sambo's second son Hamman Tukur, who was in Tibati at the time of his death, was appointed his successor. The Lāmīɗo Muhammad Lawal blessed the succession and then divided the sub-emirate into two units, and gave the northern part, as a sub-emirate with its base at Chamba,[114] to Adamu, a brother of Hamman Tukur. This was, no doubt, designed to weaken the power of the sub-emirate and make its rulers easier to manipulate.

The rightful successor to Hamman Sambo, his eldest son Hammadu Nyambula, was not only overlooked but, on his return to Tibati from a long campaign, he was expelled to Ngaundere. Nyambula, a notable warrior, was not favoured by Yola possibly because as Lamɗo, he might have proved difficult to control. Hammadu Nyambula, however, was not prepared to forego his right to succession without fighting.

While in Ngaundere, Nyambula was reconciled with his junior brother and so he returned to the sub-emirate but remained outside Tibati at Māyo-Bali. As a favourite Jauro of Tibati, on account of bravery shown in his many expeditions, the leading warriors and his brother's courtiers flocked to his camp. Even the few who remained with Hamman Tukur were morally behind Hammadu Nyambula. He had also the support of the Mbum, Bute, and Tikar. Having mobilized a formidable force, Hammadu Nyambula attacked Tibati in *c.* 1851. The Lamɗo Hamman Tukur was killed and Nyambula became ruler. In *c.* 1853, he led another expedition against his other brother, Lamɗo Adamu of Chamba, and defeated and killed him. Buba Dadi, a full brother of Hammadu Nyambula, was appointed the Khalifa in charge of Chamba.

Having ascended to the sub-emirship of Tibati and re-united the sub-emirate, Hammadu Nyambula turned his attention to the relations with Yola and with his neighbours. Tibati, a Kiri'en sub-emirate, had been co-operating fully with its neighbours, Banyo and Ngaundere, in their conquests. But in the 1850s the early co-operation gave way to conflicts arising from jealousy. Tibati and Ngaundere were in conflict over the administration of Ngan-Ha and Mbang. These had been conquered jointly by Ngaundere, Tibati, and Rai-Buba. The areas were therefore administered as common territory.[115] However, when Isa succeeded his father, Hamman Njobdi, as Lamɗo Ngaundere, he began to treat these areas as part of his sub-emirate, thereby disregarding the claims of Tibati and Rai-Buba. Tibati sent its Kaigama at the head of an expedition which attacked and destroyed Ngaundere. Tibati led a second expedition against Ngaundere but was routed at Mbi'i Pakala by Lamɗo Isa. This began the era of rivalry between the two sub-emirates which continued till the end of the nineteenth century.

There was conflict also between Tibati and its western neighbour, Banyo. Nyambula of Tibati led an expedition against Banyo when its Lamɗo, Usman, was busy in a campaign against the Baya, and devastated the town. Lamɗo Usman, on his return, invaded Tibati but was badly routed by Hammadu Nyambula at Māyo-Mbamti. Even though the reasons behind Nyambula's activities are not clear, it appears that he wanted to weaken the position of the sub-emirates neighbouring Tibati so that he would emerge the most powerful Pullo ruler in the south. The activities of Hammadu Nyambula of Tibati against his neighbours undoubtedly affected the good relations that had previously existed between the Ful6e ruling groups of the south.

The next phase of Hammadu Nyambula's activity was directed against Yola. Traditions compare Hammadu of Tibati with Bukhari of Hadejia who rebelled against the Caliph, and indeed at the time of the Tibati rebellion, Hammadu is said to have obtained aid and counsel from Hadejia.[116]

In a bid to punish his 'vassal' for his rebellion, the Lāmīɗo Muhammad Lawal separated Tinger, the northern part of Tibati, from the south by recognizing its chief as autonomous.[117] The Tinger region was vital to Tibati as its extensive Fulkumre plateau was a very fertile grazing region. At the time of the invasion of Hōsēre, Hamman Sambo Tibati had allowed Hammadu Njikira to settle on the Fulkumre plateau, but in *c.* 1849, following the death of Hamman Sambo, Hammadu Njikira revolted and declared Tinger independent of Tibati. When Hammadu Nyambula became the chief of Tibati in *c.* 1851 and brought Chamba under his control in 1853, he moved against the Tinger rebels. The region was devastated and the leading notables, including Hammadu Njikira, were captured. It was as a result of this expedition that the Fulɓe of Tinger appealed to the Lāmīɗo Muhammad Lawal to intervene. His order for the release of the Fulɓe captives was ignored; instead, Hammadu Nyambula had them executed. Following this barbaric act, the Lāmīɗo Muhammad Lawal gave Lawan Bakari a flag in *c.* 1860 and appointed him Lamɗo Tinger. Hammadu Nyambula of Tibati, however, continued to harass the Tinger Fulɓe and in *c.* 1863 he attacked and destroyed Jiga, the capital of the new sub-emirate, capturing Lamɗo Bakari and his leading lieutenants.[118]

One of the consequences of the 'Tinger affair' was war between Tibati and Yola. Hammadu Nyambula, expecting an attack from the Lāmīɗo, began to prepare, and refused the frequent summons to Yola for fear that he might be deposed and banished.

The choice before him was either to prepare and meet any attack from Yola or avoid a battle-field encounter. Militarily, Tibati was powerful enough to withstand any expedition which comprised Yola forces alone, but a Yola expedition was likely to include forces from practically all the sub-emirates which were loyal to the Lāmīɗo. Tibati on the other hand had nowhere to look for aid – Hammadu Nyambula had alienated his eastern and western neighbours and so could not expect their sympathy. Consequently, he decided to avoid a confrontation with Yola.

Hammadu Nyambula, following advice from Buba Njidda of Rai-Buba, fortified his stronghold in readiness for the inevitable expedition from Yola. All food-bearing trees were destroyed, and the inhabitants of the surrounding districts were moved into the capital with all their possessions. Finally, he built three lines of trenches outside the walls of the capital.[119] As a result of these fortifications, the expedition, led by the Lāmīɗo Muhammad Lawal himself, failed to enter Tibati; and after a long siege, they retired because of lack of food and water. For a time, Tibati, like Rai-Buba before it, succeeded in becoming fully autonomous. Its ruler continued his activities against the Fulɓe and the Hāɓe without the restraining influence of Yola.

The Lāmīɗo Muhammad Lawal did not abandon his attempt to re-integrate Tibati with the rest of the emirate. After the failure of his first expedition, he led a second one which comprised not only the Yola army but forces from Ngaundere and Banyo led by their respective Lamɓe. With this massive force behind him, Lāmīɗo Lawal met Hammadu Nyambula and the most fierce battle between the Fulɓe took place in the neighbourhood of Tibati. However, victory again eluded the Lāmīɗo, because Nyambula caused the break-up of the grand army by 'fraud, guile and lying'.[120] It has been said that during the siege of Tibati, Hammadu Nyambula sent an elephant tusk and slaves to Lamɗo Isa with the message, 'once I am captured, the Yola men shall appoint their children in Tibati; then they turn to you, subdue you and install another of their children; then our children will become common men'.[121] The Lamɗo Isa of Ngaundere feared that this might be true, and he and the chief of Banyo deserted the battle-field. With the desertion of Ngaundere and Banyo, the Lāmīɗo Muhammad Lawal was left with only the forces from Yola to withstand the superior army of Tibati. Faced also with mounting famine, he had no alternative than to retreat.

The Lāmīɗo Muhammad Lawal's failure to stop Tibati's move towards greater autonomy had serious consequences. First, the shaky authority of the Lāmīɗo over the southern sub-emirates was further weakened. Hammadu Nyambula's victory proved that it was possible to challenge the Lāmīɗo's overlordship and acquire greater autonomy by military means. Second, it demonstrated Yola's military weakness and the Lāmīɗo's reliance upon the sub-emirates for aid and support during major expeditions.

Hammadu Nyambula, however, did not declare himself independent. He continued to regard the Lāmīɗo of Fombina as a superior authority, especially on matters pertaining to the Shari'a. His rebellion was not aimed at secession, but to obtain the succession which had been denied him and then to govern the whole of Tibati sub-emirate. According to Yola traditions, he eventually sought and obtained reconciliation with the Lāmīɗo Muhammad Lawal, to whom he reaffirmed his loyalty, and resumed the dispatch of tribute and gifts to Yola.

Another challenge to the authority of the Lāmīɗo Muhammad Lawal came from the Wolarɓe of Bundang, a northern district of the sub-emirate of Ngaundere. Following the invasion of Hōsēre in the 1830s, the Bundang area was left in the charge of Mōdibbo Adama Agana, who continued in this position even when Ngaundere was developed as the sub-emirate capital. However, after the death of Hamman Njobdi, the Lamɗo Ngaundere, Mōdibbo Adama Agana, in *c.* 1845, declared the independence of Bundang. The subsequent attempts by Hamma Lamu to subdue him and regain control of Bundang were to no avail. Encouraged by his success, Adama Agana's ambition widened. It is said that he declared Bundang independent of Yola by raising the old flag which the Wolarɓe had received from Buba Yero of Gombe.[122] He also appealed to all the Wolarɓe to rally behind him.

This rebellion was very serious, since Bundang was an important pre-jihad Wolarɓe centre and any move from there was bound to have serious repercussions in other Wolarɓe areas. The raising of the old flag received from Buba Yero was the culmination of various moves by the Wolarɓe to free themselves from the control of the Ba'en.

Mōdibbo Adama Agana, a scholar educated in Borno, may have thought he was best qualified to head the emirate of Fombina. Mōdibbo Adama had been selected as the jihad leader by virtue of his Islamic learning, and after his death, another leading scholar should succeed.[123] The Lāmīɗo Muhammad Lawal was not a scholar; his appointment had not been on the basis of consultation, and he had been appointed unilaterally by Yola since the scholars outside Yola and the sub-emirs had not been consulted.

The Bundang rebellion was also a serious threat to Ngaundere, to whom control in Bundang was synonymous with control in Ngaundere itself. It was feared that Mōdibbo Adama Agana, because of his prestige as a scholar who possessed mystical powers, would rally sufficient support among the Wolarɓe to topple the house of Hamman Njobdi from the leadership of the sub-emirate.[124] At first, the Lāmīɗo Muhammad Lawal was reluctant to intervene since it was a vassal whose loyalty was shaky that was threatened. But by raising the Gombe flag, Adama Agana had gone too far.

Fearing that other Fulɓe kindred groups and scholars might emulate Adama Agana's example, the Lāmīɗo, accompanied by Hamma Lamu of Ngaundere, led an expedition against Bundang, which capitulated after fierce fighting. Adama Agana was arrested and taken to Yola, where after a period of confinement, he was set free and lived as a teacher. In order to guard against a similar occurrence, Hamma Lamu appointed his brother as the ruler of Bundang.

Rai-Buba, Tibati, Banyo, and Ngaundere selected their own rulers whom Yola had to endorse. The only real connection with Yola was common allegiance to Sokoto and so each of the four sub-emirates sent a tribute of about one thousand slaves annually to the Lāmīɗo and the Caliph. Lāmīɗo Fombina's authority in Rai-Buba and Tibati had never been strong. Banyo and Ngaundere, however, had never faltered in their loyalty to Yola, and the 'Agana affair' appears to have improved relations between Ngaundere and Yola. Banyo's reason for dependence on Yola was its internal disunity. The sub-emirate was not contiguous; its first base was Laro, then Koncha, and finally Banyo, and each of the three bases had a ruler. Mōdibbo Adama had appointed the ruler of Laro as a flag bearer, and thus, the Lamɗo Hamma Joda of Laro was independent of Hamman Dandi who became the chief of Banyo and Koncha. When Hamman Dandi died in *c.* 1864, his successors found it difficult to continue as rulers of both areas, especially when another base, Gashaka, was established. Banyo, as capital, was ruled by Usman, and his brothers ruled in Koncha and Gashaka as subordinate chiefs, but, after the death of Lamɗo Usman, the unity of the sub-emirate under a single leadership disappeared, and a succession dispute developed between Usman's brothers and his sons. The sub-emirate government of Banyo, therefore, unlike that of Tibati and Rai-Buba, was not strong enough to challenge the authority of the Lāmīɗo of Fombina.

The weak authority of the Lāmīɗo of Fombina over the sub-emirates in the south can be attributed to lack of contiguity. In fact, there were no strict frontiers between the sub-emirates, and the dominion of the Fulɓe consisted of graduated spheres of influence. Large areas between the Benue plains and

I

Hōsēre were not conquered while some conquered groups in the same region, such as those of the Galim hills,[125] regained their independence after further advance of the Fulɓe to the south. Also, the capitals of the southern sub-emirates were separated from Yola by great distances, thereby limiting the possibility of contacts between the Lāmīɗo and his vassals.

However, the greatest factor in the continued nominal overlordship of Yola was the balance of power among the sub-emirates. The rulers of the southern sub-emirates mistrusted one another; each feared the growing power of the other, especially when Hammadu Nyambula became the ruler of Tibati in c. 1849. Consequently, there were intense conflicts and rivalry between the sub-emirates, particularly in the period 1840 to 1872.[126] The Lamɓe of the south never fully succeeded in throwing off their allegiance to Yola, and co-operated with each other only in refusing to render military assistance to Yola against one of their number.

In Waila and the Benue plains, the Lāmīɗo of Fombina had greater authority. There were no struggles for greater autonomy or rebellion against the overlordship of the Lāmīɗo. These sub-emirates were more numerous and each possessed limited territory, so the Lamɓe in that region did not become very powerful. The Lāmīɗo in Yola had the power to appoint and depose most of the sub-emirate chiefs in the north, but these rights had certain limits. In all the sub-emirates, the succession to *lāmu* became hereditary among the descendants of the founding Arɗo'en (except in Holma, where Yola seems to have had a free hand in the appointment and deposition of its rulers),[127] and the Lāmīɗo of Fombina could only appoint a member of the dynasty. It was virtually impossible for the Lāmīɗo to install personal friends, relatives, slaves, or servants as Lamɓe. Similarly, he could not depose a chief without the consent and support of the leading officials of the sub-emirate concerned. Under these conditions, the exercise of control by Yola depended upon the tact, prestige, and personality of the reigning Lāmīɗo.

The Fulɓe chiefs of the sub-emirates in Waila were dependent upon Yola for military protection against Borno and Mandara. There were no powerful states in Hōsēre and so there was no threat to the sub-emirates such as had been the case in Waila. The conflicts of the Fulɓe with Borno and Mandara were long standing and the sub-emirates of Madagali, Duhu, Moda, Michika, and Uba were in the region which Mandara regarded as its sphere of influence. Similarly, Mandara's hegemony extended over the region where the Ngara'en established the sub-emirates of Marua, Mendif, and Bogo. Its sphere of influence extended as far south as Māyo Kebbi where Guider, Bibemi, Māyo-Luwe, and parts of Rai-Buba had been established by the Yillaga Fulɓe.

Relations between Fombina and Mandara had been unfriendly since the outbreak of jihad. The sultans of Mandara had never completely accepted the establishment of Fulɓe rule in the Yedseram basin in the west and the Gasawa plains to the east, and in the early years of the jihad, the Fulɓe of the two areas had lived in constant fear of Mandara attacks. Since Mōdibbo Adama's expeditions had succeeded in checking Mandara, this fear subsided and thenceforth, their relationship with the mountain kingdom was characterized by a struggle for dominance over the inhabitants of the region west of the Logone river.[128] The Lāmīd̶o in Yola, however, was at all times looked upon for protection in the event of a serious threat from Mandara, and this need governed the loyalty of the sub-emirates in Waila to the Lāmīd̶o of Fombina.

The nineteenth century witnessed the ascendancy of the Shehus who had begun to rebuild the declining empire of Borno to its former position of power and glory.[129] Some early moves by the Shehus were to check the gradual encroachment of the Fulɓe from their newly-established emirates in the west and south into the heartland of the empire. The leading emirate in the south was Fombina, and its rulers regarded Borno as a very powerful enemy which was likely to invade the emirate at any time, especially since the frontier between them was undefined throughout the nineteenth century. The absence of well defined geographical features and the homogeneity of the population between Borno and Fombina made the demarcation of definite frontiers very difficult. The government of Borno and Fombina both claimed sovereignty over the Margi on their borders and Borno used to raid the northern sub-emirates of Fombina.

The aim of the Shehu Umar (1837-80) in the years before 1846 was to regain control of the western lands lost to the empire by *c.* 1830.[130] Between 1837 and 1840, he sent expeditions against Jama'are, Misau, and Katagum, and it was then, while his attention was turned to the west, that the Fulɓe established their sub-emirates in the south and south-east of Borno. By 1846, hostilities between the Fulɓe and Borno in the west ceased as a result of Umar's improved relations with the Caliph Aliyu Babba (1842-50).[131] The attention of Borno was then turned to the south and predatory excursions against the new sub-emirates of Fombina became common. During one such raid, Ramadan, a slave officer of the Shehu Umar, penetrated well into Fombina, and ransacked and plundered Uba. Similar expeditions under Kachalla Ali Dendal plundered the Margi region.[132] The Lāmīd̶o Muhammad Lawal reciprocated by sending expeditions into southern Borno.

The border between Fombina and Borno was not settled finally until after the British conquest; till then the petty Fulɓe chiefs in the area were in no position to check the continued Borno menace, and so they maintained a strong allegiance to the Lāmīd̶o of Fombina who gave them the military assistance they required.

NOTES

1. Yola traditions.
2. R. M. East, *Stories of Old Adamawa*, (Zaria, 1935), p. 71.
3. According to M. Ahmadu Marafa Yola, July 1968.
4. East, *Stories*, p. 85.
5. Fremantle.

6. Yola traditions.
7. Ibid.
8. Ibid.
9. Migeod, p. 18.
10. 'Tarihi Rai-Buba', EMC.
11. Bata traditions.
12. H. Barth, *Travels and Discoveries in North and Central Africa*, (5 vols., London, 1857), p. 479.
13. Ibid.
14. Barth, p. 479.
15. Song traditions.
16. H. B. Ryan, 'Report on Yola Province, 1911', Yola Collected Histories, NNAK, J.2, p. 92.
17. Ibid.
18. Gazetteer, 1936, p. 144.
19. Bata traditions.
20. East, *Stories*, p. 43.
21. Ibid., p. 65.
22. Yola traditions.
23. G. B. Webster, 'Mayo Ine Assessment Papers', 1912-22, NNAK, G.2, p. 4.
24. Namtari D.N.B. (from notes prepared by W. O. P. Rosedale, in 1916) and E. A. Brackenbury, 'Namtari Assessment Report', 1910-11, NNAK, G.2, W.
25. C. C. Dunlop, 'Mayo Farang Assessment Papers', 1913, NNAK, G.2, 2H.
26. Fremantle, 'History of the Yola Emirate', 1809, NNAK, J.2, p. 63.
27. Namtari District Misc. Papers, 1923-4, NNAK, p. 8.
28. See Rosedale, 'Namtari Dist. Re-assessment Papers', 1916, NNAK, G.2, 2W, p. 6, and G. B. Webster, 'Mayo Ine', p. 4.
29. East, *Stories*, pp. 79-90.
30. Rosedale, 'Namtari District', p. 6.
31. Yola traditions; also see Nasarawo District Misc. Papers, 1925-37, NNAK, G.2, 2, p. 123.
32. Yebbi & Gurumpawo DNB, Local Authority Office, Ganye.
33. Dunlop, p. 2.
34. East, *Stories*, p. 55.
35. Chamba traditions (Sugu, Yelwa, and Gurumpawo).
36. G. M. Clifford, 'Notes on Chamba Area Re-organisation', 1933-40, NNAK, G.34.
37. Migeod, p. 19.
38. K. Strumpell, *A History of Adamawa* (Hamburg, 1912), trans. mimeo, NNAK, J.18, p. 35.
39. Barth, p. 529.
40. Ibid., p. 450.
41. Kilba traditions.
42. Yawa traditions, collected by the author, August 1968.
43. Ibid.; Migeod, p. 19.
44. Lemoigne, p. 136.
45. Yaquba Mayo Luwe, 'Tarihi Mayo Luwe', EMC.
46. Ibid.
47. Lemoigne, 'Les pays conquis du Cameroun nord', *Rens. Coloniaux Bull. Com. Afrique Française*, XVII (1918), 130-53, see p. 140.
48. L. Mizon, *Les Royaumes Foulbes du Soudan Central* (Paris, 1895), p. 11.
49. Limam Isa, 'Tarihi Ngaundere', EMC.
50. Mizon, p. 13.
51. Ibrahim Hammawa, 'Tarihi Koncha e Banyo', EMC.
52. Barth, p. 507.
53. Strumpell, p. 54.
54. Anon., 'Tarihi Koncha e Banyo', (version Meiganga), EMC.
55. Mizon, p. 14.
56. E. M. Chilver, 'Nineteenth-century trade in the Bamenda Grassfields, southern Cameroons', *Afr. u. Übersee*, 45, 4 (June 1962), 233-58, see p. 243.
57. I. Dugast, *Monographie de la tribu des Ndiki* (Paris, 1955), p. 221.

58. Mizon, p. 14.
59. M. McCulloch, 'The Tikar', in his *Peoples of the Central Cameroons*, (London, 1954), p. 24.
60. Ibid.
61. Yola traditions.
62. Ibid.
63. East, *Stories*, p. 33.
64. Yola traditions.
65. Barth, p. 450.
66. Ibid.
67. Ibid., and S. Passarge, 'The German Expedition to Adamawa' *Berlin Geographical Society*, (July 7, 1894), p. 52.
68. This title is derived from Kanuri usage – another indication of Bornoan influence – cf. *Maina* and later *Abba*, both meaning princes.
69. Strumpell, p. 35.
70. Yola traditions.
71. Yola traditions, collected by M. Last, May 1966, Adamawa File, NHRS.
72. Ibid.
73. F. Cargill, 'Provincial Recurrent Report', February 1904, NNAK, A.I.
74. Barth, p. 510.
75. E. R. Flegel, 'The Upper Benue and Adamawa Colonial Association 1885', *PBM*, (1885/6), and at p. 596.
76. Barth, p. 596.
77. A. F. I. Mockler-Ferryman, *Up the Niger* (London, 1892), p. 123.
78. Passarge, p. 53.
79. Ryan, p. 92.
80. Gowers, 'Provincial Recurrent Report', III, August 1903, NNAK, A.I., pp. 214-15.
81. Barth, p. 502.
82. Papers to and from District Officers on Tour, 1929, NNAK, Acc. 6, p. 10.
83. F. H. El Masri, ed. & trans. *Bayān Wūjub Al-Hijra by Uthman ibn Fūdi*, (Khartoum, 1977), pp. 141-6.
84. Barth, p. 502.
85. Passarge, p. 52.
86. Namtari D.N.B.
87. Rosedale, p. 8.
88. See S. Abubakar, 'The foundation of an Islamic scholastic community in Yola', *Kashim Ibrahim Library Bulletin* (ABU), 5, 2 (December 1972), 2-16.
89. S. Abubakar, 'Islam in the Upper Benue valley to *c.* 1847' mimeo, NHRS.
90. Modire traditions, recorded by Last, May 1966; the informant was Jauro Modire Ahijo; see Adamawa file (NHRS).
91. Abd al-Qadir b. Gidado, 'Majmu bad Rasa'il Amir al-Muminin Muhammad Bello', NHRS.
92. Abubakar Atiku, 'Risāla ila Jama-ᵉ at Ghundu', NHRS.
93. Abubakar, 'Islamic scholastic community', p. 11.
94. Ibid., p. 6.
95. D. M. Last, 'The recovery of Arabic script literature of the north', *2nd Interim Report*, NHRS, (1967), p. 32.
96. Abubakar, 'Islamic scholastic community', p. 6.
97. Strumpell, p. 34.
98. Muhammad Tan mo'ililal, 'Faya Fukarabe' (elegy on Raji's death) NHRS.
99. Strumpell, p. 34.
100. He died in Yola in April 1863. This is derived from Muhammad Tan mo'ililal's 'Faya Fukarabe', which says 'Zulkida jemma alata o ardi, hitande sharaf Ferol', i.e. he died on Saturday night in the month of Zulki'ida of the year 1280 A.H. For conversion see H.-G. Cattenotz, *Tables de concordance des Eres Chrestiennes et Hegirienne*, 3rd. edn., (Rabat, 1961).
101. Last, p. 32.
102. Ibid., p. 39.
103. Ibid.
104. Limam Isa, 'Tarihi Ngaundere'.

105. Ahmadu Marafa, in Yola traditions.

106. See Abubakar, 'Islam in the Upper Benue . . .'.

107. P. F. Lacroix, 'L'Islam peul de l'Adamawa' in *Islam in Tropical Africa*, ed. I. M. Lewis, (Oxford, 1966), pp. 401-7, see p. 407.

108. Strumpell, p. 71.

109. Lacroix, 'L'Islam peul', p. 407.

110. Last, *Caliphate*, p. 153.

111. The Lāmīɗo was a Ba'ajo; the Galadima was a Ngara'jo; the Kaigama was a Bolaro. Other clans, such as the Bewe'en, Kesu'en, Kitijen, Badua'en, and Kiri'en had no officials in the government.

112. Barth, pp. 502-4.

113. 'Tarihi Rai-Buba'.

114. E. Mohammadou, 'L'Histoire des lamidats de Tchamba et Tibati', *Abbia*, 6 (Août, 1964), 16-58, see 46.

115. Ibid., 47.

116. East, *Stories*, p. 51.

117. Waziri Mai, 'Tarihi Tinger', EMC.

118. Ibid. Tinger was destroyed till the 1890s when it was rebuilt by Usman b. Lāmɗo Bakari, with permission obtained from the Lāmīɗo Zubairu. Usman grew up in Tibati and so he had the support of its Lāmɗo, Hamma Lamu.

119. East, *Stories*, p. 51.

120. Ibid., p. 59.

121. Liman Isa.

122. Boyle, 'Historical Notes on Yola Province', 1909, NNAK, J.2.

123. Abubakar, 'Scholastic community', pp. 7, 10.

124. Liman Isa.

125. Mohamadou, *Abbia*, 6 (Août 1964), p. 48.

126. Chilver, p. 239.

127. Migeod, p. 16.

128. Lemoigne, p. 133.

129. See L. Brenner, *The Shehus of Kukawa*, (London, 1973), pp. 48ff.

130. Last, *Caliphate*, p. 88.

131. Ibid.

132. Barth, p. 417 and p. 402.

5. The Decline and Collapse of the Emirate: 1873–1903

The death of the Lāmīɗo Muhammad Lawal, in 1872, gave rise to the most serious succession dispute in Yola. The leading contender was the Yerima Hamidu, the eldest surviving son of the Mōdibbo Adama, and also the most learned and courageous of Mōdibbo Adama's family. Despite his strong credentials, Hamidu was passed over by the Yola Saraki'en who put forward the candidacy of his junior, Umaru Sanda, to the Caliph Abubakar-na-Rabah (1873-7) for approval.

Hamidu appealed to the Caliph; he told him, in a letter, that in 1847 he could have seized power but that he had chosen to step aside for the rightful successor, his elder brother, Muhammad Lawal. Now that he was the eldest, it was his rightful turn to become the Lāmīɗo.[1] The Caliph Abubakar saw no justification for refusing the appointment of Hamidu as the Emir and he directed the Saraki'en of Yola to appoint him.

The Yola officials refused. They wrote to the Caliph, putting forward their reasons for selecting Umaru Sanda instead of his elder brother, Hamidu. They argued that Mōdibbo Adama had stipulated the order of succession for his children and that it was his wish that Umaru Sanda should succeed the Lāmīɗo Muhammad Lawal.[2] Meanwhile, the Yerima Hamidu left Yola and encamped in the neighbourhood, fully prepared to attack Yola should he not gain the succession. The Yerima died at his camp, however, before the Caliph could reply and so Umaru Sanda was appointed the Lāmīɗo.

The Yola officials' claim that Mōdibbo Adama had stipulated the order of succession for his children was a fabrication to justify their preference of Umaru Sanda to Hamidu. (If such a stipulation had existed, the Lāmīɗo Muhammad Lawal would not have planned to abdicate in favour of his son Yerima Sudi. Similarly, Sanda himself would not have attempted to get his son, Yerima Iya, appointed the Lāmīɗo in the 1880s.[3] Both attempts had received the support of the officials and the Caliph, but neither was implemented because of strong opposition by the leading members of the dynasty and the fear of civil war.)

The Yola officials had their own reasons for wanting Umaru Sanda to succeed the Lāmīɗo Muhammad Lawal. Sanda was of weak character; he was neither very learned nor distinguished in the military field, and was unlikely to become a very powerful Lāmīɗo. His disposition was such that he would have to rely upon the officials for guidance and advice. The citizens of Yola, as well as the officials, were tired of the wars in which they had been engaged since the beginning of the jihad; in order, therefore, to avoid further wars, only a peace-minded Yerima was suited to succession. Unlike Umaru Sanda, Hamidu was military-minded and his succession would have meant the continuation of the militaristic policy. Hamidu was also a very strong personality and there was the likelihood of his becoming a very powerful Lāmīɗo just like his elder brother Muhammad Lawal. Hamidu was therefore denied the succession not because of a stipulation by Mōdibbo Adama, but because it was to the advantage of the officials to install a weak and less learned Yerima as the Lāmīɗo so that they would continue to direct the affairs of the emirate.

THE ADMINISTRATION OF UMARU SANDA

The eighteen years reign of the Lāmīɗo Sanda was marked by far reaching administrative and judicial reforms designed not only to improve the authority and influence of Yola, but also to conform to the Shari'a. According to Ahmadu Marafa, when Sanda obtained the allegiance (*mubaya'a*) of the officials and the citizens of Yola, he made a number of important declarations which can be regarded as the policies of his administration.[4] The first was that he intended to abide by the Shari'a in his pursuit of Islamic policies, and he called upon his vassals to unite and co-operate with him in the interest of Islam. Second, the Lāmīɗo informed the people that his position entailed considerable knowledge of Islam, but as he was not a scholar, he intended to work closely with the scholars (mōdiɓɓe) in Yola. He promised not to implement any policy or take any action which the mōdiɓɓe did not regard as being compatible with the Shari'a. Third, concerning the vassals who had been in conflict with Yola since the reign of the Lāmīɗo Muhammad Lawal, Sanda offered friendship and called for reconciliation. Finally, the new Lāmīɗo pledged not to continue with wars which had become concerned with destroying pagan settlements and establishing dumɗe in their place. Wars would be undertaken only after the mōdiɓɓe had agreed that they were in the interest of Islam and in accordance with the laws governing the launching of jihad.

Sanda was interested in lessening the influence of the military men in the Yola government, and enlarged the *Majalisa* with scholars, some royal members, and leaders of the immigrant communities in Yola.[5] A number of the leading scholars were appointed to the council of the Lāmīɗo, including the migrant scholars, Mōdiɓɓe Nakashiri, Abdullahi, and Safyanu, and two local scholars, Mōdibbo Abubakar Namtari and Mōdibbo Ali Bundang.

By the 1870s, the immigrant non-Fulɓe communities in the emirate had grown and each was headed by a 'Lamɗo' appointed by the Lāmīɗo of Fombina. Umaru Sanda recognized the importance of such communities, especially in the economic life of the emirate, and he felt the need for their association with the government. He, therefore, appointed the community leaders to the Council: Lamɗo Kebbi, Lamɗo Kano, Lamɗo Katagum, Lamɗo Zamfara, Lamɗo Katsina, Magaji Adar, and the Mai-Borno. Some members of the dynasty (Yerima Ali b. Mōdibbo Adama and Jijji Bakari b. Mansur b. Mōdibbo Adama) were appointed into the Majalisa possibly to strengthen the Lāmīɗo's position.

In the Council, the leading role was now played by the mōdiɓɓe, who interpreted decisions in the light of the Shari'a, which served as the basis for policy implementation or rejection. The enlargement of the Majalisa limited the influence of the traditional officials, the Galadima, Kaigama, and the Lowan Bunu, and the mōdiɓɓe, hitherto strong critics of the government, became strong supporters of the Lāmīɗo.

In previous reigns, there had not been an official vizier and the Lāmīɗo's chief adviser was the Galadima, the most senior official. Sanda created the office of Waziri when he appointed Aliyu,[6] but this did not immediately change the status of the Galadima. He was a senior half-brother of the new Waziri and was more experienced in emirate administration, so he maintained his seniority.

Another important appointment was that of the *Sarkishanu*. Muhammadu, whom the Lāmīɗo Sanda selected, became the man in charge of the pastoral nomadic Fulɓe, responsible for the collection of the zakat among the pastoralists of the metropolis and its distribution among the poor and the destitute after the Lāmīɗo's share had been deducted.

The third appointment was that of the *Magaji* of the Bata, an office created to win their support. The Bata were the main inhabitants of the Benue plains; some had submitted peacefully to the Fulɓe, but as they were not represented in the government, there may have been some resentment. The Lāmīɗo appointed as Magaji Yakubu, a descendant of the Kokumi chief who had become Mōdibbo Adama's ally at the beginning of the jihad. He became responsible for the collection of Bata tribute and the revenue derived from the ferry on the Benue. He was also the district chief of Yola responsible for the allocation of lands to people for farming and building houses. Finally, such slave offices as *Sarkin Sulke*, *Sarkin Arewa*, and *Garkuwa*[7] were also developed.

The emergence of new offices in the reign of the Lāmīɗo Sanda reflected the growing influence of the western emirates in the political evolution of Fombina. By the end of Sanda's reign, the emirate government in Yola was as elaborate as those of the other emirates of the Sokoto Caliphate.

At the time of Lawal's death in 1872, the military strength of Yola was considerable and it was virtually impossible for the vassals to challenge the Lāmīɗo's authority with any success, and in the north of the emirates, threats from Borno and Mandara made the vassals look to Yola for military protection and maintained the Lāmīɗo's overlordship. However, the Lāmīɗo Sanda, unlike Lawal, was averse to military undertakings. Throughout his eighteen year reign, only five campaigns were launched by Yola, and the Lāmīɗo went out at the head of the army only once, on the Demsa expeditions to recover cattle confiscated from nomads by the Bata.[8]

Having renounced the use of force to settle differences between Yola and the sub-emirates, the Lāmīɗo proceeded to regulate their relations with him. Some leading officials in Yola were appointed to supervise the affairs of the sub-emirates.[9] The Waziri Aliyu was appointed in charge of Madagali, Demsa, and Binder. The Kaigama Nuhu was responsible for the north-eastern sub-emirates, Marua, Mendif, Bogo, Bibemi, Guider, and Kalfu. The Galadima Faruku was the supervisor of the large and powerful southern sub-emirates, Ngaundere, Banyo, and Tibati. Finally, Yerima Bakari was placed in charge of the powerful Rai-Buba. The supervisors were in charge of tribute collection from their assigned sub-emirates, and all gifts from the vassals to the Lāmīɗo had to pass through their hands. When vassals visited Yola, they resided in the homes of their supervisors, who were regarded as hosts (*bero'en*) through whom the vassals called on the Lāmīɗo.

This was an important step towards improving relations with his vassals, but the system did not produce the expected results. The supervisors had no authority in the affairs of the sub-emirates for, although each visited his assigned areas for the annual tribute collection, he could not force the vassals to give tribute or to acknowledge the Lāmīɗo's authority.

Before 1873, the emirate judiciary was not well organized, and each sub-emirate saw itself as autonomous. By the 1870s, the Islamic scholastic community in Yola was well developed and the Lāmīɗo, possibly acting on the advice of the scholars, saw a need for judicial reforms. He divided the emirate into four zones and placed each under a leading Yola scholar as an appeal judge.[10] Mōdibbo Usman b. Raji, the Alkali Girei, was in charge of the northern sub-emirates, Mubi, Madagali, Demsa, Mendif, and Marua; the Lāmīɗo's Alkali in Yola, Mōdibbo Abdullahi, was in charge of all appeals from the metropolis and from the sub-emirates of Banyo-Koncha; Mōdibbo Abubakar Namtari was placed in charge of Balala, Gurin, Beka, Bibemi, and Rai-Buba; and the Alkali Bilkījo was appointed to take charge of Ngaundere and Tibati. These four learned judges had the power to hear cases even against the Lamɓe and the Saraki'en, and to implement the Shari'a.

At the sub-emirate level, there were local *Alkali'en* appointed by the Lamɓe whose judgements could be appealed against, first, in the court of the sub-emirate Lamɗo, then in the court of the higher appeal judge, and finally in the Lāmīɗo's court in Yola. The appeal judges had the power to try capital offences, but the passing of the death sentence lay with the Lāmīɗo. In the event of a final appeal session, all four appeal judges, as well as the other leading scholars in Yola, had to assemble before the Lāmīɗo; the case would be considered and the sentence passed after each judge and scholar had given his opinion based on the Shari'a.

The centralization of the judicial system was of advantage to Yola and the Lāmīɗo, but the system did not operate properly mainly because the majority of the non-Fulɓe peoples were not Muslims and they continued to observe local customary laws. Even among the Fulɓe, only those near or in the capitals used to refer certain cases to the Alkali'en. The majority of the Fulɓe, especially the pastoral nomads, continued to observe Fulɓe custom on inheritance and zakat; only such cases as theft, murder, disputes, and conflicts between them and the non-Fulɓe were referred to the courts, and then only when peaceful negotiations had failed.

The Lāmīɗo's policy towards the sub-emirates was one of peaceful reconciliation in the interest of Islam. The appointment of supervisors was designed to improve relations, but it was not successful. The Lāmīɗo's renunciation of the use of force to control recalcitrant vassals made some of them adopt an indifferent attitude towards him since they no longer feared him embarking upon a punitive military expedition. Some of the vassals also realized that Yola was no longer militarily powerful, since Yola had suffered a series of defeats at the hands of the Hāɓe.

Rebellions by the sub-emirates continued unabated, and some non-Fulɓe peoples seized the opportunity to became independent. In the Benue valley, the Bata, to the west of the Māyo Ine, and the Tengelen, north of the Benue near Garua, threw off their allegiance and began causing trouble to the Fulɓe.[11] The Bata resorted to highway robbery, obstructing the east-west trade route. Other non-Fulɓe groups, such as the Gulak in the Madagali area, the Gereng in the metropolis, the Daba in the Māyo Luwe region, and the Sagje in the north-east also rose in rebellion.[12] The mounting wave of non-Fulɓe rebellions compelled the Lāmīɗo to change his mind about peaceful government. He himself led the expedition to Demsa and, later, similar expeditions were sent against Gulak, Gereng, Sagje, and Gangang, though the Yola forces were not always successful. In 1885, for example, the Yola expedition against the Tengelen, who had been harassing traders, had to retreat with a loss of forty men. The Tengelen, under the leadership of Shabana, continued their activities against the Fulɓe and caravan traders, and in 1887, attacked a caravan of ivory merchants on the outskirts of Garua, killing all thirty-five traders and escaping with the booty.

Traditionally, the most stubborn vassal sub-emirate was Rai-Buba. As soon as Umaru Sanda became the Lāmīɗo, it is said that Lamɗo Buba Jurum of Rai-Buba claimed the return of the fertile lands excised from his domain at the time of its conflict with Yola under Mōdibbo Adama.[13] Buba Jurum sent about one thousand slaves to the Caliph Abubakar in order to obtain his support, and also sent a present of slaves to the Lāmīɗo Sanda and to the Yerima Iya, his eldest son. It is claimed that the Lāmīɗo approved the return of the confiscated lands to the sub-emirate of Rai-Buba.

The Mōdibbo's excision of the fertile lands had been a punishment for rebellion and was designed to weaken the Lamɗo's power by limiting his territorial control. When the lands were excised, part was merged with the sub-emirate of Bibemi and the rest divided into districts governed by Jauro'en directly responsible to the Lāmīɗo in Yola. Since then, the Jauro'en of Balda,

Wuro Māyo-Jarendi, and Mbere had been steadfast in their loyalty to Yola, not only on account of their promotion to sub-emir status, but also because they looked to the Lāmīdo of Fombina for protection against the larger and more powerful Rai-Buba and Bibemi sub-emirates. Thus when Sanda re-incorporated them into Rai-Buba, he could no longer count on their loyalty. At the same time, there was no guarantee that Rai-Buba's attitude towards Yola would change. The Lāmīɗo's action made many small sub-emirates apprehensive because it became possible for the larger ones to incorporate them and obtain the Lāmīɗo's support through gifts. It also affected Yola's relations with Bibemi. The officials there deposed Lamɓo Sulaiman and ap-pointed Mansur in his stead, possibly because Sulaiman had not protested to the Lāmīɗo about the loss of the lands. The deposition of Sulaiman and appointment of Mansur were made without Yola's knowledge. This was rebellion and the Lāmīɗo Sanda sent a delegation under his son, Yerima Iya, to seek an explanation. At Adumri, the delegates were attacked and forced to return.[14] Lamɗo Mansur never visited Yola after that and it is doubtful if he fulfilled his other obligations to the Lāmīɗo.

In c. 1880, Lamɗo Abbo of Ngaundere was directed by the Lāmīɗo Sanda to desist from indiscriminate campaigns against the Laka and the Gbaya.[15] Lamɗo Abbo refused, and Lāmīɗo Sanda, as a punishment, blockaded Ngaundere by closing the great caravan route from Yola to the south. He also recognized Bundang, a vassal district of Ngaundere, as a separate sub-emirate. Unfortunately the closure of the trade route affected Yola most, since the flow of ivory and other goods to the north into Yola ceased, thereby reducing the Lāmīɗo's income from trade, but Ngaundere continued to trade through the neighbouring sub-emirates, Tibati and Banyo, westwards to the Benue river and Hausaland. Lamɗo Abbo, like Mansur of Bibemi, also ceased sending tribute to Yola.

Yola's position in the remaining southern sub-emirates was equally weak. In Tibati, Lamɗo Buba, who had succeeded Hammadu Nyambula in c. 1872, refused to come to Yola to pay homage to the Lāmīɗo. His successor, Hamma Lamu, also abstained from his traditional obligations to the Lāmīɗo of Fom-bina. Banyo was, however, too seriously troubled by dynastic disputes to challenge Yola's overlordship.

The authority of Yola, since the foundation of the emirates, had been greater among the northern sub-emirates since the Lāmīɗo had been capable of protecting them against the raids of Mandara and Borno. In the reign of the Lāmīɗo Sanda, however, even some of the traditionally loyal sub-emirates began causing trouble, since from the end of the 1880s the north of the emirate was immune from Borno's and Mandara's threats.

The first rupture was in Madagali when in c. 1880, Buba Sujito, deposed by the Lāmīɗo Lawal nine years previously, rose in rebellion against Yola.[16] Since his deposition, he had been living among the Mbass, and with their support and that of the Gulak, Mildu, and Vemgo, he began to attack and devastate the environs of Madagali. He was captured by an expedition from

Yola and spent the rest of his life in detention. Because of this aid, the Lamɗo Bakari of Madagali remained loyal to Yola till 1903 when he was killed by German forces.[17]

In Uba, Jauro Iliyasa revolted against Sanda's appointment of his nephew, Lamɗo Belal b. Buba.[18] Like Buba Sujito, Jauro Iliyasa was captured and detained in Yola, but when he repented, Lāmīɗo Sanda forgave him and appointed him the Jauro of Mugelbu. After the death of Lamɗo Belal, Jauro Iliyasa succeeded to the Lamu Uba.

INTERNAL CRISIS AND CONFLICTS

Relations between the sub-emirates had never been harmonious; in the south, there had been struggles between the sub-emirates for greater authority and territorial acquisition, and elsewhere the authority of the Muslims was weakened by prolonged succession disputes and internal struggles for political power and influence among Fulɓe kindred groups.

In the second half of the nineteenth century, large dynasties had emerged in all the sub-emirates, and the death of the Lamɓe in some vassal states, such as Banyo and Rai-Buba, was followed by succession disputes leading to armed conflicts between the claimants.

When Banyo was established as the capital of Banyo sub-emirate, there were three other important centres which governed the districts surrounding them. The first, was Laro; before 1872, Lamīɗo Lawal accorded its ruler, Arɗo Hamman, sub-emir status. The other two centres, Koncha and Gashaka, continued as vassal districts of Banyo, under the sons of Hamman Dandi, Jauro Atiku and Jauro Sambo. After the death of Lamɗo Hamman Dandi, his eldest son, Jauro Usman, assumed the sub-emirship, but the chief of Gashaka, Jauro Sambo, refused to acknowledge his elder brother as his overlord even after Yola had intervened.[19] Sambo declared that he had the right to Gashaka as his share of his father's conquest. Lamɗo Usman attacked him in a siege lasting three years but in the end, Lamɗo Usman had to accept Gashaka's autonomy.

In *c.* 1881, following the death of the Lamɗo Usman of Banyo, his eldest son, Umaru succeeded,[20] against the claims of his uncles, Sambo of Gashaka and Atiku of Koncha. This led to the second dynastic dispute. The senior claimants argued that Umaru was too young and that it was not yet his turn to become the Lamɗo. Jauro Sambo of Gashaka led an expedition against Banyo, but he was routed at Tapawa.[21] This provoked his brother, Jauro Atiku of Koncha, into leading another attack upon Banyo, but this expedition was called off following the intervention of the Mauɓe who advised that the issue be referred to Yola.

This succession conflict lasted over ten years and during that period, the authority of the Fulɓe over a number of dependent groups was greatly weakened, and the Niam Niam of the Galim hills and the Mambilla rose in rebellion against the Fulɓe. The subsequent expedition by Banyo ended in utter disaster, and the Niam Niam and the Mambilla remained independent till the beginning of the present century when the Germans subdued them by superior arms.

Another effect of the dynastic conflict was that the sub-emirship became insecure and local officials became more powerful. It is said that after the death of Lamɗo Usman, the Waziri of Banyo, Iyawa Jauro, could have succeeded to the lamu if he had wanted to.[22] Instead, he nominated Jauro Yamba; but on learning that Yamba intended to depose him on becoming Lamɗo, the Waziri left Banyo and camped at Dou-Mayo. The majority of the Banyo people also left the town for the Waziri's camp and the new Lamɗo was left with only a very few supporters. Consequently, the Waziri revoked the selection of Jauro Yamba and appointed Umaru b. Usman, who remained under the control of his very powerful Waziri.

Another official who became powerful was the Kacalla. During the siege of Gashaka, Banyo was left in the care of the Kacalla, who then planned to seize power.[23] When Lamɗo Umaru learnt of the plan, the siege of Gashaka was abandoned and he hurried back to Banyo, but the Kacalla escaped to the neighbouring sub-emirate of Tibati.

Rai-Buba was also bedevilled by internal strife and conflicts.[24] The first sub-emir, Buba Njidda, distrusted the Fulɓe, after they had deserted him during Mōdibbo Adama's siege of Rai in the 1840s. He then built up support among the Dama, Arei, Godi, and Ndoro, all in the region of the Benue headwaters, and most of his leading officials, both civil and military, were drawn from among non-Fulɓe peoples. The sub-emirate's army was organized according to descent group, each headed by a commander. Politically, the domain was divided into two districts: the north, under Jauro Hamma Gingi, with his base at Konglong, and the south, with its centre at Chollire, under Buba Jurum. Both were sons of Buba Njidda. Thus, the Fulɓe Yillaga'en were excluded from participation in the government.

Jauro Shehu, the Lamɗo's son, seized control of the sub-emirate when his father was away on a visit to Woru Teppe. In a bloodless coup he declared his father deposed owing to old age and Buba Njidda simply moved to his Chollire fortress. However, the population of Rai began to dwindle as the non-Fulɓe gradually left and rallied behind Buba Njidda at Chollire. Within a year only the Fulɓe remained in Rai; all the other ethnic groups had moved to Chollire. Buba Njidda then led an expedition against his son and re-entered the capital. Shehu was eventually killed at Yolnde-Julol while attempting to escape to Bibemi.

After the death of Buba Njidda in *c.* 1865, a very serious conflict, which lasted till *c.* 1874, developed over the sub-emirship. The successor selected by the Rai officials was Buba Jurum, one of the sons of Buba Njidda, but his brothers refused to accept this. Two of them, Jauro Gujja! and Jauro Ma'ana Balia, moved to the sub-emirate of Lagdo-Agorma and established themselves in Wuro Yerimakona. They, then, embarked on a series of activities against the authority of the Lamɗo Rai-Buba, such as raiding villages, capturing men on farms, and confiscating cattle from nomads. Rai-Buba was thrown into a state of insecurity, and trade, agriculture, and nomadism became more and more impracticable. Lamɗo Buba Jurum was hesitant to move against his brothers, but eventually he was forced to act. While Jauro Ma'ana Balia was raiding the Mono village of Kong-Goron, he fell into an ambush and was killed. An expedition was then sent against Jauro Gujjal, and his base, Wuro Yerima-kona, was destroyed.

A more serious threat to Buba Jurum came from his elder brother, Jauro Talla. Unlike the other two claimants, Talla's claim to the succession was based on seniority. On the selection of Buba Jurum, Jauro Talla had moved to the lands of the Ka'ali and the Pam peoples and, with their support, he built up a very powerful following. He entered Chollire and declared himself the Lamɗo in succession to his father. In *c*. 1875, after Buba Jurum had dealt with his junior brothers, he turned his attention to Jauro Talla, led an expedition to Chollire, and eventually routed him.

By *c*. 1876, the dynastic dispute had come to an end, but the problems it gave rise to had to be tackled. For example, the Ngew and the Baya of Sokoto, as well as the Nyanda, taking advantage of the conflicts among the Fulɓe, had thrown off Rai-Buba's overlordship. Similarly, some Jauro'en of the Yillaga'en groups had declared their autonomy by accepting Yola's flags. Advancing by way of Laracca, Katil, and Ngawdamji, Buba Jurum reconquered the Ngew country, then proceeding through the country between the rivers Avini and Wina, he subdued the rebellious Baya. Returning to Rai, he moved north and defeated Arɗo Bamso of Mbere who had sought and obtained Yola's recognition as an autonomous ruler. These successes left Buba Jurum to govern his domain in peace for over a decade.

Prior to the jihad, the Fulɓe had lived in segmented communities, with kindred leaders (Arɗo'en) having authority only over very close relatives. They were leaders of people not rulers of territory, and the acceptance of an Arɗo's leadership was voluntary. It was not uncommon for groups belonging to the same clan (lenyol) to move separately or to co-exist as autonomous units. The succession to the *Arɗoku* was not according to primogeniture, nor was it limited to the children of the incumbent. The Mauɓe had better chances for succession because of their age and greater experience in life.

In the nineteenth century, however, the Fulɓe's concepts of sovereignty and succession began to change. The Lamɓe came to exercise authority not only over people but over lands as well, and power was expressed in terms of subjects controlled and territories possessed. These changes were due to the spread of the influence of Islam and the Lamɓe in Fombina adopted Islamic concepts in order to continue as rulers of all the territories they had conquered from the Hāɓe. The new Lamɓe built up their positions with the support of related kindred groups, and the post of Lamɗo and Saraki'en became hereditary within the families of the first holders. Other kindred groups and new immigrants had no means of entry into the political elite. At most their Arɗo'en could seek recognition as Jauro'en of their areas of residence. The position of the Fulɓe late-comers was no better than that of the Hāɓe, and in some sub-emirates, such as Rai-Buba, the position of the Hāɓe was better than that of the Fulɓe. In the others, while Fulɓe Arɗo'en could become Jauro'en, Hāɓe chiefs who had submitted could become *Arnāɓe*. The fact that political opportunities were not open to all weakened rather than strengthened the solidarity of the Fulɓe. Neither in Yola nor in the sub-emirates were all the different Fulɓe groups represented in the government.

Inter-group conflicts among the Fulɓe started during the reign of the Lāmīɗo Muhammad Lawal when Tinger revolted against the overlordship of Tibati in the 1850s. Similarly, the moves by the Arɗo'en of Balda, Adumri, Agorma, and Wuro Māyo-Jarendi, during Rai-Buba's conflict with Yola, were motivated by the desire to attain autonomous status.

The most serious conflict of this nature in the 1870s was that between Arɗo Bakari and the Lamɓe of Binder, Rai-Buba, and Bibemi.[25] Arɗo Bakari, hitherto in Binder, resented his subservience to the Lamɗo Binder; he moved north and attempted to establish himself as an autonomous ruler in the Māyo Luwe region. He was checked by the Lamɗo of Binder who claimed the area as part of his territory. Arɗo Bakari then moved to Rai-Buba where he was permitted to reside, on condition that he would acknowledge the Lamɗo's authority. He was later arrested and detained for political intrigues, and on his release, he moved to Bantaje in the sub-emirate of Bibemi. Arɗo Bakari was still not prepared to accept vassal status and so the Lamɗo of Bibemi drove him away. Finally, he moved to Goptikeri and appealed to Lāmīɗo Sanda in Yola for help. Military aid was sent from Yola, and Arɗo Bakari established the sub-emirate of Māyo Luwe.

When Arɗo Hammajam Koboshi received Yola's flag and established himself at Dembo, his junior brother, Sulaiman, also an Arɗo of his group, refused to submit to his elder's overlordship.[26] He went to Yola, obtained a separate flag, and attempted in vain to overthrow his elder brother. He then moved eastwards to establish himself at Be. Their eldest brother, Arɗo Yusufu of Mayeso, also received a flag from the Lāmīɗo and founded the sub-emirate of Basheo. Thus, the three sub-emirates, Dembo, Be, and Basheo, founded by brothers, remained as separate units and jealous of one another.

THE RISE OF MAHDISM

The expectation of *al-Mahdi* (the guided one) in the Sokoto Caliphate was encouraged by the writings of the Shehu Usman 'Dan Fodio in the early stages of the jihad. As Al-Hajj suggests, the Shehu's motive was to emphasize the prophecies, current in Islamic belief, about the End of Time in order to 'instil in his followers the love of martyrdom and the renunciation of this transitory world'.[27] Similarly, Muhammad Bello aroused further expectation when he declared that the followers of the Shehu were the Mahdi's vanguard and that 'this jihad will not end, by God's permission, until the appearance of the Mahdi'.[28] However, at a later period, the expectation which the jihad leaders had aroused became a source of anxiety and so they began to restrain their followers. As early as 1808, the Shehu declared all the prophecies about the End of Time unsupported by sunna. Even so, because his early writings had inspired widespread expectations, it became impossible to dispel the belief about the appearance of al-Mahdi.

It was believed that he would appear in the East. Fombina was the eastern-most emirate of the Sokoto Caliphate and its first Emir, Mōdibbo Adama, was charged with the responsibility for guarding the route to the East. He was also empowered by the Caliph Muhammad Bello to extend his conquest eastwards as far as Bagarmi, Wadai, and the Nile, in order to clear the way for the emigration which the Shehu had predicted.[29]

The emergence of the Mahdi was expected to be at a time of anarchy, for it was his duty to restore order and good government. Thus, whenever serious crises developed in the western emirates, the scholars interpreted them as signs of the Mahdi's advent. In the reign of the Caliph Abubakar Atiki (1837–42), Sokoto was threatened by the Gobir and Zamfara revolts, and in Gwandu, the Emir was alarmed by a Mahdist movement,[30] which gave rise to a mass movement of learned men to Fombina from the west, probably in expectation of the Mahdi's advent. The seriousness of the eastward emigration compelled the Caliph Atiku to proclaim that 'the time for the appearance of the Mahdi was not yet due'[31] in an attempt to check the eastward migration, especially of Muslim intellectuals.

Yola, the capital of Fombina, received a substantial number of immigrant scholars between *c.* 1840 and 1872. In the reign of Umaru Sanda, the mōdiɓɓe became associated with the government, some serving as councillors, some as Qadis, and others teaching throughout the emirate.

Hayat b. Sa'id, born in Sokoto after the death of his grandfather the Caliph Muhammad Bello, left for the East after Muadh's appointment as Caliph in 1877.[32] He had been in charge of the Gandi ribat, but it is said that after trouble with the inhabitants, he was recalled to Sokoto.[33] Hayat may have become disenchanted with the affairs in Sokoto after his father's failure to become Caliph, but his reaction, like that of other scholars before him, was to set out for the East. His determination may have been strengthened by the prophecy current in Sokoto that he was the Shehu's descendant who was destined to meet the Mahdi.[34]

When Hayat arrived in Yola, he was well received and lived in the house of Yerima Ali b. Mōdibbo for about four years. He engaged himself in teaching, having come with about thirty of his students and a large number of other followers. Hayat also visited a number of sub-emirates before moving to the north-east to establish himself at Balda in the sub-emirate of Bogo.

The region into which Hayat moved was different from the other parts of the emirate. First, it was a region of insecurity. For decades, the Fulɓe had failed to subdue their northern and eastern neighbours, the Musgu, Massa

132   *The Lāmī6e of Fombina*

and Sumeya. Second, it was located between two very powerful polities – Mandara to the west, and Bagarmi to the east across the Logone. Since the foundation of the sub-emirates of Marua, Bogo, Mendif, and Kalfu, conflicts with both Mandara and Bagarmi had been common, but the Ful6e had not been successful in checking the predatory expeditions from their two dominant neighbours. In addition to these external threats, the north-eastern sub-emirates were, in the 1880s, divided by rivalries, mutual fear, and jealousy. The most powerful among them was Marua under Lamɗo Sali, but the smaller and less powerful ones – Mendif, Pette, and Bogo – regarded her as a threat to their autonomy. Lamɗo Sali of Marua had always entertained the hope of subjecting the petty sub-emirates to his authority.

Balda, Hayat's base, lay eight miles from Bogo, in an unimpressive area which Hamma Gare, the Lamɗo Bogo, had permitted him to occupy. Eventually, as Hayat gained a considerable following, Balda developed into a large town. As a descendant of the Shehu Usman, Hayat was greatly respected, and common folks were eager to visit him. Second, as mōdibbo in a region where such men were rare at the time, he soon became the rallying point for other disgruntled Muslims from the various emirates of the Sokoto Caliphate.

Hayat was not the first scholar to acquire an enormous influence in the north-east of Fombina. In *c.* 1857, a Pullo marabout, Faqih Ibrahim Sharif, with his horde of supporters, failing to pass through Bagarmi, settled in the area.[35] He was eventually killed by the Musgu and his followers dispersed. A number of them may have remained in the region and later rallied behind Hayat. Similarly, in *c.* 1857, the Tijjani scholar, Mōdibbo Raji, moved from Yola to the sub-emirate of Kalfu. He too developed such enormous influence that Koiranga, the Lamɗo of Kalfu, felt overshadowed and appealed to Muhammad Lawal who persuaded the scholar to return to Yola.

Hayat soon became involved in the politics of the region. He eventually built up a very powerful cavalry with which he checked the menace of the Musgu, Massa, and Sumeya to the sub-emirates, thus earning the confidence of Lamɗo Sali of Marua. With his help, Sali succeeded in attacking Hamma Gare of Bogo for resisting Marua's control. Hayat's military victories increased his following, as more people rallied behind him for protection against Mandara and the non-Muslims of the region. In *c.* 1882, Mandara had attacked Pette, and then turned its attention towards Dukba after failing to subdue Kosewa and Pappada.[36] The Lamɗo of Pette, Lawan Dalil, and the Arɗo Borel Muhammadu became allied to Hayat for defence and protection. Sali of Marua began to view the growth of Hayat's influence with apprehension, especially because all the conquered districts, even those which in name belonged to Marua, were made to acknowledge Hayat's authority.

Hayat's career took a dramatic turn after *c.* 1883, when he declared his unreserved loyalty to the Mahdi, Muhammad Ahmed, of the Sudan. In return, Hayat was appointed an Amil (deputy) and was empowered to proclaim Mahdism in the western Sudan, summon people to the obligation of the hijra and to follow the Qur'ān and the Sunna. He also obtained a proclamation (*Manshura*) intended for the Sokoto Caliph and his Emirs.[37] This association of Hayat with the eastern Sudanese Mahdiyya marked his final break with the Sokoto establishment. On receiving the Mahdi's proclamation, Hayat immediately wrote to the Caliph, his cousin Umar b. Ali, pointing out his mission and demanding recognition as the ruler of the Caliphate. The call was not only rejected, but Hayat was also advised to desist from causing dissension in the Caliphate which his great-grandfather had laboured to build. Hayat, who had little to gain from the solidarity of the Caliphate, dismissed Umar's appeal on the ground that the Shayk had predicted the appearance of the Mahdi and he would have dissolved the Caliphate and supported the Mahdi if he had lived.

Conscious that Mahdism was a common belief in Islam and very articulate in the Sokoto Caliphate, Hayat concentrated his efforts on consolidating his position in north-eastern Fombina. Through sermons at his mosque in Balda, and skilful use of itinerant scholars, Hayat disseminated the message of Mahdism to the religious-minded and common folks. He called upon the Fulɓe Lamɓe of Waila and Fūnānge to join him in support of the Mahdi (in effect asking that they acknowledge his authority – a move which meant severing relations with Yola and the Sokoto Caliphate). In 1883, Hayat attacked Bogo and expelled Arɗo Hamma Gare.[38] He also attacked Mendif but failed to subdue it. Finally, he turned his attention towards Marua and succeeded in destroying all the villages between it and Balda. His crowning success was his victory over the combined forces of Marua and Mendif at Ginglei in *c.* 1889.

By *c.* 1890, even though a number of the local Lamɓe in north-eastern Fombina were not overthrown, Hayat had become the undeclared master of the region. The areas gained between 1883 and 1890 were largely due to the weakness of Yola under the Lāmīɗo Umaru Sanda. Both Lamɗo Sali of Marua and Hamma Gare of Bogo had for a long time known that Hayat intended to overthrow them. Consequently, they appealed to the Lāmīɗo of Fombina that Hayat was pursuing political power and territorial aggrandisement, but, Lāmīɗo Sanda remained inactive. It is said that the Lāmīɗo felt that it was wrong for Yola to fight against a descendant of the man who had removed the yoke of servitude from their necks.

Lāmīɗo Sanda's inactivity, bordering on permissiveness, encouraged Hayat to broaden his activities. More and more people rallied under his banner to seek political, social, and religious refuge, and eventually, a real Mahdist community emerged, owing allegiance neither to the Lāmīɗo of Fombino nor to the Caliph at Sokoto, but to the Mahdi in the Sudan. Moreover, even though Hayat did not call upon Lāmīɗo Sanda to follow him, the fact that he was the Mahdist representative meant that Yola had no power over him. After 1890, Mahdism became the biggest threat to the position and authority of the Lāmīɗo of Fombina.

134 _The Lāmīɓe of Fombina_

THE GROWTH OF EUROPEAN INFLUENCE

The first European to visit Fombina was Dr Barth who reached Yola from Borno in 1852.[39] He was not well received by the Lāmīɗo Lawal because he had come through enemy territory, and after four days in Yola, Barth was ordered to leave. No European visited the emirate again until in the reign of Umaru Sanda, the Church Missionary Society exploration led by Ashcroft ascended the Benue as far as Garua in 1880.[40] In subsequent years, more Europeans visited Yola either in the course of their explorations or to acquire concessions for trade in the emirate. In 1882, the German explorer, Flegel, visited Yola and claimed that he was warmly received by the Lāmīɗo Umaru Sanda,[41] but when he called on a second occasion, he was peremptorily ordered to leave.

In 1883, William Wallace, a representative of the National African Company visited Yola. He paid a courtesy call on the Lāmīɗo who, after receiving many valuable presents, permitted the Company to trade in the Yola region.[42] It is also claimed that the Lāmīɗo gave the Company a piece of land to build a trading station. However in 1884, when Wallace re-visited Yola for the purpose of establishing the trading post, Lāmīɗo Umaru Sanda refused his gifts and returned those previously given to him. He ordered the Company not to build a station but he maintained his permission for it to trade from a steamer. Consequently, the Company left an African agent in Yola with the hulk _Emily Waters_ to commence trade. However, he was not only unwelcome but was told to leave the emirate. The order was not carried out because the Benue had fallen and it was impossible for the hulk to sail down the river. After persuasion, the Lāmīɗo reluctantly allowed the hulk to be used for trade, but shortly afterwards, the operation was crippled when the Lāmīɗo ordered the Bata to blockade the hulk with their canoes.

By 1885, the most active trading organization on the Benue was the National African Company. Realizing that Fombina was a rich source of ivory, the Company became interested in establishing good relations with the Lāmīɗo Umaru Sanda of Yola, but he was reluctant to allow the Nasāra'en (Europeans) to gain a foothold in his territory. Being surrounded by scholars, Sanda must have been aware that trade with the _Ahl al-kitab_ (people of the book) was not prohibited; this may explain his verbal permission for the National African Company to trade. But in 1884, the Company's African Agent in Yola was caught intriguing with one of the ladies of the Lāmīɗo's palace.[43] This resulted in the order for Dangerfield to quit in 1885. The Lāmīɗo's coolness towards the Nasāra'en may also have been because they had not obtained the consent of the Sokoto Caliph. Also, Yola had become an important centre of trade and the government derived income through market tolls, protection of caravans and traders, who were mainly Hausa and Kanuri with representatives in the Lāmīɗo's council. These traders feared competition from the Europeans. Because the Europeans offered better prices in hard cash, they stood a better chance of monopolizing the emirate trade. The local traders transacted trade through exchange – the barter system – thus, if they were to compete against the Europeans, their business would be impaired. This would in turn deprive the Lāmīdo of the income he derived from trade and the Saraki'en from exchanging slaves for the goods they required. They may therefore have used their influence, through their representatives in the council, upon the Lāmīdo to refuse permission to the National African Company to obtain a footing in the emirate.

However, the National African Company did not desist in its efforts. In 1886, Wallace visited Yola with 'Thomson's treaty'[44] which claimed that the Caliph had ceded territories along the Benue to the Company. The Lāmīdo had been enjoined by the Caliph to encourage trade with the Nasāra'en, and so Sanda lifted his ban on the Company's trade, but when Wallace left Yola, the ban was re-imposed. Subsequently, the National African Company (which became the Royal Niger Company in 1886) suspended all attempts to obtain Lāmīdo Umaru Sanda's consent for trade on the Benue in his territory. The *Emily Waters* which had been in Yola for trade was moved up the Benue to Rai-Buba, a sub-emirate which had not been very loyal to the Lāmīdo. The venture failed, according to Ferryman, due to the misconduct of the African Agent in charge. He, too, was caught intriguing with the women of the Lamdo's palace.[45] Then, in 1887, after a letter said to be from the Caliph was presented to the Lāmīdo, he permitted the Company to transfer their hulk from Rai-Buba to Ribago, which lay to the east of the Māyo-Faro. The Lāmīdo Umaru Sanda is also said to have promised not to interfere with the Company's trade.

Lāmīdo Sanda maintained his firmness up to the end of his reign in 1890. The Royal Niger Company was allowed to trade, but not in Yola or its environs; the Company was not to build stations, but should confine its activities to the river Benue and to trade from a steamer. By 1890, the Company had only two trading posts in the emirate – one at Ribago and the other at Garua, which was founded in 1887 with the Lāmīdo's permission.

Sanda also maintained his policy of not receiving European visitors in Yola. In 1889, when a German traveller came to Yola, the Lāmīdo declined to give him audience and refused him permission to travel through Banyo to Bali in the south.[46] Later in the same year, Major Claude Macdonald visited Yola in connection with his investigations of the Royal Niger Company's operations. The Lāmīdo refused to see him and so his expedition proceeded to Garua and, after exploring the Māyo Kebbi, he returned down the Benue without stopping at Yola.[47]

REACTION AND COLLAPSE, 1890–1903

Zubairu succeeded Sanda as Lāmīdo in 1890 on the basis of seniority and inherited the various problems of his predecessor's reign: threats to Yola's overlordship; rebellion by sub-emirates and by non-Fulɓe groups against the authority of the Lāmīɗo and dynastic disputes within some sub-emirates which the Lāmīɗo had failed to resolve; and the persisting threat of Mahdism under Hayat in the north-east.

Soon after his accession to office, Zubairu began a series of wars. His first military expedition was against the sub-emirates of Bibemi which, under Lamɗo Mansur, had been virtually independent since the 1870s. Bibemi, Mansur's capital, was besieged, but the siege was lifted when he sought for reconciliation with the Lāmīɗo. Mansur then resumed normal relations with Yola.

From that time, failure to tender allegiance, failure to visit Yola from time to time by the Lamɓe, and failure to send the annual tribute regularly resulted in punitive expeditions. Consequently, the sub-emirates and other subject groups began to fulfil their obligations to the Lāmīɗo. As open rebellion meant serious consequences, some Lamɓe in the 1890s resorted to various activities designed to undermine the Lāmīɗo's authority. The most common was desertion during military campaigns jointly undertaken with the sub-emirates under the command of the Lāmīɗo. In the Konu Pugo in c. 1891, Arɗo Adamu of Be and the Lamɗo Njobdi of Gider left the battlefield so that the Lāmīɗo would be defeated and humiliated.[48] The battle ended in disaster for Zubairu – not only was his army routed but his eldest son, Sadu, was captured and tortured to death by the Pugo people. Zubairu warned Lamɗo Njobdi of Gider and deposed Arɗo Adamu of Be as punishment for desertion.

The victory of Hayat, the Mahdist Amil, over the combined forces of Marua and Mendif at Ginglei in c. 1889, seriously alarmed the emirate government. Balda, the Mahdist centre, had become the rallying point for dissident Fulɓe groups and discontented local Arɗo'en. A number of Lamɓe wanted to tender their allegiance to Hayat, not because they were Mahdist, but because apart from being a descendant of the Shehu Usman – Lāmīɗo Julɓe and the founder of the Caliphate – Hayat was believed to be more learned than Zubairu.

The advent of Rabih b. Fadrallah into the Chad basin intensified Zubairu's desire to check the activities of Hayat. A former associate of Zubair Pasha in the Sudan, Rabih had developed a very powerful slave army after the defeat of Sulaiman b. Zubair by Gessi Pasha in 1878. Then, he embarked on a career of conquest.[49] Rabih was contacted by Hayat who may have suggested the pooling of their forces against Mandara and the emirate of Fombina, which could be occupied as a base for the eventual conquest of the Sokoto Caliphate.

When Zubairu had become Emir, he had ordered Hayat to desist from attacking the districts under Marua and the other sub-emirates of the north-east, and had requested him to move into Marua if he would not return to Yola. Both requests had been turned down and Hayat had informed the Lāmīɗo that he did not consider him his overlord, saying that it was within his power to depose the Lāmīɗo and appoint another person in his place. The Mahdist state had superseded the Sokoto Caliphate, and the Caliph and his Emirs had, by rejecting Mahdism, become rebels to be subdued.

The Lāmīɗo contemplated war, but he was reluctant because Hayat was not only a scholar but also a member of the Sokoto ruling family, and Zubairu was uncertain of Sokoto's reaction should he attack Hayat. He wrote to the Caliph, Abdurrahman, informing him of Hayat's activities and sought approval to lead an expedition against him. The Lāmīɗo, also unsure whether the scholars in Yola would support his fighting against Hayat, consulted them and sent Mōdibbo Sambo b. Nakashiri to Balda to spy upon the Mahdist community, and find out how far Hayat's activities were motivated by Islam. By the time the Lāmīɗo obtained the appoval of the Caliph to fight not only against Hayat but also against any apostate (*ja'iri*), Mōdibbo Sambo had returned to Yola and informed Zubairu that Hayat was certainly a very learned scholar, a determined and uncompromising Mahdist.[50] Sambo informed the Lāmīɗo that Hayat was determined to extend his authority not only over Fombina but throughout the Sokoto empire. War became inevitable.

With the support of the Caliph and the approval of the mōdiɓɓe in Yola, Lāmīɗo Zubairu, accompanied by all his vassals and the Caliph's representative, Malam Maude, advanced to the north-east in *c.* 1892.[51] After campaigns among the Fali and the Daba, the expedition reached Marua at the beginning of the dry season, but fighting did not begin immediately. It is said that for three months Zubairu was involved in attempts to obtain the peaceful submission of Hayat. During this period, Hayat said that 'their forefathers had already foretold that they would fight' and that when they did 'he would put him to flight, slay and humiliate him'.[52] Thus, negotiations broke down. By that time, some of the Lamɓe who had accompanied the Lāmīɗo showed an inclination to depart because they were tired of waiting. Lāmīɗo Zubairu had either to fight and face the consequences or return to Yola, thereby leaving the Mahdists to pursue their policies to the detriment of the Emirate. In the battle which followed in the region between Balda and Marua, the grand army under Zubairu was defeated easily by the smaller, though more effective, forces of Balda.

It has been suggested by Al-Hajj that Hayat, being more used to large-scale warfare while in Sokoto, gained the victory by resort to stratagem, implying that warfare in Fombina had been on a small scale, involving no stratagem. This was not the case. Yola was defeated because the army under Hayat's command was well disciplined and fanatically inspired. Zubairu's grand army, on the other hand, was a conglomeration of levies from the sub-emirates, the majority of whom had nothing to gain by the Lāmīɗo's victory. Some Lamɓe, who nursed strong resentment against Yola's overlordship, had even decided to desert the battlefield to enable Hayat defeat the Lāmīɗo, to humiliate him and weaken his control over the sub-emirates. During the battle, the armies of all the sub-emirates, except Marua, deserted, leaving the Yola forces to be routed by the Mahdist. Complete victory eluded Hayat, however, for while he was busy pursuing Yola, the army of Marua under Lamɗo Sali attacked Balda, carried off women, slaves, and property, and burnt down the town.

The battle of Balda was a terrible blow to the two parties involved. For Hayat, the burning of Balda, the capture of his dependants and property, destroyed the foundation of the Mahdist community which he had laid down, and as a result he emigrated. It is said that he left Balda for Manjaffa in *c.* 1892, and joined Rabih b. Fadrallah at Dikwa. Thus, after 1892, the direct threat of Mahdism to the emirate of Fombina was at an end. The majority of Hayat's supporters joined him, and those that remained ceased to be a threat either to the Lāmīɗo or to the Lamɓe of the north-eastern sub-emirates. The dynasty of Bogo, overthrown by Hayat in the 1880s, was restored when Lāmīɗo Zubairu appointed Bakari b. Hamma Gari as Lamɗo.[53]

Balda was more than a serious set-back for Zubairu; it was a humiliation. It exposed the weakness of Fombina's emirate organization and Yola's military effectiveness, due to the unwillingness of some sub-emirates to participate in campaigns for the Lāmīɗo, and Sanda's eighteen years of comparative peace.

After removing the Mahdist threat from Fombina, Lāmīɗo Zubairu turned his attention to the other problems confronting his administration. In 1893, the Lamɗo of Kalfu, who had for a long time resented his subordination to Yola, declared his independence and conquered territories under the control of the neighbouring sub-emirates.[54] Kalfu was a very small sub-emirate and an expedition from Yola succeeded in arresting the Lamɗo who was deposed and sentenced to detention at Uba by the Lāmīɗo Zubairu. After some time, the Lamɗo repented and was restored to his position.

The Lāmīɗo was less successful, however, in his bid to subdue the large number of rebellious non-Fulɓe groups. His campaigns against the Ga'anda and Guyaku resulted in crushing defeats,[55] and he failed to re-conquer the Mundang, Binder, and the Margi of the Bazza area.[56]

The failure of the Lāmīɗo to subdue a large number of non-Fulɓe groups meant that Yola had ceased to be the military power it was during the reigns of the Mōdibbo and the Lāmīɗo Lawal. This military weakness arose because the Lāmīɗo had estranged the Saraki'en. He had dismissed most of the mōdiɓɓe from the Majalisa and taken complete control, not even allowing the traditional officials to perform their assigned functions. Consequently, while the mōdiɓɓe, once more, became critics of the administration, the Saraki'en, who had been active military leaders as well, became unwilling to render loyal service, and the military position of Yola continued to deteriorate.

Succession disputes, especially in Banyo and Rai-Buba,[57] persisted up to the end of the nineteenth century. It was the Lāmīɗo's duty to intervene, mediate, and settle such disputes, as he was responsible for the appointment and deposition of all the emirate officials. However, it was difficult for the Lāmīɗo to intervene without being called upon to do so. Sanda, for example, had attempted to settle the dynastic dispute in Banyo but had failed, and he had no other means of enforcing his selection on the sub-emirate's officials. The conflict continued till 1891 when the Banyo officials, together with the rival claimants, visited Yola for the Lāmīɗo's arbitration. Zubairu had then confirmed Umaru as the Lamɗo of Banyo and exiled Jauro Sambo of Gash-aka to Madagali. Even then, when Lamɗo Umaru returned to Banyo, his other brother, Jauro Atiku of Koncha, disputed his confirmation and de-clared the independence of Koncha. He failed to maintain his position when an expedition against him was dispatched from Banyo, and he fled to Yola. Lamɗo Umaru then appointed his cousin, Abdulkadir, as the chief of Koncha. This settled the dynastic dispute which had started in *c.* 1881 following the death of Lamɗo Usman.

In Rai-Buba, too, the Lāmīɗo was not involved in bringing to an end the civil war which followed the accession of Buba Jurum. Buba succeeded in breaking up the opposition against his succession and appointed his sons to the positions his brothers had held. Jauro Elwan was appointed the ruler of the southern district based at Chollire; Jauro Jalige was placed at Dou-Māyo to take charge of the Kali district; and Jauro Hamajam was appointed the supervisor of the trade routes to Yola and Ngaundere, and governor of the western district; Jauro Hammadu was in charge of Rai district.

Even though the leading Jauro'en were well placed, they were jealous of Muhammadu Caydo, the Waziri, a member of the ruling family on the maternal side. Lamɗo Buba allowed him a free hand in the management of the sub-emirate affairs, especially in the 1890s when Buba was very old. The Jauro'en feared that Waziri Caydo might succeed in the event of Lamɗo Buba's death or appoint a candidate of his own choice.

Led by Jauro Hamiro, they entered the Chollire palace and murdered their father, Lamɗo Buba Jurum. Jauro Jalige assumed the Lamu. Before moving into the royal house, however, he was deposed by the sub-emirate officials who feared that he might become too powerful for their control. They then appointed Muhammadu, a weak and undistinguished Jauro, as the new Lamɗo, but his appointment precipitated further conflict among the members of the ruling family. The leading claimant, Jauro Jalige, was murdered, pos-sibly by the supporters of Lamɗo Buba Jurum or those of the newly installed Muhammadu.

The remaining eight brothers appealed for redress to Lāmīɗo Zubairu in Yola. The Lāmīɗo chose not to interfere and instead cursed the Jauro'en for murdering their father. The leading claimants moved to Chollire and attemp-ted to install one of their number as a rival Lamɗo. Muhammadu dispatched an expedition to Chollire which killed all eight Jauro'en, thereby bringing the third, and most bloody, dynastic conflict in Rai-Buba to an end.

One year later, German forces attacked Rai forcing Muhammadu to flee. He eventually returned to claim his position, but he was killed by his subjects for deserting them in their hour of trouble.

Yola's military weakness being obvious, Lāmīɗo Zubairu had to explore new sources of military aid – such as the arms and ammunition of the Nasāra'en. As a result, he began to receive more Europeans, but in so doing, he created the final insoluble problem which culminated in his overthrow and the dissolution of the emirate of Fombina.

The increased presence of Europeans in Yola was largely due to colonial rivalry in the 1890s. The French had been busy establishing territorial claims between the River Congo and Lake Chad. in 1890, Cholet had reached 4°N by way of the Sanaga, and Crampel entered the Chad basin by way of Bengi.[58] In 1891, Colonel Monteil left France to reconnoitre the Say-Barua line which the Anglo-French convention of August 1890 had defined as the boundary between the British and the French 'spheres of influence'.[59]

While the French were busy in the region to the north and north-east of Fombina, the Germans were active in the south. Their occupation of the Kamerun in 1884 was followed by attempts to push their control northwards into the hinterland. In 1886, the Germans, following an arrangement with the British,[60] claimed the greater part of the emirate of Fombina as lying within their 'sphere of influence'. Thus, the German 'north policy' was designed to effect their claims through arrangements and agreements with the local rulers of the Kamerun hinterland. However, their efforts to bring the Lamɓe of the southern sub-emirates under their 'protection' failed, mainly because the Lamɓe were unwilling to enter into any agreement without the consent of the Lāmīɗo Zubairu. The Lāmīɗo had no firm control over the southern sub-emirates, but he provided a convenient excuse.

The Germans then turned their attention to Yola with a view to establishing direct contacts with the Lāmīɗo. The Germans desired to station a representative in Yola because they feared that the British would gain tremendous influence if they should gain control of the emirate capital. Thus, in the 1890s, Yola became the focus of colonial rivalry between the British, French, and Germans.

The greatest threat to the position of the Royal Niger Company in the Benue valley was the French. Following the latter's activities in the Chad basin, the Royal Niger Company became apprehensive and desired to improve its position especially in the upper Benue region. Consequently, the company contacted Zubairu and obtained his permission to trade from a hulk and to station an agent in Yola.[61] Zubairu found an occasion to withdraw his permission. In 1891, the Company's agent 'Mai Tumbi' had beaten his wife to death but the company refused to present him for trial in the Yola court.[62] Instead, he was taken to Asaba to be tried by the Company's court. Since the offence was committed in Yola, Zubairu saw no reason why the criminal should not be tried by his court. He therefore ordered the Company to leave Yola and would not permit them to establish even a fuelling station on the Benue within Fombina.

The departure of the Royal Niger Company from Yola was followed by the entry of the French. In August 1891, Mizon entered Yola but the Lāmīɗo was at first very hostile because he thought he had come as an ally of Hayat, the Mahdist leader at Balda.[63] Mizon, however, won the Lāmīɗo's confidence and the French were allowed to trade in Yola on the conditions earlier granted to the Royal Niger Company. In addition, the French agreed to pay a ten per cent levy.

Mizon was successful largely because of his Arab companions, Muhammad Meckhan and Al-hajj Mahmud Sherrif. While Zubairu regarded all Europeans, irrespective of nationality, as Nasāra'en, the fact that Mizon was accompanied by two Muslims made him more acceptable. The two Arabs in Mizon's company convinced the Lāmīɗo that Mizon was not an ally of Hayat and then lobbied the Arab community in Yola, which in turn used its influence to convince Zubairu to accept Mizon as a friend. Mizon had also promised to supply firearms to Zubairu. Consequently, the Lāmīɗo promised to sign a formal commercial treaty with Mizon if he would go back to France and return fully equipped to undertake his obligations in the proposed commercial agreement. Mizon agreed and in December 1891 he left Yola for France.

The Germans had been busy in the southern sub-emirates, but the Lamɓe were very hostile. In 1891, Lieutenant Morgan coming from the Kamerun was attacked in Tibati on the orders of the Lamɗo Hamma Lamu.[64] Similarly, in April 1892, Forneau, a French traveller, attempted to reach Yola from the south, but he was attacked at night near Ngaundere because his expedition appeared to be hostile.[65] In a letter to Zubairu, the Lamɗo of Ngaundere accused him of showing the road to one Christian who had then shown it to the others.[66] That Christian was certainly Mizon who, from Yola, had returned to France by way of the Sanaga through Ngaundere to the Congo.

The hostility of the Lamɓe of the southern sub-emirates may have been because, unlike Zubairu, they were aware of the German occupation of the Kamerun and their subsequent activities on the Bamenda grasslands. Moreover, the Germans had attempted to impose their authority over Banyo and Tibati.

In order to limit the visits of Europeans, the Lamɗo of Ngaundere closed the routes to the south. In Yola too, anti-European feeling developed after the departure of Mizon, for, in 1892, Lāmīɗo Zubairu had been defeated by Hayat at Balda and all foreigners, especially white men, were suspected of being Hayat's allies sent to spy. The hostility of the Yola'en to all Nasāra'en led to the attack of Mizon's hulk, the *René Callié* in 1892.

According to Adeleye, Lāmīɗo Zubairu had cause to fear the Germans and the French. Zubairu's apprehension of the French was not because of Mizon's activities in Muri. While in that emirate, Mizon had helped the Emir Muhammadu Nya to subdue the Kona in December 1892;[67] he had supplied arms and ammunition to the Emir and had trained local men in their use. Muri was a sister emirate to Fombina; it was not enemy territory, nor had it ever been in conflict with Fombina. Zubairu's apprehension may have been because of other Frenchmen. For example, in February 1893, De Maistre came to Garua and hurriedly passed through Yola with a party of over a hundred fully-armed soldiers.[68] This aroused fear in Yola because the expedition had all the appearances of an invading army. In the same month, it is said, Lāmīɗo Zubairu wrote to the Royal Niger Company requesting protection in return for trade concessions, including the control of the entry of foreigners into the emirate.[69]

In May, the Company's agent, Spinks, came to Yola to conclude a treaty with the Lāmīɗo. Zubairu, then in Girei, refused to sign the Company's prepared treaties (form No. 10 designed for Muslim rulers). It is said that he insisted that what he had conceded in his letter to Wallace was sufficient. Zubairu, however, according to Spinks, signed the treaty forms thereby ceding 'for ever . . . the whole of my territory' and also gave the Company 'full jurisdiction of every kind'.[70]

In Islamic law, trade with the Nasāra'en was not prohibited but the cession of territory was illegal. Thus it was not within the power of the Lāmīɗo, a Muslim Emir, to cede territory to foreigners or to give full jurisdiction to them except over their own affairs. The Royal Niger Company had wanted to enter into a formal treaty with the Lāmīɓe of Fombina for a long time, especially in the 1890s when other foreign powers were threatening its position in the middle Niger-Benue valley.

Spinks indicated that Zubairu did not understand what he had signed, believing that he gave his autograph.[71] However, instead of writing it on plain sheets, Zubairu gave the autograph on the treaty form number ten. Zubairu believed that Spinks was satisfied with the concessions given in his letter of February 1893 and he admonished Spinks that the Company should not employ runaway slaves; its employees should not tamper with native women, nor should they refuse punishment when they committed offences. Finally, Zubairu bound the Company not to preach Christianity or interfere with the principles of Islam. These conditions clearly indicate that Zubairu had entered into an agreement with the Company, but it is unlikely that he would cede his territory or surrender his judicial powers to foreigners in return for one thousand bags of cowries.

In June 1893, one month after the concessions to the Royal Niger Company, Zubairu sent to Mizon in Muri informing him that he had signed the provisional treaty with the French concluded in 1891.[72] In July, Zubairu welcomed Von Stetten and granted permission to the Germans to trade in the emirate.[73]

The Lāmīɗo's concessions to the three powers interested in establishing trade relations with him may have been due to 'an open door policy', designed to neutralize the European influences which were threatening to engulf the emirate.

In August 1893, Mizon came to Yola from Muri and obtained Zubairu's signature on the commercial treaty agreed upon during his previous visit in 1891.[74] The Lāmīɗo insisted upon some conditions just as he had when he granted concessions to the Royal Niger Company in May 1893. He bound the French not to export grain from the emirate; to pay a tax of ten per cent on all their transactions; and not to entertain local women aboard their vessels. Zubairu was thereby protecting his sovereignty and the territorial integrity of his emirate while abiding by the Maliki law which does not prohibit trade with Christians.

During the signing of the treaty in August 1893, Mizon had sold to the Lāmīdo forty rifles, two brass cannon, and ammunition.[75] A French military post was stationed in Yola, consisting of two corporals, six Senegalese *tirailleurs* (sharp shooters), with subalterns and auxiliaries to train the Yola soldiers in the use of the French weapons.

The commercial treaty with the French gave rise to a very serious dispute between the two European powers. Wallace of the Royal Niger Company had been in Yola before Mizon's arrival and on the 31st of August, Von Uechtritz and Dr Passarge arrived, barely a week after the departure of Von Stetten. The Royal Niger Company, basing its claims on the 'treaty of May 1893', regarded itself as the 'protector' of Fombina. Wallace, therefore, protested against Zubairu's treaty with the French. Von Uechtritz's protest, on the other hand, was on the grounds that under the terms of the Franco-German convention of December 1885, the emirate of Fombina lay within the German 'sphere of influence'.

Their protests carried no weight. Zubairu did not regard the Company or the Germans as anything other than trading groups which were permitted to operate in the emirate and supply him with useful goods, so, on 7 September 1893 at a meeting of the Majalisa to which all the Europeans in Yola were invited, Zubairu made a formal declaration on his relations with the Europeans. He stated that he had not ceded his sovereignty or parts of his emirate to any European power, merely allowing all to trade. Wallace of the Royal Niger Company was most upset by Zubairu's declaration and he threatened to attack the *Sgt Malamine*, Mizon's vessel in Yola.[76] Zubairu warned him that such an action would be considered a hostile act, so Wallace gave way.

When Mizon left Yola in September 1893, Wallace went to work to undo the French achievements. After telling Zubairu that he was acting on instructions from the French government, he seized the *Sgt Malamine* left in Yola by Mizon. The Company also brought pressure to bear upon the British government to influence the recall of Mizon by the French government in 1893. Finally, by bribing the Lāmīdo and his officials, 'by cajoling and intimidating members of the French posts at Yola and by other underhand means',[77] the Company prevailed upon Zubairu to agree to repatriate Muhammad Meckhan, the French Resident in Yola, in October 1895. Thus, the foundation of French influence which Mizon had laid down on the Benue was destroyed by the Royal Niger Company.

Thenceforth, Anglo-German diplomatic moves designed to check the French advance into the upper Benue basin and the Chad region resulted in an agreement which partitioned the emirate of Fombina in November 1893.[78] Germany renounced its interest in Yola in return for British recognition of German claims from the Benue river to the shores of Lake Chad. The British also conceded seven-eighths of the emirate of Fombina to the Germans. Thus, despite the fact that Germany had no treaties with the local rulers north of the Kamerun to the Chad basin, the British desire to keep the French away from the navigable portion of the Benue river made Britain willing to accept the extension of German possessions to the Chad basin.

By 1894, while Britain had protected its Benue possessions from French designs, Germany had to seek French recognition of their recent acquisitions. The French had been active in the Chad basin and along the river Logone east of the German sphere of influence. They were desperately in need of a foothold on the Benue to utilize the great waterway for their land-locked territories, so in March 1894 the two powers reached an agreement whereby the Germans ceded Bipare on the Māyo Kebbi and the sub-emirate of Binder in return for French recognition of their gains in the Chad basin.[79] Thus the French gained access to the navigable parts of the Benue and also a portion of the emirate of Fombina. This agreement ended Franco-German rivalry over the Benue and Chad regions.

The withdrawal of the French from Yola in 1895 and the confinement of the Germans to their 'sphere of influence' meant that Lāmīɗo Zubairu was at the mercy of the British Royal Niger Company. Whatever aid he might desire from the Nasāra'en in time of danger would, thenceforth, have to come from the Company, but his relations with it had deteriorated after 1894 when he believed that it was contemplating an alliance with Rabih[80] who had been active in Bagarmi since c. 1890.

In 1896, it was rumoured that Rabih had intended to push his way down to the Gongola valley and might reach the Benue.[81] Zubairu in a frantic effort to secure arms, ammunition, and military assistance in the event of Rabih encroaching upon his emirate, approached the Company, and allowed it to build stores and warehouses on the Benue within his territory.[82]

In 1897, after it was rumoured in Yola that Hayat and Rabih had sent their troops southwards to Marua, Zubairu led an expedition to the north with the intention of warding off the invasion of his domain,[83] but there had been no invasion. In the subsequent campaign against the Matakam in the north, Zubairu was defeated. During that period of rumour and anxiety, Lāmīɗo Zubairu is said to have concluded another treaty with the Royal Niger Company. The 1897 treaty is said to have corrected the omissions in the May 1893 one which did not emphasize the fact that the Company was the 'recognised agent of the British government' nor demanded the specific acceptance of the protection of the British flag.

The death of Hayat in 1897 removed much of Zubairu's fear of Rabih. Consequently, his attitude towards the Royal Niger Company began to change and relations gradually deteriorated. In 1898, after a series of interior explorations, Germany began to make its rule effective in the northern parts of the Kamerun. In April 1899, Captain Kamptz conquered Tibati and forced Ngaundere into friendly relations.[84] Tibati rebelled but was reconquered in August of the same year.

The fall of Tibati, one of the most powerful sub-emirates in Fombina, and the capture of its Lamɗo, Hamma Lamu, created a feeling of insecurity in

Yola and confusion throughout the emirate. Although the Company had never shown any desire to conquer his territory, Zubairu was highly suspicious. News of the Company's activities against Bida and Ilorin in 1897 had reached Yola and not long afterwards, the Germans started their northward advance.

Lāmīɗo Zubairu was considered by the British as the main obstacle to their control of the upper Benue region. But he had never been seriously threatened by the Company whose activities in the emirate were purely commercial; it had no military post in Yola or along the Benue within Fombina. In 1900, when Lugard instructed him to stop slave-raiding and obstructing trade, he declared that he had nothing to do with the Europeans. The death of Rabih that year had removed Zubairu's greatest fear and he had no further need of the Niger Company's help. At the beginning of 1901 he forced the Company to remove its flag, quit its stations and trade from a hulk.[85] In July, after he had been accused of being hostile to the British, he replied that they had no right to intervene in the affairs of his emirate. In the words of Lugard, 'the Emir of Yola was becoming more and more impossible'[86] and so in August 1901, the Colonial Office approved the sending of a military expedition against Yola.

On the 26th of August 1901, Colonel Moreland, accompanied by Wallace and over three hundred soldiers, sailed from Lokoja for Yola aboard *Liberty* and *Nkissi*.[87] By the end of the month, the expedition reached Yola and began negotiations with the Lāmīɗo Zubairu in order to avoid fighting. On the first of September, Dr Cargill, a member of the expedition, accompanied by the *Sarkin Turāwa* (supervisor of Europeans' affairs) called on the Lāmīɗo. During the subsequent meeting with Zubairu and his councillors, Dr Cargill accused the Lāmīɗo of breach of agreements, hostile attitude towards the British Royal Niger Company, the seizure of its property in Yola, and the destruction of its warehouse at Garua. He then informed the Lāmīɗo that the King of England had taken over power from the Company and had given it to Lugard, who was prepared for friendship provided the Lāmīɗo would abide by certain conditions. First, he should stop slave trading and raids, and those already enslaved should be allowed to redeem themselves. Second, all trade routes should be kept open and traders permitted to trade freely. Dr Cargill pointed out that the Lāmīɗo should also accept a British Resident in Yola to see to his compliance to the new arrangements and also to advise him.

Zubairu sought the opinion of his leading councillors. His Qadi, Hamma Joda, who had experienced European warfare while in the Sudan and Egypt, advised the Lāmīɗo to accept the new conditions in order to avoid war which was inevitable should he refuse the terms. The Qadi pointed out that as far as he was aware (from the situation in the Sudan and Egypt), the Europeans did not interfere with Islam. He advised that it would not be against Islam to accept the rule of the Nasāra'en if freedom of Islamic worship was guaranteed. This was, in fact, recommended in order to avoid bloodshed. If the Lāmīɗo was not in favour of capitulation, he should, on the pretext of consulting his vassals, delay taking a rush decision in order to fully examine further ways of containing the serious situation. The other officials, Waziri Pate, Galadima Faruku, and Kaigama Nuhu, held different views. They did not support the Lāmīdo's acceptance of any conditions. To submit to the Nasāra'en, they argued, meant leaving the community of believers and abandoning the authority of the Caliph. Moreover, the three officials argued, if Nupe had fought rather than accept the Nasāra'en, it would not be honourable for Yola to submit.

Lāmīdo Zubairu declined to accept the terms stated by Dr Cargill. Instead, he told M. Kiyari, the official interpreter for the expedition, to inform the Nasāra'en that he was not ready for any relations with them and that 'there is no peace between Muslims and the infidels, only war'.[88]

On the second of November, 1901, the Yola men prepared for war.[89] The cavalry and infantry advanced towards the British ship anchored at Bokki Hammapetel, but within a very short time they were beaten back by the Maxim guns. The Yola forces scattered, the Lāmīdo's palace was shelled, and the Friday mosque was destroyed. Colonel Moreland ordered his men to advance into the town towards the palace. The route leading to the palace and the palace itself was defended by the 'Yan bindiga (rifle men), most of whom were deserters from Rabih whom the French had defeated at Kusseri in 1900. These men lived in the Rabih quarter in Yola and, armed with their own weapons as well as the arms supplied to the Lāmīdo Zubairu by Mizon in 1893, they harassed the invading force. The more experienced British troops stormed the palace and gained control quite easily. The palace buildings were blown up and the two cannons, which had wrought havoc among the British troops, were seized. Yola was occupied, and Lāmīdo Zubairu fled through the western gate of the palace.

The fall of Yola hastened the German occupation of their portion of the emirate which had begun in 1899. Lāmīdo Zubairu's defeat was of advantage to the Germans, since any hope of military assistance from Yola, which some sub-emirates might entertain, was destroyed. Moreover, the defeat weakened the courage of the Lam6e to resist the Germans. When Puttkamer, the governor of German Kamerun, ordered his military commanders to advance from Tibati, they met little resistance. Before the end of 1901, Hauptmann Krämer stormed Ngaundere, Dominik entered Rai-Buba, and Nolte occupied Banyo.[90]

ZUBAIRU'S RESISTANCE

Even though Yola had fallen to the British, and the Germans had, before the end of the year, occupied the southern half of the Fombina emirate, the Lāmīdo, who had fled with his court and some loyal vassals, continued to resist the Nasāra'en.

When he had fled Yola, his intention was to go to his farm at Gurin, but the Beti river was swollen; he could not go to his farms at Māyo Ine or Girei as they lay west of Yola and it was difficult to avoid the British troops. Instead the Lāmīd̓o turned to Boli from whence he went, by way of Limadi, to Chebore which became his base for some months. While he was in Chebore, the British, who had been occupying Yola, sent envoys requesting him to return. The British were faced with the problem of reconstituting the Yola government, and as the Lāmīd̓o was accompanied in his flight by the leading officials and the majority of the Yerima'en, it was not easy to get a successor to Zubairu. They offered the emirship to Yerima Iya, the eldest son of the Lāmīd̓o Sanda, but he refused because he feared that Zubairu might return and attack him.[91] Thus the British had no alternative than to make overtures to the Lāmīd̓o Zubairu asking him to return for negotiations. He declined. The British then persuaded some officials and Yerima'en to desert and return to Yola. Bobbo Ahmadu, a younger brother of the Lāmīd̓o Zubairu, was appointed the Emir of the Yola portion of the 'Upper Benue Province' on 8 September 1901.

The fugitive Lāmīd̓o Zubairu continued his anti-European activities. He wrote a letter to Caliph Abdurrahman informing him of the fall of Yola and his escape.[92] He also wrote three identical letters to the people of Yola, Girei, and Namtari calling upon the Muslim community to emigrate and follow him to a new country.[93] He also wanted to know the views of the Yola scholars regarding the burning of the Friday mosque. Only the letter to Namtari was read after the Friday prayers and it was later sent to Yola. The letters for Yola and Girei were not opened but were passed to the Resident who directed Bobbo Ahmadu to return them to the Lāmīd̓o Zubairu. No one responded to the Lāmīd̓o Zubairu's call to emigrate so he left Chebore for that part of his domain which was still free of the Nasāra'en, and made his base at Adumri, in the sub-emirate of Bibemi.

When the Germans entered Garua, Zubairu, after failing to ally with the French, decided to attack the Germans. He still hoped to re-occupy his domain and was attempting to establish a new base not far from Yola so that he could mobilize support to continue fighting. He therefore assembled his loyal vassals, yet unconquered by the Nasāra'en – Lamd̓o Bakari of Madagali, Zubairu of Holma, and Atiku of Cheboa. Under Atiku's command, the Fulɓe force attacked the Germans under Hauptmann Krämer at Garua in November 1901,[94] but were woefully defeated, with the loss of their commander and many others.

The German force advanced to Adumri where they found that Lāmīd̓o Zubairu had escaped and they burnt down the town. The Germans consolidated their position and intensified their efforts to capture the fugitive Lāmīd̓o. They decreed that all the Lamɓe should notify the authorities whenever Zubairu entered their territories and that attempts should be made to capture him if possible. Failing that, they should refuse him safe passage. The British offered a reward of clothes to the value of ten slaves for the capture of the fugitive Lāmīd̓o.[95]

The efforts of the two powers to apprehend Zubairu failed because the

148   The Lāmīɓe of Fombina

Fulɓe and their Lamɓe sympathized with him and they were prepared to help him evade the Nasāra'en. Thus, from Adumri, Zubairu was able to travel as far north as Marua where he succeeded in organizing another force to fight the Germans.[96] Having heard of Zubairu's activities in the north, Dominik and Ratke, leading a German force, moved against Marua and succeeded in routing the Fulɓe army. Again Zubairu escaped capture by taking refuge among the Marbas, together with the Lamɗo Marua Ahmadu. He went to Madagali, but when Lamɗo Bakari refused him permission to stay for long because he feared the Germans, he proceeded to Gudu through Michika, Baza, and the Kilba country. In Michika, the Lamɗo attempted to capture Zubairu but was not successful.[97] In January 1903, Dominik entered Mubi and proceeded to Michika, intending to effect German rule and, if possible, to capture Zubairu.

By the beginning of 1903, Zubairu had to retreat to the 'British section' of his conquered emirate, because all the sub-emirates in the German portion were conquered and the only 'unconquered' part of the emirate was the British section where there had not been any military activity outside Yola. The British learnt that Zubairu had moved into their territory and was causing a great deal of political unrest in the region around Song.

Resident Barclay instructed Lieutenant Nisbet, the commander of the small British force at Yola, to undertake a military reconnaisance of the Gudu area with a view to capturing Zubairu or driving him away. On the 18th of February, 1903, the troops entered Gudu only to find that Zubairu had fled. The mounted infantry which pursued him was outdistanced and Zubairu escaped into the Ga'anda country. On the 27th of February 1903, Lieutenant Nisbet was informed by the Lala chief of Go that a group of 'Fulɓe slave-traders' had been attacked and a number of them killed near the village of Sintari. When the bodies were found, Lāmīɗo Zubairu's body was identified and carried back to Yola.

NOTES

1. R. M. East, *Stories of Old Adamawa*, (Zaria, 1935), p. 85.
2. Ibid.
3. Ibid.
4. The tradition for this section is derived from M. Ahmadu Marafa, 'Tarihin Sarautar Sanda da Zubairu' (Ms. in my possession).
5. See S. Abubakar, 'The foundation of a scholastic community in Yola', *Kashim Ibrahim Library Bulletin* (ABU), 5, 2 (December 1972), 2-16.
6. The eldest son of the marriage between Sanda's sister and Alkasum.
7. Marafa. The names of the first holders are forgotten.
8. Ibid., and East, *Stories*, p. 89.
9. Marafa.
10. Ibid.
11. C. M. Macdonald, 'Exploration of the Benue and its northern tributary the Kebbi' *Proc. Roy. Geog. Soc.*, 13, 8 (1891), 449-77.
12. East, *Stories*, pp. 91-3.
13. Migeod, p. 20.

14. 'Tarihi Rai-Buba'.
15. Yola traditions.
16. Migeod, p. 19; K. Strumpell, *A History of Adamawa*, (Hamburg, 1912), trans. mimeo, NNAK, J.18, p. 58.
17. Strumpell, p. 58.
18. Partition of the Cameroun, 1919-30, NNAK, K.5, p. 2.
19. Ibrahim Hammawa, 'Tarihi Koncha e Banyo', EMC; see also Anon., 'Tarihi Banyo', (version Meiganga), EMC, and S. H. P. Vereker, 'History of the Fulani of Banyo and Koncha' Cameroun: Assumption of Administration, 1915-17, vol. ii, NNAK, K.2, pp. 50-3.
20. Vereker, 'History', p. 53.
21. Ibrahim Hammawa.
22. Ibid.
23. 'Tarihi Banyo', (version Meiganga), EMC.
24. 'Tarihi Rai-Buba' is the main source for this section; see also Strumpell, pp. 67-72.
25. Yaquba Mayo Lume, 'Tarihi Nayo Luwe', EMC.
26. Anon., 'Tarihi Golember', EMC.
27. M. A. Al-Hajj, 'The thirteenth century in Muslim eschatology: Mahdist expectations in the Sokoto Caliphate', *Research Bulletin*, Centre of Arabic Documentation, Ibadan Institute of African Studies, 3, 2 (1967), 100-15, see p. 109.
28. Muhammad Bello, 'Infāq'ul Maisūri' trans. E. J. Arnett in *The Rise of the Sokoto Fulani*, (Kano, 1922) at a meeting of the eastern emirs in 1805/6 at Birnin Gada.
29. 'Abd al-Qādir b. Gidado, 'Majmu bad Rasa'il Amir al-Muminin Muhammad Bello', NHRS.
30. D. M. Last, *The Sokoto Caliphate*, (London, 1967), pp. 67-8.
31. Abubakar Atiku, 'Risāla ala Jama'at Ghundu', NHRS.
32. Last, Caliphate, p. 122; see also A. G. Sa'id, 'Mahdist in Northern Nigeria: Tensions of Teaching and Society', B.Sc. research essay, ABU, June 1972.
33. M. Z. Njeuma, 'Adamawa and Mahdism: the career of Hayat ibn Sa'id in Adamawa, 1818-1898', *JAH*, XII, 1 (1971), 61-77.
34. Sa'id, pp. 5ff.
35. G. Nachtigal, *Sahara und Sudan*, (Berlin, 1881), vol. II, pp. 72ff.
36. Strumpell, p. 39.
37. Letters between the Mahdi, Muhammad Ahmad and Hayat have been published by the union of Young Fulani Ansar of the Sudan as *Min al-Khitabat al-Mutabadala baina al-Imam al-Mahdi was Shayk Hayat* (Khartoum, 1962, 3rd reprint). The manshura is in possession of Alhaji (Dr) Junaidu b. Muhammad al-Bukhari, Wazirin Sokoto.
38. Strumpell, p. 39. He had already obtained the support of Lawal Dalil, the Lāmdo Pette, and the Ardo Borel Muhammadu Tukur.
39. For the account of his Yola expedition see Barth, pp. 357ff.
40. A. F. I. Mockler-Ferryman, *Up the Niger*, (London, 1892), p. 64. However, before this expedition, Dr Baikie had, in 1854, ascended the Benue up to the emirate of Hamarua. He did not reach Yola because the water level had fallen: see W. B. Baikie, *Narrative of an Exploring Voyage up Rivers Kwóra and Binue . . . in 1854*, (London, 1856); T. J. Hutchinson, *Narrative of the Niger, Tshadda and Binue Exploration*, (London, 1855); and S. A. Crowther, *Journal of An Expedition up the Niger and Tshadda . . . in 1854*, (London, 1855).
41. H. R. Rudin, *Germans in the Cameroons 1884-1914*, (London, 1938), p. 76.
42. Mockler-Ferryman, p. 90. For the activities of thr National African Company (later Royal Niger Company) on the Benue see J. E. Flint, *Sir George Goldie and the Making of Nigeria*, (London, 1960).
43. Mockler-Ferryman, p. 91.
44. Said to have been concluded by Thomson on behalf of the National African Company with the Caliph in 1885. Adeleye says that this treaty was forged: R. A. Adeleye, *Power and Diplomacy in Northern Nigeria, 1804-1906*, (London, 1971), pp. 133-4.
45. Mockler-Ferryman, p. 91.
46. B. Zintgraff, *Nord-Kamerun* (Berlin, 1895).
47. MacDonald, p. 463, and Mockler-Ferryman, p. 94.
48. Modibbo Nyako, 'Tarihi Guider', EMC, and Anon., 'Tarihi Be'.
49. He occupied Bagarmi in 1891 and two years later he conquered Borno. See J. S. Trimingham, *A History of Islam in West Africa*, (London, 1962), p. 218, and A. D. Babikir, *L'Empire de Rabeh*, (Paris, 1950).

50. Njeuma, p. 73.
51. Strumpell, p. 40.
52. Yola traditions; the mediators were Yerima Alim b. Mōdibbo Adama, Magaji Yakubu, Lawan Bakari, Lāmɗo Bogo and Lāmɗo Mubi.
53. Lāmīɗo Muhammadu, 'Tarihi Bogo', EMC.
54. G. B. Webster, 'Mayo Ine District Assessment Papers', 1912-22, NNAK, G.2.
55. East, *Stories*, pp. 99ff.
56. Migeod, p. 20.
57. See 'Tarihi Rai Buba' and 'Tarihi Banyo' (version Meiganga), EMC.
58. Adeleye, p. 151, quoting ANSOM Afrique, VI, 82C.
59. Ibid. For the terms of the 1890 Anglo-French convention, see E. Hertslet, *The Map of Africa by Treaty*, 3rd edn. (3 vols., London, 1967), pp. 739ff.
60. For the Anglo-German arrangement of 1886 see Hertslet, pp. 880ff.
61. Adeleye, p. 152, quoting ANSOM Afrique III, file 14, 18/11/1893.
62. Ibid., p. 152; also Flint.
63. Adeleye, p. 152, quoting ANSOM Afrique III, file 15a, Mizon to French Secretary of State for the Colonies.
64. Ibid., p. 153.
65. Ibid., ANSOM Afrique III, 16b.
66. Ibid., pp. 153-4.
67. J. M. Fremantle, *Gazetteer of Muri Province* (London, 1922).
68. A. H. M. Kirke-Green, *Adamawa Past and Present*, (London, 1958), pp. 36-7.
69. Flint, p. 177, quoting FO27/3160, RNC to FO, 15/6/93 enc. Zubairu to Mai Gashi, Wallace, 20/2/93.
70. Ibid., p. 178, quoting FO. 27/3161, RNC to FO encl. 'Adamawa treaty'.
71. Ibid., quoting Spinks' Report, 7/5/93.
72. Adeleye, p. 156.
73. Kirk-Greene, *Adamawa*, p. 35.
74. Flint, p. 179; see Adeleye, pp. 156-7 for the terms of the treaty, ANSOM Afrique III, file 14.
75. Adeleye, p. 157.
76. Ibid.
77. Ibid.
78. See Hertslet, pp. 913ff.
79. Ibid., pp. 657ff.
80. Flint, p. 296. Egyptian emissaries came to Yola *en route* to Borno on a British mission, but they were detained by Lāmīɗo Zubairu for six months in 1893. Eventually they returned to Ibi and then proceeded to Borno by way of Bauchi.
81. Adeleye, p. 201.
82. Kirk-Greene, *Adamawa*, p. 44.
83. Ibid., p. 49.
84. CO 446/5, F. Lascalles to Salisbury, 4/10/1899: also Strumpell, p. 56. Tibati fell on 11 March 1899.
85. CO 446/15, Wallace to CO 6/8/1901.
86. Migeod, p. 21.
87. CO 446/16, Wallace to CO, encl. Moreland's Report also SNP 7/2, NNAK, Acc. No. 2363/1901.
88. Yola traditions.
89. Moreland's Report.
90. Liman Isa; 'Tarihi Ra-Buba'; and Ibrahim Hammawa.
91. Yola traditions.
92. H. F. Backwell (ed.), *The Occupation of Hausaland, 1900-1904*, (Lagos, 1927), p. 67.
93. F. Cargill, 'Provincial Recurrent Report', Oct. 1901, NNAK, A.1.
94. Alhaji Abdullahi, 'Tarihi Garua', EMC, and Garua traditions; see also CO 446/22, Lugard to CO, 19/2/1902.
95. G. N. Barclay, 'Monthly Reports', 1902, NNAK, A.1.
96. Anon., 'Tarihi Marua', EMC.
97. Yola traditions.

6. Twentieth-Century Developments in Fombina

Unlike the other emirates of the Sokoto Caliphate, the emirate of Fombina was conquered by two powers – Britain and Germany. Thus, while Nupe, Ilorin, Kano, Zaria, and Bauchi, among others, continued to function as single units after British conquest, the emirate of Fombina could not continue as a single political unit and the emir could not continue as a ruler of a divided domain under different powers. From the moment a new emir was appointed by the British at Yola, his policy was the reunification of Fombina. Lāmīɗo Bobbo Ahmadu made a number of attempts to obtain German recognition of his authority over the Fulɓe rulers in Cameroun, but nothing was achieved and so, frustrated by his new position, he became openly hostile and unfriendly to the British who finally deposed him in 1909.[1]

The abolition of slavery in the emirate by the British caused great discontent. The Lamɓe and Sarāki'en had always depended on tribute and slave labour for their food requirements. Nowhere was this dependence more pronounced than in the metropolis where the Lāmīɗo and his leading Sarāki'en had their dumɗe. After the fall of Yola, the British declared that slavery was abolished and slaves had the right to be free.[2] As a result of the declaration, some of the enslaved dumɗe cultivators began to desert their masters' farmsteads. The abolition of slavery meant that thenceforth the Fulɓe had to face the difficult task of farming in order to raise their own food. This marked the beginning of a new era which was generally called the period of hardship (zamanu bone). In Yola, resentment mounted and in May 1902, while the Resident was on tour, the populace of the town attacked the British fort.[3]

Apart from Fulɓe discontent, the British had to deal with troubles from the non-Fulɓe, who saw the coming of the British as ushering in an era of freedom. After the fall of Yola to the British, many non-Fulɓe groups who had hitherto lived in peace due to fear of expeditions against them from Yola, began raiding caravans and disrupting trade. The Bata and Bachama to the west of Yola, the Yendam Waka of Māyo-Balwa, and the Kilba-Margi of the north closed the trade routes passing through their territories by active highway robbery. This greatly affected trade which the British wanted to promote. In order to restore peace, a detachment from Yola was sent to traverse the Bachama country in 1902, and by 1903 a permanent military base was stationed at Numan.[4] This stabilized the situation and brought the Bata

under control. Another military base was established at Wamdeo in the north
to reopen the trade route from Borno and to deal with the recalcitrant groups.
When the force was temporarily withdrawn, the Margi and the Kilba plundered a government caravan and closed the Borno road again. For the British,
the problem after the fall of Yola centred around the restoration of law and
order for trade to prosper. This was done by friendship and conciliation with
the non-Ful6e peoples. The creation of independent pagan districts[5] and the
recognition of non-Ful6e chiefs by the British gained for them the support
which they needed.

The Germans, too, had problems over trade in their part of the emirate.
As already pointed out, long before the German conquest of their 'sphere of
influence', they made several attempts to participate in the interior trade,
especially in ivory. The most important traders in the emirates were Hausa
who carried the ivory to the west via the Taraba valley or northwards to Yola.
Thus, ivory and other products of the German colony went to the British.
This disturbed German traders who wanted the colony's wealth for themselves.
To alter the pattern of trade became one of the policies of the newly established German administration. They exercised toleration towards Muslim
institutions partly to win sympathy for their rule and partly to obtain the
confidence of Hausa traders so that they could trade with them rather than
with the British via Yola or by way of the Taraba valley.

Ful6e opposition to European rule also arose from the partition of the
emirate. Seven-eighths of the emirate was under German rule after 1901. The
boundary between the British and German possessions did not follow the
boundaries of the sub-emirates,[6] and some sub-emirates, such as Uba, Michika, Holma, and Zummo, were divided into two parts each under a different
colonial government. In some cases only the capitals remained under their
rulers and a number of villages were separated from their farmlands and
grazing grounds. Before the partition, nomads moved freely from one grazing
ground to another and from plains to plateaux. But after partition, strict
control of nomadic movements was exercised for the collection of cattle tax
(*Jangali*). Thus, the division of the emirate into two parts aroused bitterness
among the Ful6e Shi'e for depriving them of their farmsteads and among the
Ful6e ruling group for dividing their domains. The ruler most affected was
the Lāmīd̃o of Fombina. Apart from the partition of the emirate, the metropolis was also divided. It is said that Bobbo Ahmadu lamented 'they have left
me merely the latrines of my kingdom' after the demarcation of the Anglo-
German boundary. In the south, the Nasarāwo plains were divided into two
parts: the German section under Maigari, and the British under his father,
Bobbowa b. Hamidu b. Mōdibbo Adama. To the east of Yola, districts of
the metropolis beyond the Faro were transferred from the Emir's control to
Lamd̃o Garua.

Apart from ceasing to be the ruler of the whole emirate or the whole of the
metropolis, the partition of the emirate limited the Lāmīd̃o's source of income.
The colonial proclamation against the sale and gift of slaves deprived the

Lāmīɗo and his Sarāki'en of one of their chief sources of income. Similarly, the Lāmīɗo could not collect any form of tax from traders, nomads, and artisans.[7] However, he was compensated by being allowed to retain all the other taxes collected. In 1903, however, a quarter was paid to the government and by 1906, the share of the Lāmīɗo was reduced to half of the taxes collected.[8] This income could not be compared to what the Lāmīɓe had once received from their vassals in the form of tribute or gift. With no tribute coming from the sub-emirates and with no more slaves to cultivate the dumɗe, the Lāmu was shorn of its laurels.

From the moment of his appointment, Bobbo Ahmadu's preoccupation was the reunification of Fombina under his leadership. As early as March 1902, barely seven months after he was appointed, he sent large presents to the German Commissioner at Garua requesting recognition as the Lāmīɗo of the German portion of the nineteenth century emirate, but this was refused.

While the Lāmīɗo resented the division of the emirate, his former vassals who were conquered by the Germans welcomed it. Even before the coming of the Europeans the majority of the Lamɓe resented their subservience to Yola and were only nominal vassals of the Lāmīɗo. For such Lamɓe the conquest of Yola and the partition of the emirate brought to an end their vassalage to the Lāmīɗo.

The Germans, too, were opposed to the idea of the Lāmīɗo at Yola continuing as overlord of the Fulɓe rulers in Cameroun, and the initial policy of the German administration was aimed at breaking all former ties between the Lāmīɗo of Fombina and the Fulɓe rulers in Cameroun so that they could win the loyalty that was formerly accorded to the Lāmīɗo. To this end, the Germans conceded considerable independence of action to the Fulɓe rulers. Throughout the territory, there were only German Commissioners (at Garua and Ngaundere) whose functions were mainly advisory. The Lamɓe continued to govern their domains as of old and without the restraining influence of Yola.

The Germans also avoided policies that offended the Fulɓe rulers whose military organization was an asset in holding in subjection the various non-Fulɓe peoples. Unlike in the British possessions where slavery was abolished, the Germans merely assured protection to slaves, but there was no move to end slavery. It is said that this was because the Germans did not want to upset any institution that experience had made fundamental to the Fulɓe way of life.[9] But it appears that the Germans stood to gain by allowing slavery to persist. The colonial government of the Cameroun had only slight control in the north and to have tampered with the institution of slavery at that time would have been to invite trouble. Moreover, the Fulɓe rulers were expected to supply workers for German plantations and public works. Such workers could not be obtained from among free men who looked upon manual labour as indignity, and therefore people who were in slavery were put to this work.

Lāmīɗo Bobbo Ahmadu, soured by loss of territory, power, and prestige, became not only intractable but also unwilling to work with the British. It is therefore not surprising that he was deposed in 1909 for misrule.[10] His successor, the Lāmīɗo Iya, abdicated in 1910 after only eighteen months in office because he did not want to continue as a Lāmīɗo only in name.[11] Bobbo Ahmadu and Iya belonged to the generation when the Lāmīɓe lived in affluence and power, and the new situation was unacceptable to them.

It was not until the appointment of Abba as the Lāmīɗo in 1910 that the British began to obtain the full co-operation of the Lāmīɓe of Yola. Even so, the Lāmīɓe still regarded the expression 'Yola Province' and 'Emir of Yola' as diminutive, and the moves for a reunited Fombina continued. For example, in 1949, the Lāmīɗo, in a petition to the trusteeship council, called for the 'total dissolution of Trusteeship and annexation of Adamawa Emirate . . . all the portion now British and French Territory formerly belonging to Adamawa.'[12] In 1955, the Lāmīɗo informed a U.N. Visiting Mission that 'in his land the concept of Trust territory was little more than Greek to him and that his people looked on Northern Nigeria as their country.'[13] Finally, during the plebiscite in 1960, the Lāmīɗo campaigned for Northern Cameroun's continued unity with Adamawa emirate. But because the people of the territory did not wish to continue associating with Yola, they voted for separate existence till 1961 when they voted for union with Nigeria.

The decision of the people of Northern Cameroun to decide their future at a later date was tantamount to a refusal to remain within Adamawa Native Authority. Had they voted in 1960 to remain as part of Nigeria they would have remained subordinate to Yola. Thus, with the attainment of independence by French Cameroun early in 1960 and the separation of British Northern Cameroun later in the same year, a final blow was dealt to the unification of Fombina.

In 1961, a massive campaign was inaugurated by the former Northern Nigerian Government in order to retain Northern Cameroun. One of the promises made to the people was that should they vote to remain as part of Nigeria, they would constitute a province, and there would be no question of their reunification with Adamawa emirate. After the plebiscite in 1961, the people voted overwhelmingly to remain as part of Nigeria. Subsequently, they became Sardauna Province with Mubi as its headquarters and the former Lamɗo Mubi, once a vassal district chief of the Lāmīɗo, was awarded second-class chief status.

In 1961, the problem of reunification of the emirate under centralized leadership became a dead issue, but the problem of harmonious relations between the Fulɓe and the non-Fulɓe persisted. The separation of the Trust Territory from Adamawa Native Authority through self-determination was a blow to its efforts to maintain its corporate existence. Other non-Fulɓe still within the authority were encouraged to demand separation. The Kilba, Yungur, and the Margi in the region north of the Benue were most vociferous in their demand for a separate Native Authority since the creation of Sardauna Province. The Northern People's Congress, the party then governing Northern Nigeria, because of its connection with the major Native Authorities, refused to give in to these demands, but the Adamawa Native Authority began to give way to more and more non-Fulɓe participation in the highest organ of local Administration – the Native Authority Council.

With the overthrow of the civilian regime by the military, and the subsequent national crisis, the situation whereby the Fulɓe dominated local administration in the emirate was bound to change.

In 1967 new states were created and in 1969 following administrative reforms in North-Eastern State, the domination of the Fulɓe in the emirate was swept away. Adamawa emirate was divided into two Development Areas: Little Gombi and Māyo-Belwa. Similarly, representation in the Local Authority Council was based on district, thereby making it possible for the non-Fulɓe to be fully represented in the highest body of Local Government – a major development in the improvement of Fulɓe–non-Fulɓe relations in what remains of the nineteenth-century Fombina emirate.

NOTES

1. Migeod, p. 22.
2. F. D. Lugard, *Annual Reports. Northern Nigeria. 1900-11*, (London, 1907), pp. 49-55, 131-3, and 180.
3. G. N. Barclay, Monthly Reports, 1902, NNAK, A.I.
4. Ibid.
5. These are the Chamba and the Bata-Bachama country.
6. The proper demarcation of the Anglo-German boundary was started in 1904 when a Boundary Commission undertook astronomical and triangulation work from Yola to Lake Chad. See C. L. Jackson, 'Yola to Lake Chad Boundary Demarcation', *JRGS*, XXVI. Between 1907 and 1909 Colonel Whitlock surveyed the region between Yola and Obikum on the Cross River and in 1912/13 another Boundary Commission demarcated the region. See W. V. Nugent, 'The geographical results of the Nigeria-Kamerun Boundary Demarcation Commission of 1912-13,' *Geog. Journ.*, XLIII (1914), 630-51.
7. Lugard, *Annual Reports*, pp. 293-5.
8. Income of Chiefs, NNAK 462/1905.
9. Barclay.
10. Migeod, p. 22.
11. Provincial Reorganisation, 1926 Memo and Papers, NNAK.
12. A. H. M. Kirk-Greene, *Adamawa Past and Present*, (London, 1958), p. 86, U.N. Document T/Pet. 4/21.
13. Ibid.

Glossary

Ar. Arabic; F. Fulfulde; H. Hausa; K. Kanuri

Abbasid	a Caliphate in Islamic history
afo	first born
Afon	governors of districts conquered by the Tikar
ainol dīna	strict observance of true religion
ajia	keeper, treasurer
Alfālūji (sing. alfālu)	inherited customs
Alkāli (pl. Alkāli'en) (F. form of Ar.)	judge
Amāna (Ar.)	trust, friendship pact
Amana'en	trustees
al-Mahdi (Ar.)	the expected one, the one who will come to guide
amīl (Ar.)	executive officer of an Emir
amir al-jaish (Ar.)	army commander
amir al-Muminin (Ar.)	leader of the Muslims
Amir al-Yaman (Ar.)	Lāmīɗo of Fombina
Arɗo (pl. Arɗo'en)	kindred leader
Arɗoku	kindred leadership
Arnāɗo (pl. Arnāɓe)	leader of non-Fulɓe groups
Atanto	Tikar palace officials
bacci	children
bandirāgu	consanguinity
Banjeano	vizier of Gang of Yebbi
barāde	warriors
Barāya	new Yola office created by Lāmīɗo Muhammad Lawal
Barguma	courtier, palace official of the Till Hong
Barguma	civil official of the Gudur
Barkuma	chief official of the Muvya government
Batari	executive official of the Till Hong
bauɗe	power
Belaka	chief of the Mbum
bero'en	hosts
Bikkoi	children
Biratada	courtier, palace official of the Till Hong

Birawol	executive official of the Till Hong
Birma	palace official of the Gudur
bone	hardship
chēde	money (cowrie shells)
Chiduma	governor
chūsu	courage
Dainyatil	judicial official of the Till Hong
Darakiras	religious official of the Gudur, concerned with day-to-day affairs of state
daura	native woven cotton cloth
daurōɓe	decision maker, war cabinet
defte	Islamic books, books on religious sciences
dīna	religion
Disku	religious official of the Gudur, concerned with day-to-day affairs of state
doutāre	obedience
Dubukuma	judicial official of the Till Hong
dumɗe	see under *rumnde*
eggol	migratory drift, nomadic wanderings
Fate-Llidi	civil official of the Gudur; father-substitute of the Llidi
firki	a boggy loam
Fon	Tikar ruler
Furu'a (Ar.)	branch of Islamic learning, the political sciences
Gang	priest-chief of Chamba chieftaincy
Gangtoma	regent of Sugu
Ganguramen	war leader of the Gang of Sugu
Ganta	chief priest and adviser of the Gang of Gurumpawo
Garga	a principal cult of the Kilba, centred on the royal family
Garkuwa	new Yola office created by Lāmīɗo Sanda
Guva	counsellors of the Hemen/Homon
Hāɓe (*s. Kāɗo*)	non-Fulɓe
hadith (Ar.)	traditions of the Prophet
hakke	rights
hakkīlo	sense, care and forethought
Hedima	chief adviser
heferɓe (*s. kefero*)	unbelievers
hombondu	ostracism
Homon/Hemen	chief of the Bata
horɓe (*s. korɗo*)	female slaves
Hōsēre	mountain, plateau
huya'en	settled Fulɓe
Imam (Ar.)	leader in congregational prayer
irths (Ar.)	inheritance

iwaibe	young women
Jagurni	a principal cult of the Kilba, centred on the royal family
ja'iri (Ar.)	apostate
jama'a (Ar.)	community
Jangani	religious cult of the Chamba
jantinirdu	Mbororo girls initiation
Jauro	leader of a group of settled Fulɓe
Jihad (Ar.)	holy war
jizya (Ar.)	poll-tax, tribute from non-Muslims
jomol	tax
Kadagimi	executive official of the Till Hong
Kadakaliya	courtier, palace official of the Till Hong
Kadlla	courtier, palace official of the Till Hong
Kaigama-ishi	head of the Mban
Kamandimen	collector of tributes and taxes for the Gang of Sugu
Kamen	executive council of the Gang of Gwumpawo
Katashawa	a religious cult among the Kilba
Khalif (Ar.)	successor to the prophet Mohammed
kharaj (Ar.)	land tax
khums (Ar.)	one-fifth of any booty
kofnol	greetings, gifts
konu	war
kori'en	newly wed among Mbororo'en
Kpana	commander of the army, custodian and administrator of the Homon's/Hemen's wealth
Krama	mountain community of Kilba
Kuni	judge in the Chamba chieftaincy of Gurumpawo
Kurndasu	a religious cult among the Kilba
Lamɓe (*s. Lamɗo*)	chiefs
Lamɗo Konu	official commander
Lamidats	sub-emirates, chieftaincies
Lāmīdo (*pl. Lāmīɓe*)	Emir
Lāmīdo Julɓe	Commander of the faithful; i.e. Caliph (of Sokoto)
lāmu	authority of an Emir or chief; chieftaincy
lawan (*pl. lawan'en*)	leader of territory
lāwol pulāku	the Fulɓe way of life
lenyol (*pl. le'i*)	clan
leppi	hand-woven cloth
Llagama	civil official of the Gudur
Llidi	chief of Sukur
Lligun	palace official of the Gudur
Lli-Sukur	religious official of the Gudur, concerned with day-to-day affairs of state
Lluffu	leading civil official of the Gudur

maccuɓe	male slaves
Magāji	new Yola office created by Lāmīɗo Sanda
mairamjo (K.)	princess
majalisa (H.)	council
Majidāɗi	new Yola office created by Lāmīɗo Muhammad Lawal
Makarama	civil official of the Gudur
mangingo	respect for elders
manshura (Ar.)	proclamation
maral hōre	independence
Mauɓe (*s. maudo*)	elders
Māyo	river
Mban	advisers of the Gang of Gurumpawo
Mbanbengi	head of the Jangani cult of the Chamba
Mbangaji	chief priest of Gang of Sugu
Mbanshem	the Gang's vizier in Gurumpawo
Mbanshi	priest of the Jangani cult
Mbansoro	royal proclaimer of the Gang of Gurumpawo
Mbantem	intermediary between the Gang of Gurumpawo and village heads
Mbanvaso	adviser to the Gang of Gurumpawo, in charge of royal burials
Mboi	priest of the Gudur
Mbosofui	religious official of the Gudur, concerned with day-to-day affairs of state
Mbuga	leaders of Gudur clans
Medella	civil official of the Gudur
mērājo/mērējo	idler, one not concerned with cattle husbandry
Midala	executive official of the Till Hong
mōdiɓɓe (*s. mōdibbo*)	scholars
M'tar	middle class of the Nsaw, freeborn
mubāya'a	allegiance
munyal	patience, fortitude
mutūru	humpless cattle
Na'ib (Ar.)	deputy
nasārājo (*pl. nasāra'en*)	European, Christian
naye'en	men over the age of 40
Ndallata	religious official of the Gudur, concerned with day-to-day affairs of state
ndotti'en	men over the age of 40, men to be respected
Ndowi'en	settled Fulɓe
Ngara'en	a Fulɓe clan
Ngau	a principal cult of the Kilba, centred on the royal family
Ngeylu	religious cult among the Mbula
ngorgi	age mate (male)

nguron (s. wuro)	villages
Ngwirong	Tikar police force
Nshilif	slaves, the lowest class of the Nsaw; Tikar servants
nuwwāb	lieutenants of the Caliphate
Nyagang	warleader of the Gang of Sugu
nyāmtol	fine, payable in cattle
perībe	refugees
peral	migration
pulāku	morality, code of conduct of the Fulɓe
Q'adi (Ar.)	Judge
reuɓe tēle	married women
ribāt (Ar.)	border stronghold
rigi	servants
rumnde (pl. dumde)	slave farmstead, agrarian slave settlement
sangējē	war camps
sappa	age mate (female)
sarāki'en	officials
Sarki Yayi/ Sarki Yaki (H.)	official commander
Sarkin Arewa (H.)	new Yola office created by Lāmīɗo Sanda
sarkin dillālai (H.)	chief hawker
sarkin karo (H.)	official responsible for collection of caravan tolls
sarkin kāsuwa (H.)	market chief
sarkin pāwa (H.)	chief butcher
Sarkin-shanu (H.)	new Yola office created by Lāmīɗo Sanda
Sarkin Sulke (H.)	new Yola office created by Lāmīɗo Sanda
semtē'nde	shyness, modesty
shāhu	gifts
Shamaki (H.)	new Yola office created by Lāmīɗo Muhammad Lawal
Shantaru	a religious cult among the Kilba
Shari'a (Ar.)	Muslim Law
sharo	test of manhood by beating
Shell	royal prince of the Kilba
siyāsa	politics, administration
sukāɓe	young men
sukkulki	ceremonial gifts
sulāɓe	concubines
sunna (Ar.)	practice of the Prophet
Sunoma	courtier, palace official of the Till Hong
tafsir (Ar.)	commentary on the Qur'ān
tāje	iron bars
Tali'i/Tali'ihi	judicial official of the Till Hong
Tauhid (Ar.)	theology
Tawong	priest of the Fon
Tdif	palace official of the Gudur

Till Hong	chief of Hong
Till-Krama	chief of the mountain community of the Kilba
toröbe	worshippers, devotees
tsa'afi	fetish practices
Tulli	court officials of the Mokule government
turkudi	cloth, dyed with indigo
ulama (Ar.)	malams, scholars
umarā (Ar.)	lieutenants of the Caliphate
Vibai	inner council of Tikar chieftaincy
Vidigal	a principal cult of the Kilba, centred on the royal family
wāldēru	age group association
wali-al-shurta (Ar.)	chief of police
wamgo	non-Fulɓe settlement
wariwari-en	immigrants
wazīri (Ar.)	executive official, deputy, vizier
wēndu (*pl. beli*)	lake
Wiri-e-Fon	highest class of Nsaw
wullitol	appeal (to a higher court)
'yarnol	Mbororo boys initiation ceremony
Yedima	senior officials of the Till Hong
yerduye	trust, guarantee, consent
yerīma (*pl. yerima'en*)	prince
Yewung	priest of the Fon
'yölde	rising ground
zakāt (Ar.)	obligatory alms
Zarma	executive official of the Till Hong; palace official of the Gudur
Zomodogbaki	counsellor of the Hemen/Homon
Zumoto	head courtier of the Hemen and intermediary between the people and the Hemen

Notes on Sources

Contemporary sources are the books and journals of European travellers who visited the emirate or neighbouring regions in the nineteenth century. The first to enter Fombina was Dr Barth in 1851, although Denham had visited Mandara in 1822 and mentioned the activities of Fulɓe there. No European set foot in the emirate since Dr Barth until Ashcroft, at the head of a Church Missionary Society expedition, explored the Benue as far as Garua in 1880. An earlier expedition led by Dr Baikie had not reached Yola, but stopped at Hamarua; Dr Baikie followed the Benue up to Djen, less than a hundred miles from Yola.

During the last quarter of the nineteenth century, more Europeans visited the emirate. The accounts of such travellers as Flegel, Zintgraff, Morgen, Stetten, Üchtritz, Mizon, Maistre, and Passarge provide contemporary information about various areas and events. Other useful accounts are those of Macdonald and Mockler Ferryman who visited the emirate in connection with the investigations into the activities of the Royal Niger Company in 1890. It should be borne in mind however that the Europeans obtained some of their information through third parties and interpreters, and thus their opinions and judgements on historical situations, as opposed to the facts they record, cannot always be taken as gospel truth. Also only some parts of the emirate were visited. The British and French limited their activities to the region along the Benue, and the Germans confined themselves to the south, thus the sub-emirates of Rai-Buba, Guider, Bibemi, Kalfu, Māyo Luwe, Bogo, Pette, Gawar, Marua, and Mendif were not visited, nor were Song, Holma, Zummo, Gurin, and Malabu.

European travellers' accounts are vital, however, for the reconstruction of Fombina history, especially in view of the scarcity of contemporary Arabic sources. The accounts are also useful for checking and determining the chronology of events derived from oral accounts.

Other contemporary accounts are books and articles by colonial administrators (German, French, and British), using travellers' accounts and their own investigations. Migeod's *Provincial Gazetteer* and Temple's *Notes on The Tribes etc.* were compiled from material supplied by a number of provincial officials; Kirk-Greene's *Adamawa Past and Present* was compiled from archival sources. Meek's *Northern Tribes* was written after extensive field work

by the author when he was a government anthropologist in Northern Nigeria.
One of the most useful sources for reconstructing the history of Fombina
is East's *Stories of Old Adamawa* (the Hausa version is *Labarun Hausawa da
Makwabatansu*), compiled from oral traditions and Arabic manuscripts col-
lected by the staff of the Yola Middle School (including Taylor, Alhaji Bello
Malabu, and Malam Muhammadu Mayine).

ARABIC MANUSCRIPTS

Arabic works on the history of the Sokoto Caliphate provide more information on Sokoto itself but some contain accounts relating to the whole of
the Caliphate, e.g. Muhammad Bello's 'Infaku'l Maisuri', giving detailed
accounts of the jihad; Abd al-Qadir b. al-Mustafa's 'Raudthat' ul afkari',
containing annalistic accounts of the first 25 years of the jihad; and Gidado
Dan Laima's 'Raud al-Jinan', which includes a list of the lieutenants of the
Shehu. Arabic sources dealing with the organization of the jihad and emirate
governments include 'Kitab al-Farq', 'Wathiqat ahl al-Sudan', and 'Bayān
Wūjub al-hijra', by the Shehu.

Arabic sources with direct bearing on Fombina are very limited. Those
available are 'Buba Yero of Gombe', trans. Abraham, and 'Tabyin amr Buba
Yero na'a ummalihi wa-Ashabihi', which gives an account of Buba Yero's
activities in the Gongola valley and some parts of Fombina. A contemporary
Arabic manuscript of Fombina origin is Adama Agana's 'Marthiyyat Amir
Modibbo Adama', written after the Mōdibbo's death. He gives the date for
this as Saturday night 27th Safar 1263 A.H., a firm date from which subsequent events in the emirate can be dated.

Finally there are letters from the Lāmīɓe in Fombina to the Caliphs in
Sokoto and vice versa. Two were by Lāmīɗo Sanda and the rest by Zubairu
(see Backwell, *Occupation of Hausaland*); letters from the Caliphs to the
Lāmīɓe Fombina at present available are those by Muhammad Bello to
Mōdibbo Adama, in Abd al-Qadir b. Gidado's 'Majmu bad Rasa'il Amir
al-Muminin Muhammad Bello' (NHRS).

ARCHIVAL MATERIAL

The records in the Nigerian National Archives, Kaduna, include numerous
reports such as intelligence, assessment and re-assessment, organization and
re-organization reports, special reports, ethnological notes, studies on various
tribes as well as memoranda and other papers. These archival records were
compiled by government officials on the instructions of the government for
its use and there were established procedures for collection of data, compila-
tion, and transmission to headquarters. At the beginning of the British
administration of the Northern States, political officers were instructed to

investigate and record tribal customs, mythology, and language; these records were sent to senior officers, usually resident, who commented or amended them, then sent them to the Secretary, Northern Provinces for his comments or approval.

By the time the material reached the Secretary, the originality, form and meaning of the collected materials may have been lost through amendments and explanations and answers to queries.

It was the undeclared policy of the early British colonial government that accounts that might arouse indignation in any section of the population should not be included in historical reports.

The compilers of the reports were aliens who knew little about the people among whom they worked; they lived apart from the local community and there was also a language problem. Although the early political officers were encouraged to learn the local languages and were required to pass proficiency tests in them, the diversity of the peoples in the vast Northern provinces made it impossible for any official to learn all the languages.

Only certain things could be told to the British for fear of disclosing the secret of the community. For some years after the British occupation of Yola, the Ful6e were afraid of telling certain things to the Europeans because they feared that the power of the Emir and the Saraki'en over certain areas would be curtailed should they indicate that such areas were not under the Emir's authority. The non-Ful6e used to deny ever being under the control of the Emir so that they would not be placed under the Adamawa Native Authority.

The most useful archival materials are the assessment and re-assessment reports which studied people from the village level to ensure that the tax they paid was fair and just. Each report contains a brief geographical introduction of the district assessed, its population density, ethnic groups, and the history of each, also notes on agriculture, local industry, trade routes, and economic products. The value of such information is that apart from the historical section, it was derived from observation during extensive touring.

Other archival materials such as notes on tribes and intelligence reports (mainly anthropological) were compiled by government anthropologists, the most outstanding of whom was Meek, whose reports form the basis of his later publications. These were compiled after brief tours of the provinces from information supplied by the elders of the communities he studied, though their names are not mentioned.

Provincial reports, usually compiled by residents, are of four types: monthly, quarterly, half-yearly, and annual reports outlining the events which took place in the province during the period. The provincial reports and the other reports discussed formed the basis for the *Gazetteer of Yola Province* (published in 1927) and the unpublished anonymous one of 1936 which is in the archives. Materials for the historical section of the gazetteers came from oral traditions compiled by Boyle, Brackenbury, and Fremantle among others. These are contained in 'Yola Collected Histories'.

Finally, mention should be made of Strumpell's *Histoire des Peuls de*

L'Adamaua, an English version of which is in the archives as *The History of Adamawa*. Strumpell, a German administrator in Northern Cameroun, compiled his book from oral traditions collected by himself and other German officers from Fulɓe elders in 1912. Among his leading informants were Lāmɗo Rai-Buba and Liman Isa of Ngaundere. The book covers the whole of Fombina and treats the history of the emirate, sub-emirate by sub-emirate.

LOCAL AUTHORITY RECORDS

These are mainly District Notebooks, district reports, and miscellaneous notes on various tribes. At the Divisional office, Yola, there are twelve district notebooks, and at the local authority office, Ganye, there are two, and two miscellaneous files on Sugu district and Jada-Binyeri areas. At the Divisional office, Jalingo, there are notes by Meek on the Chamba and the Jukun.

District Notebooks contain brief histories of districts and their inhabitants as well as the genealogy of the District rulers. They were written by touring officers, and later by district scribes, members of the local authority staff. Other information on the districts includes economic products, population distribution, and village areas. The Chief Scribes of the local authorities were in charge of the books and part of their duties was to see that further information was added to the notebooks from time to time.

At Yola, there is also a book called 'Dossier, the Chiefs' Book' containing the genealogies of the Lāmɓe who were formerly under the Emir, each accompanied by brief historical notes on the ruling house. The authenticity of such historical notes is vouched for by the *Wakilin Offis*, the head of the local authority's central administration, Yola.

UNPUBLISHED WORKS

Unpublished works used in the preparation of this book are 'Tarihin Maiha' by Ibrahim Dodo, 'Tarihin Sarautar Lamido Sanda da Zubairu' by Malam Ahmadu Marafa, and a number of Fulfulde poems. 'Tarihin Maiha' was written in 1936 by M. Ibrahim, an Arabic Teacher at Yola Middle School, and it deals with the origin of Maiha, the organization of the people, the coming of Islam to Maiha, the campaigns of Buba Yero in the region, the relations between the Fulɓe and Maiha people and the history of Maiha and Garwa. There are also brief histories of Holma, Vokna, Nguli, Lukdira, Hudu, the Fali people, and Mōdibbo Adama's relations with Aji Maiha, the pagan chief of the region at the time of the jihad in Fombina. Photocopies of these are available at the NHRS centre in Zaria. The information was obtained from elders after a period of investigation which took over eighteen years. The names of his informants are not indicated.

Ahmadu Marafa, also the author of *Ranar Tabbatar Da Lamido* (Zaria

1956) an account of the installation of the Lāmīd́o Aliyu Musdafa in 1953, compiled the 'Tarihi' from oral traditions. His informants include Magaji Nenne Manu and Wakili Kawu, both of Yola. He also derived information from his relatives among whom were Alkali Hamma Gabdo and Alkali Mahmud both Chief Alkali of Yola.

ORAL TRADITIONS

Oral traditions are the most extensive source for the nineteenth century history of Fombina. The traditions used for this book are those collected by Eldridge Mohamadou of the Cultural and Linguistic Centre, Ya'ounde, and my own collection in Adamawa, Sardauna province of Nigeria, and in the northern parts of the Cameroun Republic. The archival sources relating to history can also be termed oral traditions since these were collected through interviews by British colonial officers with elders and chiefs. This information may be more reliable since the informants are the parents or grandparents of present day oral historians. Because the majority of these people did not understand the motives behind such collections, we should be cautious in accepting some of their accounts. While making my own collection, a number of communities mistook me for an investigator sent by the government to look at their connections with Yola so that they could be accorded local authority status. Such impressions have to be corrected before one can get reliable information. The collections of the early colonial officials may have been falsified by the informants to promote the image of their community. Thus, while the Fulɓe could quite easily claim that all the non-Fulɓe in the emirate were subject to the Lāmīɓe before the advent of the British so that they could continue to govern them under the British, the non-Fulɓe could also claim independence long before the British came so that they would not be placed under the Lāmīd́o in Yola.

The oral traditions collected by Eldridge Mohamadou covered the greater part of Fombina. A Pullo from Māyo Luwe, he collected traditions in Fulfulde between 1965 and 1967 and these cover all the nineteenth-century sub-emirates now in Cameroun Republic. When I visited Ya'ounde in 1969, I read the transliterated Fulfulde versions of his collection and translated them into English. The traditions are recorded on tapes and preserved at the Cultural Centre, Ya'ounde.

My collections in Adamawa and Sardauna Provinces in 1968 are translated into English from Fulfulde. For easy reference the various traditions have been classified according to town, village or ethnic name viz: 'Yola traditions' or 'Kilba traditions' followed by the names of the people who supplied the information, as indicated below.

Yola Traditions: The leading people interviewed are Magaji Nenne Manu, a great grandson of Mōdibbo Adama on the maternal side; M. Ahmadu

Marafa, a member of the family of the Alkali Hammajoda; M. Wakili Kawu, a member of the Ba'en in Yola. The late Galadima Aminu, a descendant of Mōdibbo Raji; the interviews took place in July, 1968.

Song Traditions: Information obtained from the late ex-Arɗo Song Alhaji Babbawa, a descendant of Mōdibbo Hamman Song, and from Jauro Mulon Abdurrahman in Song.

Uba Traditions: The leading elders interviewed were the Galadima, M. Bello Kaga, M. Usman Uba, M. Hamma Maifoni, Kaigama Atiku, M. Umaru Sarki Yayi and M. Ahmadu Garaji, all in Uba, August, 1968.

Chamba Traditions: Collected from the elders in Sugu and Yelwa. These are Gang Phillip Maken II; Gang Turaki, ex-chief of Yebbi; Gang Veren, ex-chief Gurumpawo; Kaigama Ishi of Gurum, Kaigama Ganzonen; Kaigama Bansam Gurum, Jimilla Gurum; Jimilla Dimbiwerd; Wakili Hamma Yebbi; Damori Gurum; Someri Yelwa and Clarkson of Yelwa. The elders in Sugu were Wakili Dala; Barde Sugu; Jauro Sugu; Mana Baleri; Mai Limilla; Burmani Sugu; Lawan Sugu and Bako.

Kilba Traditions: The leading Kilba elders interviewed comprised the Yedima, M. Buba Hong; M. Hassan Hong; Yerima Tawa Abdullahi; Yerima Bakari Pella; Muhammadu Toma Bangshika; Yerima Ahmadu Bangshika; Pastor Shall Holma of Pella; Yerima Uliyaduma Pella; Malam Nuhu Hong; Jauro Sulai Hong, Janwusu Adamu and Yahya Muhammadu Nyabandanya, in August, 1968.

Margi Traditions: Collected from those in Uba District under the Till Sillo. The elders were Arɗo Bobbo; Shall Kwallang; Bulani Javini; Daba Wamgo Uba, Wandida; Ndabanyi and M. Wabilari.

Higi Traditions: The leading informants were Malam Umaru Ngikki of Michika; Malam Dandi Oaya, a Local Authority Councillor in Mubi; and M. Zira Wamughi of Bazza.

Mubi Traditions: The people from whom information has been obtained included M. Sanusi Dogari; Malam Baba Taundire; also Arɗo Yawa in Yawa Traditions.

Lamorde Traditions: The leading elders interviewed were Alhaji Adamu; Arɗo Lamorde; Liman Yaro; M. Hole; M. Usman Ndaka; Yerima Ndanewa; Yerima Adamu; Wakili Abibakar, and M. Abubakar Lamorde.

Madagali Traditions: Collected from Albasi Madagali; Yerima Hamma Jalo, the son of the late Hamman Yaji, Lāmɗo Madagali, and from his brother.

Ganye Traditions: The leading informants were the Arɗo Nama of Ganye and M. Bobbo Wuro Toungo also in Ganye.

Jada Traditions: The elders interviewed were Arɗo Hamma Yaj, Lamɗo Jada; M. Bakari Sinna, the Alkali Jada, and M. Muhammadu Laido, the District Head, Jada.

Bata Traditions: The chief informant was the ex-chief of Bata, Enoch Swade, who is perhaps the leading authority on the history of the Bata. Another reliable informant was M. Hammanjam, the Magajin Yola, a Bata by descent. Information on the other Bata groups came from Jauro Mulon Abdurahman of Song.

Mbula Traditions: Collected in Jimeta from Yonana Monongo; Mr Raymond Bayo and Mr Yustus Offah, in September, 1968.

Garua Traditions: The leading elders interviewed in Garua in June 1969 were Mōdibbo Ahmadu Bassoro; Mōdibbo Muhammadu b. Hamman Gabdo; Mōdibbo Ahmadu Muhammadu; Galadima Sa'adu Sabana, and Yerima Mamman Tukuru.

Marua Traditions: The chief informant was Mōdibbo Nasuru Goni Bello in the presence of M. Ibrahim Muhammadu and M. Adamu Dalil, in Marua, June, 1969.

The traditions are preserved in the Adamawa file, Northern History Research Scheme (NHRS), Zaria.

DATES

One of the problems in using oral traditions is the question of chronology. Generally, informants associate certain events with the reigns of particular Emirs; they can tell how long an Emir reigned but they cannot tell when his reign started or ended. For example, the traditions give the reign of Mōdibbo Adama as forty years. Nothing is said about when the Mōdibbo came to power or when the reign ended. Moreover, the years given by the informants are according to the lunar calendar. Similarly, on the question of the beginning of the jihad, informants point out that the Mōdibbo visited the Shehu and received a flag five years after the Shehu had started his jihad. Therefore, in attempting to fix the dates of events described by oral traditions, one has to look for external sources or contemporary written ones. As regards the latter, only one is at present available. This is the 'Marthiyyat Amir Modibbo', written by Adama Agana. In it, it is pointed out that the Mōdibbo died 'in the night of Saturday the 27th of Safar / In the year *junhi bishrin* (1263) of the

Hijra'. Since the Mōdibbo is said to have reigned for forty years, then, the jihad was started in 1223 A.H. (A.D. 1808/9). This is based on the assumption that my informants are correct.

The second way of fixing dates is by the use of external sources. Traditions say the Mōdibbo received the Shehu's flag five years after the start of the Sokoto jihad. Since we know that the Sokoto jihad was started in 1218 A.H., then, Mōdibbo received his appointment from the Shehu in 1223 A.H. (A.D. 1808/9). In fixing the reigns of the Emirs of Fombina whose years in office are given by informants, I worked from the date given in the 'Marthiyyat'. I also used it to determine the dates of other important events. These are converted from A.H. to A.D. by the use of the *Tables de Concordance des Eres Chretiennes et Hegiriennes* by H-G. Cattenotz (3rd edition, Rabat 1961).

Bibliography

ABBREVIATIONS:

Adam. Prov.	Adamawa Province
Afr. u. Übersee	Afrika and Übersee
Bull. IFAN	Bulletin de l'Institut français d'afrique noire
Bull. et Mem. Soc. d'Anthrop.	Bulletin et Mem. de la Société d'Anthropologie
Bull. Soc. Et. Cam.	Bulletin de la Société d'études camerounaises
BSOAS	Bulletin of the School of Oriental and African Studies
DKB	Deutsches Kolonialblatt
EMC	Eldridge Mohamadou's collection, Cultural Centre, Yaounde
DNB	District Note Book
Et. Cam.	Etudes Camerounaises
Geog. Journ.	Journal of the Royal Geographical Society
JAH	Journal of African History
JAS	Journal of the African Society
JHSN	Journal of the Historical Society of Nigeria
JRAI	Journal of the Royal Anthropological Institute
JSA	Journal Société des Africanistes
MAJ	Muri Archives, Jalingo
Mem. IFAN	
NHRS	Northern History Research Scheme
NNAK	Northern Nigeria Archives, Kaduna
PGM	Petermanns Geographische Mitteilungen
Proc. Roy. Geog. Soc.	Proceedings of the Royal Geographical Society
Rens. Coloniaux Bull. Com. Afrique Française	Renseignements Coloniaux Bulletin de la Comité de l'Afrique Française
SNP	Secretary, Northern Provinces

PUBLISHED MATERIAL

ABUBAKAR, S., 'The establishment of Fulbe authority in the upper Benue Basin, 1809-47', *Savanna*, 1, 1 (June 1972), 67-80

'The foundation of an Islamic scholastic community in Yola', *Kashim Ibrahim Library Bulletin* (ABU), 5, 2 (December 1972), 2-16

ADELEYE, R. A., *Power and Diplomacy in Northern Nigeria, 1804-1906*, London, 1971

AHMED IBN FARTUA, *History of the First Twelve Years of the Reign of Mai Idris Alooma of Bornu (1571-83)*, trans. H. R. Palmer, Lagos, 1926

ALEXANDER, B., 'From the Niger, by Lake Chad, to the Nile', *Geog. Journ.*, 2 (August 1907), 119-49

AL-HAJJ, M. A., 'The Fulani concept of Jihad', *Odu*, 1, 1 (July 1964), 45-58

'The thirteenth century in Muslim eschatology: Mahdist expectations in the Sokoto Caliphate', *Research Bulletin*, Centre of Arabic Documentation, Ibadan Institute of African Studies, 3, 2 (1967), 100-15

172 *Bibliography*

AL-MAWARDI, A. A. M., *Al-Akham al-Sultaniyya*, Bonn, 1853

ANDERSON, J. N. D., 'Islamic Law in African Colonies', *Corona*, 3, 7 (1951), 262-6

ARMSTRONG, J. G., 'The development of kingdoms in negro Africa', *JHSN*, 2, 1 (1960), 27-39

ARMSTRONG, R. G., *The Study of West African Languages*, Ibadan, 1964

ARNOLD, T. W., *The Caliphate*, London, 1965

ARNOTT, D. W., 'Proverbial lore and word-play of the Fulani', *Africa*, 27, 4 (Oct. 1957), 379-96

BABIKIR, A. D., *L'Empire de Rabeh*, Paris, 1950

BACKWELL, H. F. (ed.), *The Occupation of Hausaland 1900-1904*, Lagos, 1927

BAIKIE, W. B., *Narrative of an Exploring Voyage up Rivers Kwóra and Binue . . . in 1854*, London, 1856

BAKARI, M., 'Histoire des Sultans de Maroua', *Abbia*, 3 (1963), 77-92

BAKER, R. T., 'The Higis of Bazza Clan', *Nigeria Magazine*, 47 (1955), 213-222

BARTH, H., *Travels and Discoveries in North and Central Africa*, 5 vols., London, 1857

BASSORO, H., 'Un manuscript peul sur *L'Histoire de Garoua*', *Abbia*, 8 (1965), 45-75

BAUER, F., *Die Deutsche Niger-Benue-Tsadsee Expedition, 1902-1903*, Berlin, 1904

BIOBAKU, S. O., 'The problem of traditional history with special reference to Yoruba traditions', *JHSN*, 1, 1 (Dec. 1956), 43-7

BOURDILLON, H. H., *The Future of the Colonial Empire*, London, 1945

BOVILL, E. W., *Caravans of the Old Sahara*, London, 1933

BOYLE, C. V., 'Historical notes on Yola Fulanis', *JAS*, 10, 37 (October 1910), 73-92

BRACKENBURY, E. A., 'Notes on the "Bororo Fulbe" or nomad "Cattle Fulani" ', *JAS*, 23, 91 (April 1924), 208-17; 23, 92 (July 1924), 271-7

BRENNER, L., *The Shehus of Kukawa*, London, 1973

BUISSON, E. M., 'Caractères descriptifs de quelques Foulbé nobles de Maroua (Haut-Cameroun)', *JSA*, 3, 2 (1933), 283-8

BURDON, J. A., *Northern Nigeria: Historical Notes on Certain Emirates and Tribes*, London, 1909

'The Fulani Emirates of Northern Nigeria', *Geog. Journ.*, 24 (July-December 1904), 636-51

CAMPBELL, M. J., 'Cameroons under Germany Part II: Consolidation and Downfall', *West African Review*, XXXI, 386 (1960), 57-9

CATTENOTZ, H-G., *Tables de Concordance des Eres Chrestiennes et Hegiriennes*, 3rd edn., Rabat, 1961

CHILVER, E. M., 'Nineteenth century trade in the Bamenda Grassfields, southern Cameroons', *Afr. u. Übersee*, 45, 4 (June 1962), 233-58

COOK, A. N., *British Enterprise in Nigeria*, Philadelphia, 1943

CROWDER, M., *Pagans and Politicians*, London, 1959

CROWTHER, S. A., *Journal of an Expedition up the Niger and Tshadda . . . in 1854*, London, 1855

CROZIER, F. P., *Five Years Hard. Being an Account of the Fall of the Fulani Empire*, London, 1932

CULLEN, A. A., 'Adamawa Province', *Nigeria Magazine*, 19 (1939), 224-7

DAVIES, J. G., *The Biu Book*, Zaria, 1956 (mimeogrpph)

DENHAM, D., CLAPPERTON, H. and OUDNEY, Dr, *Narrative of Travels and Discoveries in Northern and Central Africa, in the years 1822, 1823 and 1824*, London, 1826

DE ST CROIX, *The Fulani of Northern Nigeria*, Lagos, 1944

DOMINIK, H., *Vom Atlantik zum Tschadsee*, Berlin, 1908

DRAKE ST C., 'Traditional authority and social action in former British West Africa', *Human Organisation*, 19, 3 (1960), 150-8

DUGAST, I., 'Inventaire ethnique du Sud-Cameroun', *Mem. IFAN* (Centre du Cameroun), Serie: Populations, 1 (1949), xii + 159
Monographie de la tribu des Ndiki (Banen du Cameroun), vol. 1, Paris, 1955

DUGAST, R., 'Essai sur le peuplement du Cameroun', *Et. Cam.*, 1, 21/2 (Juin-Sept. 1948), 19-33

EAST, R. M., *Stories of Old Adamawa*, Zaria, 1935
'Sharo: cruelty or discipline?', *West Africa Annual*, 1950, 90

EL MASRI, F. H., 'The life of Shehu Usuman dan Fodio before jihad', *JHSN*, 2, 4 (1963), 435-48
Bayān Wūjub Al-Hijra, by Uthman ibn Fūdi, Khartoum, 1977

FEGAN, E. S., 'Some notes on the Bachama', *JAS*, 29, 115 (1929), 269-79; 29, 116 (1929), 376-400

FLEGEL, E. R., 'Der Benue von Djen bis Ribago', *PGM*, 1880, 146-53
'Rob. Ed. Flegel's expedition nach Adamaua. Reisebriefe vom Januar bis März 1882', *PGM*, 1882, 227-30
'Rob. Ed. Flegel's Reise nach Adamaua, März 1882 bis März 1883', *PGM*, 1883, 241-9
'The Upper Benue and Adamawa Colonial Association 1885', *PGM*, 1885/6

FLINT, J. E., *Sir George Goldie and the Making of Nigeria*, London, 1960

FORDE, D. and KABERRY, P. M., *West African Kingdoms in the Nineteenth Century*, London, 1967

FOURNEAU, J., 'Une tribu païënne Nord-Cameroun: Les Guissiga (Montouroua)', *JSA*, 7, 2 (1938), 163-95

FREMANTLE, J. M. (ed.), *Gazetteer of Muri Province*, London, 1922

FROELICH, J. C., 'Le commandement et l'organisation sociale chez les Foulbé de l'Adamoua', *Et. Cam.*, 45-6 (Sept.-Dec. 1954), 3-91
'Notes sur les Mboum du nord-Cameroun', *JSA*, 29, 1 (1959), 91-117
'Ngaunderé: la vie économique d'une cité-peule', *Et. Cam.*, 43-4 (Mars-Juin 1954), 3-65

GAUTHIER, J. C., 'Notes sur la religion des Fali', *Abbia*, 3 (1963), 48-54

GIBB, H. A. R. and BOWEN, H., *Islamic Society and the West*, Oxford, 1950

174   Bibliography

GIFFORD, P. and LOUIS, W. R. (eds.), *Britain and Germany in Africa*, London, 1967

GOWERS, W. F., *Gazetteer of Kano Province*, London, 1921

GREENBERG, J., 'Studies in African linguistic classification: II The classification of Fulani', *Southwestern Journal of Anthropology*, 5, 3 (1949), 190-8
The Languages of Africa, The Hague, 1963
'The influence of Islam on a Sudanese religion', *American Ethnographic Society, monograph no. 10*, New York, 1946

HAFFENDEN, W. J. R., *The Red Men of Nigeria*, London, 1930
'Ethnological notes on the Shuwalbe group of Bororo Fulani', *JRAI*, 57 (1927), 275-93

HAMPATÉ BÂ, A., 'The Fulbe or Fulani of Mali and their culture', *Abbia*, 14-15 (July-December 1966), 55-87
'Fulah Culture', *Présence Africaine*, 8-9-10 (1956), 84-96

HERTSLET, E., *The Map of Africa by Treaty*, 3 vols., 3rd edn., London, 1967

HISKETT, M., 'An Islamic Tradition of reform in the Western Sudan from the sixteenth to the eighteenth century', *BSOAS*, 25, 3 (1962), 577-96
'Material relating to the state of learning among the Fulani before their Jihad', *BSOAS*, 19, 3 (1957), 550-78

HODGKIN, T. L., 'Kanem and Northern Nigeria; remarks on the history of Northern Nigeria', *West African Review*, 30, 378 (1959), 169-71
Nigerian Perspectives, London, 1960
'Uthman dan Fodio', *Nigeria*, 1960, 75-82
'Islam and national movements in West Africa', *JAH*, 3, 2 (1962), 323-7
'Islam, history and politics', *Journal of Modern African Studies*, 1 (1963), 91-7

HOFFMANN, C., *A Grammar of the Margi Language*, London, 1963

HOGBEN, S. J., *The Muhammadan Emirates of Nigeria*, London, 1930

HOGBEN, S. J. and KIRK-GREENE, A. H. M., *The Emirates of Northern Nigeria*, London, 1966

HOPEN, C. E., *Report on the study of Field Fulani*, Kaduna, 1955
'Note on Alkali Fulfulde', *Africa*, 34, 1 (1964), 21-7
The Pastoral Fulbe Family in Gwandu, London, 1958

HUTCHINSON, T. J., *Narrative of the Niger, Tshadda and Binue Exploration*, London, 1855

HUTTER, F., 'Explorations dans l'hinterland septentrional de la colonie du Cameroun', *Bull. et Mem. Soc. d'Anthrop.*, Paris, 5, 4 (1903), 505-32

VON KAMPTZ, 'Berich des Hauptmanns von Kamptz über die Fortschritte des Wute-Adamaua-Expedition', *DKB*, 1899, 339
'Erstürmung der Stadt Tibatis am 13 März 1899 durch die Shutztruppe', *DKB*, 1899, 401
'Gefangennahme des Lamidos von Tibati durch den Hauptmann von Kamptz', *DKB*, 1899, 693

JACKSON, C. L., 'Yola to Lake Chad Boundary Demarcation', *JRGS*, XXVI

JEFFREYS, M. D. W., 'Some notes on the customs of the grassfield Bali of Northwestern Cameroons', *Afr. u. Übersee*, 46, 3 (May 1963), 161-8
'Traditional sources prior to 1890 for the grassfield Bali of Northwestern Cameroons', *Afr. u. Übersee*, 46, 3 (May 1962), 168-99; 46, 4 (Sept. 1962), 296-313
'Banyo; a local history note', *Nigeria Field*, 18, 2 (1953), 87-91
'Speculative origins of the Fulani language', *Africa*, Jan. 1947, 47-54
'Some notes on the Fulani of Bamenda', *Abbia*, 14-15 (July-December 1966), 127-34
'L'origine du nom "Fulani" ', *Bull. Soc. Et. Cam.*, 5 (1944), 5-24
JOHNSTON, H. A. S., *The Fulani Empire of Sokoto*, London, 1967
JOOS, L. C. D., 'Note sur le traité entre l'Allemagne et le Lamidat de Tibati', *Et. Cam.*, 53-4 (1956), 18-19
JUNAIDU, A. M., *Tarihin Fulani*, Zaria, 1957
KABERRY, P. M., 'Notes on Nsaw History and social categories', *Africa*, 22, 1 (1952), 72-5
KHADDŪRĪ, M., *War and Peace in the Law of Islam*, Baltimore, 1955
KIRK-GREENE, A. H. M., *Adamawa Past and Present*, London, 1958
'Expansion on the Benue, 1830-1900', *JHSN*, 1, 3 (1958), 215-37
'The Kingdon of Sukur', *Nigeria Field*, 25, 2 (April 1960), 67-96
'Von Uechtritz's expedition to Adamawa 1893', *JHSN*, 1, 2 (1957), 86-98
'Tax and travel among the hill-tribes of Northern Adamawa', *Africa*, 26, 4 (October 1956), 369-78
KIRK-GREENE, A. H. M. and SASSOON, C., *The Cattle People of Nigeria*, London, 1959
KOELLE, S. E. (ed.), *African Native Literature*, London, 1854
LACROIX, P. F., 'Matériaux pour servir à l'histoire des peuls de l'Adamawa', *Et. Cam.*, 5, 37-8 (Sept.-Dec. 1952), 3-61; 6, 39-40 (Mar.-July 1953), 5-40
'L'Islam peul de l'Adamawa', in *Islam in Tropical Africa*, ed. I. M. Lewis, Oxford, 1966, 401-7
LARGE, W. H., 'Over the hills to Yola', *Nigeria Magazine*, 29 (1948), 180-221
LAST, D. M., *The Sokoto Caliphate*, London, 1967
'An aspect of the caliph Muhammad Bello's social policy', *Kano Studies*, 1, 2 (July 1966), 56-9
'The recovery of Arabic script literature of the north', *2nd Interim Report*, NHRS, 1967, p. 32.
LAST, D. M. and AL-HAJJ, M. A., 'Attempts at defining a moslim in 19th century Hausaland and Bornu', *JHSN*, 3, 2 (Dec. 1965), 231-40
LEMBEZAT, B., *Les Populations païennes du Nord-Cameroun et de L'Adamaoua*, Paris, 1961
'Kirdi, les populations païennes du Nord-Cameroun', Doula: *Mem. IFAN* (Sér. Populations, no. 2), 1950
LEMOIGNE, C., 'Les pays conquis du Cameroun nord', *Rens. Coloniaux Bull. Com. Afrique Française*, XVII, (1918), 94-114; 130-53
LE VINE, V. T., *The Cameroons from Mandate to Independence*, California, 1964

LEWIS, I. M. (ed.), *Islam in Tropical Africa*, Oxford, 1966

LUGARD, F. J. D., *The Diaries of Lugard*, ed. M. Perham, 3 vols., London, 1959

Annual Reports, Northern Nigeria, 1900-11, London, 1907

MACDONALD, C. M., 'Exploration of the Benue and its northern tributary the Kebbi', *Proc. Roy. Geog. Soc.*, 13, 8 (August 1891), 449-77

MACLEOD, O., *Chiefs and Cities of Central Africa*, London, 1912

MACCALL, D. F., *Africa in Time-Perspective*, Worcester, 1961

McCULLOCH, M., 'The Tikar' in *Peoples of the Central Cameroons*, London, 1954

MEEK, C. K., *The Northern Tribes of Nigeria*, 2 vols., London, 1925

Tribal Studies in Northern Nigeria, 2 vols., London, 1931

A Sudanese Kingdom, London, 1931

Land Tenure and Land Administration in Nigeria and the Cameroons, London, 1957

'The Fulani', *Man*, 59 (Oct. 1959), art. 287, p. 182.

MIGEOD, C. O., *Gazetteer of Yola Province*, Lagos, 1927

MIGEOD, F. W. H., 'The British Cameroons, its tribes and natural features', *JAS*, 23, 91 (April 1924), 176-87

Through British Cameroons, London, 1925

MIZON, L., *Les Royaumes Foulbes du Soudan Central*, Paris, 1895

MOCKLER-FERRYMAN, A. F. I., *Up the Niger*, London, 1892

MOHAMADOU, E., *L'Histoire de Tibati*, Yaounde, 1965

'Pour servir à l'histoire du Cameroun: Chronique de Bouba Njidda Rey', *Abbia*, 4 (Dec. 1963), 17-55

'Introduction à la littérature Peule du Nord-Cameroun', *Abbia*, 3 (1963), 66-72

'L'Histoire des lamidats de Tchamba et Tibati', *Abbia*, 6 (Aout 1964), 16-58

'Pour une histoire du Cameroun central: les traditions historiques des Vouté ou "Babouté" ', *Abbia*, 16 (Mars 1967), 59-127

MONTELL, V., 'Contribution a la sociologie des Peuls (le "Fonds Veillard")', *Bull. IFAN*, 25(B), 3/4 (Juil.-Oct. 1963), 357-414

'Reflexions sur le probleme des peuls', *JSA*, 20, 22 (1950), 153-92

MORGEN, C. VON, *Durch Kamerun von Süd nach Nord*, Leipzig, 1893

MOSELEY, L. H., 'Regions of the Benue', *The Geog. Journal*, XIV (1889), 630-7

MURDOCK, G. P., *Africa: its Peoples and their Culture History*, New York, 1959

MVENG, E., *Histoire du Cameroun*, Paris, 1965

MYRES, J. L., 'Nomadism', *JRAI*, 71 (1941), 19-42

NACHTIGAL, G., *Sahara und Sudan*, Berlin, 1881

NJEUMA, M. Z., 'Adamwa and Mahdism: the career of Hayatu ibn Sa'id in Adamawa, 1878-1898', *JAH*, XII, 1 (1971), 61-77

NOLTE, L., 'Bericht des Stationschefs von Joko, Oberleutnants Nolte, über einen Besuch beim Sultan von Tibati', *DKB*, 1900, 284

NUGENT, W. V., 'The geographical results of the Nigeria-Kamerun Boundary Demarcation Commission of 1912-13', *Geog. Journ.*, XLIII (1914), 630-51

OMER-COOPER, J. D., 'The question of unity in African history', *JHSN*, III, 1 (1964), 103-12

PALMER, H. R., *Sudanese Memoirs*, 3 vols., Lagos, 1928
'An early Fulani conception of Islam', *JAS*, 13, 52 (1914), 407-14; 14, 53 (1914), 53-9; 14, 54 (1915), 185-92
'The "Fulas" and their language', *JAS*, 22, 85 (Oct. 1922), 121-8
'Western Sudan History: the *Raudthât'ul afkâri*', *JAS*, 15, 59 (April 1916), 261-73
The Bornu Sahara and Sudan, London, 1936

PASSARGE, S., *Adamaua*, Berlin, 1895
'Adamawa', *Geog. J.*, 5, 1895, 50-3, paper read to the Geographical Society, Berlin, 1894, p. 52

PFEFFER, G., 'Prose and poetry of the Ful'be', *Africa*, XII, 3 (1939), 285-307

REED, L. N., 'Notes on some Fulani tribes and customs', *Africa*, V, 4 (1932), 422-54

RELLY, H., 'Grandeur et décadence du lamidat de Tchamba', *Report de Tournee Administration*, Poli, Juin 1954

ROWLING, C. W., *A Study of Land Tenure in the Cameroons Province*, London, 1948

RUDIN, H. R., *Germans in the Cameroons, 1884-1914*, London, 1938

SALASC, L., 'Le Bebenda, formation du Lamidat de Bibemi', *Et. Cam.*, 3, 31/32 (Sept.-Dec. 1950), 201-6

SCHULTZE, A., *The Sultanate of Bornu*, trans. P. A. Benton, London, 1913

SMITH, H. F. C., 'A neglected theme of West African history: the Islamic revolutions of the 19th century', *JHSN*, 2, 2 (1961), 169-85

SMITH, M. G., *Government in Zazzau, 1800-1950*, London, 1960

STAPLEDON, J., 'In their end is their beginning: a Fulani crisis', *Nigeria Field*, 13, 2 (Oct. 1948), 53-9

STENNING, D. J., *Savannah Nomads*, London, 1959
'Transhumance, migratory drift, migration; patterns of pastoral Fulani nomadism', *JRAI*, 87 (1957), 57-73

VON STETTEN, 'Bericht des Rittmeisters von Stetten über seinen Marsch von Balinga nach Yola', *DKB*, 1895, 110-14

SURET CANALE, J., 'Zur historischen und sozialen Bedeutung der Fulbe-Hegemonie', *In Geschichte und Geschichtsbild Afrikas*, 1960, 29-59

TAUXIER, L., *Mœurs et histoire des Peuls*, Paris, 1937

TAYLOR, F. W., *A First Grammar of the Adamawa Dialect of the Fulani Language, Fulfulde*, Oxford, 1921

TELLI, D., 'Le divorce chez les Peuls', *Présence Africaine*, N.S., 22 (1958), 29-47

TEMPLE, C. L., *Native Races and their Rulers*, Cape Town, 1918

TEMPLE, O., *Notes on the Tribes, Provinces, Emirates and States of the Northern Provinces of Nigeria*, ed. C. L. Temple, Lagos, 1922

TRIMINGHAM, J. S., *A History of Islam in West Africa*, London, 1962

URVOY, Y. F. M. A., 'Chronologie du Bornou', *JSA*, 11, 1-2 (1941), 31-2
Histoire des Populations du Soudan Central, Paris, 1936
Histoire de l'Empire du Bornou, Paris, 1949

VANSINA, J., *The Oral Tradition: A Study in Historical Methodology*, London, 1965
'A comparison of African kingdoms', *Africa*, 32, 4 (1962), 324-5

VIVIEN, A., 'Essai de Concordance de cinq tables généalogiques du Baguirmi (Tchad)', *JSA*, 37, 1 (1967), 25-39

VOSSART, J., 'Histoire du Sultanat du Mandara', *Et. Cam.*, 35/6 (1952), 19-52

WALIMAN, M. R., 'The Fulani Jihad: a reassessment', *JAH*, VI, 3 (1965), 333-55
'A note on the ethnic interpretation of the Fulani Jihad', *Africa*, 36, 3 (July 1966), 286-91

WHITLOCK, G. F. A., 'The Yola-Cross River boundary commission, Southern Nigeria', *Geog. Journ.*, 36 (Oct. 1910), 426-38

YELD, E. R., 'Islam and social stratification in Northern Nigeria', *British Journal of Sociology*, XI, 2 (1960), 112-28

ZADROZNY, J. T., *Dictionary of Social Science*, Washington, 1959

ZELTNER, J. C., 'Notes relatives à l'histoire du Nord Cameroun', *Et. Cam.*, 4, 35/6 (1952/3), 5-18

ZINTGRAFF, E., *Nord-Kamerun*, Berlin, 1895
Min al-Khitabat al-Mutabadala baina al-Imam al-Mahdi was Shayk Hayat, Khartoum, 1962, 3rd reprint

ARCHIVAL MATERIAL

NNAK: Nigerian National Archives, Kaduna; MAJ: Muri Archives, Jalingo; DNB: District Notebook; SNP: Secretary, Northern Province.

BARCLAY, G. N., Monthly Reports, 1902, NNAK, A.1

BERKELEY, H. S., 'The Chamba', 1905, extracts from provincial correspondence jacket, PCJ. 345/1922, MAJ, file no. 34
'Chamba District Notes', 1907, MAJ, file no. 48

BOYLE, 'Historical Notes on Njobolio, Beti and Ribadu', 1909-10, NNAK, J.2
'Historical Notes on Yola Province', 1909, NNAK J.2

BRACKENBURY, E. A., 'History of Goila', 1910, NNAK, G.2 E
'Goila District Miscellaneous Papers', 1910-36, NNAK, G.2
'Cameroun: Assumption of Administration', 1915-17, NNAK, K.2
'Namtari Assessment Report', February 1910-11, NNAK, G.2 W

CARGILL, F., 'Provincial Recurrent Report', February 1904, NNAK, A.1

'Provincial Recurrent Report', October 1901, NNAK, A.1
CLIFFORD, G. M., 'Notes on Chamba Area Reorganisation', 1933-40, NNAK, G.3 A
'Chamba Area Reorganisation', 1933-40, Vol. 1, NNAK, Adamprof.
DUNLOP, C. C., 'Mayo Farang Assessment Papers', 1913, NNAK, G.2, 2H
FREMANTLE, J. M., 'History of the Yola Emirate', 1908, NNAK, J.2
'History of the Emirate of Yola', 1908, NNAK, J.1
'The Fulani: Collected Papers and Correspondence', 1910-34, NNAK, J.2
GOWERS, 'Provincial Recurrent Report', III, August 1903, NNAK, A.1
LOGAN, PERCIVAL and SHAW, Notes in Sugu District Notebook, Local Authority Office, Ganye
MCALLISTER, 'The Kona', MAJ, file no. 34
MCBRIDE, D. F. H., Notes in Uba DNB
'Wollarbe History', Pagan Administration, vol. ii, 1933-5, NNAK, F.4
'Report on Northern Margi Area', 1936, in Uba DNB
MEEK, C. K., 'The Kona', 1928, MAJ, file no. 34
MOORE, W. C., 'Balala District Assessment Report', 1917, NNAK, G.3 Y
PERCIVAL, D. A., 'Notes on the Tikar Tribe', 1938, NNAK, Adamprof.
'History of Mayo Farang', 1907-13, NNAK
'Mayo-Balwa, Mayo-Farang, Yendang-Waka District Miscellaneous Papers', 1907-47, NNAK, G.2, 2F
PATTERSON, R. J., 'Special Report on Uje District', Ethnology Mbum, NNAK, 2700
ROSEDALE, W. O. P., 'History of Balala', 1926, NNAK, Acc. 77
'Yungur District Miscellaneous Papers', 1923-9, NNAK, G.19
'Notes on Balala History', Balala DNB
'Namtari District Re-assessment Papers', 1916, NNAK, G.2, 2W
RYAN, H. B., 'Report on Yola Province', 1911, Yola Collected Histories, NNAK, J.2
SHAW, J. H., 'Madagali District', 1935, NNAK, 25073 Report on Uba
'Yungur District Miscellaneous Papers', 1935-40, NNAK, G.20
'Report on Madagali District', 1935, NNAK, 25073
SHIRLEY, W. R., 'Malabu and Belel District Miscellaneous Papers', 1917-46, NNAK, Adamprof.
SKELLY, J., 'Ethnology Gudu', 1928, NNAK, SNP, 2710H
STRÜMPELL, K., *A History of Adamawa* (Hamburg, 1912), trans. mimeo, NNAK, J.18
TALBOR, A. C., 'Belel and Malabu Districts Miscellaneous Papers', 1917-46, NNAK, G.2, H
VEREKER, S. H. P., 'The Kitijen', Fulani Collected Papers and Correspondence, 1910-34, NNAK, J.2
'Cameroun War Campaigns', 1915-17, NNAK, SNP, K.2
'Precis of Yola Local History', Partition of the Cameroun 1910-30, NNAK, K.5

N

'History of the Fulani of Banyo and Koncha', Cameroun Assumption of Administration, 1915-17, vol. ii, NNAK, K.2
'Notes on the History of Koncha and Banyo', Partition of the Cameroun, 1919-30, NNAK, K.5
WEBSTER, G. B., 'Historical Notes on Ribadu District', Pagan Administration, Vol. 1, 1910-27, NNAK, F.3
'Mayo Ine District Assessment Papers', 1912-22, NNAK, G.2
'Papers to and from District Officers on Tour', 1929, NNAK, Acc. 6
Anon., 'Nasarawo District Miscellaneous Papers', 1925-7, NNAK, G.2, 2
Various Nassarawo Miscellaneous Papers, 1925-37, NNAK, G.2, 2
Binyeri DNB, Divisional Office, Yola
'Dossier, the Chiefs' Book', Divisional Office, Yola
Belel DNB
Zummo DNB
Uba DNB
Gazetteer 1936
Namtari DNB, from notes prepared by W.O.P. Rosedale in 1916
Namtari District Miscellaneous Papers, 1923-4, NNAK
Yebbi and Gurumpawo DNB, Local Authority Office, Ganye
Income of Chiefs, NNAK, 462/1905
Provincial Reorganisation, 1926, Memo and Papers, NNAK
CO 446/5, F. Lascalles to Salisbury, 4/10/1899
CO 446/16, Wallace to CO, 6/8/1901
CO 446/16, Wallace to CO, encl. Moreland's Report, also SNP, 7/2, NNAK, Acc. No. 2363/1901
CO 446/22, Lugard to Co, 19/2/1902
Moreland's Report

UNPUBLISHED MATERIAL

EMC: Eldridge Mohamadou's collection, Cultural and Linguistic Centre, Yaoundi

Alhaji Abdullahi, 'Tarihi Garua'
Anon., 'Tarihi Be'
Anon., 'Tarihi Golembe'
Anon., 'Tarihi Koncha e Banyo', version Meiganga
Anon., 'Tarihi Marua'
Ibrahim Hammawa, 'Tarihi Koncha e Banyo'
Lāmīdo Muhammadu, 'Tarihi Bogo'
Liman Ngaundere Isa, 'Tarihi Ngaundere'
Mōdibbo Nyako, 'Tarihi Guider'
'Tarihi Bibemi'
'Tarihi Rai-Buba', (version officiale)

Waziri Mai, 'Tarihi Tinger'
Yaqubu Mayo Luwe, 'Tarihi Mayo Luwe'

NHRS: Northern History Research Scheme, Ahmadu Bello University, Zaria

D. M. Last, 'Notes' in Adamawa File
Garbosa II, 'Labarun Chamba da Alamuransu'
Ibrahim Dodo, 'Tarihin Maiha'
Muhammad Tan Mo'ililal, 'Faya Fukarabe'

Other Mss

Jauro Goila, 'History of the Origin of Kilba District', May 1950, Kilba DNB
M. Ahmadu Marafa, 'Tarihin Sarautar Sanda da Zubairu', Ms. in my possession
'Tarihin Marwa', in possession of Mōdibbo Nasura Goni Bello
Yerima Balla, 'Tarihin Kilba', Secondary School, Hong

Theses and Research Essays

ALIYU, Y. A., 'The establishment and development of Emirate government in Bauchi, 1805-1903', unpublished Ph.D. thesis, Ahmadu Bello University, 1974
BALOGUN, S. A., 'Gwandu emirates in the nineteenth century, with special reference to political relations: 1817-1903', unpublished Ph.D. thesis, Ibadan University, 1970
BENISHEIK, A. K., 'The Galadimas of Bornu', unpublished B.A. research essay, Ahmadu Bello University, Zaria, 1972
CHASKDA, G. 'The establishment of a Government-General among the Kilba', unpublished B.A. research essay, Ahmadu Bello University, Zaria, 1972
MAIYAKI, R. M., 'The emergence of chieftainship among the Mbula', unpublished B.A. research essay, Ahmadu Bello University, Zaria, 1972
MASON, M., 'The Nupe Kingdom in the nineteenth century: A Political History', unpublished Ph.D. thesis, Birmingham University, 1970
SA'ID, A. G., 'Mahdist in Northern Nigeria: Tensions of Teaching and Society', unpublished B.A. research essay, ABU, 1972

Arabic Manuscripts

'UTHMĀN B. MUHAMMAD FŪDĪ
'Kitab al-Farq: a work on the Habe kingdoms attributed to Uthman dan Fodio', M. Hiskett, *BSOAS*, 23, 3 (1960), 558-79
'An early Fulani conception of Islam – "Tanbīhu'l Ikhwān" ', H. R. Palmer, *JAS*, 13, 52 (1914), 407-14; 14, 53 (1914), 53-9; 14, 54 (1915), 185-92

'The Wathīqat ahl al-Sūdān, a manifesto of the Fulani jihad', trans. A. D. H. Bivar, *JAH*, 2, 2 (1961), 235-43

'ABDULLĀH B. FŪDĪ

Tazyīn al-Waraqāt, trans. M. Hiskett, Ibadan, 1963

Ḍiyā, Al-ḥukkām (Ms., NHRS Collection, and Hausa trans., Gaskiya Corporation)

MUḤAMMAD BELLO

'Infaku'l Maisuri of Sultan Mohammed Bello', E. J. Arnett in *The Rise of the Sokoto Fulani*, Kano, 1922

al-Gayth al-Sh'ibūb fī Tawṣiyyat al-Amīr Ya'qūb, KEN, 123, NHRS Arabic Collection

'ABD AL-QADIR B. AL-MUṢṬAFĀ

'Western Sudan History: the Raudthât' ul Afkâri', H. R. Palmer, *JAS*, XV, 59 (1916), 261-73

GIDADO DAN LAIMA

Rauḍ al-Jinān, trans. Harris, NNAK, Kadcap. I: 23

'ABD AL-QĀDIR B. GIDADO

Majmu' ba'ḍ Rasā'il Amīr al-Muminīn Muḥammad Bello etc., NHRS Collection

IDRĪS B. IBRĀHĪM

Biography of Būba Yero of Gombe, trans. R. Abraham, NNAK K. 5051

ABŪ BAKR AL-'ATĪQ

Risāla ala Jama' at Gandu, NHRS Collection

ADAMU AGANA

Marthiyyat Amīr Modibbo Adama, NHRS Collection

ANONYMOUS

Tabyīn amr Būba Yero ma'a 'Ummalihi wa-Aṣhābihi, H. F. C. Smith's Collection

Index

Index of Names

Printed in Great Britain by Robert MacLehose and Company Limited
Printers to the University of Glasgow

R. Hadejia

R. Gongola

R. Benue

CAMEROON
MTS

ATLANTIC OCEAN